ANALYTIC T

ANALYTIC THEOLOGY

New Essays in the Philosophy of Theology

Edited by
OLIVER D. CRISP AND MICHAEL C. REA

OXFORD
UNIVERSITY PRESS

OXFORD
UNIVERSITY PRESS

Great Clarendon Street, Oxford OX2 6DP

Oxford University Press is a department of the University of Oxford.
It furthers the University's objective of excellence in research, scholarship,
and education by publishing worldwide in

Oxford New York

Auckland Cape Town Dar es Salaam Hong Kong Karachi
Kuala Lumpur Madrid Melbourne Mexico City Nairobi
New Delhi Shanghai Taipei Toronto

With offices in

Argentina Austria Brazil Chile Czech Republic France Greece
Guatemala Hungary Italy Japan Poland Portugal Singapore
South Korea Switzerland Thailand Turkey Ukraine Vietnam

Oxford is a registered trade mark of Oxford University Press
in the UK and in certain other countries

Published in the United States
by Oxford University Press Inc., New York

© Oxford University Press 2009

The moral rights of the authors have been asserted
Database right Oxford University Press (maker)

First published 2009
First published in paperback 2011

All rights reserved. No part of this publication may be reproduced,
stored in a retrieval system, or transmitted, in any form or by any means,
without the prior permission in writing of Oxford University Press,
or as expressly permitted by law, or under terms agreed with the appropriate
reprographics rights organization. Enquiries concerning reproduction
outside the scope of the above should be sent to the Rights Department,
Oxford University Press, at the address above

You must not circulate this book in any other binding or cover
and you must impose the same condition on any acquirer

British Library Cataloguing in Publication Data
Data available

Library of Congress Cataloging in Publication Data
Library of Congress Control Number: 2008942635

Typeset by SPI Publisher Services, Pondicherry, India
Digitally printed and bound in Great Britain by
CPI Antony Rowe, Chippenham and Eastbourne

ISBN 978–0–19–920356–7 (Hbk)
ISBN 978–0–19–960042–7 (Pbk.)

For Mathilda Anais Crisp,
who has already shown herself to be 'mighty in battle'
and
For Christina Brinks Rea,
who came with gentleness and peace, and love in abundance.

Contents

Notes on Contributors ix

Introduction 1
Michael C. Rea

I. IN DEFENSE OF ANALYTIC THEOLOGY

1. On Analytic Theology 33
   Oliver D. Crisp
2. Systematic Theology as Analytic Theology 54
   William J. Abraham
3. Theology as a Bull Session 70
   Randal Rauser

II. HISTORICAL PERSPECTIVES

4. A Conception of Faith in the Greek Fathers 87
   John Lamont
5. 'As Kant has Shown...': Analytic Theology and the Critical Philosophy 117
   Andrew Chignell
6. Schleiermacher's Theological Anti-Realism 136
   Andrew Dole
7. How Philosophical Theology Became Possible within the Analytic Tradition of Philosophy 155
   Nicholas Wolterstorff

III. ON THE DATA FOR THEOLOGY: SCRIPTURE, REASON, AND EXPERIENCE

8. On Understanding Scripture as the Word of God 171
   Thomas McCall

9. On Believing that the Scriptures are Divinely Inspired 187
   Thomas M. Crisp

10. The Contribution of Religious Experience to
    Dogmatic Theology 214
    Michael Sudduth

11. Science and Religion in Constructive Engagement 233
    Michael J. Murray

IV. ANALYTIC APPROACHES RECONSIDERED

12. The Problem of Evil: Analytic Philosophy and Narrative 251
    Eleonore Stump

13. Hermeneutics and Holiness 265
    Merold Westphal

14. Dark Contemplation and Epistemic Transformation:
    The Analytic Theologian Re-Meets Teresa of Ávila 280
    Sarah Coakley

Index 313

Notes on Contributors

William J. Abraham is Albert Cook Outler Professor of Theology and Wesley Studies and Altshuler Distinguished Teaching Professor at the Perkins School of Theology, Southern Methodist University.

Andrew Chignell is Assistant Professor in the Sage School of Philosophy at Cornell University.

Sarah Coakley is Norris-Hulse Professor of Divinity at Cambridge University.

Oliver D. Crisp is Reader in Theology at the University of Bristol.

Thomas M. Crisp is Associate Professor of Philosophy at Biola University.

Andrew Dole is Assistant Professor of Religion at Amherst College.

John Lamont is Lecturer in Theology at the Catholic University of Sydney.

Thomas McCall is Assistant Professor of Biblical and Systematic Theology at Trinity Evangelical Divinity School.

Michael J. Murray is Arthur and Katherine Shadek Professor in Humanities at Franklin and Marshall College.

Randal Rauser is Associate Professor of Historical Theology at Taylor Seminary.

Michael C. Rea is Professor of Philosophy at the University of Notre Dame.

Eleonore Stump is Robert J. Henle Professor of Philosophy at Saint Louis University.

Michael Sudduth is Lecturer in Philosophy at San Francisco State University.

Merold Westphal is Distinguished Professor of Philosophy at Fordham University.

Nicholas Wolterstorff is Emeritus Noah Porter Professor of Philosophical Theology at Yale University.

Introduction[†]

Michael C. Rea

In recent decades, philosophers of religion in the so-called 'analytic tradition' have gradually turned their attention toward the explication of core doctrines in Christian theology. The result has been a growing body of philosophical work on topics that have traditionally been the provenance of systematic theologians. Despite this theological turn, however, the results haven't, in general, been warmly received by theologians. This is in large part due to the fact that many theologians seem to have very different ideas from analytic philosophers about how theology (and philosophy) ought to be done, and about the value of analytic approaches to theological topics.

Whereas philosophy in the English-speaking world is dominated by analytic approaches to its problems and projects, theology has been dominated by alternative approaches. For reasons that I shall try to sketch below, many would say that the current state in theology is not mere historical accident, but is, rather, how things *ought* to be. Others, however, would say precisely the opposite: that theology as a discipline has been beguiled and taken captive by 'continental' approaches, and that the effects on the discipline have been largely deleterious.[1]

The methodological divide between systematic theologians and analytic philosophers of religion is ripe for exploration. It is of obvious theoretical importance to both disciplines, but it also has practical import. The climate in theology departments for analytic theologians is much like the climate in English-speaking philosophy departments for continental philosophers: often chilly.[2] Moreover, the methodological divide is surely the most significant

[†] I would like to thank Michael Bergmann, Jeff Brower, Andrew Chignell, Oliver Crisp, John Lamont, Michael Murray, Merold Westphal, and Nicholas Wolterstorff for helpful comments on an earlier draft of this chapter. Also, both Oliver and I would like to thank Alex Arnold for help preparing the index for this volume, and the Institute for Scholarship in the Liberal Arts in the College of Arts and Letters at the University of Notre Dame for funding that made Alex's work possible.

[1] The idea that theology has been taken captive is made explicit in R. R. Reno, 'Theology's Continental Captivity', *First Things*, 162 (2006), 26–33.

[2] Often, but not always. In some philosophy departments, continental dominates; and in a few—like the philosophy department at the University of Notre Dame—both continental and analytic are strongly represented, and relations among their practitioners are generally quite positive. But this is the exception rather than the rule. From all I can tell, the same is true—except with continental approaches in the dominant position—in the field of theology.

obstacle to fruitful interdisciplinary dialogue. The problem isn't just that academics with different methodological perspectives have trouble conversing with one another. Rather, it is that, by and large, the established figures in both disciplines don't even view mutual conversation as worth pursuing. They ignore one another. They (implicitly or explicitly) encourage their students to ignore one another. They allow their methodological preferences to play a very large role in their judgments about hiring and about the quality of papers they referee for professional journals. And the divide only grows deeper. No doubt many (on both sides) will think that all of this is perfectly legitimate. Maybe it is, but that is beside the point; its legitimacy shouldn't just be taken for granted. It is an open and interesting question whether theology can sensibly be done in the analytic mode.

The present volume represents an attempt to begin a much-needed interdisciplinary conversation about the value of analytic philosophical approaches to theological topics. It is a largely one-sided attempt insofar as most of the essays herein are at least sympathetic toward, if not defensive of, the enterprise we are calling *analytic theology*. But we have aimed to provide some balance by including a few essays that offer more critical perspectives on analytic theology. Also in the service of balance, I shall attempt in the present essay to summarize and explain what seem to be some of the most important objections against analytic theology.

I shall begin by trying to explain what I mean by the terms 'analytic philosophy' and 'analytic theology'. The contributors to this volume do not have a precise or even entirely uniform vision of what analytic theology amounts to (though there is certainly broad agreement on what it would involve). But this, I think, is to be expected in light of the fact that the nature of analytic philosophy also eludes precise and uniform characterization.

Next, I shall present what is essentially an analytic theologian's perspective on the most salient objections against the enterprise of analytic theology. I do this for the following reason. Much has been written in both philosophy and theology that can plausibly be invoked in defense of broadly non-analytic approaches to theological topics. Here I'm thinking, for example, of work by Don Cupitt, John Hick, George Lindbeck, Jean-Luc Marion, D. Z. Phillips, and Merold Westphal—to name just a few, very diverse thinkers whose writings either point toward defects in analytic approaches, or seem in other ways to speak in favor of going a different way.[3] But the methodological

---

[3] I don't mean to suggest that these figures are intentionally trying to discredit analytic philosophy or theology. Some are, no doubt; but others might simply be following a different path (as Merold Westphal put it to me in correspondence). In Ch. 13 e.g. Westphal recommends a hermeneutical phenomenological alternative to analytic theology, but without declaring analytic theology to be defective. Still, his work does provide reasons which deserve to be taken seriously for favoring his alternative path; and so his work (like the work of these other figures) might sensibly be *appropriated* by critics who *do* want to discredit analytic theology, even if he himself is unwilling to go that far.

import of a lot of this work has gone largely unappreciated by those interested in analytic theology. Part of the problem is that many (though hardly all) of the arguments that would speak against analytic theology are couched in a rhetorical style that analytic philosophers and theologians (henceforth, 'analytics') will find objectionably opaque. But it is also because the arguments in this literature often depend upon claims and attitudes which are handed down from figures largely dismissed by analytics and which many analytics find to be inaccurate, insufficiently motivated, or wholly unintelligible. The result is that the critics are largely preaching to the choir—and this despite the fact that, in my opinion anyway, some of their arguments and objections deserve serious engagement.

My own efforts, then, will be directed at articulating in my own terms what the main objections seem to be. I hope to express them in ways that will resonate with those who embrace them, while at the same time helping analytics to appreciate their force more fully. I also hope that, to the extent that I miss the mark in characterizing the objections, critics of analytic theology will take what I say here as an open invitation to clarify, and to replace inadvertent caricature with real substance. I shall not attempt to respond to the objections here. Some responses will come in the chapters that follow, and in the closing section I comment briefly upon those. But the main purpose of this introduction is just to open up dialogue on the issues discussed herein, not to provide a defense of my own perspective.

ANALYTIC PHILOSOPHY AND ANALYTIC THEOLOGY

It is commonplace now to express skepticism about the usefulness of trying to distinguish between analytic and non-analytic philosophy, in no small part because the label is misleading: quite a lot of analytic philosophy has little or nothing to do with conceptual analysis. Nevertheless, the term is still in regular use, and people seem to have a fairly good idea about what sort of thing it refers to, even if they can't define it very well. Roughly (and I think that 'rough' is the best that we can do here), it refers to an approach to philosophical problems that is characterized by a particular rhetorical style, some common ambitions, an evolving technical vocabulary, and a tendency to pursue projects in dialogue with a certain evolving body of literature. Obviously it would be impossible to try to specify in detail the relevant literature and technical vocabulary. The point is just that these factors play a role in determining whether a piece of work falls within the analytic tradition. But the rhetorical style and ambitions of analytic philosophy are somewhat easier to characterize.

The ambitions seem generally to be to these: (i) to identify the scope and limits of our powers to obtain knowledge of the world, and (ii) to provide such true explanatory theories as we can in areas of inquiry (metaphysics, morals, and the like) that fall outside the scope of the natural sciences. The first ambition overlaps the ambitions of many non-analytic philosophers, the difference lying partly in the mode of pursuit, but also partly in expectations about the outcome. Many in the analytic tradition have sought to explain how knowledge of a certain kind, or knowledge in general, is possible—often with an eye to refuting skeptics and showing that we in fact possess such knowledge. This project might be loosely (and, many of us would say, inaccurately) described as a quest for the 'foundations' of knowledge—a quest that, thus described, obviously takes for granted the *existence* of foundations. This, the non-analytic philosophers will say, is the part of the attempt to identify the scope and limits of our powers to obtain knowledge that is distinctive of the analytic tradition, and it is the part that needs to be given up. On the other hand, many others in the analytic tradition have pursued more critical projects, aiming to show that knowledge of a certain kind is problematic, or impossible, or, at any rate, unobtainable by humans under current epistemic circumstances. Projects of this sort are pursued by analytic and non-analytic philosophers alike. The difference between Bas van Fraassen's critique of metaphysics or of the 'false hopes of traditional epistemology' on the one hand, and those offered by folks like Jean-François Lyotard or Jean-Luc Marion on the other lies not so much in the overall aim or thesis as in the style of argument, the choice of targets and conversation partners, and the suppositions and vocabulary that are taken for granted.[4]

The second ambition includes the quest for 'local' explanations of particular phenomena—morality, causation, and composition, for example. It also includes the quest for some sort of 'global' explanation that identifies fundamental entities and properties and helps to provide an account of human

---

[4] Compare van Fraassen, 'The False Hopes of Traditional Epistemology', *Philosophy and Phenomenological Research*, 60 (2000), 253–80 and *The Empirical Stance* (New Haven: Yale University Press, 2002) on the one hand, and, on the other hand, Lyotard, *The Postmodern Condition: A Report on Knowledge*, tr. Geoff Bennington and Brian Massumi (Minneapolis: University of Minnesota Press, 1984), and Marion, *God Without Being*, tr. Thomas A. Carlson (Chicago: University of Chicago Press, 1991); 'Metaphysics and Phenomenology: A Relief for Theology', tr. Thomas A. Carlson, *Critical Inquiry*, 20 (1994), 572–59; and 'The Idea of God', pp. 265–304 in D. Garber and M. Ayers (eds.), *The Cambridge History of Seventeenth-Century Philosophy*, i (Cambridge: CUP, 1998). This isn't, of course, to minimize differences between the overall agendas of these philosophers, but just to identify a certain affinity in their views about 'traditional' epistemology.

cognitive structures and their abilities to interact with and theoretically process facts about the fundamental objects and properties. Accomplishing the latter goal would amount to providing the ontological underpinnings of a final epistemological theory. Thus, the ambitions of analytic philosophy are intimately connected; and so skepticism about our ability to fulfill one of them will inevitably translate into skepticism about our ability to fulfill (completely) the other.

Characterizing the rhetorical style is a bit more complicated. Making no claim either to completeness or universality, the analytic style might roughly be characterized as a style paradigmatic instances of which are distinguished by conformity (more or less) to the following prescriptions:

> P1. Write as if philosophical positions and conclusions can be adequately formulated in sentences that can be formalized and logically manipulated.[5]
> P2. Prioritize precision, clarity, and logical coherence.[6]
> P3. Avoid substantive (non-decorative) use of metaphor and other tropes whose semantic content outstrips their propositional content.[7]
> P4. Work as much as possible with well-understood primitive concepts, and concepts that can be analyzed in terms of those.

---

[5] I don't mean to suggest that it's part of analytic philosophy always to carry out the formalizations or to lay entirely bare the logical relations among one's claims. But analytic philosophers generally think that, absent special circumstances, something is very amiss if a philosophical view is expressed in such a way that it has no clear logical consequences.

[6] In correspondence, Nicholas Wolterstorff pointed out to me that one obvious distinctive feature of analytic philosophy is the heavy use of counterexamples, including bizarrely imaginative ones. I take this to be one of the primary manifestations of the prioritization of precision. As for prioritization of clarity, this claim can seem ironic in light of the fact that quite a lot of analytic philosophy is very difficult even for specialists, and totally inaccessible to non-specialists. But the idea that analytic philosophers prize clarity has, I think, less to do with prizing accessibility to non-specialists (or even to specialists) and more to do with the fact that analytic philosophers place a high premium on spelling out hidden assumptions, on scrupulously trying to lay bare whatever evidence one has (or lacks) for the claims that one is making, and on taking care to confine one's vocabulary to ordinary language, well-understood primitive concepts, and technical jargon definable in terms of these.

[7] There is controversy in the literature on metaphor over the question whether and to what extent metaphors have determinate propositional content. Here I am taking it for granted that metaphors often, even if not always, have cognitive significance that outstrips whatever propositional content they might have. See e.g. David Cooper, *Metaphor* (Oxford: Basil Blackwell, 1986) and Josef Stern, *Metaphor in Context* (Cambridge, Mass.: MIT Press, 2000), both of which defend, in different ways, the view that the cognitive significance of a metaphor is not to be identified with whatever propositional content it might have. Also, I do not mean to deny that metaphors get used in analytic theorizing to put forward models, or to otherwise 'support' various kinds of (literal) theoretical claims. But in such cases, I think, it is the models or the supportive claims that play the more substantive role. (For defense of the view that metaphors can be 'reality depicting' and can 'support metaphysical claims' in both religion and science, see Janet Martin Soskice, *Metaphor and Religious Language* (Oxford: Clarendon Press, 1985), esp. chs. 7 and 8.)

P5. Treat conceptual analysis (insofar as it is possible) as a source of evidence.

More might be added, of course. But my 'official' list stops at P5 because most of what else I would add wouldn't really count as prescriptions that *divide* analytic from continental philosophers. P1–P5 are contentious, however. By my lights, they are prescriptions that non-analytic philosophers either reject as unimportant or actively aim to violate, and for principled reasons.

On the surface, these prescriptions might seem to be just stilted expressions of fairly commonsensical virtues that we all (even postmodern philosophers) aim to inculcate in our undergraduates: reason coherently; write clearly; say what you mean and mean what you say; try to express your ideas in terms that your audience will understand; try not to express your arguments and conclusions in overly 'poetic' language; understand the terms that you're employing and rely on your understanding of those terms to draw out the implications of what you say and what you presuppose; and so on. Thus construed, it is hard to imagine how anyone could sensibly object.

In fact, however, each of the prescriptions (or the presumption that each can be followed when treating some philosophical or theological topic) expresses or presupposes views that can very reasonably be questioned. And I think that it is precisely the deep-seated reservations that many non-analytic philosophers have about the views underlying these prescriptions that explains a lot of the current hostility toward analytic approaches to theological topics. (The third section of this chapter, 'Against the Analytic Style' is devoted to unpacking this last remark in some detail.)

I have gone on for a bit now about what analytic philosophy is. Hopefully it is also becoming clear what analytic philosophy is *not*. Nothing in my characterization of analytic philosophy has wedded it to a particular theory of truth. Nor have I saddled it with commitment to a particular epistemological theory. Contrary to what various critics of analytic philosophy have suggested, there are analytic philosophers aplenty who reject (for example) the correspondence theory of truth; there are also analytic philosophers who reject foundationalism. Analytic philosophers are not, as such, committed to belief in propositions (at least not where propositions are considered to be abstract entities that stand in the *is expressed by* relation to sentences). Nor are they committed to any brand of metaphysical realism or moral or metaphysical absolutism.[8] In fact, so far as I can tell, there is no substantive philosophical thesis that separates analytic philosophers as such from their rivals.

---

[8] Some seem to think that the grand explanatory ambitions of analytic philosophy commit it to a brand of realism, or at least to 'absolute metaphysical truth'. But this is manifestly false. If metaphysical realism is false, then that fact will be part of the 'grand explanation' that we're all striving for. If there is no absolute truth (whatever exactly that means), then there won't be a

To be sure, analytic philosophers typically write as if certain metaphilosophical theses are true—in particular, whatever theses underlie the prescriptions sketched above. Moreover, it is reasonable to think that both foundationalism of a certain kind and metaphysical realism lurk in the background of a lot of analytic theorizing (more on foundationalism in the next section below). But my point here is that analytic philosophy as such carries no *commitment* to these theses. It is easy enough to imagine an analytic philosopher objecting to any one of them, and doing so more or less in the analytic style and in the service of some of what I have called the ambitions of the analytic philosophical tradition. It is, I think, a failure to recognize this fact that has led to so many of the embarrassing caricatures of analytic philosophy in the contemporary literature.

So much, then, for analytic philosophy. What about analytic theology? As I see it, analytic theology is just the activity of approaching theological topics with the ambitions of an analytic philosopher and in a style that conforms to the prescriptions that are distinctive of analytic philosophical discourse. It will also involve, more or less, pursuing those topics in a way that engages the literature that is constitutive of the analytic tradition, employing some of the technical jargon from that tradition, and so on. But, in the end, it is the style and the ambitions that are most central. For this reason, analytic theology as an enterprise stands or falls with the viability of its ambitions and with the practical value of trying to do theology in a way that conforms to the prescriptions that characterize analytic philosophical writing.

AGAINST ANALYTIC AMBITIONS

In the opening paragraph of Louis Berkhof's *Introductory Volume to Systematic Theology*—chosen for discussion here almost entirely at random from among several older systematic theologies on my shelf—the aim of the systematic theologian is characterized as follows:

There was little or no attempt in the first two centuries of the Christian era to present the whole body of doctrinal truth, gathered from the Word of God, in a systematic way. Yet the urge of the human mind to see the truth as much as possible as a whole could not long be suppressed. Man is endowed with reason, and the human reason cannot rest satisfied with a mere collection of separate truths, but wants to see them in

unique 'grand explanatory theory', but analytic philosophy can proceed from different perspectives and starting points just as it always has. These two points seem not to be sufficiently appreciated by those who would criticize analytic philosophy.

their mutual relationship, in order that it may have a clearer understanding of them.... God certainly sees the truth as a whole, and it is the duty of the theologian to think the truths of God after Him. There should be a constant endeavor to see the truth as God sees it, even though it is perfectly evident that the ideal is beyond the grasp of man in his present condition.[9]

Berkhof's characterization represents an entirely common, traditional view of the task of the systematic theologian. These words might just as easily express the collective ambition of many who are engaged in the analytic theological enterprise. Of course, much that will qualify as analytic theology—for example, projects that aim to revise our concept of God in light of reason rather than scripture—falls outside the scope of Berkhof's vision. Nevertheless, we all can recognize in his remark about the 'theologian's duty' an ambition distinctly in keeping with the analytic tradition and decidedly contrary to what critics of the tradition will recognize as a proper or sensible goal for a theologian.

One point of contention here will be the idea that we can, even in principle, have access to 'the truth as God sees it'—i.e. absolute, perfectly objective truth. Objections to this idea come from two quarters. Some say that there simply is no such thing as 'the truth as God sees it'—that (in the words of Don Cupitt) 'reality [is] a mere bunch of disparate and changing interpretations, a shifting loosely-held coalition of points of view in continual debate with each other'.[10] Others are prepared to grant the existence of such a perspective but vehemently deny that we can occupy it.[11] These claims are familiar territory, widely discussed both within and without the analytic tradition. I won't comment further on them here except to note the obvious: both are in tension with analytic ambitions, and so both will be sources of objection to analytic theology.

One can, of course, challenge both of these suppositions while remaining in the analytic mode. As I said earlier, analytic theology as such carries no commitment to substantive theories about truth or epistemology. But those who do challenge these suppositions will not think that any sort of *robust* theology can be developed in the analytic mode. It is in this way, then, that the

---

[9] *Systematic Theology: New Combined Edition* (Grand Rapids, Mich.: Wm. B. Eerdman's, 1932/1996), 15.

[10] Don Cupitt, 'Anti-Realist Faith', repr. in his *Is Nothing Sacred? The Non-Realist Philosophy of Religion* (New York: Fordham University Press, 1987), 34.

[11] See e.g. Merold Westphal's 'Appropriating Post-Modernism', *ARC: The Journal of the Faculty of Religious Studies, McGill University,* 25 (1997), 73–84, and 'Overcoming Onto-Theology', pp. 146–69 in J. D. Caputo and M. J. Scanlon (eds.), *God, the Gift, and Postmodernism* (Bloomington, Ind.: Indiana University Press, 1999), both of which are reprinted in Westphal, *Overcoming Onto-Theology: Toward a Postmodern Christian Faith* (New York: Fordham University Press, 2001). See also Westphal's 'Father Abraham and His Feuding Sons', pp. 148–75 in *Overcoming Onto-Theology,* and 'Taking Plantinga Seriously: Advice to Christian Philosophers', *Faith and Philosophy,* 19 (2002), 173–81.

objections just mentioned count against analytic theology: they are objections against what we might call a *non-minimalist* conception of analytic theology.

I do not, however, think that these claims are the *main* source of objection to analytic ambitions. The arguments simply aren't good enough. Like many philosophical arguments, those that motivate denials of the existence and accessibility of absolute truths work much better as rationalizations for positions already held than as positive stimuli to conversion. Thus, I think that the best explanation for the nearly wholesale rejection of analytic ambitions on the part of theologians lies not so much in their success or failure in assessing a certain range of arguments, but rather in a more or less collectively held *positive vision* about the proper aims of theology that is antecedently at odds with the goals of the analytic theologian. Let me now make an effort at unpacking and justifying this claim.

Merold Westphal notes that, '[i]n postmodern contexts, onto-theology is one of the seven deadly sins' ('Overcoming Onto-Theology' (1999), 13). As I understand it, onto-theology involves primarily two tendencies. First, it treats God primarily as an explanatory posit, so that (as Westphal puts it), 'God's *raison d'être* has become to make it possible for human reason to give ultimate explanations' (ibid. 11). Second, it involves theorizing about God in a way that presupposes that reason is a reliable tool for arriving at *clear* knowledge of God, so that reasoning about God can ultimately remove divine mystery.[12] To put it in other terms, the view of the onto-theologian is that we can (and sometimes do) believe *exactly the truths about God*, undistorted by our own human circumstances, that God himself believes.[13] Now, it is easy enough to see that if the God's-eye point of view is wholly inaccessible (or, worse, non-existent), the hope of the onto-theologian is a non-starter. Moreover, I suspect that most analytic theologians nowadays will think that, in any case, the suppositions of the paradigmatic onto-theologian are narrow-minded and optimistic at best. Mystery is inevitable, and God is clearly much more than a mere explanatory posit. Still, those who are theologizing with analytic ambitions typically and naturally find explanatory roles for God to play, and they will typically share the supposition that we can arrive at *clear* knowledge of God, even if that knowledge is not *complete* and some mysteries remain.[14]

---

[12] Correspondence with Westphal and attention to his work have helped me to sharpen my understanding of onto-theology; but if misunderstandings linger, they are my fault and not his.

[13] Cf. 'Overcoming Onto-Theology', pp. 6 ff., and 'Taking Plantinga Seriously', pp. 177 ff. In the latter article, Westphal seems to suggest that belief in *propositions* somehow promotes or encourages onto-theology thus construed. But I do not find that suggestion plausible. One can have substantially the same view of our cognitive powers without believing in propositions; and one can believe in propositions while also affirming that God is utterly mysterious, that no proposition is absolutely true, and so on.

[14] Typically, but not inevitably. See below, pp. 19–21 on the relation between analytic theology and apophatic theology.

Thus, analytic theology shares affinities with onto-theology, even if the two enterprises are not to be identified.

But Westphal and others speak as if the very aspiration to onto-theology is not just a little misguided, but bad, dangerous, inimical to the life of faith, and so on. Why would it be so? In 'Overcoming Onto-Theology', Westphal tells us that, according to Heidegger,

> the goal of theology 'is never a valid system of theological propositions' but rather 'concrete Christian existence itself.'... [B]ecause its goal is the *praxis* of the believer as a distinctive mode of existence, '*theology in its essence is a practical science.*' Unlike onto-theology, theology properly understood is 'innately homiletical'... It is as if Heidegger is saying, I have found it necessary to deny theory in order to make room for practice. (16; emphasis in original)

In glossing the meaning of this last remark, Westphal refers us to the story of Cupid and Psyche as (in his view) it is retold in Wagner's *Lohengrin* and C. S. Lewis's *'Till We Have Faces*. In each of these tales, a certain kind of loving relationship is undermined by a woman's desire to possess forbidden knowledge about her lover—knowledge which will give her a kind of control over her beloved, or (as Westphal puts it), will put him 'at her disposal'. He writes:

> [In each of these stories] the challenge of faith is the same: the believer is called upon to sustain a beautiful and loving relationship through trust in a lover about whom she remains significantly (though not totally) in the dark and who, though he gives himself to her freely, is not at her disposal. The relationship is destroyed when the beloved... insists on Enlightenment, on dissipating the darkness of mystery with the light of human knowledge, on walking by sight and not by faith.
>
> To be able to resist this temptation, faith must deny theory, or, to be more precise, the primacy of insight. For such faith, Plato's divided line and Hegel's modern vision thereof as the movement 'beyond faith' to knowledge are not the ascent from that which is inferior... to that which is superior...; they are rather the withdrawal from the site at which alone is possible a loving, trusting relation with a God before whom one might sing and dance...
>
> This love, this trust, this relationship—these are the practice for the sake of which it was necessary to deny theory. This is not to abolish theology. It is to see that theology's task is to serve this life of faith, not the ideals of knowledge as defined by the philosophical traditions. ('Overcoming Onto-Theology', 27)

On Westphal's view, then, the duty of the theologian is emphatically *not* to 'think God's thoughts after Him' (*pace* Berkhof) but rather to serve the life of faith. In order to do this, however, it must always respect the transcendence of God and refrain from the temptation to try to 'put God at our disposal'—i.e. to try to see God with clear intellectual vision, believing about God the absolute truths that God believes about himself. And, again, the issue isn't just that we are *unable* to attain such a clear vision. Rather, the point is that the *effort* both implicitly denies the transcendence that theology ought to respect and aims at a goal that, if accomplished, would undermine the life of faith and would thus work at cross purposes with the true goal of theology. If this is correct, then much of what would count as analytic theology is fundamentally misguided, predicated upon a wrong view about what is in keeping with the goals of theology. And if we take seriously the animadversions against the existence or accessibility-in-principle of 'absolute truth', then analytic theology (conceived in a non-minimalist way) is also predicated upon a false view about what is even *possible* for theology. This, then, is our first substantive objection against analytic theology.[15]

Westphal's vision of the goals of theology is articulated in a way that, so far as I can tell, is fully consistent with traditional, creedally orthodox Christian belief. But it is important to bear in mind that substantially the same vision can and does arise out of very different points of view as well. In his essay, 'A Remarkable Consensus', for example, Michael Dummett laments what he takes to be a general loss of faith among Catholic theologians—a loss reflected in what Thomas Sheehan refers to as the 'liberal consensus':[16]

In Roman Catholic seminaries... it is now common teaching that Jesus of Nazareth did not assert any of the messianic claims that the Gospels attribute to him and that he died without believing that he was the Christ or the Son of God, not to mention the founder of a new religion.

Nor did Jesus know that his mother, Mary, had remained a virgin in the very act of conceiving him.... Most likely Mary told Jesus what she herself knew of his origins: that he had a natural father and was born not in Bethlehem but in Nazareth, indeed without the ministrations of angels, shepherds, and late-arriving wise men bearing gifts. She could have told her son the traditional nativity story only if she had managed to read, long before they were written, the inspiring but unhistorical Christmas legends that first appeared in the gospels of Matthew and Luke fifty years after her son had died.

Moreover, according to the consensus, although Jesus had a reputation as a faith healer during his life, it is likely that he performed very few such 'miracles', perhaps only two. (Probably he never walked on water.) ('A Remarkable Consensus', 428–9)

It is no doubt an overstatement to say that these claims are really a matter of *consensus* among theologians (Catholic or otherwise). But it is probably not

---

[15] The respect for divine transcendence and the corresponding preference for apophatic modes of discourse that motivates this objection also motivates objections against the analytic *style*. See below, the section 'Against the Analytic Style'.

[16] Thomas Sheehan, Review of Hans Kung's *Eternal Life*, *New York Review of Books*, 31 (14 June 1984), quoted in Michael Dummett, 'A Remarkable Consensus', *New Blackfriars*, 68 (1987), 424–31.

far off the mark to say that such claims are widely endorsed by contemporary theologians. The point, in any case, is that exactly the same sort of positive vision for theology that Westphal articulates—one according to which theology's task is primarily practical, aimed at bolstering the life of faith rather than providing a true explanatory theory—will as naturally arise out of a theological perspective like this one as out of Westphal's or any of a variety of other perspectives.

The second objection pertains to a perceived link between the adoption of postmodern approaches to theology and the rejection of *foundationalism*. This is a complicated matter to discuss, however, because there seems to be a great deal of confusion among theologians and some postmodern philosophers about what foundationalism actually is. The problem (and I am hardly the first to point this out) is that many writers seem to confuse what most of us would call 'classical foundationalism' (roughly, the view that a belief is justified only if it is self evident, incorrigible, evident to the senses, or deducible from premises that satisfy at least one of those three conditions) with foundationalism *simpliciter*.[17] Classical foundationalism is almost universally rejected nowadays. Other kinds of foundationalism, on the other hand, are thriving. But many of the writers I have in mind seem to think that the death of classical foundationalism was nothing more or less than the death of foundationalism *simpliciter*. This is far from the truth.

Matters are further complicated by the fact that relatively few writers distinguish between *doxastic foundationalism* and what might be called *source foundationalism*. Doxastic foundationalism is the (entirely commonsensical, even if not universally held) view that some of our beliefs are *properly basic*. Basic beliefs are those that are not based on other beliefs. Properly basic

---

[17] Stanley Grenz and John Franke write: 'In its broadest sense, foundationalism is merely the acknowledgment of the seemingly obvious observation that not all beliefs we hold ... are on the same level, but that some beliefs ... anchor others. ... In philosophical circles, however, "foundationalism" refers to a much stronger epistemological stance than is entailed in this observation about how beliefs intersect. At the heart of the foundationalist agenda is the desire to overcome the uncertainty generated by our human liability to error and the inevitable disagreements that follow. Foundationalists are convinced that the only way to solve this problem is to find some means of grounding the entire edifice of human knowledge on invincible certainty' (*Beyond Foundationalism: Shaping Theology in a Postmodern Context* (Louisville, Ky.: Westminster/John Knox, 2001), 29–30). But as anyone acquainted with the contemporary literature in epistemology is aware, this characterization is simply false. Grenz and Franke cite W. Jay Wood (*Epistemology: Becoming Intellectually Virtuous* (Grand Rapids, Mich.: InterVarsity Press, 1998), 84) as their source for the characterization; but Wood does not characterize *foundationalism* as they do. Rather, as one might expect, he applies a description like the one given by Grenz and Franke to *classical* (or, what he calls *strong*) foundationalism (Wood, pp. 84–5). The characterization of classical foundationalism that I have given is the one found in Alvin Plantinga and Nicholas Wolterstorff (eds.), *Faith and Rationality: Reason and Belief in God* (Notre Dame, Ind.: University of Notre Dame Press, 1983).

beliefs are those that are rationally or justifiably held in the basic way. Perceptual beliefs, for example, are usually thought to be justifiably based on experiences rather than beliefs. Thus, they are typically considered to be examples of properly basic beliefs. Source foundationalism, on the other hand, is the view that some of our sources of evidence are privileged in the sense that (*a*) they can rationally be trusted in the absence of evidence of their reliability, and (*b*) it is irrational to rely on other sources of evidence unless they are somehow 'certified' by the privileged sources.[18] Classical empiricism and rationalism are both examples of source foundationalism. Distinguishing between these two brands of foundationalism is important, because doing so will help us to get a sense for what the connection between postmodernism and non-foundationalism is supposed to be.

Pick up any of a variety of postmodernish texts inveighing against foundationalism, and you will find something like the following story. The modern period was dominated by an obsession with certainty and a quest for indubitable, incorrigible foundations for knowledge. Rational beliefs were supposed to be just those beliefs that were part of the indubitable and incorrigible foundation, together with those that were deducible from the former. But, alas, subsequent work in philosophy demonstrated that the quest was in vain, that foundations of this sort are not to be had. Thus, foundationalism is no longer viable.

The story about what follows from the alleged death of foundationalism (both historically and logically) is variously told, but at least two consequences seem to be fairly widely heralded. First, it is said that we must give up on the idea that there are universal standards of rationality, and we must see facts about rationality and 'the deliverances of reason' as being in some way dependent upon historical and cultural factors. Second, it is said that the death of foundationalism has now put us into what Lyotard characterizes as the 'postmodern condition'—namely, a state of 'incredulity toward metanarratives' (Lyotard, *The Postmodern Condition*, p. xxiv). A metanarrative, as I understand it, is a grand story aimed at the 'legitimation' of some broad field of inquiry (e.g. empirical science). It is, in other words, an account that aims to show—once and for all, as it were—that a certain mode of inquiry is reliably truth-aimed.

---

[18] *Rejecting* source foundationalism, then, will be a matter of rejecting at least one of the two components that I have just identified. Note, however, that those who reject source foundationalism might still *treat* various sources of evidence as basic, in the sense that (*a*) they rely on those sources in the absence of evidence for their reliability, and (*b*) they treat other sources as in need of certification by the sources they privilege. Doing this does not count as accepting source foundationalism because it does not involve the belief that doing otherwise is irrational, nor does it necessarily even involve beliefs about the reliability of the sources that one in fact treats as basic.

But why should these consequences be taken as somehow natural or inevitable consequences of the death of foundationalism? And what have they to do with analytic ambitions? Regarding the first question, I suggest that the details might be filled in as follows. Remember that the modern quest for secure foundations for knowledge also included a quest for what Roderick Chisholm would call a *criterion* of knowledge: a mark possessed by all and only beliefs that count as knowledge (or, alternatively, by all and only beliefs that belong in the foundation).[19] For Descartes, the mark was 'clarity and distinctness': beliefs that possess the mark are foundational; beliefs that don't are justified only if they are derivable from foundational beliefs. Notoriously, however, Descartes faced real problems providing a defense (or, one might say, a *legitimation*) of his criterion. The criterion could be circularly defended, or simply accepted without any defense; but it is hard to see any way of 'getting behind' it, so to speak, and defending it without relying on it or on some other, similarly indefensible criterion. Thus, if one is persuaded that circular defenses are wholly unacceptable, the prospects for this part of the Cartesian project look dim.

Of course, the claim that we can find and provide a non-circular defense of a criterion of knowledge is no part of doxastic foundationalism as such. But it is easy to see why one might think that the failure of Descartes' quest points to a general problem with finding criteria for knowledge. And it is easy to see how skepticism about criteria would translate into incredulity toward metanarratives. If we can't find criteria, then, ultimately, we can't demonstrate the reliability of *any* of our putative sources of knowledge (reason, sense perception, religious experience, etc.). Thus, any grand story we tell in defense of some mode of inquiry will ultimately rely on suppositions about our sources that we can't defend. Metanarratives, one and all, will be nothing more than castles in the air.

This spells trouble for source foundationalisms like empiricism and rationalism. If we can't legitimate any of our sources then it's hard to see how we could have any basis for privileging one over the others as empiricists and rationalists have traditionally wanted to do. For exactly the same reason, it spells trouble for the prospects of *defending* an alleged universal standard of rationality. Source foundationalisms offer, at least implicitly, such standards. But so too does coherentism—very roughly, the view that beliefs are justified by virtue of their coherence with other beliefs we hold. Thus, all of these views will have to be tossed out as indefensible, and we will have to move to a position according to which decisions about which sources to trust and which

---

[19] See Chisholm, *Foundations of Knowing* (Minneapolis: University of Minnesota Press, 1982), esp. ch. 1.

standards of rationality to adopt are simply ungrounded pragmatic choices.[20] In moving to this sort of position, it is not inevitable that we give up on universal standards of rationality. There *being* such a standard is consistent with our not being able to *defend* any particular standard. But to avoid giving up on universal standards, we must take a very optimistic view either of our ability to hit on the correct standard by accident (evolutionary or otherwise) or by divine design.[21]

I have been moving quickly here, and painting with a broad brush; but I think that something like what I have just said is a reasonable reconstruction of how many thinkers manage to move from the failure of classical foundationalism to some of the postmodern distinctives that might otherwise seem rather remote from it. But now how does all of this hook up with a decision to reject analytic approaches to problems in philosophy and theology?

I said earlier that source foundationalisms lurk in the background of a great deal of analytic philosophical theorizing. Philosophical naturalism has dominated the contemporary philosophical landscape and, though I do not myself think that it is a version of source foundationalism, there is no denying that many naturalists have characterized it as such.[22] Moreover, many of the research projects undertaken by analytic philosophers can be characterized as contributions to large-scale efforts to work out the explanatory/theoretical consequences of adherence to some particular brand of source foundationalism. Crudely, we can think of many projects as trying to help answer questions like, 'Suppose the methods of science and those methods alone are the only sources of knowledge that need not be certified by other sources. How then should we think about consciousness?' Likewise in theology. Again crudely, one might think that many projects in systematic theology (traditionally construed) are aimed at answering questions like, 'Suppose Reason and the Bible are sources of knowledge that need not be certified by other sources. How then should we think about the metaphysics of the incarnation?' But for those who have given up on source foundationalisms, these sorts of projects can seem rather pointless. Different communities will rationally adopt different standards of evidence and rationality; and so they

---

[20] This is a position I have defended elsewhere. See ch. 1 of my *World Without Design: The Ontological Consequences of Naturalism* (Oxford: Clarendon Press, 2002). Note, however, that in saying that it is via *pragmatic choices* that we determine which sources to trust and which standards of rationality to adopt, I do not mean to suggest that our trust in those sources or our adoption of those standards is *merely* pragmatically (as opposed to epistemically) rational. This is discussed ibid., esp. chs. 1 and 3.

[21] Ibid., ch. 1, for further discussion of this point.

[22] I do not think that it is a version of source foundationalism because source foundationalism is a *view* according to which we have certain privileged sources, and naturalism, as I understand it, is not a view at all. For defense of this claim, ibid., esp. chs. 2 and 3.

will naturally—and rightly—think differently from one another about theological matters. The project we *ought* to engage in, one might think, is a more conversational project—one which aims to assess each of the different 'traditions' by its own standards and then to bring the best in all of them into dialogue with one another. The analytic ambition of going to the sources and working out a single grand explanatory theory is myopic at best.

It is important to pause here, however, and note that there are *quite a lot* of presuppositions and questionable inferences in the movement I have traced from the failure of classical foundationalism to the abandonment of analytic ambitions. Though many of the moves I have described seem natural in one way or another, and maybe even philosophically defensible, the movement as a whole still seems to me to be far from inevitable, despite the way in which many 'post-foundationalist' philosophers and theologians seem to talk. But even if it is not a logically inevitable movement, there might be further motives in play.

The sorts of 'further motives' I have in mind are pragmatic. For instance: The majority opinion among contemporary philosophers (analytic and continental alike) seems to be that neither of the source foundationalisms—empiricism and rationalism—that have dominated the history of philosophy is especially friendly toward religious belief. There are, of course, plenty of philosophical arguments (both empirical and a priori) for the existence of God and even for particular doctrines of Christianity, like the resurrection of Jesus. Moreover, many of these arguments are still avidly defended. Even so, the arguments are widely regarded even among religious philosophers as impotent to convince the unconvinced. One response to all of this has been, effectively, a move in the direction of a new brand of source foundationalism—one that admits religious experience, or something like a special faculty for producing religious beliefs (such as Calvin's *sensus divinitatis*), as an additional basic source of evidence.[23] But a natural alternative response—especially in light of the suggestion that Descartes's failure spells trouble in general for source foundationalism—is to look with despair upon the prospects for developing a

---

[23] So-called 'Reformed Epistemology' is part of this trend. (See, esp., the essays in Plantinga and Wolterstorff, *Faith and Rationality*.) The 'core' of Reformed Epistemology is the view that certain kinds of religious beliefs (e.g. belief that God exists) are properly basic—i.e. that they are justifiably held in the absence of propositional evidence. Saying this implies a rejection of the traditional source foundationalisms; but, of course, it isn't equivalent to affirming any *new* brand of source foundationalism. Indeed, it is consistent with an outright rejection of source foundationalism. Still, it seems fair to characterize it (as I have) as a step in the direction of a new brand of source foundationalism. See also Plantinga's *Warranted Christian Belief* (New York: Oxford University Press, 2000) and William P. Alston's *Perceiving God* (Ithaca, NY: Cornell University Press, 1991). On the *sensus divinitatis* in particular, see Plantinga, *Warranted Christian Belief*, esp. pp. 170–84, and John Calvin, *Institutes of the Christian Religion*, bk. I, ch. iii, pp. 43–6 in *Calvin: Institutes of the Christian Religion*, ed. J. T. McNeill and tr. F. L. Battles (Philadelphia, Pa.: Westminster Press, 1960).

satisfying theology within source-foundationalist constraints, and to decide simply on pragmatic grounds to embrace a different methodological tradition altogether. As I see it, this second response arises not so much out of a cold logical inference from the demise of classical foundationalism to the rejection of analytic ambitions, but just out of a sense that one has seen the breach in the hull, as it were, and ought therefore to abandon ship.

Summing up, I have discussed two main objections to analytic ambitions. First, those ambitions seem to presuppose a false view about what theology can actually accomplish. Second, the grand explanatory aims of analytic theology seem to fit best within a tradition that takes some version of source foundationalism for granted; but the alleged death of classical foundationalism, together with the widely perceived tension between religious belief and the dominant source foundationalisms in the analytic tradition, provide a rather complicated impetus toward alternative modes of theorizing. In the next section, I turn to objections against the analytic *style*.

AGAINST THE ANALYTIC STYLE

In *Continental Philosophy: A Very Short Introduction*,[24] Simon Critchley argues that the original aim of philosophy was not theoretical knowledge (as, he thinks, it is today) but rather *wisdom*. Philosophy, he says, was an 'eminently practical activity' (p. 1), whereas now it has been relegated to the role of 'an under-labourer to science, whose job is to clear away the rubbish that lies in the way to knowledge and scientific progress' (p. 5). Analytic ambitions naturally place philosophy in the latter role, since it will be mostly in the sciences rather than in philosophy that we will find the details of the grand explanatory theory that analytic philosophers are collectively (more or less) working toward. The contribution made by philosophers is precisely that of clarifying, drawing out consequences, and building theories that, as Quine puts it, 'fill out interstices of [scientific] theory and lead to further hypotheses that are testable'.[25] By contrast, '[t]he appeal of much that goes under the name of Continental philosophy', Critchley says, 'is that it attempts to unify or at least move closer together questions of knowledge and wisdom, of philosophical truth and existential meaning' (p. 9).

Analytic philosophers will naturally protest that this alleged difference is *at best* an accident of history. Even if it is true that the explanatory ambitions of

---

[24] Oxford: OUP, 2001.
[25] 'Naturalism, or: Living Within one's Means', *Dialectica*, 49 (1995), 251.

the analytic tradition push it toward scientistic metaphysics rather than toward wisdom and the knowledge of how to live rightly, and even if we ignore all of the work that is being done every year in (say) applied ethics and political philosophy (to name just two among several practically oriented subfields), there is still no reason why analytic philosophers couldn't turn their collective attention away from science-related projects and toward the discovery of wisdom.

But my impression is that critics of analytic philosophy will see this response as entirely missing the point. True, the 'analytic ambitions' described above don't characterize everything that falls within the tradition; and true, there is nothing to prevent a bunch of metaphysicians from deciding one day to start writing analytic philosophical books about the meaning of life. But, the objector will say, the *prescriptions* that characterize the analytic tradition reflect the wrong set of priorities. The problem with analytic philosophy is that it prioritizes clarity and precision *at the expense of everything else,* and it ignores the fact that sometimes, in order to attain wisdom and understanding, we have to rely substantively on metaphor and other literary tropes. Analytic philosophers are unwilling to step outside the box of what is cognitively familiar—their own 'well-understood primitives', reasoning in accord with the canons of logic, and so on—for the sake of wisdom, philosophy's traditional prize.

It is easy to see how this sort of objection would resonate with theologians. Recall the Heideggerian claim, referred to earlier, that 'theology in its essence is a practical science'. Theology even more than philosophy, one might think, ought to be aimed at the pursuit of wisdom, right living, and related ideals. It ought, moreover, to be aimed at *cultivating* these things. Thus, to approach it in a way that prioritizes clarification and precision over more poetic rhetorical virtues might be seen as, again, rather myopic (or worse). Clarity and precision are nice; but poetic virtues are often better tools for inspiring and persuading. To the extent that the latter goals are part of the theological task, then, it might well seem foolish for theologians to restrict themselves to the former virtues in an effort to appear more tough-minded and 'scientific'.

As with other objections that I am discussing in this chapter, I will not attempt to respond to this one here. But I cannot resist noting that, despite the superficial attractiveness of the idea that philosophers and theologians ought to be aiming in the direction of wisdom and moral improvement, Christian philosophers as such, and theologians as well, might in fact have some reason for resisting this idea. Recently, a student from another (religious) university emailed me and asked, among other things, what philosophy books or articles I'd recommend for the purpose of helping him to grow in wisdom. My answer was that I wouldn't recommend philosophical texts for that purpose at all; rather, I'd recommend scripture. If philosophy as a discipline (or theology) were to aim its efforts at the production of a self-contained body of wisdom, or at a general theory of right living, it would (I think) be aiming at the production of a *rival* to scripture. And that is a project that I think Christian philosophers and theologians ought to try to avoid. Indeed, to my mind, this sort of project involves just as much hubris as onto-theology is said to involve. Thus, it seems to me that the right *theoretical* task for Christian philosophers and theologians to pursue is in fact one that involves clarifying, systematizing, and model-building—precisely the sort of project that analytic philosophers are engaged in.

In any case, the upshot of what I have said so far is that one objection to what I am calling the 'analytic style' is that it imposes constraints upon theorizing that, in the eyes of objectors anyway, actually *prevent* philosophers from doing their traditional task—namely, pursuing wisdom. It is important to note, furthermore, that the objection is really twofold. The prescriptions that favor clarity and well-understood primitives and that proscribe substantive use of metaphor partly constrain our *choice* of topics. So, in other words, part of the concern is that philosophers will miss out on the pursuit of wisdom simply by ignoring rich and messy topics in favor of ones that admit of neat, precise, and literal discussion. But the prescriptions also reflect contentious presuppositions about the nature of language and about the nature of the topics with which we deal. For one thing, they presuppose, to borrow a remark from H. H. Price, that 'whatever can be said, can be said clearly' ('Clarity is Not Enough', 40). Moreover, they presuppose that none of the objects of philosophical inquiry transcends human thought and categories in the way that God is thought to do by those in the tradition of apophatic theology.

This latter point is absolutely critical to understanding the present objection to analytic theology. As noted earlier, one might easily practice analytic theology while fully acknowledging that there are divine mysteries far beyond our ken. But enjoining theologians to avoid substantive use of tropes whose semantic content goes beyond their propositional content presupposes that we can have propositional knowledge about God, and so it presupposes that God is not *totally* mysterious. Many philosophers and theologians, however, will balk at these presuppositions; for many are inclined to think that divine transcendence places God beyond *all* human categories—so much so that it is a mistake even to say that God *exists* (for God is beyond Being in just the way in which God is beyond everything else), much less to say anything else positive about God.[26] Admittedly, it is not impossible to do

---

[26] See e.g. William Franke, 'Apophasis and the Turn of Philosophy to Religion: From Neoplatonic Negative Theology to Postmodern Negation of Theology', *International Journal for Philosophy of Religion*, 60 (2006), 61–76; Marion, *God Without Being*; Thomas Carlson, 'Postmetaphysical Theology', pp. 58–75 in Kevin Vanhoozer (ed.), *The Cambridge Companion to*

analytic theology in a way that respects the scruples of apophatic theologians. But one can't do *much* analytic theology in that way. Apophatic analytic theology is, of necessity, extremely thin. The reason is simple: if God really does transcend human categories, then the propositional content of our positive discourse about God will always be, strictly and literally speaking, false. Thus, evocative language—richly metaphorical language, for example, that can be used to convey a sort of non-propositional understanding—will be an integral part of any sensible theological project. So those who favor apophatic discourse about God will quite naturally think that the analytic style is exactly the wrong style for doing theology.[27]

Note too that it is not just the injunction against metaphor that the apophatic theologians will reject. The prioritization of clarity and logical rigor will naturally be rejected as well. This might seem odd: what could possibly be wrong with trying as hard as possible to be clear and coherent? But here, I think, it helps to bear in mind the reasons why we analytics not only strive for clarity, but *prioritize* it. H. H. Price is illuminating on this score:

> It is true that our modern clarifiers have more to say about words and sentences than their predecessors had, and even profess sometimes to be concerned with nothing else. But they are only interested in words and sentences because words and sentences are what we think with.... No doubt the sentences which are nowadays selected for clarification are in themselves trivial, and even sometimes rather ridiculous. As Dr. Joad points out, it does seem peculiar to worry oneself overmuch about the sentence 'this is a rocking-horse covered with pink spots'.... All the same, I should like to quote against Dr. Joad what the poet says of the flower in the crannied wall. If we could really be clear about the meaning of this sentence concerning the rocking-horse, which bristles with philosophical puzzles, I do not say that 'we should know what God and man is', but I think we should be in a much better position for finding out.[28]

Postmodern Theology (Cambridge: CUP, 2003); and Paul Tillich, *Systematic Theology*, i (Chicago: University of Chicago Press, 1951), esp. pp. 235 ff. Also illuminating on the subject of apophaticism generally are the readings and introductory essays in William Franke (ed.), *On What Cannot be Said: Apophatic Discourses in Philosophy, Religion, and the Arts*, i and ii (Notre Dame, Ind.: University of Notre Dame Press, 2007).

[27] So I say, anyway. But my co-editor objects that one might respond as follows (these are my words, not Oliver's; but he is the one who pressed me to consider an objection like this). An apophatic theologian will surely take issue with an analytic theologian who claims to have arrived at a definitive and comprehensive understanding of divine mysteries. But she needn't object to one who claims merely to be producing 'approximations' of the truth about God, and striving for constant, even if faltering, improvement in her approximations. If so, then an apophatic theologian could practice analytic theology after all. I am not so sure that this response is viable, though. I am inclined to think that the 'typical' apophatic theologian will think that the analytic theologian here described is not really apophatic *enough* to deserve the label.

[28] H. H. Price, 'Clarity is Not Enough', repr. in H. D. Lewis (ed.), *Clarity is Not Enough: Essays in Criticism of Linguistic Philosophy* (London: George Allen & Unwin, 1945), 31–2.

In short, Price seems to think that clarity of expression, and clear, precise thinking about what our words mean, is a route to understanding. But this is true, it seems, only if one has hope of reaching the sort of understanding that can be expressed propositionally. The apophatic theologians have given up on this ambition; and they have wholeheartedly embraced a mode of discourse that demands free and creative use of evocative language. Clarity when possible might be nice; but to prioritize it in apophatic discourse—at any rate, in apophatic discourse that aims to be robust and interesting—makes no sense whatsoever.

The twofold objection considered thus far—that the analytic style subverts the proper goals of theology by both restricting our choice of topics and encouraging us to use what may well be the wrong rhetorical tools—primarily targets prescriptions P2, P3, and P4 listed earlier.[29] Now I'd like to turn to two further objections, one against P1 and the other against P5.

P1 recommends that we operate under the assumption that positions and conclusions can be formulated in sentences that can be formalized and logically manipulated. One might object, however, that this prescription misconstrues the nature of philosophical and theological positions. Consider empiricism, for example. This position is notoriously problematic when thought of simply as a thesis about sources of knowledge. It is significantly less so when thought of as somehow involving attitudes, preferences, dispositions, and so on.[30] Though no one that I know of has said exactly this, one might easily imagine someone claiming that empiricism simply cannot be understood apart from extensive familiarity with the writings of various historical empiricists. Any attempt to distill the position down to a thesis would inevitably fail; any attempt to express it propositionally and reject it on the basis of its alleged 'logical consequences' would be wholly misguided.[31] And the problem would be that all such attempts are objectionably 'ahistorical'. They leave out the historical circumstances (whatever they might be—facts about particular authors and their intellectual climates, facts about what the position at various times is being defined in contrast with, and so on) that help constitute the position as whatever it is, and so they set up a mere caricature as an object of discussion or target for attack. Nobody that I am aware of has actually accused critics of empiricism of being 'ahistorical' in just

---

[29] See p. 5 above.
[30] For defense of this claim, see esp. van Fraassen, *Empirical Stance*, ch. 2.
[31] One might concede that empiricism could be propositionally *described*—say, at book length, in a way that amounted to tracing out its history and development, its contours at various times in history, and so on. But, of course, this sort of 'propositional characterization' of empiricism is not one that would facilitate projects that aim to draw out the logical consequences of empiricism, or to test it for internal coherence, or any such thing. Thanks to Sam Newlands and Jim Beilby for helpful conversation on this point.

this way; but the charge has been leveled against (for example) analytic philosophers who treat fundamental doctrines of Christianity in the way prescribed by P1. Such philosophers are often mystified by the criticism, in no small part because many of us often comment on (and thus show awareness of) the history of the relevant doctrines in the course of our philosophical treatments of them.[32] But the objection lingers, I think, precisely because we do not regard the history as in any meaningful sense *determinative* of the doctrines.[33]

Other views about the nature of philosophical and theological positions will also cause trouble for the attempt to conform to P1 in theological writing. For example, George Lindbeck has argued that doctrinal sentences (e.g. 'Jesus is the Son of God', or the sentences that comprise the Nicene Creed) are not to be regarded as expressing the propositions that they would if interpreted at face value.[34] Rather, they are to be seen as providing a 'grammar' for religious discourse—analogous, perhaps, to a system of uninterpreted axioms and inference rules in a formal logic. On Lindbeck's view (as I understand it), the claim that Jesus is the Son of God can be interpreted by Christians in all manner of different ways, so long as it coheres with whatever interpretations are given to other 'axiomatic' sentences, and so long as the right sorts of inferences are preserved.[35] If this is right, then doctrinal claims as such do not express determinate propositions, and there is no guarantee that they will do so even once they have been interpreted. On some interpretations, for example, the claim that Jesus is the Son of God might be an evocative metaphor with very minimal, if any, propositional content. As a *general* strategy for doing theology, then, P1 will be wholly off-target.

Lastly, I turn to an objection against P5. A common complaint against 'metaphysical' theorizing about God is that it is idolatrous. As I see it, the rationale behind this complaint amounts, in the end, to a rejection of the idea that conceptual analysis is to be treated as a source of evidence. Let me explain why.

---

[32] Such is the reaction of H. H. Price to this sort of objection. See 'Clarity is Not Enough', 22.

[33] The first clear expression of this idea that I encountered was in Beau Branson's dissertation proposal (unpublished). I do not know whether he would endorse it exactly as I have articulated it here, however.

[34] *The Nature of Doctrine* (Louisville: Ky., Westminster/John Knox, 1984).

[35] Presumably a further constraint is that each term must be uniformly interpreted throughout the system. Thus, though Lindbeck doesn't explicitly say anything to rule out our interpreting 'Jesus is the Son of God' as having the same meaning as '2 + 2 = 4', I take it that the demand for uniform treatment of terms *will* rule out such interpretations. For, given the uniform-treatment constraint, a mathematical interpretation of 'Jesus is the Son of God' would force at least a partially mathematical interpretation of (say) the Apostle's Creed and the Nicene Creed; but it would be extremely difficult, at best, to provide consistent interpretations of that sort.

In *The Empirical Stance,* Bas van Fraassen raises two main objections against the enterprise of analytic metaphysics. One objection (which I won't discuss here) is that analytic metaphysicians posit objects and properties to do *explanatory* work—a practice which he regards as rationally indefensible. The other is that the practice of analytic metaphysics results in the creation of 'simulacra' which then replace, as our primary objects of discourse, the things about which we actually *meant* to be talking—the things that we actually care about when we ask philosophical questions.

One gets the impression that Van Fraassen thinks explanation via theoretical posit is what results in the creation of simulacra.[36] But upon further reflection it looks as if conceptual analysis is the real culprit. Thus, for example, he argues that when philosophers ask the question 'Does the world exist', what they inevitably do is to make the question rigorous with technical definitions of 'world' and related terms that map onto some but not nearly all uses of the term 'world', and then they stipulate that the world exists if, and only if, the world *as they have defined it* exists. On his view, the 'world as they have defined it' is a simulacrum (*The Empirical Stance,* 27–8). But what makes it the case that the 'world of the philosophers' is a simulacrum isn't the fact that it is *postulated.* For, after all, if the technical concept had turned out to be identical to the ordinary concept, then the postulated world would have been nothing other than the real world—not a simulacrum at all. Rather, what makes the world of the philosophers a simulacrum (if anything does) is just the fact that satisfying a philosopher's analysis of the concept world is, in general, a different thing from *being a world.* But this can be right only if there is something inherently defective about treating conceptual analysis as a source of evidence. The idea seems to be that, in trying to answer the question 'Does the world exist?', metaphysicians will *inevitably* analyze the concept of a world in a way that illegitimately privileges some aspects of the concept over others as being central, or essential. (And likewise with other concepts.) Thus the result will always be that satisfying a metaphysician's analysis of a concept is different from satisfying the concept itself. But if this is right then it is an illegitimate use of conceptual analysis rather than postulation that results in the shift from talking about things we care about to mere simulacra.

On van Fraassen's view, the same sort of shift occurs when we theologize like analytic metaphysicians. We do with God what he accuses us of doing with 'the world': we effectively introduce a new term, one which is 'intelligibly related to [the old one] taking over a carefully selected family of uses, regimenting them, and is then used to make new, logically contingent, fully intelligible assertions' (ibid. 27). But, again, the *referent* of the new term is not

---

[36] See esp. *Empirical Stance,* pp. 25 ff.

the same as the referent of the old; talk of 'the God of the philosophers' simply replaces talk about God. Thus, the God of analytic metaphysical discourse is a simulacrum as well—or, in theological terms, an idol.

Van Fraassen doesn't defend this charge in any detail. Presumably he takes his earlier discussion of metaphysical discourse about 'the world' as providing ample evidence that the charge is apt. But the same sort of objection has been raised by others, and they do fill in some of the details. Thus, for example, Marion argues that 'metaphysics' is brought to an end when the quest for an 'ultimate ground of being' is abandoned; and he goes on to say, in effect, that the end of metaphysics spells the death of the God of the philosophers, for the God of the philosophers is posited precisely to serve as the ultimate ground ('Metaphysics and Phenomenology', 579). But, Marion argues, this 'death of God' isn't really the death of *God*; for, by this point, 'God is no longer at issue—but rather "God", who by his quotation marks is stigmatized as an idol' (ibid.). As with Van Fraassen, this looks initially to be an objection simply against explanation via theoretical posit. But the fact is that one arrives at this particular posit ultimately by way of something like conceptual analysis: unpacking our concept of God (as the sort of thing capable of serving as ultimate ground), our concept of contingent being (as something in need of a ground), and so on.

Of course, one might well point out that Marion's point will have purchase only on those who (unlike most of us nowadays, I should think) are inclined to think of God as something whose existence is *posited* as the 'ground of all being'. But in fact the point is broader than this. In 'The Idea of God', Marion claims that, by the seventeenth century, God had become 'a term in a demonstration, and no longer the assumed goal of a journey towards him' (p. 265). He goes on to argue that the various conceptions of God (or, as he puts it, 'names of God') that are presupposed in proofs of his existence such as those given by Descartes conflict to varying degrees. Thus, for example, in Descartes's proofs, God is seen as (i) a transcendent, incomprehensible, infinite substance, (ii) a perfect being who possesses to a maximal degree all of the (same) perfections possessed by finite creatures and whose essence includes his existence, and (iii) the first cause, the ground of all being. But, Marion argues, if we make positive affirmations about God and God's essence, as we do in conceiving of God in the second way, then we give up on our conception of him as transcendent and incomprehensible. Likewise, if we invoke the Principle of Sufficient Reason in defending the third conception, we '[impose] a precondition as to what is possible and what is not upon the supposedly transcendent God' (ibid. 277). Thus, (i) and (iii) appear to conflict as well. On the other hand, Marion notes that, in the course of offering the proof of God's existence as ground of all being, Descartes characterized God's power as 'immense and incomprehensible power'—in line with (i), but in conflict with (ii) if the divine perfections are to be understood as the perfections of finite beings taken to a maximal degree (ibid. 276–8).

Suppose Marion is right in thinking that Descartes was having a problem maintaining consistency in the premises of his natural theological arguments. Suppose also that he is right in thinking that we have somehow moved beyond trying to show that there is a 'ground of all being'. At this point, I think that sympathizers with analytic theology will object that showing these things is a far cry from showing that the 'God of the philosophers' is a simulacrum or an idol. True enough; but to stop there, I think, would be to miss what I think is the real import (for our purposes) of what Marion, Van Fraassen, and others are trying to show. The problem in short is that God falls, analogically at least, under a variety of concepts—some philosophical, some not. God is the perfect being and the first cause; but God is also our heavenly father, the stern employer of the parable of the talents, the righteous judge, our companion in paradise, and the Ancient of Days seated on the throne of fire. Theorizing about God via conceptual analysis, as we in the analytic tradition often do, involves attributing properties to God based on our intuitions about how best to analyze these concepts. But to do that coherently, we must privilege some ways of conceiving of God over others. We must also determine the *extent* to which the relevant concept applies—whether it applies fully and literally, or only analogically; and if only analogically, then how quickly the analogy breaks down, etc. The assumptions that determine the privileging, as well as the assumptions that determine the extent to which each concept applies—not to mention the intuitions that determine the analysis of a concept like *perfect being*—will all be highly contentious. And different sets of assumptions along these lines will result in very different characterizations of God. Hence the concern about constructing 'simulacra'. The methodological worry here is, I think, genuine; and it is one that analytic theologians ought to take seriously.[37]

This completes my survey of what I take to be the main objections against the enterprise of analytic theology. Not all of the objections seem to me to be of equal strength; but all do seem serious and widespread enough to merit more attention in the literature—both by those who embrace them and by those who reject them. It is the hope for such further open discussion that gave birth to the present volume.

---

[37] Thanks to Daniel Howard-Snyder for raising some helpful objections to an earlier version of this paragraph.

THE CHAPTERS

As indicated earlier, the contributors and co-editors of this volume do not share a perfectly uniform vision about the nature of analytic theology, about the shape or relative import of the 'main' objections against it, or even about what one ought to do (if anything) to find a place for it in the academy. Despite that, the collective vision is at least roughly homogeneous; and the chapters that follow touch in various and interesting ways upon the objections just described.

The first three chapters are aimed explicitly at the defense of analytic theology. Oliver Crisp and William J. Abraham articulate similar visions of analytic theology and then proceed to address concerns about and objections against the enterprise. According to Crisp, analytic theology is an approach that is characterized by (*a*) explanatory/metaphysical ambitions that prioritize explanations marked by rhetorical features like clarity and (*b*) a commitment to the view that there are theological truths that are accessible to human beings. He also emphasizes that analytic theology as such carries *no* commitment to the view that reason is a source of 'fundamental knowledge' (rather than merely a tool for exploring the relations among ideas). Abraham's vision is similar, even if somewhat narrower: on his view, analytic theology is 'systematic theology attuned to the deployment of the skills, resources, and virtues of analytical philosophy'. On Crisp's view, concerns about analytic theology are likely to arise out of misconceptions about its commitments—e.g. that it is committed to a form of what I have here been calling 'source foundationalism', or to a particular theory of truth, or to seeing philosophy as authoritative over theology. Much of his chapter is devoted to dispelling these misconceptions. Abraham also addresses objections against analytic theology, but more of his contribution is devoted to exploring what analytic theology might actually look like.

Randal Rauser's chapter, 'Theology as a Bull Session', is more polemical and, to put it mildly, provocative and controversial. It aims at combating two important 'alternatives' to analytic theology: Sallie McFague's 'persuasive metaphor' model of theology, and Jürgen Moltmann's 'perpetual conversation' model. Drawing on recent philosophical analyses of—yes—the concept of *bullshit*, Rauser argues that both of these models make theological discourse out to be precisely that: idle and fruitless conversation, nothing more than mere bullshit.

In the next Part, we turn to historical perspectives on a variety of issues relevant to the viability of analytic theology. The section opens with a chapter by John Lamont on the notion of faith in the Greek Fathers. According to Lamont, the view under discussion traces back to Clement of Alexandria, exerted influence on the Greek Fathers, anticipated ideas in Aquinas, and was later brought to completion in the work of the seventeenth-century Puritan John Owen. It is a view according to which faith is grounded in divine testimony, where testimony is construed as a basic source of rational belief separate from (and in no need of certification by) sense perception and reason. It is also a view according to which knowledge of God can be obtained by rational reflection upon truths believed on faith. Though Lamont does not discuss analytic theology directly, the significance of his chapter in light of the foregoing should be plain. Lamont is identifying a view of faith and theological reflection that rejects the traditional rationalist/empiricist dichotomy (and which in some figures seems to carry no commitment to any sort of source foundationalism as it was understood above) and yet leaves room for substantive knowledge of God by way of reason.

The next two chapters, by Andrew Chignell and Andrew Dole, focus on a pair of figures who might well be thought to be driving forces behind a great deal of contemporary opposition to analytic theology: Kant and Schleiermacher. Kant is widely regarded as having shown things that imply that the substantive theological ambitions of analytic theologians are unattainable. Likewise, Friedrich Schleiermacher has 'frequently been accused of "emptying" Christian faith of its (metaphysical) content and reducing it to a "merely individual and subjective" phenomenon' (Dole). But Chignell argues that 'Kant doesn't exactly hold what "Kant has shown"', and Dole rejects the idea that, on Schleiermacher's view, religious doctrines do not make truth claims. According to Chignell, Kant engages in substantive theology himself and wouldn't stand in clear opposition either to the project of providing analyses of religious concepts (including our concept of God), or to the application of the tools and methods of analytic metaphysics to theological topics. Dole argues that Schleiermacher would oppose the metaphysical/explanatory ambitions of analytic philosophy as a component of theology; but he provides reasons for doubting that analytic theologians ought to follow him in this.

Finally, Nicholas Wolterstorff examines how developments in the analytic tradition during the twentieth century not only made room for analytic philosophical theology, but contributed to its flourishing. Wolterstorff does not make it an explicit goal to respond to the objections against analytic theology outlined above. Nevertheless, one important feature of his chapter is that it goes some distance toward showing how several of the objections discussed thus far rest on misconceptions or caricatures of analytic philosophy as it is practiced today.

Part III examines what might be called the 'data' for theology. Earlier I noted that one concern about the analytic tradition is its apparent obsession with source foundationalisms. And one motive for adopting alternative approaches to theology is a certain sort of skepticism about our ability to acquire information or genuine evidence about the character and attributes of God. The chapters in this part address issues in this neighborhood.

I said earlier that some (like Merold Westphal) are concerned about approaches to theological topics that imply or take for granted the idea that God is somehow 'at our disposal'. According to Thomas McCall, this is a concern shared by Karl Barth; and the concern partly motivates his view of scripture, according to which scripture is not 'on its own' (so to speak) the Word of God, but rather only 'becomes' the Word of God as God reveals himself to those who engage with scripture. McCall engages with this idea and argues that the concerns that motivate Barth in this direction can be addressed without giving up the classical view of scripture, according to which scripture's status as the Word of God does not depend upon additional revelatory acts. One consequence of his view (not explicitly drawn) is that those who object to the idea that God might somehow be placed 'at our disposal' in certain ways need not object to the idea that divine truths can be communicated in a way that makes them fully accessible to human beings without special additional acts of revelation. If this is right, then it will go a long way toward addressing some of the concerns raised in earlier sections of this introduction.

In the next two essays, Thomas Crisp and Michael Sudduth, respectively, explore the ways in which sources other than reason and sense perception function in the formation and rational grounding of important theological beliefs. Crisp argues that belief in the inspiration of scripture is warranted for many, maybe most, Christians by what he calls 'authoritative testimony' rather than by natural theological arguments or the 'internal testimony of the Holy Spirit'. And Sudduth argues that dogmatic theology—the 'examination and systematic development of dogmas, ecclesiastically formulated and sanctioned core theological beliefs ostensibly based on scripture'—must take account of the role played by religious experience as a source of justification for theological beliefs. In the course of making their arguments, furthermore, Sudduth argues that religious experience plays a vital role in *natural* theology (the enterprise of trying to arrive at knowledge of God by way of a priori or empirical argument), and Crisp argues against the idea that natural theology warrants belief in the inspiration of scripture. Together, these two chapters help to provide a corrective to the idea that analytic theology is wedded to an overly optimistic view about the power of pure reason to provide grounds for theological beliefs.

Next Michael Murray examines the relationship between theology and science. On Murray's view, the most promising model of the interaction between theology and science is one of 'constructive engagement': theologians ought to take account of developments in science in the course of working out their theories, but likewise, religious believers at any rate ought to recognize that 'authoritative religious teaching can and does have consequences for the natural world, consequences which yield empirically testable conclusions'. Theology and science might thus be seen (by religious believers, at least) as working cooperatively toward a unified explanatory theory. Here too, then, we find a model for understanding theology that retains analytic ambitions without either embracing an objectionable rationalism or forcing theology somehow to accommodate the strictures of empiricism.

In the last part of the volume, we have placed three chapters that offer what might be thought of as 'correctives' to analytic theology. One way to offer a corrective to a theoretical enterprise is to point out methodological shortcomings. Another way is to suggest alternatives. The first way is taken by Eleonore Stump, who argues that one shortcoming of analytic philosophy is *hemianopia*: a narrow focus on left-brain processing skills. Because of this, she thinks, analytic philosophers end up ignoring important sources of information. One such source, she thinks, is narrative. On her view, narratives that relate one person's experience of another convey non-propositional information about the person (or about persons generally) that might, in principle, function evidentially in philosophical argument. This is of particular importance, obviously enough, in theology; for the Bible is a rich source of narratives relating the experiences *of God* that have been had by various people. If she is right, then an approach to theology that ignores the evidential value of narrative *as such* will be severely limited.

The second way is taken by Merold Westphal. The alternative that Westphal proposes is a theology which takes hermeneutical phenomenology, rather than analytic philosophy, as its ally. As noted earlier, one of Westphal's concerns about analytic approaches to theology is that they seem to encourage (indeed, they might seem to be fixated on) the idea that we can, with our limited human cognitive apparatus, come to know eternal, non-perspectival, objective truths about God and the world. This idea naturally attends a conception of the primary theological task as one of *theoretical understanding*—a conception which, as I have already indicated, is central to the enterprise of analytic theology. A theology which takes hermeneutical phenomenology as its philosophical ally, however, will think of the primary theological task as one of interpretation, and as one whose goal isn't so much theoretical understanding as practical wisdom—right living or, as Westphal puts it, holiness.

This, according to Westphal, is a conception of theology that fits better with, among other things, the fact of human finitude.

In the final chapter, Sarah Coakley looks at the mystical writings of St Teresa of Ávila with an eye to providing certain correctives to analytic appropriations of St Teresa's work. Earlier in this essay, I noted that one way of responding to the collapse of classical foundationalism within the analytic tradition has been to move toward a brand of source foundationalism that treats religious experience as a basic source of knowledge. In partial support of this move, analytic philosophers have turned to the writings of Christian mystics like St Teresa.[38] According to Coakley, however, analytic work on the writings of mystical theologians tends to be insensitive to their apophatic character, which the continental tradition understandably celebrates. Moreover, she argues, the analytic tradition has not sufficiently appreciated the way in which the 'experiential turn' in contemporary religious epistemology is, effectively, a turn toward the exploration of stereotypically feminine ways of knowing. Accordingly, it has left much of the epistemological significance of St Teresa's work unexplored. Toward filling this lacuna, Coakley considers the way in which St Teresa's work might suggest important roles for both *contemplative practice* (as opposed to isolated religious experiences) and apophatic sensibilities in the epistemology of religious belief. In this way, she closes our volume with a project whose aim is 'not so much to adjudicate between [continental and analytic] philosophical projects as to nudge creatively beyond them'.

[38] See esp. Alston, *Perceiving God*.

I

In Defense of Analytic Theology

1

On Analytic Theology

Oliver D. Crisp

There is nothing true in divinity which is false in philosophy, or the contrary.

(Benjamin Whichcote)

Some contemporary theologians bewail the fact that much modern systematic theology seems mired in theological prolegomena and never gets on to the more constructive task of explicating the content of Christian doctrine. Thus David Tracy: '*the* problem for the contemporary systematic theologian, as has often been remarked, is actually *to do* systematic theology'.[1] But this is surely an overstatement. Constructive systematic theology is being engaged in, as even a casual glance at the literature will show.[2] However, there is also a preponderance of work dealing with questions of theological method, one central aspect of traditional theological prolegomena.[3] There is good reason for this. A number of contemporary theologians have, for various reasons, been trying to find new ways of presenting Christian doctrine in the current intellectual climate, and that inevitably raises methodological issues.

This chapter represents one such contribution to the current discussion of theological method. In it I will outline a possible research programme that could provide a fruitful means of thinking theologically. The primary aim is to recommend a particular theological methodology, not to advocate one particular construal of that methodology. However, in the course of setting

---

[1] David Tracy, *Blessed Rage for Order: The New Pluralism in Theology* (Chicago: Chicago University Press, 1996 [1975]), 238; emphasis original.

[2] This was true even in the mid-1970s when Tracy's book was first published. Representative examples of recent constructive systematic theology include the work of Jürgen Moltmann, Wolfhart Pannenberg, Eberhard Jüngel, Thomas Torrance, John Webster, Colin Gunton, Robert Jenson, Millard Erickson, and many others.

[3] Two recent North American examples are the postliberal theological agenda expressed by George Lindbeck in *The Nature of Christian Doctrine* (London: SPCK, 1984) and the postconservative theology advocated by Stanley Grenz in *Revisioning Evangelical Theology: A Fresh Agenda for the Twenty-first Century* (Downers Grove, Ill.: IVP, 1993). In the UK, John Hick's work in religious pluralism might be construed as a project in theological method, or as having important methodological implications.

out this methodology, including a number of different ways in which analytic theology could be understood, I shall try to indicate where my own sympathies lie.

The theological model under consideration draws upon one stream of current philosophical thinking, namely, analytic philosophy of religion, hence the title of this chapter.[4] To some (especially, to some theologians) the idea of 'analytic' theology might look like a Trojan horse, by which I mean a method of smuggling into the citadel of theology potentially destructive alien ideas. However, I will argue that this need not be the case, if analytic theology is rightly understood.[5] This is, therefore, a plea to theologians to give this particular way of doing theology a fair hearing. But it might also be of interest to those philosophers already engaged on something akin to analytic theology.[6]

WHAT IS ANALYTIC THEOLOGY?

In theology, procedural issues that are usually found in discussions of prolegomena fall into one of two categories: methodological, or formal concerns about the way theologians should approach substantive matters in Christian doctrine, and substantive, or material concerns about the nature of Christian doctrine.[7] This is a distinction that can be found, in various forms, in much traditional theological literature, particularly the literature indebted to a

---

[4] The term 'analytic theology' is broader than 'Analytic Thomism' as it is understood by John Haldane (see the issue of *Mind*, edited by Haldane, which sets out some issues in Analytic Thomism). Whereas Haldane is interested in a particular research programme associated with Thomist studies in particular, I am interested in the application of analytical tools that might have a much wider remit than this.

[5] Of course, not declaring one's philosophical assumptions in theology might also be a Trojan horse. But that is not the concern here.

[6] A similar plea is made by Brian Hebblethwaite in *Philosophical Theology and Christian Doctrine* (Oxford: Blackwell, 2005), ch. 1, which offers an interesting survey of the current state of the literature in philosophical theology. For a recent assessment of philosophical theology that is very much akin to analytic theology, see Gijsbert van den Brink and Marcel Sarot, 'Contemporary Philosophical Theology', in Van den Brink and Sarot (eds.), *Understanding the Attributes of God* (Frankfurt am Main: Peter Lang, 1999).

[7] Alister McGrath distinguishes between Christian doctrine and theology. Whereas the former is the activity of a particular community, the Church, individuals may practise the latter with no commitment to a particular ecclesiastical body. Sometimes theologians also make a distinction between doctrine and dogma, where the former is the expression of a particular theologian and the latter reflects the teaching of the Church Catholic, e.g. the propositions of the Nicene–Constantinopolitan Creed. In this essay I shall not observe these distinctions since I am interested in the way theologians and churches formulate their discussion of Christian teaching, not the nature of that teaching. For McGrath's comments on these matters, see *The*

scholastic theological method.[8] More often than not debates about theological method incorporate aspects of both of these, although discussions focused on the nature of Christian doctrine predominate. To many familiar with analytic philosophical literature, the words 'analytic theology' will probably conjure up a particular mental image of a philosophical procedure—or, at least, the results of such a procedure set out in a rather dry, orderly, and logical fashion on paper. However, as I shall use the term, analytic theology has aspects that are both procedural and substantive. The procedural element concerns a particular analytic style of pursuing theology, including certain assumptions about why this procedure and not some other currently on offer is better suited to the task of theologizing. The substantive element includes several features that are interrelated: the presumption that there is some theological truth of the matter and that this truth of the matter can be ascertained and understood by human beings (theologians included!), and an instrumental use of reason.

Let us begin by considering the procedural component of the proposal. I have said that the 'analytic' component to analytic theology is borrowed from current analytic philosophy. But what does this analytic component consist in?[9] Analytic philosophy describes a certain method used by some philosophers, characterized by a logical rigour, clarity, and parsimony of expression, coupled with attention to a certain cluster of philosophical problems. But

Genesis of Doctrine: A Study in the Foundation of Doctrinal Criticism (Grand Rapids, Mich.: Eerdmans, 1990), ch. 1. Cf. Colin Gunton's comments in 'Historical and Systematic Theology', in *The Cambridge Companion to Christian Doctrine* (Cambridge: CUP, 2000), 4.

[8] See e.g. the discussion of this point in the theological method of Gisbertus Voetius (1589–1676) and Johannes Coeccius (1603–69), in Willem van Asselt, 'Coeccius Anti-Scholasticus?', and Luco J. van den Brom, 'Scholasticism and Contemporary Systematic Theology', in Willem J. van Asselt and Eef Dekker (eds.), *Reformation and Scholasticism: An Ecumenical Enterprise* (Grand Rapids, Mich.: Baker Academic, 2001). See also Richard A. Muller, *Post-Reformation Reformed Dogmatics*, i. *Prolegomena to Theology*, 2nd edn. (Grand Rapids, Mich.: Baker Academic, 2003), ch. 4.

[9] There has been considerable interest in philosophical theology in the modern period. Various strands of existentialism influenced a number of theologians writing philosophical theology in the mid-20th cent. Examples include the influence of Martin Heidegger's thought on Rudolf Bultmann (see e.g. David Fergusson, *Bultmann* (London: Geoffrey Chapman, 1992), ch. 4), as well as Karl Rahner and Paul Tillich. Some have claimed that existentialism influenced the work of Karl Barth, although this is contested. Contemporary continental theologians, unlike most of their Anglo-American counterparts, have been willing to read and incorporate some aspects of analytic philosophy into their work, although this does not always include attention to the philosophy of religion. See e.g. the work of Ingolf Dalferth, or Wolfhart Pannenberg. Dutch theology is interesting because it has been influenced by both the Anglo-American and continental ways of doing theology—this is particularly true of the 'Utrecht School' of philosophical and systematic theologians (see Brink and Sarot (eds.), *Understanding the Divine Attributes*, passim). In the English-speaking world most theology is written with an eye to one or other continental school of philosophy. But there are exceptions to this. For instance, postliberal theologians have been keen to utilize the work of the later Wittgenstein.

beyond this, it is difficult to say precisely what analytic philosophy is. On one way of characterizing the analytic philosophical project problems are broken down into their constituent parts, analysed, and then reformed in an argument that attempts to make sense of the original problem. Here the analytic philosopher is rather like a mechanic who decides to strip an engine down in order to understand why is it making a peculiar rattling sound. He analyses the parts of the engine, cleans them up, and then reassembles the machine having satisfied himself that he has addressed the problem so that the engine will work properly once reformed.

Something of this approach can still be detected in contemporary analytic philosophy. But, without qualification, this picture could be misleading. It suggests the sort of analysis in vogue during the 1950s, when the subject matter of Anglo-American philosophy was ordinary language, which had to be analysed in order to ascertain in which circumstances a particular sentence, or phrase, was meaningful. Such ordinary-language philosophers had little time for metaphysics (or theology, for that matter). But, arguably, contemporary analytic philosophy is more concerned with building metaphysical worldviews than analysing problems (in this narrow, linguistic sense at least), as philosophers in this tradition did during the heyday of ordinary-language philosophy. According to Richard Swinburne, 'the goal is now metaphysical: to give a correct account of what are the ultimate constituents of the world and how they interact. "Analytic" is merely a title for this kind of philosophy inherited from its ancestry.'[10] This raises an important point: the anti-metaphysical *animus* of much mid-twentieth-century analytical philosophy (in both the logical positivist and linguistic phases) is now in the past. Metaphysics is once again a central concern of philosophers in the Anglo-American tradition. Although the constructive metaphysical project of contemporary analytic philosophy presents new challenges to theologians, there is what we might loosely characterize as a shared 'metaphysical' concern that was not typical of an earlier stage in the analytic philosophical tradition.[11] In what follows, I shall take analytic theology to be concerned with analysis in this 'metaphysical' sense—not in the narrower, linguistic sense applied to the earlier phases of analytic philosophy.

---

[10] Richard Swinburne, 'The Value and Christian Roots of Analytical Philosophy of Religion', in Harriet A. Harris and Christopher J. Insole (eds.), *Faith and Philosophical Analysis: The Impact of Analytical Philosophy on the Philosophy of Religion* (Aldershot: Ashgate, 2005), 35.

[11] But caution should be exercised here. The early phase of analytic philosophy characterized by Russell and Wittgenstein's logical atomism was certainly metaphysical, and there were metaphysical issues discussed by philosophers in the mid-20th century, such as Arthur Prior or H. H. Price. For discussion see the introduction to Michael J. Loux and Dean W. Zimmerman (eds.), *The Oxford Handbook of Metaphysics* (Oxford: OUP, 2003).

But this 'metaphysical turn' in analytic philosophy makes it more difficult to distinguish from so-called 'continental' approaches to philosophy, much of which has been motivated by metaphysical concerns, for example, Martin Heidegger's interest in *sein* (being). And since most contemporary theologians take their philosophical cues from continental philosophy, the distinction between contemporary 'metaphysical' analytic philosophy and continental philosophy will be important for analytic theology. Perhaps one way of distinguishing these two philosophical traditions has to do with which intellectual virtues are to be most prized in philosophy. On this view, analytic philosophy is less to do with the sort of argument atomizing of the mechanic example and more to do with the *ends* of philosophy, or what the point of philosophy is supposed to be. Continental philosophers might think that clarity and rigour are intellectual virtues to be pursued. But it may be that continental philosophers are less optimistic than analytic philosophers that analysis can yield the dividends it promises. (Perhaps some issues are just too messy or tangled for analysis to be effective, or perhaps the issues are somehow 'larger' than analysis can allow for, or perhaps analysis fails to take into consideration the interconnections between different topics, or between philosophy and the wider concerns of life.) It may also be that certain topics less amenable to careful analysis are the sorts of issues continental thinkers are more drawn to than analytic thinkers. Or at least, a 'continental' approach to such topics ('being' comes to mind) is more likely to be better suited to the broader, more evocative approach of many 'continental' thinkers than the analytical penchant for tying down concepts and definitions.

I do not wish to comment on the merits or demerits of continental philosophy. But it seems to me that the analytic method of philosophizing does have a number of intellectual virtues. As William Hasker observes in the context of discussing the development of analytic philosophy of religion,

> [t]his approach to philosophizing offers the best means yet available for clarifying the meaning of religious claims and for assessing the reasons for and against the truth of those claims. Those who are uninterested in clarity and truth as applied to religious assertions will naturally find this style of philosophizing uncongenial. Those who do care about such matters may well find it indispensable.[12]

The 'analytic' component to analytic theology, like contemporary analytic philosophy, involves the use of certain tools like logic to make sense of theological issues, where metaphysical concerns are central. And like analytic philosophy, analytic theology will prize intellectual virtues like clarity, parsimony of

---

[12] William Hasker, 'Analytic Philosophy of Religion', in William Wainwright (ed.), *The Oxford Handbook of Philosophy of Religion* (Oxford: OUP, 2005), 443.

expression, and argumentative rigour. It will also, where appropriate, seek to deal with complex doctrinal concerns by dividing them into more manageable units, or focusing on providing a clear expression of particular theological terms that inform particular doctrines in important respects, for example, 'substance', 'perichoresis', or 'person'. In fact, analytic theology is about redeploying tools already in the service of philosophy to a theological end.

The benefit of an analytic approach to systematic theology should be obvious. It provides a means by which complex problems can be made sense of with logical rigour within a metaphysical framework of thought for decidedly theological purposes. But it might be objected that an analytic approach to theological problems suggests a kind of 'atomism'. What if it turns out that certain doctrines are the theological equivalent of uncrackable molecules, the complexity of which makes them unsuited to analysis?

There are two things to be said by way of response to this. The first is, it is difficult to say in advance of investigation whether or not a particular theological problem, once analysed, will turn out to be composed of 'uncrackable theological molecules'. In any case, theological doctrines have been subjected to different sorts of analysis for long periods of the history of the Church. It would be strange to think that the analysis proposed here would turn up problems of this sort that had never appeared before in the Christian tradition. There will be issues that analysis is unable to resolve because they are mysterious (in the sense of being beyond human reasoning, not contradictory or false). But that is another matter entirely, which does not necessarily present problems peculiar to analytic theology.

Secondly, even if some theological questions are not amenable to analysis, many will be. To take one example, the threeness–oneness problem associated with the doctrine of the Trinity may be approached by dividing it up into smaller parts: what do we mean by 'divine person'; what is meant by 'trinitarian perichoresis'; what can be said about 'divine substance', and so forth. A resolution of these issues that are elements of the larger threeness–oneness problem, will certainly help the theologian to make sense of the whole (to the extent one can make sense of this doctrine).

As I have already indicated, there is nothing novel in the idea that theologians might make use of the latest in philosophical thinking to help them express the great things of the Gospel in a contemporary idiom. Theologians in every age of the Church have done just this.[13] Sometimes this has led to

---

[13] On occasion theologians of the past have characterized their own approach to theological problems in a way that sounds startlingly like analytic theology. Compare the English Puritan, Richard Baxter: 'I was never more weary of learned men's discourses, than when I heard them wrangling about unexpounded words or things, and eagerly disputing before they understood

mistakes (although these mistakes are occasionally the fault of the theologian, not the philosophical ideas he or she has (mis)appropriated), and, of course, philosophical notions used in the theology of yesterday have a habit of looking rather outdated today. (The same could be said of the scientific concepts taken up by theologians in the past—just read some of the prolegomena of nineteenth-century divines on this score.) But the use of philosophical tools in past theology has also brought about great advances in our understanding of particular doctrines. Take, for example, the metaphysical language that helped forge the Catholic Creeds, or the logical acuity of the work of Augustine, Anselm, or Aquinas. For all their shortcomings, these theologians have shaped the sort of theology we do today, and in no small part this is due to the philosophical notions they borrowed, baptized, or redeployed for their own theological purposes.

There is already work being done by theologians that utilizes aspects of analytic philosophy. One obvious example is the use made of speech-act theory in contemporary biblical hermeneutics.[14] There is also a growing body of literature in analytic philosophical theology that analyses Christian doctrine in a manner that theologians should welcome. The philosophers engaged in this project tend to defend their work by saying that this sort of theology, though very similar to the sort of approach classical theologians of the past have adopted, is not being done by contemporary theologians. So the philosophers have stepped in to do it for them.[15] Unfortunately, there is more than a grain of truth in this assertion. Theologians have been slow to seize upon the great benefits offered by an analytic approach to matters theological,

each other's minds.... I never thought I understood anything till I could anatomize it, and see the parts distinctly, and the conjunction of the parts, as they make up the whole. Distinction and method seemed to me of that necessity, that without them I could not be said to know; and the disputes that forsook them, or abused them, seemed but as incoherent dreams.' Cited in William G. T. Shedd, *A History of Christian Doctrine,* i (Eugene, Oreg.: Wipf & Stock, 1999 [1864]), 93 n.

[14] See e.g. Kevin Vanhoozer, *The Drama of Doctrine: A Canonical Linguistic Approach to Christian Theology* (Louisville, Ky.: Westminster John Knox, 2005), 65–8, and Richard Briggs, *Words in Action: Speech Act Theory and Biblical Interpretation* (Edinburgh: T&T Clark, 2001).

[15] Compare Alvin Plantinga: 'Philosophical theology... is a matter of thinking about the central doctrines of the Christian faith from a philosophical perspective; it is a matter of employing the resources of philosophy to deepen our grasp and understanding of them.... The theologians don't seem to be doing the work in question. I therefore hope I will not be accused of interdisciplinary chauvinism if I point out that the best work in philosophical theology—in the English-speaking world and over the past quarter century—has been done not by the theologians but by philosophers.' Alvin Plantinga, 'Christian Philosophy at the End of the 20th Century', in James Sennett (ed.) *The Analytic Theist: An Alvin Plantinga Reader* (Grand Rapids, Mich.: Eerdmans, 1998), 340–1. Similar comments are made by William Lane Craig in *The Only Wise God* (Grand Rapids, Mich.: Baker, 1984), introd.

although there are some encouraging signs of the beginnings of such an engagement.[16]

Part of the reason for this hesitancy might be due to the concern that an analytic approach is reductionistic, in that analysis tends to focus in on the minutiae of a particular problem, without considering other, wider concerns. (This is connected to the persistence of an outdated linguistic conception of analytic philosophy in some theological circles.) It seems to me that, if one is faced with a particular problem that is difficult to resolve, one obvious consideration (though not the only one) is to break that problem down into simpler parts that might yield a solution more easily than the whole. Thus, if I am attempting to assemble an Ikea chair but find that I am confused by the instruction manual and end up with something that looks more like a cubist painting than an object I can sit on in comfort, I might think the best way of resolving the problem is to take the chair to pieces and make sure I have all the right parts, before carefully reassembling it. But no one would think me guilty of a reductionistic method of chair assembly if this were to take place. However, if I were to say 'there is no such thing as a chair. There are only these parts, arranged chair-wise', I might be guilty of reasoning that looks more like a sort of reductionism.[17] But there is no reason to think that analytic theology is like the second of these examples. Which is not to say that someone who holds a particular thesis about the nature of theological problems might not take analysis in this direction. But that is no reason to object to the right use of analysis in Christian theology. It is only a reason to object to its misuse.

There is a second, related objection in the neighbourhood of this one. It is that the whole notion of dealing only with 'problems' in philosophy or theology is reductionistic. Some philosophers may, like the early Wittgenstein, have thought of philosophy merely as a series of problems that need resolution. And it may be a concern from some theological quarters that this is just what analytic theology would turn out to be: reducing theology to some set of problems to be solved, rather than as the doctrinal concerns of a way of life. But one need not think this to find the method of problem-solving fruitful in philosophy or theology. Treating some of the most intractable theological issues facing the Christian as problems that might be amenable to analysis is, I think, a method that is at least worthy of consideration

---

[16] See e.g. the essays by Ann Loades and Harriet Harris in *Faith and Philosophical Analysis*, the essays in Brink and Sarot, *Understanding the Attributes of God,* and the much discussed book by Bruce Marshall, *Trinity and Truth* (Cambridge: CUP, 2000).

[17] But even then, it would not be sufficient to simply dismiss my assertion if I had a good argument for my position. A reductionism argued for is a reductionism that needs to be refuted, not scorned.

by theologians and has already shown itself to be extremely fruitful in contemporary philosophical theology. To return to the analogy of the Ikea chair: my decision to take the chair to pieces in order to work out where I went wrong in my first attempt to assemble it does not necessarily mean I think that the only important thing about the chair is getting its assembly right. Surely I want to assemble the chair in the right way in order *to use it*. Similarly, it seems to me that the analysis of Christian doctrine may be a way of making sense of what we are capable (in the face of divine mystery), in order to rightly deploy the doctrines concerned in the life of the Church.

We come to the second characteristic of analytic theology, having to do with the use of reason. Here we will need to consider some aspects of traditional theological prolegomena in order to grasp that, for the analytic theologian, understanding a matter is independent of believing it. This simple point is crucial to a right understanding of the nature of the analytic theological project, as we shall see.

The instrumental use of reason in theology is one aspect of what we might call the 'handmaid' approach to thinking about the relationship between theology and philosophy, where philosophy is thought of as the handmaid to theology. A handmaid is a helper, not a hindrance, and certainly a servant, not a superintendent to her mistress. Analytic theology could be thought of as a rationalistic programme that attempts to domesticate theology, by annexing it to philosophy. But it would be a mistake to think that it is somehow inevitable that analytic theology ends up going in this direction, or that there is something inherent in analytic theology that would lead that way.

To see why, consider the distinction between a procedural and substantive use of reason in theology. The substantive use of reason depends on a highly contentious thesis, that reason alone, or reason and the senses, give us fundamental and general non-trivial knowledge about the world around us that every rational person can understand, or is capable of understanding, and on the basis of which every rational person is able to make sense of the world. Theology, on this view, must conform to reason in order for it to be taken seriously as an intellectual discipline. Contrast this strong use of reason in theology with the weaker, procedural sense. On this way of thinking, reason is a tool for establishing the logical connections between different propositions, for distinguishing what I am talking about from what I am not, and whether what I am saying makes sense, or is incoherent. Such reasoning also enables me to consider the validity of a particular argument that is put forward, and whether or not it is subject to less obvious defects of reasoning, like question-begging or affirming the consequent, and so on. As Paul Helm points out, 'Any reasoning about anything requires the acceptance, the use, of procedural reason. We are continually making judgements of what, given certain assumptions about how the world is, is likely to happen next, or what is likely to be true, and reason is necessary for making or assessing such claims.'[18]

It seems to me that analytic theology is entirely consistent with either a substantive or procedural use of reason. One could use well-formed, logical arguments to defend a rationalistic approach to theology, consistent with a substantive use of reason, or, indeed, some other philosophical notion whose theological redeployment theologians may be right to regard with suspicion. But one need not. Analysis may also be part of a much more modest use of reason, such as that found in the procedural approach. Such a use of reason in theology provides, amongst other things, an argumentative framework within which theological discussion can take place. But an instrumental use of reason is not just about teasing out the internal logic of a given doctrine. If I argue that the internal logic of a particular construal of Chalcedonian Christology is internally consistent, that will have implications for other doctrines, such as the Trinity. It will also have implications for wider issues, such as realism and anti-realism, or scepticism about metaphysical truth. Thus, even this modest use of reason raises issues beyond that of the coherence of particular doctrines, including within its scope matters that are properly apologetic, or prolegomenal (about which, more presently). In a similar way, the tools needed to assemble my Ikea chair may be used to destroy it as well. But the fact that the same tools can be used in an improper fashion is hardly an argument for not using them at all.

When this is understood, it becomes apparent that analytic theology is not intended as a vehicle by which theology may become enslaved to philosophy. Instead, it is a means of making sense of substantive theological claims (as well as raising substantive issues). This brings me to the issue of understanding a matter without necessarily believing it. Peter Strawson, in his book *Individuals*, speaks of two sorts of metaphysics.[19] The first is descriptive. It offers an account of certain notions and problems in order to describe how things stand. The second is revisionist. It offers an account of metaphysics that seeks to explain how the conventions and concepts in current usage are mistaken, in order to present an alternative way of thinking metaphysically. As I envision it, analytic theological method is rather like Strawson's descriptive metaphysics. The end to which such analysis is put is entirely at the disposal of theology, the objective being to make clear certain notions and

---

[18] See Paul Helm, *Faith and Understanding* (Edinburgh: Edinburgh UP, 1997), 7. I owe the distinction between substantive and procedural reason to Helm's ch. 1.

[19] P. F. Strawson, *Individuals: An Essay in Descriptive Metaphysics* (London: Methuen, 1959), 9–10.

problems in order to see how things stand with respect to a particular theological doctrine.

It is also descriptive in a second, related sense, to do with the way in which theology is an intellectual discipline that is self-consciously part of a tradition. One virtue of analytic theology as I understand it is that it attempts to make sense of matters theological in a way that is conscious of, and sympathetic to, the Christian tradition, and traditional ways of doing theology. This is consistent with an analytic theologian being critical of the tradition in important respects. One could be critical of substantive matters within one particular stream of the Christian tradition and do so using an analytic theological method. For instance, an analytic theologian might have considerable difficulties with certain doctrines about the sacraments, though such understandings of the sacraments are supported by a venerable Christian tradition. And one could be critical of certain ways of doing theology that might be part of the Christian tradition, without being revisionist in the Strawsonian sense. After all, 'living' traditions are capable of change and adaptation, unlike traditions that are dead. The Christian can be part of the process of making sense of her particular stream of the tradition in a way that is sympathetic to what has gone before whilst also being creative within that tradition. No modern person can say the same about the Philistine cult of Dagon, a religious tradition long dead.[20]

So analytic theology is not necessarily a revisionist exercise (it might be; but that is not how I am construing it). It need not attempt to rewrite theology according to some prior agenda or programme. It is in fact one way in which a faith seeking understanding approach to theology might be had.[21]

This instrumental use of reason, as part of a 'handmaid' approach to theology, has not gone unnoticed in recent discussion of theological method. For instance, the English Reformed theologian Colin Gunton prefaces his own explanation of something very like the procedural and substantive uses of reason by saying that, contrary to some assumptions, 'what we mean by reason is by no means straightforward or agreed'. Moreover, 'differences in conceptions of what reason is able to do *on its own* affect conceptions of the

---

[20] This should also underline the point that the analytic theology I have in mind is analytic *Christian* theology. But there is nothing preventing other theistic religions taking up and adapting much of the following to their own purposes. I suppose a Muslim might find much in an analytic theological method that is agreeable.

[21] Compare the comments of Van den Brink and Sarot, concerning the way in which the 'Utrecht School' attempts a specifically Christian approach to the subject matter of philosophical theology, which acknowledges that, 'in the end...our knowledge of God...[is] dependent upon God's self-revelation'. *Understanding the Divine Attributes*, 19.

nature of systematic theology in various ways, especially in determining the place and relation of 'natural' and 'revealed' theology'.[22]

And here we come to an important consideration for theologians. It might be thought that the use of what Gunton calls 'general terms, argument, logic and the rest' is perfectly harmless—in fact, that such things are intellectual virtues all academic disciplines should exemplify in their methods of reasoning. If 'analytic' theology boils down to a recommendation that theologians make every effort in their reasoning to provide well-formed, pellucid arguments then it might be thought that there is nothing to argue over, apart from the fact that such 'recommendations' are likely to appear rather condescending. Surely, all parties can agree that it is perfectly appropriate to expect certain standards of argument in an intellectual enterprise, irrespective of the subject matter? But problems arise when we begin to ask what counts as a 'good' or 'well-formed, pellucid' argument. The standards one advocates may well depend on one's goals. For the analytic theologian, clarity and precision of argument, coupled with attention to possible objections to one's position, will be very important considerations, as they are in analytic philosophy. But not everyone will agree that such matters should be paramount, and some theologians (like some philosophers, perhaps) may think that such concerns are unhelpfully narrow, or somehow fail to deal with wider, or prior concerns (e.g. that the language of theology is inherently metaphorical in nature and cannot be translated into propositions without loss of meaning). So what is meant by 'well-formed, pellucid argument' is not as obvious as it might first appear.

Gunton points out that being *systematic* in one's theology can mean more than one thing. It could mean setting forth clear, well-formed arguments for one's views; it could be a thesis about the scope of theology—that it should embrace an entire system of Christian doctrine; it could even be a recommendation that theologians shape their work according to a particular theological or philosophical template, such as the austere, Euclidean beauty of Spinoza's *Ethics,* or the loci-ordered theology of much post-Reformation dogmatics, or perhaps the unrelenting Teutonic orchestration of Karl Barth's *Church Dogmatics.*

There is one way of reading what Gunton says about the nature of systematic theology that is perfectly in accord with what I am recommending: what is meant by 'reason' is rather slippery at times, and how we use reason in theology will have important implications for the shape and content of theology. And, although I am recommending analysis (taken in its contemporary,

---

[22] Colin Gunton, 'Historical and Systematic Theology', in *The Cambridge Companion to Christian Doctrine* (Cambridge: CUP, 2000), 13.

worldview-building form) as a method for tackling theological problems, this is consistent with more than one way of doing theology, although it will also be inconsistent with some ways in which theology might be pursued. But there are two issues that his discussion raises that are more controversial. The first concerns the relationship between natural and revealed theology. The second has to do with the different forms systematic theology might take.

As to the first concern, Gunton is right to suggest that the place of reason in theology may affect the place and relation of natural to revealed theology. But analytic theology's procedural use of reason is consistent with at least some ways in which natural theology has been understood in theology. For instance, one could hold to an analytic theological method as I have been suggesting, and think that God reveals himself in the created world around us, or has given human beings a *sensus divinitatis*, in a way consistent with John Calvin's thought, or with contemporary Reformed Epistemology. On this way of thinking, though natural revelation does take place, our ability to apprehend that revelation is blunted by the noetic effects of sin, and we are incapable of coming to a saving knowledge of God via natural revelation, in the absence of special revelation.

This, of course, is a Reformed way of thinking about the relationship between analytic theology, and natural and special revelation. I offer it as an illustration of one way in which this relationship could be construed, not as the only way in which it can. There is nothing about analytic theology that precludes the theologian from using it as a method by which to establish a much less sanguine view of the nature and place of natural theology in Christian thinking. For instance, the analytic theologian might argue that parts of theology, perhaps large parts of it, are beyond reason, by arguing that every effort to articulate a particular doctrine leads to paradox, or antinomy, or even self-contradiction. In other words analytic theology could be used to define a boundary of inquiry beyond which we are unable to go.[23] The converse is also true. Analytic theology could describe a way of doing theology that was much more optimistic about the prospect of natural theology than John Calvin. Perhaps a kind of Swinburnian version of analytic theology might look like this.

In any case, my point is just that (*a*) analytic theology is consistent with (at least one construal of) natural theology, and (*b*) the use of an analytic theological method does not, in and of itself, determine the nature and place of natural and

---

[23] I know of at least one recent attempt to argue in an analytic fashion that any attempt to articulate a coherent version of central Christian doctrines like the Trinity or Incarnation are bound to end up in paradox because of the limitations of theology. See James Anderson, *Paradox in Christian Theology: Its Presences, Character, and Epistemic Status* (Milton Keynes: Paternoster Press, 2007).

revealed theology. Another way to put the same thought would be to say that the 'worldview-building' forms of contemporary analysis, including a procedural use of reason, do not in and of themselves preclude more than one way of making sense of natural and revealed theology. Nevertheless, to the extent that particular analytical-theological accounts of Christian doctrine imply substantive issues of a more apologetic or prolegomenal nature (including, no doubt, issues concerning natural theology) analytic theology does involve making judgements that will have implications for the place of natural and revealed theology.

The response to the second controversial matter Gunton raises, to do with different ways in which theology can be 'systematic', takes a similar form. Analytic theology as a method is consistent with more than one way of producing systematic theology, although it might be inconsistent with certain sorts of theology. If someone were to write theology in imitation of Euclidean geometry, like Spinoza, the result might be analytic theology (it might also be a very bad piece of dogmatics). It is more difficult to see how a Barth-like method might be analytic. His whole approach to theology, as John Webster suggests, is much more like a fugue that uses variations on a theme in different parts of the work to make sense of a theological topic.[24] But analytic theology is certainly amenable to the loci approach to theology pioneered by Philip Melanchthon and Protestant Scholasticism, which treat of theology according to its various topics and how they interrelate. Even more—it is amenable to the sort of scholastic *disputatio* from which both Melancthon and the Protestant Scholastics borrowed. Which is not to say that analytic theology is identical to school theology. It is not.

So Gunton's concerns about the theological use of reason and his desire to make room for different ways of being 'systematic' in theology are perfectly consistent with an analytical method. Of course, adoption of an analytic theological method is no guarantee that the conclusions for which a particular theologian argues are true. An analytic theologian might end up holding doctrine that is unorthodox, or even heretical, and have argued for this in an impeccably analytic fashion. But this should not be terribly surprising. After all, one can have a valid argument with a false conclusion.

We come to the third component of analytic theology. This has to do with truth in theology. There are a number of different, competing theories of truth at present, and this variety of approaches to truth is reflected in recent discussion of theological method. It seems to me that analytic theology, at least as I understand this method, is compatible with a range of theories of

---

[24] See John Webster, *Karl Barth* (London: Continuum, 2002), 50. Cf. Jenson's characterization of God as a fugue in *Systematic Theology*, i. 236.

truth. One such theory or family of theories is the deflationary theory of truth. On this sort of view there are no truths as such, if we mean by that some property possession of which gives a sentence the truth function of being true. Sentences of the form 'p is true', where p is some sentence expressing a proposition, have (it is said) an equivalent content to sentences that make no claim about the truth or falsehood of what is being stated. Truth is redundant; it is merely a speech act that I perform when I affirm 'p is true', or a means of demonstrating my assent to a particular assertion. An analytic theologian might take this sort of approach to truth. Then, asserting that the sentence 'Jesus of Nazareth is God Incarnate' is true is just a matter of performing a particular speech act, or is equivalent to saying 'I agree with the notion that Jesus of Nazareth is God Incarnate'. I do not find this approach appealing, but some who are sympathetic to an analytic theological method might.

But analytic theology might also be consistent with an epistemic theory of truth, which has to do with the relation between a particular proposition and, say, the community of believers, and whether those believers are justified in holding as true certain beliefs they have. Postliberal theologians seem to hold to an epistemic theory of truth, or something very like it.

In his influential book, *The Nature of Doctrine*[25] the postliberal theologian George Lindbeck claims, amongst other things, that theology is actually a second order discourse concerned with the grammar of a certain form of life. He characterizes his position as a 'cultural-linguistic' theological method, according to which the function of Church doctrines 'is their use, not as expressive symbols or as truth claims, but as communally authoritative rules of discourse, attitude, and action'. He speaks of this view of doctrine as 'rule theory',[26] because on this way of thinking doctrine has a merely regulative function. It stipulates what it is meaningful to say within the Christian community; it does not necessarily correspond to some metaphysical truth of the matter. To be fair to Lindbeck, he does say that the grammar of theology might correspond to the actual metaphysical truth of the matter, but our understanding of this cannot be binding because, on his way of thinking, we cannot be sure which particular 'grammar' of theology is actually the right one, this side of the eschaton: 'Rule theory does not prohibit speculations on the possible correspondence of the Trinitarian pattern of Christian language to the metaphysical structure of the Godhead, but simply says that these are

---

[25] George A. Lindbeck, *The Nature of Doctrine, Religion and Theology in a Postliberal Age* (London: SPCK, 1984).
[26] Ibid. 18. Further references to Lindbeck's book are given parenthetically in the body of the text.

not doctrinally necessary and cannot be binding' (Lindbeck, *Nature of Doctrine*, 106).

He is quite happy to accept the consequence of this view:

> If the doctrine is a rule or conjunction of rules for, amongst other things, the construction of Trinitarian theories, then both types of theory we have mentioned [i.e. theories concerning whether or not the immanent and economic Trinity is the same or not] can be doctrinally correct, providing they conform to the same rules. If, however, the doctrine is a proposition with ontological reference, only one type of theory has a chance of being true because the theories disagree on what the ontological reference is. (ibid. 106–107)

Such a proposal concerning the nature of Christian doctrine might be consistent with analytic theology. For a postliberal sympathetic to analytic theology, theological method has to do with ensuring a particular theologian is playing according to the rules of the game. The question of whether or not the theologian concerned is articulating the truth of the matter remains *sub judice,* until these matters are made known in the next world. So, a postliberal could be a theological realist, but also a fallibilist in epistemology. She could use reason to articulate her communitarian theology, setting to one side the question of whether or not her theology (in whole or part) is in fact the sober truth of the matter.

This does require a particular way of thinking about the 'understanding is independent of believing' principle, mentioned earlier in the context of discussing the procedural use of reason. On an epistemic theory of truth like the postliberal one, understanding might be independent of believing, if one is faced with two different 'grammars' of theology that both adhere to the rules of the game. I might believe that my 'grammar' makes best sense of, say, the Nicene-Constantinopolitan Creed, although my liberal theological colleague thinks his view does better. Lindbeck wants us to believe that both the liberal theologian and I might 'play by the rules' of the game. Then, provided I understand the difference between my view and my colleague's, and see that both work according to a Lindbeckian account of doctrinal language-games, one might be able to say 'I understand your view is not mine, and I believe my view not yours, despite the fact that both views correspond to a common theological grammar' (assuming they do both correspond to a shared theological grammar and that both views are consistent with that common grammar).

But is this also consistent with a descriptive account of theology as per what was said earlier about the analytic use of procedural reason? Although a creative Lindbeckian might want to make this case, I think it would be difficult to sustain. There is not the space to develop this here, but I think it is not difficult to see that Lindbeck's account of doctrine is a revisionist one, in the Strawsonian sense. His view of the nature of Christian doctrine is not that of classical theologians like John of Damascus, Augustine, Anselm, Aquinas, or the theology of the Reformation and post-Reformation Orthodox. At the very least, the onus is on the Lindbeckian to show that her position is consistent with the tradition, if the Lindbeckian were to contest this point (which I doubt she would). So there is an important sense in which at least one current proposal for theological method (the postliberalism of Lindbeck) could not be a *consistently* analytic theology. It may be that other epistemic theories of truth could overcome this, if they were able to satisfy the condition that analytic theology be descriptive.

One last comment on this: the claim that analytic theology is descriptive not prescriptive might be contested—who is to say that analytic theology may not *prescribe* what theology should look like?[27] I suppose one could jettison this requirement, as per my suggested Lindbeckian construal of analytic theology (or, indeed, some other way of thinking about analytic theology). But this is not, to my mind, an entirely satisfactory way of thinking about such a theological method. For one thing, a prescriptive theological method does not appear to sit very easily with a procedural use of reason.

A much more satisfactory way of thinking about analytic theology is in the context of a correspondence theory of truth, according to which a proposition is true just in case it corresponds to a fact about the world to which it refers. Such theories of truth are commonly called 'realist'.[28] This theory of truth appears compatible with the 'understanding is independent of believing' criterion of the procedural use of reason. It is also consistent with analytic theology as a descriptive, rather than prescriptive, method in theology. Finally, the correspondence theory is commensurate with the notion that there is such a thing as truth (about Christian doctrine) and that human beings are capable of apprehending what that truth is. It may be that we

---

[27] This point was put to me in conversation by Vincent Brümmer.

[28] They are called realist because they are said to 'refer' to a world independent of the person using the sentence. But this is not sufficient to render a theory of truth realist. So I shall not equate the two. In fact, correspondence theories are compatible with idealism as well as realism. A proposition may 'refer' to a world that is independent of the person uttering the sentence, but not a world that is mind-independent or person-independent. This would be true where truth is not mind-independent. As Plantinga points out, 'the fundamental intuition—that truth is not independent of mind—is indeed correct. This intuition is best accommodated by the theistic claim that necessarily, propositions have two properties essentially: *being conceived by God* and *being true if and only if believed by God*.' So, it would appear that one can be both a correspondence theorist and an anti-realist, provided one is also a theist! See Plantinga, 'How to be an Anti-Realist', *Proceedings and Addresses of the American Philosophical Association*, 56 (1982), 70.

cannot apprehend all there is to know about a particular matter. But there is nothing inconsistent in saying that analytic theology uses a correspondence theory of truth and that there are limits to the use of reason in theology. One could hold both of these things together with a robust doctrine of divine mystery and be engaged in an internally consistent theological method.

It may be that one could hold to a rather austere version of the correspondence theory as an analytic theologian. In which case, one might think that there are truths of the matter, but that we may not be in a position to know the truth in every instance. Applied to theology, one might say 'the Chalcedonian "definition" of the person of Christ is the best way we have of thinking about the Incarnation'. But this is consistent with saying 'whether the Chalcedonian definition gives us the *truth* of the matter or not, we cannot say'. Such a position might be taken in a Lindbeckian direction, coupled with an epistemic theory of truth. But it might also be taken along the lines of a correspondence theory of truth. It could be that we simply do not know (perhaps, cannot know) whether the canons of Chalcedon correspond to the facts of the matter, although there are facts of the matter—it is just we might not be able to apprehend them in the absence of further divine revelation.

So, it would seem that plotting the course of analytic theology is not an entirely straightforward matter, and may be taken in one of several directions, depending on the use of made of reason, and the theory of truth one opts for.

OBJECTIONS TO ANALYTIC THEOLOGY

We come to objections that might be raised about this proposal for theological method. Here I intend to deal only with those criticisms that might be raised with analytic theology *as a theological method*. There are objections that might be raised about this method that are also objections to analytic philosophy of religion. One oft-repeated objection of this sort is that analytic philosophy of religion is ahistorical and does not pay sufficient attention to the social and cultural factors that shape Christian doctrine. Such an objection might also be raised in the context of analytic theology. If it were, we could offer the same response offered by analytic philosophers when the objection is raised in the context of philosophy: although this criticism has some purchase, it is not a reason to reject an analytic approach outright. It is a reason to correct the way in which an analytic method is used. In any case, there is much work in analytic philosophy of religion that is historically sensitive, and there is no reason to think that analytic theology would be any different (perhaps, if theologians are pursuing this project, this sort of objection may be met even more effectively).[29]

A second objection has to do with whether analytic theology is really a theological enterprise at all. Here a further point of clarification may help. As I have characterized analytic theology, it is primarily a faith-seeking-understanding project, where 'metaphysical' analysis is the means by which theologians make sense of what they already believe. In short, the main task of analytic theology as it has been characterized thus far is primarily metaphysical. If it is a project that deals with epistemological matters, these are secondary to its primary goal. So analytic theology does not address the question that has bedevilled much modern theology in the wake of Kant's Copernican Revolution in philosophy, namely: how is knowledge of God possible?[30] It is much more concerned with other kinds of questions. How can the doctrine of the Trinity be coherent? What does it mean to say 'Christ

---

[29] Two other objections raised against analytic philosophy of religion that could also be raised in connection with analytic theology: the claim that analytic work pretends to a 'God's eye view' that is impossible, and that hides a will to power (in the Nietzschean sense); and that analytic work is a very androcentric, narrowly focused activity that fails to take into account broader concerns which are at play, such as the role of feelings. The first of these objections is recognizably postmodern. The second is feminist. I do not see why analytic theology hides a 'will to power' or pretends to a God's eye view: I have already conceded that an analytical theologian could be an epistemological fallibilist. As to the feminist objection, this seems rather beside the point. What is at issue is whether an analytic method can get at the truth of the matter. If there is a truth of the matter to be had, the gender of those in quest of it is irrelevant. There are wider issues involved in all academic activities, and personal factors are among them. But an analytic philosopher or theologian need not ignore these matters. For discussion of these issues, see Basil Mitchell, 'Staking a Claim for Metaphysics', in *Faith and Philosophical Analysis*, 21–32.

[30] In this regard, Nicholas Wolterstorff is instructive: 'Kant is a watershed in the history of theology. Ever since Kant, the anxious questions, "Can we? How can we [know that there is a God]?" have haunted theologians, insisting on being addressed before any others. This is the agony, the Kantian agony, of the modern theologian. Since Kant, a good many of our theologians have spoken far more confidently about the existence of the Great Boundary [between the phenomenal and noumenal] than about the existence of God.' Wolterstorff, 'Is it Possible and Desirable for Theologians to Recover from Kant?', *Modern Theology*, 14 (1998), 15–16. Cf. Plantinga, *Warranted Christian Belief* (Oxford: OUP, 2000), ch. 1. There is not the space to explore how one might be able to 'move beyond' Kant (as Wolterstorff puts it). But this has to do in part with the incoherence of Kant's claim to know one cannot know anything about the unknown world beyond our subjective experience. Kant's certainty that there is a Great Boundary between the phenomenal world, the contents of which we give structure to, and the noumenal world beyond this, about which we can say nothing, requires that Kant knows at least one thing about the noumenal: that we can *know* nothing about it. But how can he know this if he can know nothing beyond the Great Boundary of which he speaks? Moreover, Richard Swinburne claims the atomic theory of chemistry has shown 'in precise detail some of the unobservable causes of phenomena—the atoms whose combinations give rise to observable chemical phenomena'. For this reason, it can no longer be doubted that we can have access to (at least some of) Kant's 'unobservable causes' of phenomena. See Swinburne, 'The Value and Christian Roots of Analytical Philosophy of Religion' in *Faith and Philosophical Analysis*, 39.

died for our sins'? How is eschatology related to God and time? Taken in this way, analytic theology seems a lot more traditional than it might appear at first glance. For these are precisely the sorts of questions that classical theologians addressed themselves to.

But this will not be a recommendation of analytic theology to at least two sorts of people. The first sort is the person who maintains that theology is really nothing more than a branch of philosophy. If this is the case, then the whole idea of analytic theology is misguided, because it assumes that theology is a distinct discipline from philosophy. But I think this is mistaken. Theology is a variegated and complex discipline that is distinct from philosophy, although both disciplines share overlapping concerns. It would be wrong to think that theology may be reduced to philosophy because theologians make use of philosophical tools and notions, just as it would be wrong to think that biology can be reduced to physics, just because biologists make use of physics in biological science.[31]

A second sort of person will object that the characterization of analytic theology as principally a metaphysical, not epistemological enterprise is to put the theological cart before the horse. One cannot begin to ask questions about the nature of God before establishing whether we are able to talk about the nature of God in any meaningful sense. This, of course, is one way in which the Kantian spirit of much modern theology manifests itself. But, as Nicholas Wolterstorff points out,

> If one believes that one's car is in good running order, one does not spend the whole day tinkering under the hood to determine whether it could possibly be in good running order, and if so, how. One gets in and drives off. Along the way one might discuss with one's passengers how it is that this old car runs—especially if *they* thought it wouldn't!ced[32]

A third objection has to do with the relevance of this method to contemporary theology. Why should theologians take this seriously? One reason for

---

[31] Some theologians go in the opposite direction to this. For instance, Robert Jenson characterizes philosophy as a potentially rival *theological* discipline: 'The secular mood by which some forms of "philosophy" contrasts with Christian theology and that tempts us to take them for a different kind of thinking is simply a character [sic] of Olympian religion itself, which pursued a divinity purged of mystery. Insofar as western philosophy is not now reduced to the pure study of logic, it is still in fact theology, Christian or Olympian-Parmenidean. Theologians of Western Christianity must indeed converse with the philosophers, but only because and insofar as both are engaged in the *same* sort of enterprise.' Jenson, *Systematic Theology*, i. 10; author's emphasis. However, the fact that a discipline has its roots in another is not sufficient to conclude that it is identical with that other. Modern chemistry has its roots in medieval alchemy, but this does not make the modern chemist the equivalent of the alchemist in search of the Philosophers' Stone!

[32] Wolterstorff, 'Is it Possible?', 18.

doing so is that this promises a method for approaching theology that reflects the character of much traditional theology. Another reason is that the analytic method has already proved a powerful tool in contemporary philosophy. The work in contemporary philosophical theology is evidence of how effective this can be. Not all theologians will find this method amenable, just as some philosophers reject the analytic tradition in preference for so-called 'continental' approaches. That is grist to my mill. I am not suggesting that this is the only way of doing theology, just that it is one way, and a way that promises to be most useful in the prosecution of the theological task.[33]

[33] Thanks are due to audiences at the Society for the Study of Theology conference at Leeds University, 2006, the APA Central Division Meeting in Chicago, 2006, Heythrop College, University of London and St Mary's College, University of St Andrews, where earlier versions of this chapter were read. It has also benefited from the comments of Gavin D'Costa, Paul Helm, Matt Jenson, Randal Rauser, and Mike Rea.

2

Systematic Theology as Analytic Theology

William J. Abraham

Over its history systematic theology has delivered its goods under many names and in many forms. Generally the discipline has sought to provide a carefully constructed, coherent, interrelated articulation of Christian teaching that is apt for its particular time and space. However, the term is also used rather loosely. So systematic theology has been identified as dogmatic theology, constructive theology, and the interpretation of the Christian message. It has branded itself in terms of biblical theology, philosophical theology, existential theology, process theology, and the like. It has been linked to the achievement of great figures, as in Thomist theology, Calvinistic theology, and Wesleyan theology. Over the last two centuries it has been tied to various movements in Christianity such as liberal theology, evangelical theology, feminist theology, and liberation theology; or to various places as represented by Princeton theology, Third World theology, and the New Yale theology. Systematic theology has been a malleable and moveable feast that develops a great variety of modes of thought and sensibility. The emergence of systematic theology as analytic theology was then an accident waiting to happen. Christian theologians have deployed the resources of many modes of philosophical thinking from the beginning; the turn to analytic philosophy as a source for systematic theology should neither surprise us nor initially trouble us.

In this chapter I shall explore a vision of systematic theology as analytic theology, describe in general terms what that might involve, deal with some objections, and illustrate how it might proceed by taking up two loci of systematic theology and showing what analytic theology might look like in practice. I shall end with some suggestions on the division of labor between analytic theology and the epistemology of theology as this crops up in the place of prolegomenon in systematic theology.

Analytic theology can usefully be defined as follows: it is systematic theology attuned to the deployment of the skills, resources, and virtues of analytic philosophy. It is the articulation of the central themes of Christian teaching illuminated by the best insights of analytic philosophy. One reason for proceeding with cautious cheerfulness in the development of analytic theology is that analytic philosophy, while it often deploys highly technical tools and skills, has from the beginning sought to illuminate our everyday concepts and modes of thought. To use the felicitous comment of Harry G. Frankfurt, 'Surely one need not have been trained in any very distinctive philosophical tradition and skill in order to be able to think clearly, or reason carefully, and to keep one's eye on the ball.'[1] This good sense can apply immediately to the prospects of analytic theology. To be sure, as analytic philosophy migrated and began exploring more specialized fields of discourse, say, in science, education, and history, philosophers of necessity had to be acquainted with what was going on in these domains. Yet the commitment to clarity and persuasive argument never wavered in this migration, and the fruits across the last century as seen in a host of disciplines have been intellectually invaluable.

The drive into theology is a natural one, even though some theologians are wont to complain that analytical philosophers are likely to oversimplify, to be historically insensitive, and to foster theological naiveté. The scattered work on Christian doctrine to date by philosophers gives cause for quiet optimism, for analytic philosophers of religion have been probing the contours and central themes of Christian theology for at least two generations. It would be inflated to say that students in systematic theology would be delivered from many intellectual vices were they to be initiated into the rigors and clarity of analytic philosophy; analytic philosophy is not a holy labor-saving device, and analytic theology will no doubt have its own liabilities and vices. Yet the confusion that abounds in contemporary systematic theology is likely to diminish if theologians and their students come to terms with the virtues of the analytic tradition.[2]

As a discipline systematic theology has a set of topics or loci that are constitutive of its nature. While there are variations here and there, the set network of topics is something like this: prolegomenon, the existence of God (attributes, Trinity), Christology, pneumatology, creation, providence, the human condition, ecclesiology, soteriology, and eschatology. The evidence for the claim that these topics and their internal themes represent the hard-drive of systematic theology is both empirical and normative. On the one hand, these are the topics that standard textbooks invariably take up and the

---

[1] Harry G. Frankfurt, *Necessity, Volition, and Love* (Cambridge: CUP, 1999), p. xi.
[2] The conceptual problems and intellectual sloppiness that bedevil contemporary systematic theology are highly visible in William C. Placher (ed.), *Essentials of Christian Theology* (Louisville, Ky.: Westminster/John Knox Press, 2003). This is one of the best readers currently available, yet one has only to compare it with standard readings in philosophy texts for undergraduate students to become aware of the difference in intellectual standards. It is pleasing to record an exception that proves the rule in John Webster, Kathryn Tanner, and Iain Torrance (eds.), *The Oxford Handbook of Systematic Theology* (Oxford: OUP, 2007).

conventional topics generally pursued by theologians. On the other hand, omission of any of these topics is a cause for substantial failure.[3]

These topics were clearly originally drawn from the great creeds or proto-creeds of the Church. They were not invented by theologians seeking tenure in the modern university. The first great systematic theologians, like Origen, the Cappadocians, and Augustine, were not starting from scratch in their work as theologians. They had already been baptized into the faith of the Church and found themselves driven by the inner logic of that faith to explore, expand, and enrich its central doctrines. They were engaged in a massive exercise of faith seeking understanding.

On the surface, dependence on the creeds as indispensable background music appears initially to be intellectually disastrous for analytic theology. It looks as if the early theologians were cooking the books in advance; and so the same criticism applies *mutatis mutandis* to the analytic theologian in relying on their labors. Have we not already decided in favor of the truth of the faith? Is not theology a massive exercise in question-begging crucial truth claims that simply cannot be take for granted? Of course, if we define systematic theology in merely descriptive terms, this objection will not bother us. However, theologians have rightly been concerned with the truth of their claims rather than simply their authenticity or Christian identity. They have operated at the level of the normative and the prescriptive, seeking to articulate what we ought to believe rather than simply what has been believed. In other words, the task of apologetics and proof, while they have been conceived in radically different ways, has always been in the neighborhood. So the objection raised here has to be taken seriously; and I will return to this sort of query later.

Suffice it here to say that the worry initially is mere appearance. Conversion and baptism where one encounters and receives the creed were themselves a quest for truth. To be sure, it was a truth hidden from the world that had crucified in its earthly wisdom the Lord of Glory, but it was truth they had encountered, and it was truth that motivated their manifold labors.[4] Indeed the problem faced by the systematic theologian was how to come to terms with the truth of God revealed in Christ and brought home by the Holy Spirit. Systematic theology arose precisely because one had crossed over into the

---

[3] *Essentials of Christian Theology* e.g. omits the whole topic of the Holy Spirit. Things fare even worse with Serene Jones and Paul Lakeland (eds.), *Constructive Theology* (Minneapolis: Fortress Press, 2005), which omits the sacraments, providence, the Trinity, and eschatology. As we shall see, great theologians like Jürgen Moltmann can get away with ignoring prolegomenon; this is a very illuminating omission of keen relevance to the work of analytic theology.

[4] The truth of faith was not, of course, detached from participation in the life of God or from growth in sanctity, for it was truth that set the sinner free to discover their true destiny in creation and live a life of love to God and neighbor.

strange new world of the Church and the Bible and was compelled to think through systematically what one had gotten oneself into in one's Christian initiation. Within that initiation confession of the substance of the creeds as later canonically adopted at Nicea-Constantinople was not an optional issue; it was constitutive of baptism and conversion.

Donald Mackinnon captures both the challenge and commitment that stems from this feature of Christian existence.

> One who, like the present writer, is a professional philosopher is hardly likely to be tempted to underestimate the importance of the task of the Christian scholar. But it is, and must remain, a subordinate task, that is, to the proclamation of the everlasting Gospel of the mercy of God. It is always the temptation of the intellectual to resent the restriction laid upon him by the fact of the Gospel. To him the fact is scandalous, that is, a stumbling block, in a quite peculiar sense. Its 'fleshiness' oppresses him with an intensity that is manifested in the ingenuity wherewith he seeks to escape its burden. It is he who is aware of dogma (in the strict theological sense) as a restriction. Its presence inhibits him from erecting into an absolute a prevailing mood of thought. It is not those, who in the eyes of the world, are accounted poor and simple, that crave release from the cramping frame of Christian institutions. To them the giant affirmations of the Nicene Creed are not tiresome restraints imposed by an arbitrary authority. They are the lasting signpost to the fact that they were so loved by God that he gave them his only-begotten Son.[5]

Commitment to this kind of robust version of Christianity broke down in the modern period. In fact, the material content of systematic theology virtually disappeared in some quarters due to a Third Schism in the Church in which the canonical faith was deconstructed from within in the name of credibility and relevance.[6] The motives were good; theologians wanted to speak in a fitting manner to the intellectual and political challenges of the day. The problem was that so little doctrinal content was left by the time the theologians were finished speaking. This development in part explains the disarray within much contemporary systematic theology. If the deep truths of the Gospel and the central elements of the Nicene Creed are constitutive of the Christian faith, then much modern and contemporary theology is really the invention of various forms of post-Christian religion. Some theologians have, of course, been tempted to blame the breakdown within systematic theology on this or that philosopher or this or that philosophical mistake; but the role of philosophy in any proposed narrative of fall from grace is itself informed by philosophical judgment, so we should take the theological blame-game with a

---

[5] D. M. MacKinnon, *The Church* (London: Dacre Press, 1940), 50.

[6] I provide one narrative of this transition in *Canon and Criterion in Christian Theology* (Oxford: Clarendon Press, 1998).

pinch of salt. The truth of the matter is complex, but there is no denying that the multiple attempts to revise the constitutive doctrines of Christianity have resulted in confusion and disarray within theology as an academic discipline. It is no surprise that theology has become thoroughly marginalized if not outright dismissed as a serious intellectual enterprise within the contemporary university.[7]

The issues at stake here are straightforwardly conceptual and spiritual. The Christian faith really does have a content that cannot be set aside without losing the faith itself. Given the concern about conceptual clarity within analytic theology, it is not at all surprising that many talented analytic philosophers have gravitated towards robust forms of Christian theism. They do not want to be accused of not dealing with real Christianity; they have a sharp eye for equivocation and conceptual sleight of hand. Nor is it surprising that they have turned to doing theology themselves. They are intellectually and spiritually tired of having been offered stones when they asked for bread.[8] It is true that, because of the theologically conservative cast of much analytic philosophy of religion, there has been a tension between theologians and philosophers that is not likely to dissolve in the near future. Theologians think that the philosophers are theologically naive;[9] philosophers think that theologians have given away the store for no good reason.[10] No doubt there is need for greater understanding on both sides of this divide. Analytic philosophers have had very good reasons for digging in on their side of the ditch; we can expect that much analytic theology will generally share this disposition.

However, this is not the whole story, for one can also read the development of analytic philosophy of religion and of analytic theology as a natural development from within philosophy itself. After the collapse of logical positivism with its strident polemic against the cognitive content of religious

---

[7] The issue is taken up with characteristic depth and originality by John Webster in *Theological Theology* (Oxford: Clarendon Press, 1998).

[8] I recall vividly when I was a graduate student at Oxford attending during the same term the lectures of John Macquarrie and of A. J. Ayer. After complaining about the lack of substance and rigor in Macquarrie's lectures, I was chided by a friend from South Africa for my impatience and hasty judgments. So I repented and stayed the course. Three weeks later we left Macquarrie's lectures and, coming down the steps of Christ Church, I impishly said that if I had a choice between going to heaven with Macquarrie or to hell with A. J. Ayer, I was headed for hell. My friend immediately responded that he would be happy to come to hell with me.

[9] See e.g. Sarah Coakley, ' "Persons" in the "Social" Doctrine of the Trinity: A Critique of Current Analytic Discussion', in Stephen Davis, Daniel Kendall, and Gerald O'Collins (eds.), *The Trinity* (Oxford: OUP, 1999), 123–44.

[10] See e.g. Alvin Plantinga, 'Sheehan's Shenanigans: How Theology Becomes Tomfoolery', in James F. Sennett (ed.), *The Analytic Theist: An Alvin Plantinga Reader* (Grand Rapids, Mich.: Eerdmans, 1998), 296–315.

claims, a network of exceptionally able philosophers in Britain and North America took up philosophy of religion in the 1950s and 1960s in a way that forced others to take notice.[11] As philosophy of religion revived, more believers entered the profession; others came out of hiding; other philosophers bored by work in other fields and impressed by the freshness and boldness of the new work joined the fray as astute critics.[12] The result was an extraordinary renaissance of philosophy of religion that readily spilt over into work in philosophical theology and from thence over into theology proper.

I have already proposed an initial definition of analytic theology. It is systematic theology attuned to the deployment of the skills, resources, and virtues of analytic philosophy. This, of course, is just a beginning. How might we fruitfully proceed from here? One obvious way forward is to make some general comments on the nature of systematic theology developed with an analytic perspective. Beyond that we can look at some preliminary work on specific doctrines.

First, analytic theology will put a high premium on conceptual clarity in exploring the doctrines taken up within the various loci. Very generally this will mean coming clean on the concept of God at play throughout the loci. My own preference at this point is to conceive of God in terms of personal agency, rather than, say, Process, Being, the Absolute, and Spirit. In doing so I am not conceiving of God as simply a bigger and better version of human agents. At its core the idea of agency as applied to God signifies an agent who possesses all the standard attributes, who transcends space and time, and who exists in an utterly mysterious reality as three Persons in One Substance. The critical feature of agency in play here is that of acting on various intentions and purposes. We might say that God is that agent than which nothing greater can be thought, who has created and redeemed the world through His Son Jesus Christ in the activity of the Holy Spirit, and who will bring the redeemed creation to final glory in the future.

Second, analytic theology will naturally deploy the notion of narrative in spelling out the activity of God in creation and redemption. Beyond the ambivalent impact of Alasdair Macintyre this has not happened to date,[13]

---

[11] Two collections of essays and two books became landmark texts: Antony Flew and Alasdair MacIntyre (eds.), *New Essays in Philosophical Theology* (London: SCM, 1995); Basil Mitchell (ed.), *Faith and Logic* (London: George Allen & Unwin, 1957); Alvin Plantinga, *God and Other Minds* (Ithaca, NY: Cornell University Press, 1967); Basil Mitchell, *The Justification of Religious Belief* (London: Macmillan, 1973).

[12] See e.g. Richard M. Gale, *On the Existence and Nature of God* (Cambridge: CUP, 1991).

[13] Alasdair MacIntyre's stress on narrative in *After Virtue* (Notre Dame, Ind.: University of Notre Dame, 1981) and beyond has had a profound impact on contemporary theology through the work of Stanley Hauerwas and his students. However, MacIntyre, while his work clearly bears the hallmarks of analytic philosophy, has been scathing in his criticisms of analytic

but it is easy to see why narrative is a crucial concept. The heart of Christian theology is a drama of creation, freedom, fall, and comprehensive renewal. Narrative matters at this point because it is through narrative, that is, through the careful delineation of action, intention, and purpose, that the works of God are articulated and rendered intelligible.[14] Theological explanations are not scientific; they are inescapably personalistic and teleological; they involve personal causation rather than event causation. Narrative, to be sure, is a slippery notion so it can be deployed in a way that seeks to evade issues of truth and falsity. There is no equivocation at this point here; fictional and mythological narratives that carry deep theological truth are commonplace in the scriptures and the tradition of the Church; so there is no need to be squeamish or defensive about the complexity of narrative in the Christian tradition. However, the metanarrative of systematic theology is clearly intended to be read as true rather than as expressions of emotion, or as avowals to lead, say, an agapeistic way of life. It is the grand, reality-depicting narrative of creation, freedom, fall, and redemption that I have in mind when I suggest that analytic theology will take narrative with radical seriousness.

Third, analytical theology will bring to bear all the resources of conceptual clarification where appropriate to each of the doctrines articulated in the classical loci. It is hard to think of any doctrine from creation to eschatology where conceptual issues are not extremely important. It will be sufficient in a programmatic essay to draw attention to the kind of work that has already been done and further work that waits to be done in the future. For the moment I shall eschew comments on issues in prolegomenon for reasons that will become clear later. But if we do not begin with prolegomenon, where can we begin?

Analytic theology can begin by standing inside the circle of Christian faith and seeking to articulate the deep contours of the vision of God that is to found in the Church. We speak here unapologetically of the Christian God, the God of creation and redemption, whose saving acts are laid out in the Nicene Creed and in the manifold practices of the Church.[15] Within this

---

theology because of its lack of historical depth and sociological sensitivity; and Hauerwas, in part because of his strong Barthian sensibilities, has been reluctant to deploy the resources of analytic philosophy.

[14] Contrary to what is widely held at the moment, this means that attempts to develop general theories of divine action yield only limited dividends in theology. A general theory of divine action does little to throw light on the meaning of specific action predicates as applied to God. What we need at this level is the creative deployment of analogical modes of thought that aptly explore how action predicates as applied to God do and do not match action predicates as applied to human agents.

[15] For a delineation of what this means see William J. Abraham, Jason E. Vickers, and Natalie B. Van Kirk (eds.), *Canonical Theism* (Grand Rapids, Mich.: Eerdmans, 2008).

horizon let me visit two distinct loci of systematic theology and see what emerges. I shall look at the doctrine of God and at the doctrine of grace and freedom. The aim overall is to indicate the kind of work that will come naturally to the analytic theologian.

Consider how analytic theology might proceed in articulating a robust doctrine of God. At present there is stout resistance in some theological circles to deploying philosophical skill in articulating a Christian vision of God that has multiple sources. There is, at the outset, the long-standing contrast that pits the god of the philosophers over against the God of Abraham, Isaac, and Jacob. From as far back as Tertullian and at least from Pascal onwards in the modern period we have been told that there is the dead, abstract god of the philosophers and the living God of scripture and faith.[16] Karl Barth's arguments against natural theology have aided and abetted this contrast sharply and made it the staple diet of three generations of theologians. To reach for the god of the philosophers is to seek to justify ourselves by our works; it is to invent an idol rather than turn to the one true God of divine revelation; and it is to make revelation subordinate to human reason.[17] In addition it has been suggested from the side of recent liberation theology that the omnipotent, omniscient, omnipresent god of the philosophers is the top-down god of the masters, the god of empire.[18] An omnipotent god will end up, like it or not, being brought in to support the unilateral omnipotence of empire. Thus the god of the philosophers is, if only by default, in synch with the new North American, neo-colonial empire. From another angle the god of the philosophers is a god one comes to know through cold, clinical logic divorced from genuine spirituality and from the special revelation through whom God is supremely known and loved. So the god of the philosophers is really the god of pagan thinking rather than the God known and worshipped in the faith of the saints and martyrs.

These are certainly extremely interesting moves, but taken either singly or together they are not at all persuasive. On the contrary, we need the help of analytic theology to do justice to the God we meet in the worship of the Church. We can cut to the chase by noting that the God we have identified in our initial orientation is not some idol cooked up by philosophers, but precisely the God and Father of our Lord Jesus Christ, the triune God of Christian Creed and worship. The warrant for this move is simple: this is the

---

[16] For a recent expression of this tradition see Justo L. Gonzalez, *Mañana, Christian Theology from a Hispanic Perspective* (Nashville, Tenn.: Abingdon, 1990), ch. 6.

[17] I have discussed this at greater length in *An Introduction to the Philosophy of Religion* (Englewood Cliffs, NJ: Prentice Hall, 1985), ch. 7.

[18] This is an important theme in Joerg Rieger, *Christ and Empire* (Minneapolis: Fortress, 2007), 240, 249, 254.

way God is named and identified in the Church. To be sure this God can also be identified as the one and only Creator of the universe; and this God is also the God of Abraham, Isaac, and Jacob. However, our quarry is not the God of mere theism, but the God of the Gospel as identified and named over time in the Church canonically; it is the God of revelation, faith, and worship that matters in our doctrine of God. Thus the first task of a doctrine of God in analytic theology is to unpack as fully as possible what is involved in confessing that we believe in the triune God of the Church. In doing so we can draw extensively on recent work on the nature of identity and we can explore metaphysical possibilities that would otherwise be overlooked or not taken seriously.[19]

What then about the classical attributes of God? Should these be included in our doctrine of God? Are we not including alien material if we look at omnipotence, omniscience, omnipresence, and the like? If we deal with them at all, should we not confine ourselves to the sparse and meager references to them that show up in scripture? The response to this worry has long been available to us in the work of Anselm. Clearly Anselm began his thinking about God inside the faith. He was not in search of God or in search of a proof of God; he already had come to know God for himself in the life of the Church. What his stunning discovery in the *Proslogion* makes clear, however, is that the One he has encountered in the faith of the Church can also aptly be identified as nothing less than that than which nothing greater can be conceived. Hence in order to do justice to the God he knows and loves Anselm has judiciously hit upon a conceptual means for expanding his vision of God. He is not just at liberty to explore the classical attributes of God as an exercise in abstraction or mere semantics; he is required to stretch his mind to the limits in order to work out how he may now speak appropriately of God as omniscient, omnipotent, omnipresent, all-good, totally worthy of worship, and so on. In turn, this will require the analytic theologian to investigate how these attributes of God relate to God's work in creation, providence, and miracle, and to other relevant topics like natural and moral evil, human freedom, and God's sovereign control over all things.[20] At its limit Anselm eventually comes to the conclusion that the very idea of God requires his

---

[19] See e.g. Bruce M. Marshall, *Trinity and Truth* (Cambridge: Cambridge University Press, 2000), and Richard Swinburne, *The Christian God* (Oxford: Clarendon Press, 1994). For a penetrating discussion by a leading analytic philosopher on the doctrine of the Trinity see William P. Alston, 'Substance and the Trinity', in Stephen Davis, Daniel Kendall, and Gerald O'Collins (eds.), *The Trinity* (Oxford: OUP, 1999), 179–201.

[20] For a fine exploration of these matters see Thomas V. Morris, *Our Idea of God* (Notre Dame, Ind.: University of Notre Dame, 1991).

existence. This God is such that his non-existence is inconceivable; he differs so radically from all else in creation that he must exist.[21]

In my teaching of systematic theology to totally new believers in Kazakhstan I initially hesitated to introduce them to Anselm's vision of God. When I first did it, I noticed the lights go on in the mind of one of the brightest students present and asked afterwards why he was so excited about what had been said. He immediately replied that in thinking of God as that than which nothing greater can be conceived he had at long last found an apt way of describing that God of the Gospel who had saved his life and whom he gladly worshipped in the services of his local church. In this instance spirituality and theology were brought together in a pleasing harmony. I have seen this repeated again and again in my teaching of new converts in the Third World.

Moreover, we can add that to seek to prove the existence of this God in no way reduces God to an idol. The property of being proved is a Cambridge property; it takes nothing away from the subject in question. One can see this immediately by noting that proving that my daughter exists in no way turns her into an idol or diminishes my love and devotion towards her. Equally, it is inappropriate to confuse commitment to the God described in this robust Anselmic fashion with commitment to any political philosophy, whether to that of some empire or some other favored constituency. On the contrary, one can see how those committed to this vision of God are given resources to stand up to tyranny wherever it occurs. Commitment to a God who has entered into the brutality of human evil in the cross and who is also omnipotent should be more than enough to provide lavish moral and spiritual resources in standing up to political and social evil.[22] So we can set aside the widespread aversion to putting rigorous philosophical analysis to work in exploring the rich contours of the Christian doctrine of God.

We can also begin to see how such analysis might help us both clarify and resolve a long-standing conundrum buried deep within the Christian doctrine of salvation. There are many elements at issue in the Christian doctrine of salvation. Initially they cluster in and around how to understand justification and sanctification. In turn these concepts open up the question of how we should think of the interrelation between divine and human action in salvation. One way to pose the issue is this: what is the relation between grace and freedom? On the one hand, we want to say that we are saved by grace; we depend on divine action to initiate, provide, and sustain the new life that

---

[21] For a very important examination of this issue see Robert Prevost, *Probability and Theistic Explanation* (Oxford: Clarendon Press, 1990).
[22] For a stirring example of this see *Father Arseny, 1893–1973: Priest, Prisoner, Spiritual Father* (Crestwood, NY: St Vladimir's Seminary Press, 2004).

Christ brings to us. There is no question of our being saved by our own works, by our own merit, or by our own worthiness. God alone saves us. On the other hand, we are not coerced into salvation; God does not save us against our wills; we are free to say no to God in salvation; and in the Gospel we are called upon to repent, put our faith in Jesus Christ, to take up our crosses, to attend to the sacraments of the Church, and the like. So how can we at one and the same time say that God alone saves us and that we have an indispensable role to play in the total process of salvation?

The Western tradition as a whole, following Augustine, has come heavily down on the side of grace. Grace operates from beginning to end; even the first move towards repentance is made possible by prevenient grace; and faith itself is a gift of God. This line has run so deep as to lead to the development of a vision of double, unconditional predestination in which God elects some to salvation and sees to it that they receive it and elects others to damnation and sees to it that they get what they deserve. This in turn has led either to a denial of freedom altogether or to compatibilist doctrines of freedom that does not baulk at insisting on divine determination of all that happens. While modern theologians are reluctant to go this far, the shadows of the logic of grace remain in the theological undergrowth and in much half-baked, popular piety. Any move to take seriously a more robust doctrine of freedom or to take seriously genuine human action in salvation will be greeted as a form of Pelagianism.

This is clearly one area where conceptual analysis is vital in unraveling the theological issues that need attention. To speak of grace is to enter the domain of causation. To say that we are saved by grace is to insist that we are saved by divine agency; we are explaining salvation in terms of the actions of God both in history and in the human soul. As J. R. Lucas has pointed out, however, it is easy at this point to be misled by the diverse ways in which we use causal language.[23] Explanations are extraordinarily varied, but we can make progress by distinguishing two relevant types. There are those kinds of explanations where we supply full causal explanations of phenomena by means of natural laws and antecedent conditions. In this instance we are wedded to determinism; if we knew all the antecedent conditions and causal laws, then the outcome is determined. In these circumstances to explain the cause of what happened is to identify the complete cause. However, we also speak of causation in a quite different way, that is, we think of causation in terms of the most significant cause of the event in question. Here we select the cause of the event by picking out one factor as the critical factor, leaving aside for the moment all the other antecedent conditions that are pertinent. Thus we

---

[23] J. R. Lucas, *Freedom and Grace* (London: SPCK, 1976), 2.

set aside standing conditions and negative conditions and focus in on this or that factor as the cause of what happened or what is going on. We do this most characteristically when we want to assign credit or responsibility to this or that causal agent.

With this distinction in hand we can begin to see what has gone astray in the debate about freedom and grace. What began as an effort to give credit to God in salvation has taken the language of most significant cause and stretched it to mean the complete cause. In the latter case there can be no room for human agency for the complete cause has been identified with God and the corollary of this is obvious: there can be no other causes, including human actions. Hence human agency must be eliminated completely or become so anemic as to be non-existent. Moreover, given the fat relentless human ego that is ever ready to take credit for anything we do, we are all too ready to seize on any human action in salvation and construct grandiose schemes of credit and merit that quickly become schemes of salvation by works. In this instance the logic of our language and our sinful perversity feed off each other and the drift into Pelagianism becomes irresistible. However, once we trace the issue back to the complex causal and explanatory discourse that is operating as relevant background music, we can cut off such moves and begin to take seriously both genuine human freedom and agency in the total process of salvation. We are well on our way to solving the Augustinian—Pelagian controversy.

This conclusion will immediately seem far-fetched even to many analytic theologians; perhaps we have the glimmerings of a way forward rather than being well on our way to solving one of the deepest mysteries of the faith. Our optimism is a matter of degree at this point; for my part I am amazed at the progress that is already possible. However, I agree entirely that this optimism may be misplaced. Moreover, I also agree that there is much more to be done in the unraveling of this long-standing problem in Christian theology. We need a careful phenomenology of Christian conversion in all its teeming diversity. It is surely no accident that many are drawn to the Augustinian position because they are aware of how they were worn down by God in the journey home; without the relentless hound of heaven they would never have made it. However, we also need to look with care at other kinds of conversion narrative where the role of human action and the sense of human freedom are much more pronounced. In and around this we need a much more nuanced account of what is at stake in speaking of freedom or free will. It is clear that when Luther spoke of the bondage of the will he did not mean to treat human agents as mere mechanisms or automatons who acted out of total necessity. We can be in bondage to, say, bigotry or jealousy, and still be free to express our bigotry or jealousy in a host of ways. Likewise, there are a host of actions that we cannot will to do even though logically and humanly we are free to do them, as when we insist that we cannot do those things that run headlong into confrontation with those values and things we really care about.[24] So we need a much deeper account of the character of human agency and the dynamics of human action that crop up initially around disputes about free will. Finally, we need a more sensitive reading of the rhetoric involved in the call to human action and endeavor. When we tell our teenagers that they need to get their act together, that they can do much better than their current conduct suggests, we are not falling into a superficial vision of the human predicament. We are manifesting a complex interplay of human relations that have a genuine place for exhortation and inspiration. Likewise, when we are called upon to repent or to take up the cross, we are not falling into some kind of Pelagian doctrine of works righteousness. We are taking seriously the role of human response to the commands of God, even as, in those commands and exhortations, God is aiding us to do what we cannot do on our own.[25]

Thus far I have made some preliminary and descriptive comments about the nature of analytic theology and briefly explored what analytic theology might look like were it to take up the doctrine of God and the relation between grace and freedom. Yet plunging straight like this into the content of Christian theology may frustrate even the most sympathetic reader. What about the question of truth? What about the justification of these theological claims? What about the criteria of theological inquiry? Surely, it will be said, it is these questions that ought to be foremost in the work of analytic theology. In fact it seems perverse not to tackle these questions up front, given that they are taken up within systematic theology itself in the opening section on prolegomenon. So why have I held back in raising them to this closing section?

It is certainly not because I think these questions unimportant. Nor am I belittling the wealth of recent work done on these issues by philosophers. My concerns are threefold. First, theologians become so consumed with epistemological issues that they never really get beyond the worries that arise once these issues are given a privileged position in the opening exercise in prolegomenon. Theologians never get over their initial doubts and skeptical impulses; and students become intellectually paralyzed and lose their confidence. Second, and alternatively, these questions are so difficult and complicated that it is very tempting for the theologian to reach for the nearest

---

[24] For an very important treatment of this issue see Harry G. Frankfurt, *The Importance of What We Care About* (Cambridge: CUP, 1988).

[25] I leave aside the need to develop an appropriate doctrine of sin, original and otherwise, at this point; but that issue too would benefit from careful philosophical analysis.

answer that lies to hand or to cut and paste this or that item in epistemology and hope that this will hit the target.[26] Either way, we are offered unsatisfactory solutions to a network of problems that deserve far more attention than can be given to them within the boundaries of a prolegomenon. Worse still, students offer up schoolboy solutions to problems in epistemology and develop a false sense of security in doing so. Third, as hinted earlier, the history of modern theology shows that a host of epistemologies deployed within prolegomenon have hindered rather than helped in systematic theology. They have acted as a form of intellectual birth control in which the faith of the Church has been prematurely aborted rather than allowed to come to full term. They operate as artificial and inappropriate forms of thought control within the borders of systematic theology.[27]

There is no easy solution to the problem I am identifying. Some theologians, like Jürgen Moltmann, have simply ignored it and left it to be taken up at the end of their careers. Others, like Barth, have realized the magnitude of the task and devoted hundreds of pages to tackling it, but then found themselves unable to finish their work. It is very tempting, of course, to hand the whole affair over to philosophy of religion and simply leave it at that. However, philosophers of religion all too often restrict themselves to the standard queries about the validity and soundness of natural theology and natural atheology and thus leave a host of important epistemological topics unattended.[28] Besides, they have other issues to discuss. So this will only offer marginal assistance.

What we sorely need at this point is the creation of a new subdiscipline in the borderlands between philosophy and theology, namely, the epistemology of theology. What I envisage is a systematic, self-critical, historically informed

---

[26] Nowhere is this more visible than in the lazy and dogmatic use of the so-called Wesleyan quadrilateral of scripture, tradition, reason, and experience.

[27] It is clear e.g. that the restriction of warrant to religious experience has inhibited the development of robust doctrines of the Trinity, most famously in Friedrich Schleiermacher's great work in Christian theology, where the doctrine is relegated to an appendix. See *The Christian Faith* (Edinburgh: T &T Clark, 1928). The brilliant work of Schubert M. Ogden in the last generation also comes to mind, where similar effects can be seen in the field of Christology. See his *The Point of Christology* (Dallas, Tex.: Southern Methodist University Press, 1982). John Macquarrie's widely used *Principles of Christian Theology* (New York: Scribner, 1966, 1977) represents a similar trend where the constraints in this instance are derived from a heavy allegiance to a Heideggerian epistemology and ontology.

[28] It is rare nowadays to find the whole topic of revelation taken seriously; yet discussion of divine revelation is vital to the interests of systematic theology. For a fine exception see Sandra Lee Menssen and Thomas D. Sullivan, *The Agnostic Inquirer: Revelation from a Philosophical Standpoint* (Grand Rapids, Mich.: Eerdmans, 2007). It is clear that if it is the pure in heart who see God, then philosophers will need to pay attention to the place of the theological virtues of faith, hope, and love in discussions of the place of virtue epistemology in the epistemology of theology.

inquiry into the epistemological issues that crop up in theology.[29] Such work will require the efforts of both philosophers and theologians; neither need confine themselves to the crumbs that fall from each other's tables; we need a new table where both can bring a full plate of food and their recipes to the feast. The theologians will be crucial because without them the subject matter of theology, namely, God, will never get the attention it deserves. The philosophers will be crucial because without them we will not have the full range of resources within epistemology at our disposal. Within this work we must let the subject matter of our inquiry in all its plenitude of being play a vital role in sorting out what counts as relevant evidence, justification, and warrant. Equally we must examine any and every proposal in this domain for its epistemological validity and fruitfulness. In doing so we are also under obligation to take up relevant matters about the nature of language and truth that naturally impinge on resolving epistemological questions that crop up within systematic theology. Nothing short of this, in my judgment, will suffice to deal adequately with vital and inescapable questions on the nature of norm and truth that are currently sorted out in the prolegomenon to systematic theology.[30]

Should we then reform systematic theology and eliminate the prolegomenon from systematic theology entirely? It is certainly tempting to take this step; there is a pleasing simplicity about this move. We could still, of course, retain an initial introductory section in which the analytic theologian provides relevant preliminary remarks to get the show up and running. 'Prolegomenon' generally means quite simply the words that come at the beginning; so we can still use that term to cover an opening section that indicates the nature of the work to follow, the kind of questions that will be pursued, the assumptions that are already in play, and the like. We might even indicate in a cursory way the norms that will be deployed, noting that the full treatment of these matters must be taken up in their own right elsewhere. Such a move would dovetail nicely with the invention of a new section at the end, the postlegomenon, where we might take up again the bearing of our theological investigations on important questions in the epistemology of theology. This would be especially apt given that the analytic theologian will be deploying

---

[29] Clearly this work will overlap with work that currently flies under the banner of 'the epistemology of religious belief'. The difference with this work will be two-fold: it will be confined to reflection of epistemological issues related to Christian theology (rather than to religion generally or to religions other than Christianity); and it will have space for the work of theologians as well as philosophers.

[30] I have pursued the epistemology of theology in *Crossing the Threshold of Divine Revelation* (Grand Rapids, Mich.: Eerdmans, 2006).

all sorts of arguments and reasons in working through those loci that rightly occupy the attention of the systematic theologian.

However we resolve the challenge of what we do in prolegomenon, we cannot cut and run when it comes to the central themes of systematic theology as these have been identified and explored across the centuries. The subject matter of systematic theology has its own integrity. In the end the theologian must come to grips with the questions that arise in and around the activity of God in the great drama of creation, freedom, fall, and redemption. This is as true for analytic theology as it is for any other kind of theology. Within analytic theology the theologian will deploy the skills, resources, and virtues of analytic philosophy in clarifying and arguing for the truth of the Christian Gospel as taken up in the great themes of the creeds of the Church.[31] No doubt the analytic theologian can develop and display other interests and skills as garnered, say, from biblical studies, historical investigation, and cultural commentary. Moreover, there is no reason why the analytic theologian cannot keep an eye on the role of theology in the fostering of deep love for God; indeed that should be a concern of any theology whatever its virtues or vices.[32] There is ample evidence to hand to suggest that the time is ripe for the emergence of analytic theology; there is also sufficient evidence to suggest that this work will bear much fruit in the years ahead.

---

[31] For a fuller account of my own vision of the various tasks of systematic theology see my 'Canonical Theism and Systematic Theology', in *Canonical Theism*.

[32] For a point of entry into this arena see Robert C. Roberts, *Spiritual Emotions* (Grand Rapids, Mich.: Eerdmans, 2007).

3

Theology as a Bull Session

Randal Rauser

Our culture is full of it. It fills the bloated claims of advertising and the spin of public relations, it pervades the bluster of political discourse, and it even lurks in the feigned profundity and conviction of a beauty contestant's speech.[1] Although it is called many things—balderdash, poppycock, bunk, humbug—within academic discussion the standard term was fixed by Harry Frankfurt's ground-breaking analysis in the aptly titled essay 'On Bullshit'.[2] While this term is admittedly coarse, so is the reality to which it refers, and so the choice of a more polite term might, ironically, mask the offense of the topic itself. (As such, there is more to the use of the term bullshit than a mischievous attempt to interject sailor talk into highfalutin' academic discourse.) While bullshit is pervasive in society, we might hope to gain some respite from it in the confines of academia, but alas, here too it is not hard to find. William Lycan recounts with bemusement a philosophy book that promised 'Eleven new ways in which negation negates itself',[3] an example which recalls Martin Heidegger's sober pronouncement that 'The nothing *noths*.'[4] And then there is the famous case in which physicist Alan Sokal impugned the standards of the peer-reviewed cultural studies journal *Social Text* by successfully submitting for publication an essay of nonsense ostentatiously titled 'Transgressing the Boundaries: Toward a Transformative Hermeneutics of Quantum Gravity.'[5]

---

[1] See Laura Penny, *Your Call is Important to Us: The Truth About Bullshit* (Toronto: M&S, 2005).

[2] Frankfurt's essay was originally published in *The Raritan Review*, 6/2 (1986) and later reprinted as *On Bullshit* (Princeton: Princeton University Press, 2005) in which form it became a *New York Times* bestseller. All references are to the book edn.

[3] William G. Lycan, *Philosophy of Language: A Contemporary Introduction* (London and New York: Routledge, 1999), 128.

[4] See Gary L. Hardcastle, 'The Unity of Bullshit', in Hardcastle and George A. Reisch (eds.), *Bullshit and Philosophy* (Chicago and LaSalle, Ill.: Open Court, 2006), 143.

[5] *Social Text*, 46–7 (1996), 217–52. For a discussion see Alan Sokal, *The Sokal Hoax: The Sham that Shook the Academy* (Lincoln, Neb.: University of Nebraska, 2000).

While such examples serve to illustrate the grosser indulgences of academia, at the same time they raise a serious question: how is it that academic discourse comes to provide fertile ground for bullshit? Undoubtedly there are many reasons.[6] Consider for instance the effect of the demand to 'publish or perish'. The fact is that few of us have the Wittgensteinian luxury of polishing our academic gems until they are truly ready to go on display. Need it be said that, if the only pressure were to 'publish when perfect', the amount of academic bullshit would be greatly reduced? Frankly this demand for productivity places an enormous burden on academics to produce something to distinguish themselves. But as Hilary Putnam (speaking to philosophers) reminds us, 'A philosopher's job is not to produce a view X and then, if possible, to become universally known as "Mr. View X" or "Ms. View X."'[7] The reminder is crucial since the professional pressures of academia constantly draw individuals into jostling for the recognition of peers and employers at the expense of the tireless pursuit of truth.[8]

A second impetus to academic bullshit, and the one on which I shall focus in this chapter, arises from skepticism. As Cornelis de Waal observes, 'Part of the reason behind the prevalence of bullshitting and the ease with which it is accepted is a lack of confidence that genuine inquiry is worth pursuing, or even possible.'[9] The point is not that people explicitly abandon truth for bullshit; rather, adopting a broad skepticism about the prospects of a given field of enquiry makes one who remains within the discipline liable to bullshit. Our specific focus here concerns how the types of skepticism currently affecting theology lead to bullshit. To that end I shall begin by summarizing the two basic types of bullshit, the intention-based and the product-based. Next I shall consider two skeptical approaches to theology: Sallie McFague's view of theology as persuasive metaphor and Jürgen Moltmann's view of theology as perpetual conversation. Both are skeptical in nature because they deny either that there is special revelation or that we can have

---

[6] Alan Richardson discusses the letter of reference as a refined type of bullshit: 'I can write that "Mortimer's Ph.D. thesis offers a counterfactual account of causation that is a significant contribution to our understanding of causation" without fear that I have engaged in gratuitous and counter-productive bullshit. Indeed, if I am Mortimer's advisor, I am supposed to write this, even though the number of Ph.D. theses in philosophy that are significant contributions to anyone's understanding of anything is vanishingly small.' 'Performing Bullshit and the Post-Sincere Condition', in *Bullshit and Philosophy*, 87.

[7] Putnam, *Representation and Reality* (Cambridge, Mass., and London: MIT Press, 1988), p. xii.

[8] This attitude originates in the classroom, as students strive to distinguish themselves over against their peers. See Henri Nouwen, *Creative Ministry* (New York: Image Books, 1991), 8.

[9] De Waal, 'The Importance of Being Earnest: A Pragmatic Approach to Bullshitting', in *Bullshit and Philosophy*, 99. Sokal traces the degeneration of cultural studies to postmodern skepticism. See 'A Physicist Experiments with Cultural Studies', *Lingua Franca* (May/June 1996), 62–4.

knowledge of it. Consequently, I will argue that each view tends to predispose those who hold it to a specific type of bullshit: those who hold McFague's view are susceptible to intentional bullshit while advocates of Moltmann's view are liable to product bullshit. I shall close by noting that, despite their significant differences, both McFague and Moltmann's skepticism effectively reduces theology to something akin to a perpetual bull session.

We begin then with an analysis of bullshit itself. Not only did Harry Frankfurt fix the terminology, but he also forwarded an especially influential theory of the phenomenon with his intriguing thesis that the essence of bullshit is not deception but rather bluffing: 'although it is produced without concern with the truth, it need not be false. The bullshitter is faking things. But this does not mean that he necessarily gets them wrong.'[10] As such, the bullshitter may in fact say something true, but if she does it is merely incidental because she doesn't *care* about the truth either way. All she is concerned with is eliciting an effect, be it selling a product, protecting someone's feelings, or improving her image as a profound thinker. This is quite different from the deceiver who, in his deceptive intent, is in fact very concerned with the truth (and thus leading us away from it). Interestingly, Frankfurt argues that the bullshitter's alethic ambivalence makes the practice even more subversive of truth than lying, given that the liar at least *cares* about what is true.

While there is a general consensus that Frankfurt's theory has identified one crucial aspect of bullshit, it runs into difficulties when we attempt to apply it to all cases. One significant problem is that it requires us to know an author or speaker's intention before we can identify his/her statement as bullshit. Certainly in many cases this presents no problem: I confidently dismiss the claim of a certain carbonated soft drink to be 'the real thing' as bullshit because I know that advertisers ultimately have a single intent: sell the product. But when I come to a putative case of academic bullshit things are not so clear. Indeed, in the vast majority of cases in academia I simply do not know enough about an individual's intentions to conclude that he/she was *intending* to bullshit. Nonetheless, it seems in many cases in academia one can reasonably identify a statement as bullshit without knowing anything of the speaker/writer's intentions. If this is correct then not all bullshit is the result of an intentional act.[11] Along these lines G. A. Cohen proposes that in addition to Frankfurt's bullshit there is a type where the bullshit lies not in the intention but the product. In confirmation of this thesis he points out that

---

[10] Frankfurt, *On Bullshit*, 47–8.

[11] Frankfurt admits that one may bullshit without intention insofar as one repeats a bullshit statement while believing it to be profound. Frankfurt, 'Reply to G. A. Cohen', in Sarah Buss and Lee Overton (eds.), *The Contours of Agency: Essays on Themes from Harry Frankfurt* (Cambridge, Mass.: MIT Press, 2002), 341.

the *OED* includes two basic definitions of bullshit: (1) nonsense or rubbish (Cohenian bullshit) and (2) insincere talking or writing (Frankfurtian bullshit).[12] So while many types of bullshit are rooted in intentionality (e.g. advertising, public relations) others are unintentional nonsense.[13] As Cohen puts it, 'Bullshit as insincere talk or writing is indeed what it is because it is the product of something like bluffing, but talking nonsense is what it is because of the character of its output, and nonsense is not nonsense because of features of the nonsense-talker's mental state.'[14]

Cohen's analysis, which focuses upon the characteristics of bullshit in academic discourse, is rooted in his memories spending hours as a young scholar attempting to dissect the obscurity of certain French Marxists: 'I attributed to it more interest or more importance...than it had, partly, no doubt, because I did not want to think that I had been wasting my time.'[15] This of course is a common human response: when we invest in something we persist in trying to vindicate the initial commitment (who has not suffered through a bad movie simply because you paid the money to watch it and thus were determined to 'get your money's worth'?).[16] Cohen then observes that having committed to finding something profound in a text, academics occasionally imbue profundity into whatever tidbits they can salvage from their efforts: 'Someone struggles for ages with some rebarbative text, manages to find some sense in it, and then reports that sense with enthusiasm, even though it is a banality that could have been expressed in a couple sentences instead of across the course of the dozens of paragraphs to which the said someone has subjected herself.'[17] Unfortunately, this simply perpetuates the cycle as relatively unimportant claims are imbued with more significance than they ever deserved. As Hans Maes and Katrien Schaubroeck warn, such opaque academic prose is a serious threat to the integrity of academia itself: 'Academic discourse should always aim for the truth and texts that are so obscure that the question of truth becomes irrelevant are a threat to any serious academic enterprise.'[18]

---

[12] Cohen, 'Deeper into Bullshit', *Bullshit and Philosophy*, 120.

[13] And still other statements might be both. An advertiser could make a claim of Frankfurtean bullshit which is believed and repeated by an individual, at which point it becomes Cohenian bullshit.

[14] Ibid. 121–2.

[15] Ibid. 118.

[16] Preti comments: 'Anyone who slogged through graduate school is familiar with the psychological tension Cohen describes: the hours spent poring over some obscure text, justifying the hours of work by believing—even arguing—that the work in question is deeply important and terribly profound; the more so, because of its obscurity.' 'A Defense of Common Sense', *Bullshit and Philosophy*, 20–1.

[17] Cohen, 'Deeper into Bullshit', 118.

[18] Maes and Schaubroeck, 'Different Kinds and Aspects of Bullshit', *Bullshit and Philosophy*, 179.

While Cohen points out that product bullshit comes in different varieties, he focuses upon one type prevalent in academia, 'unclarifiable unclarity', which he defines as discourse 'that is not only obscure but which cannot be rendered unobscure, where any apparent success in rendering it unobscure creates something that isn't recognizable as a version of what was said'.[19] Dare we suggest that some theologians, despite their undeniable brilliance, occasionally lapse into unclarifiably unclear statements?[20] Karl Rahner for one was a famously obscure writer,[21] and this obscurity is readily on display in 'Rahner's Rule': 'The immanent Trinity is the economic Trinity and the economic Trinity is the immanent Trinity.'[22] In the search for evidence of this text's unclarifiable unclarity, one need simply observe that forty years after Rahner wrote the rule there is still no consensus as to its meaning. Of course one could always argue that there is some supremely profound point buried therein, but forty years of commentary suggest the prospects are not bright.[23]

While Cohen suggests that unclarifiable unclarity is the central mark of academic bullshit, Mark Evans identifies other types which are germane to academic work including 'clarifiable unclarity' and 'irretrievable speculation'.[24] One important mark of clarifiable unclarity is found when a relatively straightforward or simple claim is cloaked in a cascade of unnecessarily technical nomenclature. (Incidentally, the previous sentence comes close to qualifying.) Such obscurity is often accompanied by a second mark: verbosity. As Cohen puts it, 'a banality that could have been expressed in a couple sentences instead of across the course of...dozens of paragraphs'. Stanley Grenz unwittingly provides an example of clarifiable unclarity when he summarizes the consensus of recent Trinitarian theology: 'any truly helpful explication of the doctrine of the Trinity must give epistemological priority to

---

[19] Cohen, 'Deeper into Bullshit', 130. Unfortunately, Cohen is pessimistic about the prospects for defining clarity which, as Frankfurt points out, renders the concept of clarity itself liable to the charge of being unclarifiably unclear. See 'Response to G. A. Cohen', 341.

[20] This is one explanation for Nicholas Wolterstorff's apparent difficulty in understanding Moltmann: 'My own view—and Moltmann's also, if I understand him'; 'His proposal, as I understand it—possibly I *mis*-understand it'; 'If I understand Moltmann's proposal correctly—and let me say, once more, that it may well be that I do not'. 'Public Theology or Christian Learning?', in Miroslav Volf (ed.), *A Passion for God's Reign* (Grand Rapids, Mich.: Eerdmans, 1998), 68, 72, 73.

[21] Stanley Grenz and Roger Olson describe a cartoon Rahner once received which depicted him lecturing as a 'theological nuclear physicist' with a puzzled Jesus in the audience who afterward confesses 'I don't understand.' *Twentieth Century Theology: God and the World in a Transitional Age* (Downers Grove, Ill.: InterVarsity, 1992), 238.

[22] Rahner, *The Trinity*, tr. Joseph Donceel (Tunbridge Wells: Burns & Oates, 1970), 22.

[23] See Randal Rauser, 'Rahner's Rule: An Emperor without Clothes?', *International Journal of Systematic Theology*, 7/1 (2005), 81–94.

[24] Evans, 'The Republic of Bullshit', *Bullshit and Philosophy*, 198–9. Cf. Cohen, 'Deeper into Bullshit', 131–2.

the presence of the trinitarian members in the divine economy but reserve ontological primacy for the dynamic of their relationality within the triune life'.[25] Shorn of technical verbiage and wordiness, Grenz seems to be saying that, while we know God through the economy of revelation, there is more to God than what is revealed in the economy, a statement so platitudinous that I cannot think of one notable theologian who would have denied it. Clarifiably unclear statements also occasionally evince a 'bait and switch' quality such that on one reading the statement is controversial—even absurd—while on another it is mundane or even tautological. This is rhetorically effective, for when critics turn up the heat on the controversial reading one can always retreat to the tautology. Take the case of Jacques Derrida who, after being thoroughly critiqued by John Searle and others for his claim that 'there is nothing outside the text', later explained that he just meant there is nothing outside a context.[26] We should keep in mind that, insofar as we classify such cases as Cohenian bullshit, we are denying that there is any intentional strategy to dodge the critics; rather, one may accidentally produce this kind of ambiguous statement and later capitalize on the ambiguity.[27] (At the same time, the bait and switch would also be a great strategy for the Frankfurtean academic bullshitter.)

Evans argues that irretrievable speculation occurs when a claim has no possible means of verification. Frankly that definition seems too strong since there are statements that are possibly verifiable but still overly speculative. Further, it is potentially vulnerable to the self-referential problem with the verificationist criterion of meaning.[28] As such, we might do better with a more open definition that includes a broad swath of overly speculative statements, recognizing that we thereby gain flexibility at the expense of precision. While there may be many ways to identify overly speculative statements, I would submit that one sure mark is 'indifference to negation'. As Cohen defines it, this occurs when 'adding or subtracting (if it has one) a negation sign from a text makes no difference to its level of plausibility'.[29] For instance, Heidegger initially took the position that Being exists independently of beings, but later changed his mind and concluded that Being does *not* exist

---

[25] Stanley Grenz, *Rediscovering the Triune God: The Trinity in Contemporary Theology* (Minneapolis: Fortress Press, 2004), 222. Grenz's summary of the theological contributions of Hans Urs von Balthasar (196) and Thomas Torrance (212) likewise appear trivial.
[26] See Jacques Derrida, *Limited Inc* (Evanston, Ill.: Northwestern University Press, 1988), 136.
[27] Rahner's rule is a plausible candidate for this kind of clarifiable unclarity since the two most obvious readings are trivial and absurd. See Rauser, 'Rahner's Rule'.
[28] Hence the problem if we cannot possibly verify the statement that 'all ultimately unverifiable statements are overly speculative bullshit'.
[29] Cohen, 'Deeper into Bullshit', 132. Cohen however offers this criterion as a mark of unclarifiable unclarity.

independently of beings. Paul Edwards comments: 'It seems clear that there cannot be any reason either way and that Heidegger's option... is totally arbitrary and illustrates the "anything goes" character of his philosophy.'[30]

Even as we warn against unbridled speculation it should be pointed out that judgments of Cohenian bullshit are at least in part relative to one's prior metaphysical commitments. For instance, a naturalist is likely to dismiss debates about the *filioque* or Chalcedonian definition as unclarifiably unclear, irretrievably speculative, or both. The classic case here may be David Hume's call to commit every volume of metaphysics and theology to the flames as mere sophistry and illusion. A more recent example is found in the campaign of logical positivism against the 'nonsense' of theology, metaphysics, and ethics.[31] While the theologian might find a legitimate challenge in some of these critiques, she would surely be mistaken to seek to eliminate from her discipline all that Hume or Neurath would call bullshit, for that would be the elimination of theology altogether!

Having distinguished intentional and product bullshit, we can now proceed to consider how these are fostered by two types of theological skepticism that are currently in vogue, beginning with Sallie McFague's view of theology as persuasive metaphor. McFague's view is rooted in her skeptical claim that 'there is no uninterpreted access to reality; hence, we are not dealing, on the one hand, with "reality as it is" and, on the other hand, with views of it; but solely with the latter'.[32] Based on this presupposition, she denies that we have any access to revelation of God, a view which leads her to reinterpret purported instances of divine revelation as humanly constructed metaphors: 'All language about God is human construction and as such perforce "misses the mark."'[33] While McFague predictably denies that God revealed himself as 'Father', she adds that even the description of God as *personal* is a metaphor.[34] As a result, she shifts the work of theology from reflection on revelation to

---

[30] *Heidegger's Confusions* (Amherst, NY: Prometheus Books, 2004), 36.

[31] Gary Hardcastle characterizes logical positivism as an 'anti-bullshit philosophical program': 'The Unity of Bullshit', 141.

[32] Sallie McFague, *Metaphorical Theology: Models of God in Religious Language* (Philadelphia: Fortress Press, 1982), 134.

[33] McFague, *Models of God: Theology for an Ecological, Nuclear Age* (Philadelphia: Fortress Press, 1987), 23; cf. 26. Given the complete rejection of revelation in McFague's thought, Colin Gunton *understates* the problem when he observes, 'The systematic weakness of *Metaphorical Theology* and its successor [*Models of God*] is the inadequacy—indeed, almost absence—of the author's concept of revelation.' 'Proteus and Procrustes: A Study in the Dialectic of Language in Disagreement with Sallie McFague', in Alvin F. Kimel, Jr. (ed.) *Speaking the Christian God: The Holy Trinity and the Challenge of Feminism* (Leominster: Gracewing; Grand Rapids, Mich.: Eerdmans, 1992), 70.

[34] McFague, *Models of God*, 82–3.

remythologizing the God/world relation through metaphorical 'description': 'As remythologization, such theology acknowledges that it is, as it were, painting a picture. The picture may be full and rich, but it *is* a picture. What this sort of enterprise makes very clear is that theology is *mostly* fiction: it is the elaboration of key metaphors and models.'[35] With revelation having been rejected, the ground of theology shifts to experience: 'Our primary datum is not a Christian message for all time which becomes concretized in different contexts; rather, it is experiences of women and men witnessing to the transforming love of God interpreted in a myriad of ways.'[36] This notion of 'transforming love' provides a key to McFague's assessment of theological accounts of God and his (her, its) relation to us. In short, while theology is 'mostly fiction' we judge which fiction is preferable in a given instance based on its adequacy 'both for human habitation and as expressions of the gospel of Christian faith at a particular time'.[37] That is, we choose our metaphors of God and the God/world relation based on their emotive power to shape behavior in a way that aids human flourishing.[38] For example, while the metaphor of father may have been useful at one time, it has long been used to justify the oppression of women and abuse of the earth and so must be replaced (or at least supplemented) by other metaphors.[39] Not surprisingly, all traditional fixed points of 'orthodoxy' are open to being replaced in an ongoing re-evaluation of doctrines relative to our current needs and ends: 'Theological constructions are "houses" to live in for a while, with windows partly open and doors ajar; they become prisons when they no longer allow us to come and go, to add a room or take one away—or if necessary, to move out and build a new house.'[40]

While I reject McFague's Kantian presuppositions, my specific concern here is to identify the basis on which her view of theology tends to produce bullshit. For point of illustration consider the case of James Frey whose bestselling memoirs *A Million Little Pieces* were chosen by Oprah for her book club. When it emerged that Frey had fictionalized significant portions of the book, Oprah initially defended him by arguing that the work was still 'inspirational'. Fortunately, she later recanted and joined the masses in decrying Frey's dishonesty for presenting fiction as real life.[41] In doing so, Oprah was admitting that there is no justification to inspire under false pretenses. As Consuelo Preti points out, 'if I think that your specific story *S* is true, and I am

---

[35] Ibid., p. xii. [36] Ibid. 44. [37] Ibid., p. xii.
[38] Ibid., p. xiii. [39] Ibid. 21. [40] Ibid. 27.
[41] See George A. Reisch and Gary L. Hardcastle, 'On Bullshitmania', *Bullshit and Philosophy*, p. xi; Preti, 'A Defense of Common Sense', 22–4.

inspired by it, *then to discover it isn't true, is to discover that there is nothing in it* by which to be inspired'.[42] As a result the fictionalized portions of Frey's book, embellished simply to tell a good tale, are classic examples of Frankfurtean bullshit. It is my claim that McFague's theology is structurally parallel to Frey's book and thus also produces intentional bullshit. There is however one glaring difference: McFague does not misrepresent her theology in the way that Frey misrepresents his memoirs. On the contrary, she is clear that theology is about metaphorical swapping rather than reflection on revelation, and thus that the *point* of theology is the transformation of the individual rather than knowledge about God. But despite that crucial difference, I will argue that McFague's theology still produces, or at least predisposes us to produce, theological bullshit.

The central problem arises when we ask how McFague's theology (or any other for that matter) can be expected to inspire individual transformation. Since she rejects the propositional content of theology, one might think that the inspiration is to come from a pure, non-propositional aesthetic experience, rather like the effect that Beethoven's Fifth Symphony has upon Helen, a character in *Howard's End*:

Helen pushed her way out during the applause. She desired to be alone. The music had summed up to her all that happened or could happen in her career. She read it as a tangible statement, which could never be superseded. The notes meant this and that to her, and they could have no other meaning, and life could have no other meaning.[43]

This performance of music transformed Helen without providing her with any propositional information. Might McFague's theology function similarly by fostering a transformative aesthetic experience? This is unlikely for McFague's books, well written though they are, have nothing like the aesthetic quality of Beethoven's Fifth (or even the Bee Gees' 'How Deep is Your Love'). The problem is that discursive prose is not the *kind* of thing to foster pure aesthetic experience.[44] Perhaps one might reply that McFague actually intends for her theology to foster verbal aesthetic experience like a great romantic poem (e.g. Wordsworth's 'Tintern Abbey'). But of course McFague's writing is not poetry, it's academic theology.

If McFague's theology is to inspire, it will do so because of the truths that it communicates. Undoubtedly the most inspiring (and potentially transformative) metaphors of God are not impersonal (e.g. rock, gate) but rather personal (e.g. father, mother, friend, lover). These are inspiring, and

[42] Preti, 'A Defense of Common Sense', 23.
[43] Cited in Colin Lyas, *Aesthetics* (Montreal and Kingston, ON: McGill-Queen's University Press, 1997), 3.
[44] Though a great rhetorician may express herself with aesthetic sophistication.

potentially transformative, precisely because they depict God as a *personal agent* with whom we can enter into relationship and whose perfections we can strive to emulate in our other relationships. Unfortunately, McFague's Kantian rejection of revelation obliges her to deny that God really is personal: this too is but a metaphor. But once we recognize that God is not really personal, the power of all these personal metaphors is emasculated in the same way as Frey's fabricated experiences: this too is inspiration under false pretenses. How, after all, are we to be transformed in our parental love by our heavenly mother/father when we realize that God is not even personal, let alone parental? Alvin Plantinga's critique of John Hick's constructivist approach to doctrine applies to McFague as well: 'Once I am sufficiently enlightened, once I see that those doctrines are not true, I can no longer take the stance with respect to them that leads to the hoped-for practical result.'[45] That is, I cannot be transformed in my personal being by a transcendent, impersonal abstraction. Hence, McFague's apophatic conception of deity seems doomed to failure. Or to turn it around, the one chance for it to succeed is found in misleading people into thinking that God really is in some sense personal. For McFague's theology to have the best shot at facilitating transformation, one must *at least* believe that the metaphors of mother, lover, and friend mediate a *personal* reality. What is more, in light of McFague's belief that theology involves the use of 'mostly fiction' to facilitate 'transforming love', it is not a stretch to conclude that such a misleading procedure would be encouraged, even required.[46] As a result, McFague is little different from the used car salesperson who cares not about providing me with factual information on that rusty old Ford Cortina, but rather with getting me to buy it. Just as the salesperson's job description ensures that closing the deal trumps truth telling, so on McFague's view of 'theo-poetic persuasion', the theologian's final obligation is not to inform but to persuade (even as she makes it *appear* that she informs). Whether or not you agree that this practice of depicting God in a variety of personas to facilitate transforming love is justified does not change the fact that it is intentional bullshit.

While a number of 'metaphorical theologians' share McFague's presuppositions, this type of skepticism is still very much in the minority. In contrast, there is a much wider skepticism which is having a great impact on contemporary theology. This approach to theology, which builds on the central image of conversation,[47] is skeptical of the traditional use of reason in

---

[45] *Warranted Christian Belief* (Oxford and New York: Oxford University Press, 2000), 61.
[46] The situation reminds one of Voltaire's practice of sending the servants out of the room before broaching the topic of atheism.
[47] Conversation is determinative for McFague's view of metaphorical development as well, though she tends to opt for the metaphor of a quilt. See Shannon Schrein, *Quilting and Braiding:*

theology, particularly in systematic theology. One finds skepticism about theological reasoning among many self-described postmodernists, postliberals, and emergent church leaders like Brian McLaren who speaks derisively of 'modern Christians, who do not build cathedrals of stone and glass as in the Middle Ages, but rather conceptual cathedrals of proposition and argument. These conceptual cathedrals—known popularly as systematic theologies—were cherished by modern minds...'[48] McLaren's point seems to be that the age of systematic theologies which attempt to provide a 'comprehensive' theology is past. Now the best that theology can aim for is to be coherent, contextual, and *conversational*: 'never attempting to be the last word, and thus [to] silence other voices, but rather inviting ongoing dialogue in the search for truth'.[49]

Diverse though proponents of this skeptical perspective may be, Moltmann could launch a plausible claim to being their theological patron saint. His own skepticism toward systematic theology begins in his pervasive suspicion of power, in this case the power that the systematic theologian seeks to wield which would effectively exclude or suppresses dissonant voices that do not fit the accepted system of theology.

In several European languages, understanding a thing means 'grasping' it. We grasp a thing when 'we've got it'. If we have grasped something, we take it into our possession. If we possess something we can do with it what we want. The motive that impels modern reason *to know* must be described as the desire to conquer and to dominate.[50]

Moltmann adds that reason's aspiration to control is bound to fail because the more we attempt to grasp abstract timeless concepts, the less the concepts we grasp transcend their concrete historical applications:

From experiences which are historically changeable and unrepeatable we abstract those which can be more or less repeated, and for these we form the timeless *concept*, which transcends history and hence is continually applicable. If we hold the phenomena of time fast in the concept, the concept then eliminates time and itself has no time,

---

The Feminist Christologies of Sallie McFague and Elizabeth A. Johnson in Conversation (Collegeville, Mich.: Liturgical Press, 1998).

[48] McLaren, *A Generous Orthodoxy* (Grand Rapids, Mich.: Zondervan, 2004), 168.
[49] Ibid. 169.
[50] Moltmann, *The Trinity and the Kingdom: The Doctrine of God*, tr. Margaret Kohl (London: SCM Press, 1981), 9. Moltmann believes that, since Bacon and Descartes, 'to know has meant to dominate. I want to perceive nature outside myself in order to dominate it. I want to dominate it in order to acquire it for myself. I want to acquire it for myself in order to do what I like with my possession. That is a thinking with the rapacious hand: I grasp that—I've mastered it—I've got it—I've seized the meaning—I have it.' Moltmann, *God for a Secular Society: The Public Relevance of Theology*, tr. Margaret Kohl (Minneapolis: Fortress Press, 1999), 139.

because it must not be altered but must always remain unequivocally the same. In this way concepts acquire a rigidity which does not befit the life embraced by the concepts. This makes it clear that there can be no concepts for 'the living God', that source of life which continually brings forth what is new.[51]

This pessimism derives from Moltmann's belief that the modern view of reason depends upon the premise that 'like seeks after like'.[52] Moltmann argues in platonic fashion that this principle leads to the doctrine of recollection in which true learning is impossible as all knowledge is derived from a prior experience with the forms: 'The principle of correspondence does not lead to any increase in knowledge, but only to the continually reiterated self-endorsement of what is already known.'[53] But Moltmann recognizes that while one may construct an internally consistent theological system along these lines, it will always be unconnected to the world and thus ultimately sterile. Such isolated systems (e.g. those of Thomas Aquinas and Jonathan Edwards) may be self-consistent but they are also irrelevant, 'like fortresses which cannot be broken into but cannot be broken out of either, and which are therefore in the end starved out through public disinterest. I have no wish to live in such a fortress'.[54] Consequently, Moltmann believes that this view of reason as looking within supports individualism, frustrates dialogue, and breeds stagnant homogeneous (and xenophobic) communities. As a result the pursuit of reason frustrates true learning for 'what is other and alien in nature remains for ever hidden from it'.[55] In short, we are doomed to see only that which fits within our preconceived notions.

The surrender of timeless absolutes means that the theologian 'cannot therefore aim to say what is valid for everyone, at all times and in all places'.[56] Instead, he has the humbler task of setting 'himself, with his own time and his own place, within the greater community of theology'.[57] At this point, Moltmann introduces a Hegelian view of theological reason as an historical threefold process involving assertion, conflict, and resolution. As he cryptically puts it, 'how do we perceive this other? Not through its correspondence

---

[51] Moltmann, *Experiences in Theology: Ways and Forms of Christian Theology*, tr. Margaret Kohl (Minneapolis: Fortress Press, 2000), 169.
[52] Cited in Moltmann, *The Crucified God: The Cross of Christ as the Foundation and Criticism of Christian Theology*, tr. John Bowden and R .A. Wilson (London: SCM Press, 1974), 26. In Plato see *Meno* 80d–e.
[53] Moltmann, *God for a Secular Society*, 139.
[54] Moltmann, *Experiences in Theology*, p. xx; cf. Moltmann, *The Spirit of Life: A Universal Affirmation*, tr. Margaret Kohl (Minneapolis: Fortress Press, 1992), 226.
[55] Moltmann, *God for a Secular Society*, 140.
[56] Moltmann, *Experiences in Theology*, p. xii.
[57] Ibid.

but through its contradiction.'[58] For Moltmann, this threefold process is rooted in the triune history of God who comes to be through the distinction of the Son from the Father and the resolution of the two in the Spirit.[59] The theological community thus reflects the glory of God as historical and diverse insofar as it gives voice to the oppressed and reconciles the other within a community of diversity. The image of God is found not in the rational individual but rather in the community-in-dialogue.[60] This brings us to Moltmann's central image of congenial conversation: 'For me, theological access to the truth of the triune God is through dialogue. It is communitarian and co-operative. *Theologia viatorum*—the theology of men and women on the way—is an enduring critical conversation'.[61] Moltmann takes this to mean that one's doctrinal work is never the last word, but rather always a *contribution* to the wider conversation.[62] In the following passage he contrasts the individual rationalistic system builder with the free, egalitarian community:

Theological systems and assertive dogmatics can hardly bring out this aspect of truth. They exert coercion where free assent can be expected and given. They leave the individual mind little room for creative fantasy. They allow no time for individual decisions. But it is only in free dialogue that truth can be accepted for the only right and proper reason—namely, that it illuminates and convinces *as* truth. Truth brings about assent, it brings about change without exerting compulsion. In dialogue the truth frees men and women for their own conceptions and their own ideas.[63]

While Moltmann's theology begs critical reflection at a number of points, my focus here is on how it tends to produce Cohenian bullshit. The core problem is that Moltmann's repudiation of reason removes the critical safeguards that weed out bullshit. For point of analogy, imagine what would happen if the USDA and FDA declared that all standards for the raising, slaughter, and processing of cattle would henceforth be strictly voluntary. No doubt some ranchers and meat packers would attempt to retain good practices (e.g. testing for BSE, treating workers humanely, abstaining from feeding meat by-products to ruminants) but the overall effect on the industry would

---

[58] Moltmann, *God for a Secular Society*, 144. Further, 'It is through dissonance, not consonance, that we become alive to the new', 144. 'It is first in the distance, even more in the difference, and then lastly in the contradiction that we perceive the other, and learn to value it', 144–5.

[59] As Richard Bauckham notes, 'It seems as though in *The Crucified God* Moltmann meant to say that the Trinity is actually constituted by the event of the cross.' Bauckham, *The Theology of Jürgen Moltmann* (Edinburgh: T&T Clark, 1995), 155. Bauckham adds however that Moltmann 'quickly retreated from that position to the view that God is eternally Trinity', 155.

[60] 'The trinitarian concept of community envisages *diversity in unity* from the outset.' Moltmann, *The Spirit of Life*, 219–20; cf. Moltmann, *Trinity and the Kingdom*, 198.

[61] Moltmann, *Experiences in Theology*, p. xvii.

[62] Moltmann, *Trinity and the Kingdom*, p. viii.

[63] Ibid., p. xiii.

surely be devastating. Those strictures are in place precisely as checks and balances to ensure rigor and honesty against the baser profit motives of the market system. Academic theology requires its own checks and balances and these are found in the rigorous demands of closely reasoned analysis. As Mark Evans puts it, 'an anti-bullshit discursive culture may develop if there is greater practice of, and respect for, the techniques of a good old-fashioned analytic-philosophical style, which prizes clarity of exposition and rigor of analysis in pursuit of truth and the "best argument" objectively understood'.[64] Just as we need laws to regulate beef, so we need laws to regulate bull.

It is precisely the regulative demands for clarity of exposition and rigor of analysis that Moltmann decries as a tacit grab for power. But in rejecting these standards of clarity and rigor Moltmann thereby rejects crucial bullshit filters. Is it a coincidence that Moltmann's own style of prose is frequently turgid and his arguments frustratingly resistant to analysis? Ironically, Moltmann's model of perpetual conversation may contribute to precisely what he repudiates: the abuse of power. Moltmann does not appreciate the pure discursive meritocracy that is secured by the analytic theologian's demand for rigor, concision, and clarity from all. Within this discursive culture the appeal of your rhetoric, impenetrability of your prose, and security of your reputation matter nothing if your arguments are poor. It is on this egalitarian and iconoclastic ground that upstart Bertrand Russell could write his famous 1903 letter shooting down Frege's Basic Law V. Now try to imagine this dazzling exercise of analytic reasoning if Frege had written with Heideggerian obfuscation. In such a climate, Russell could easily be dismissed as a smarmy upstart whose temerity to challenge such a profoundly difficult thinker could only come from youthful ignorance. Hence, Moltmann's dismissal of carefully reasoned analysis as a hubristic power grab could easily become a means to indemnify the academic elite against criticism. And since it is poor fashion to question the elites, who is to call them to account when they do not follow their own claims? Note that just a few pages after proffering his ideal of communal dialogue, Moltmann states his intention 'to demolish some explicit objections and some tacit inhibitions' regarding a particular understanding of the Trinity.[65] Now how does such a demolition fit with the paradigm of non-coercive 'creative fantasy' and 'dialogue'? That of course is just the point: when necessary, Moltmann strikes out on tactical sorties to demolish contrarian positions, but then when the polemic is turned back on him, he beats a hasty retreat back behind the wall of congenial conversation.

---

64 Evans, 'Rhetoric of Bullshit', 200.
65 Moltmann, *Trinity and the Kingdom*, 2.

This brings us to our final point: despite their significant differences,[66] both McFague and Moltmann essentially reduce the discipline of systematic theology to a perpetual bull session. The bull session is an informal discussion that invites the sharing of different stories or ideas.[67] Robert Gorrell comments that both 'bull session' and 'shoot the bull' 'refer to talk, often empty, nonsensical, exaggerated, or lengthy'.[68] However, the bull session may serve a higher purpose by functioning as a brain-storming session where new ideas are suggested in an open forum of exploration. It is precisely this non-committal, experimental space that makes the bull session valuable for trying out new ideas. In this sense there is nothing wrong *per se* with a bull session, and indeed it can be a valuable heuristic tool, but *only* if one is committed to closing the loop by discerning which of the results are worth keeping and which should be discarded. That is, we need to be open to the possibility that while some of the products of the bull session will fail, others might move from idea to implementation, thereby providing genuine advances in understanding. As Cornelis de Waal puts it, 'what distinguishes a brainstorming session from an evening of bullshitting is that the participants in the former are interested in discovering something, a desire that is altogether absent among bullshitters'.[69] Perhaps one might speak more appropriately not of desire, but rather of expectation. That is, a bull session devolves into bullshit when it is assumed that the various ideas and arguments to be shared can have no final probative significance, but instead must remain a group of tales, told by theologians, signifying nothing.[70]

---

[66] For Moltmann's critique of projection theologies like McFague's, see *God for a Secular Society*, 142. Moltmann expresses his specific disagreement with Sallie McFague in *Experiences in Theology*, 165.

[67] Christine Ammer observes: 'This expression originally referred to an exchange of opinions and anecdotes, including stories of sexual prowess, by men, and then came to be used more broadly.' 'Bull Session', *The American Heritage Dictionary of Idioms* (Boston and New York: Houghton Mifflin, 1997), 87. See Frankfurt's discussion in *On Bullshit*, 39–40.

[68] Robert M. Gorrell, *Watch your Language! Mother Tongue and her Wayward Children* (Reno, Nev.: University of Nevada Press, 1994), 35.

[69] De Waal, 'Importance of Being Earnest', 110.

[70] Thanks to those colleagues and friends who picked out instances of unclarifiable unclarity in earlier drafts, including Oliver Crisp, Andrew Dole, Tom McCall, Ryan Murphy, and Michael Rea whose comments rivalled the paper in length.

II

Historical Perspectives

4

A Conception of Faith in the Greek Fathers

John Lamont

A frequent complaint about the application to theology of ideas from analytic philosophy is that such applications are unhistorical; they impose anachronistic concepts and questions upon issues from the Christian theological tradition, while ignoring vital elements of this tradition that do not fit into analytic ways of thinking. This chapter will consider a subject where this accusation is the opposite of the truth. It will use a contemporary debate in analytic philosophy, that of the nature of testimony as a source of knowledge, to gain a better understanding of an important theological tradition on the nature of Christian belief. This tradition, developed by the Greek Fathers, is not only illuminated but supported by current arguments for testimony as an autonomous source of knowledge. Since the notions of faith and knowledge are intimately connected, this illumination also requires and contributes to a better understanding of faith's goal, which is the knowledge of God.

THE MOTIVES FOR CREDIBILITY AND REDUCTIONIST/NON-REDUCTIONIST VIEWS OF TESTIMONY

The term 'motives of credibility' was coined by scholastics to designate the reasons that can be offered to unbelievers to defend the truth of the claim that the Christian faith is revealed by God, and that appeal to objectively rational considerations that are discoverable solely by natural human reason. Thus, for example, an appeal to miracles or to the fulfilment of prophecy would be an appeal to motives of credibility, whereas an appeal to prophecies themselves—assumed to be divinely revealed—would not. By the nineteenth century, these motives had taken on a fairly standard structure. A first step would be proving the existence of God, which would then be followed by arguing for the necessity of worshipping God, the possibility of a divine revelation that would tell us how we are to worship him, the need for such a revelation on the part of humankind, the criteria by which such a revelation can be recognized—usually consisting in miracles and the fulfilment of prophecy—the satisfaction of these criteria by Christianity, and hence the truth of the claims of Christianity to be divinely revealed. The work of Richard Swinburne is the most comprehensive contemporary example of such argument. Protestants will usually stop at the claim that the teachings of the scriptures are divinely revealed and hence should be believed, but Catholics will continue to argue that the Roman Catholic Church is divinely guided in its teachings, and hence that what the Church describes as divinely revealed (which includes, but is not limited to, the scriptures) should be taken to be so, and believed as such.

Divine revelation of the Christian gospel was simply assumed, prior to the eighteenth century, to consist in God's speaking to humankind to announce this gospel, and faith was assumed to involve believing God when he spoke. The Christian message uttered by God was taken to be the basis for Christian theology. This understanding of faith and theology is now largely rejected by theologians, although it continues to be the teaching of many Christian bodies, most notably the Roman Catholic Church. I have argued elsewhere that this rejection is a mistake,[1] but the question of its rightness or wrongness is not directly at issue in our historical investigation, since none of the figures we will look at thought of questioning it; their discussions of faith all proceeded on the assumption that it was true.

If Christian faith involves believing God's testimony, this raises the question of the relation of the motives of credibility to such belief. Three main answers have been given to this question. A first answer, which can be called the Latitudinarian one, holds that the belief that God speaks to announce the Christian revelation is based on inference from the motives of credibility. The name given to this position arises from the fact that it reached its full development in the work of the seventeenth-century Latitudinarian school of Anglican theology, although it seems to have first been proposed by Abelard. A second view, which has come to be called the Thomist view, holds that faith is not inferred from the motives of credibility. Believers accept the Christian revelation because God tells them, and this reason for belief is not based on any other grounds. A third view, first fully elaborated by Duns Scotus, holds that, although faith is not inferred from the motives of credibility, these motives are nonetheless necessary for faith, because without them it would not be rational. The Scotist view, which arises from the attempt to reconcile theological views held by the Thomists with philosophical

---

[1] In John Lamont, *Divine Faith* (Ashgate: Aldershot, 2004), ch. 2. That work concentrates on exposition and defence of the Thomist view of faith, whereas this chapter is intended to give a deeper examination of its history and its relation to the patristic conception of knowledge.

views held by the Latitudinarians, is not very convincing, and will not be discussed here.[2]

The question about testimony that concerns us has to do with the debate between reductive and non-reductive accounts of learning through accepting the testimony of others.[3] A classic expression of a reductive position is that given by Hume:

we may observe, that there is no species of reasoning more common, more useful, and even necessary to human life, than that which is derived from the testimony of men, and the reports of eye-witnesses and spectators. This species of reasoning, perhaps, one may deny to be founded on the relation of cause and effect. I shall not dispute about a word. It will be sufficient to observe than our assurance in any argument of this kind is derived from no other principle than our observation of the veracity of human testimony, and of the usual conformity of facts to the reports of witnesses.[4]

The non-reductive position is thus expressed by Peter Geach in his discussion of the theological virtue of faith:

The idea is as ludicrous as it is widespread that a man can in principle justify his rational beliefs by memory, observation and induction: his trust in the testimony of others is supposed to be inductively guaranteed. But none of us has any rational grounds of the sort described for trusting in the testimony of others in the way that we do and to the extent that we do. This point is concealed by a slippery use of the words 'observation' and 'experience' to mean now the observation and experience of a given individual, now human observation and experience: Hume is a conspicuous offender over this. But a moment's thought shows that a man's observation and experience cannot get him far and that the observations and experience of mankind generally are available to him only on trust and authority.[5]

Michael Dummett, in presenting the non-reductionist position, compares belief in testimony to memory as a fundamental source of knowledge:

The analogy between memory and testimony is very strong. In forming a belief, or adding an item to one's stock of knowledge, on the strength of a memory, one does not, in the normal case, arrive at it by any process of inference.... Exactly the same holds good for coming to believe or to know something by being told it. In the normal case, this is not effected by any process of inference. There are, again, special cases.

---

[2] Ibid., ch. 4, for an account of the history of these views.

[3] For an introduction to the non-reductive view of testimony, see C. A. J. Coady, *Testimony: A Philosophical Study* (Oxford: OUP, 1992); J. Lackey and E. Sosa (eds.), *The Epistemology of Testimony* (Oxford: OUP, 2006); Jonathan Adler, 'Epistemological Problems of Testimony', in *The Stanford Encyclopedia of Philosophy*, ed. Edward N. Zalta (Summer 2007 edn.), <http://plato.stanford.edu/archives/sum2007/entries/testimony-episprob/>.

[4] David Hume, *An Enquiry Concerning Human Understanding*, 3rd edn. (Oxford: Clarendon Press, 1975), 111.

[5] Peter Geach, *The Virtues* (Cambridge: CUP, 1977), 33–4.

I may know, from experience, that a particular informant is generally unreliable, through dishonesty or proneness to error, or that he is especially unreliable about a certain subject-matter. I may therefore consider, concerning something he has told me, the probabilities that he is mistaken or deceiving me, and decide that, in that specific case, the probability of either supposition is low, and so conclude to the probable truth of what he said. But such reflections are exceptional.[6]

Dummett, with his example of the unreliable informant, helpfully brings out the fact that some belief in testimony can be based on inference from non-testimonial knowledge. The existence of such belief in testimony is not incompatible with non-reductionism, which only denies that belief of this sort is typical of belief in testimony, or can make up more than a very small part of it. Geach and Dummett briefly indicate the main reasons that have been given for rejecting the reductionist view, which are that we do not in fact perform the inferences it presupposes when we form beliefs based on the testimony of others, and that we do not and could not have the evidence that would be necessary to justify such inferences, at least to the extent required by the beliefs we rationally possess. An important part of the case against reductionism lies in bringing out how much of our beliefs depend on testimony—those connected with history, geography, most of science, when we were born, etc.—and the degree of certainty we attribute to them, which in some cases is not significantly less than the certainty attributed to mathematical claims. It is accepted that a speaker's testimony in normal circumstances no longer constitutes reason to believe what the speaker says, if one comes to believe that the speaker is ignorant or dishonest in that particular instance. However, it is pointed out that this does not imply that positive evidence of knowledge or honesty is required to justify belief in testimony; the belief that a speaker is ignorant or dishonest undermines belief in his testimony because it is a defeater for that belief, rather than because it implies a lack of the positive evidence needed for accepting testimony.

A satisfactory non-reductionist view will not simply maintain the default rule that testimony is to be accepted in the absence of defeaters. The inadequacy of such an approach is apparent from the fact that in believing something on the basis of someone's testimony, we do more than follow such a rule; we also credit the speaker with being knowledgeable and honest in making the assertion we believe. That is why ignorance or dishonesty in a speaker constitute defeaters for their testimony. On the non-reductionist view, we must therefore credit those speakers we believe with knowledge and honesty, without basing this evaluation of them on evidence. Believers

---

[6] Michael Dummett, 'Testimony and Memory', in Bimal Krishna Matilal and Arindam Chakrabarti (eds.), *Knowing from Words* (London: Kluwer, 1994), 260–1.

in a reductionist view of testimony focus their objections on this claim: the existence of ignorance and deceit, they say, makes this view of testimony irrational. The debate over this objection is the crucial issue in the philosophy of testimony. The non-reductionist answer to it generally takes the form of asserting that the function of assertions of the relevant sort just is to communicate the speaker's knowledge, and that the hearer is entitled to accept that this function is being performed in the absence of indications to the contrary.[7] An analogy can be drawn with frowning; this is an expression whose natural function is to express displeasure of some sort, and an observer is entitled to believe that it is performing this function in the absence of evidence to the contrary. There are of course disanalogies here as well—most notably the fact that assertions are normally expressed by conventional means—and explaining exactly how such assertions function is the main task for the non-reductive theorist. I can only claim that the prospects of such explanation are hopeful, while the prospect of giving a reductionist account of knowledge from testimony is clearly hopeless, and on these grounds proceed on the assumption that a non-reductive account of testimony is correct.

The connection between this dispute about testimony and the dispute over the functions of the motives of credibility is evident. If a reductionist view is correct, the Thomist view cannot be right, since it holds that believing God is not based on inference. But if the non-reductionist view is right, the Thomist view can be right; and it is made more plausible by a non-reductionist view, since it presents belief in God's testimony as conforming to the normal pattern of belief in testimony generally.

Although debate on the role of the motives of credibility in faith only really began in the Middle Ages, a position on the role they play was explicitly taken early on, in Clement of Alexandria. This position is substantially identical with the Thomist one (which makes the name of the position somewhat inappropriate, but we will retain it as it has made a place for itself in theological discussion; its use dates back to the defence of it by baroque scholastics who identified themselves as Thomists). It became the characteristic position of the Greek Fathers; and it is the background and later history of this characteristic position, and the theology of faith within which it is contained, that I will be examining.

---

[7] An early version of such an answer is given by Thomas Reid, in his *Inquiry into the Human Mind*, ch. 6, s. 24, in *Works*, ed. Sir William Hamilton (Edinburgh: Maclachlan & Stewart, 1972; repr. Elibron Classics, 2005), pp. 194–201. Lamont, *Divine Faith*, ch. 6, also develops such an answer.

BACKGROUND TO PATRISTIC THOUGHT ON FAITH

In order to understand the view of the Greek Fathers, we need to look at its philosophical context. It should be kept in mind that the ancient world did not distinguish between philosophy and religion in the way that we do. Concerns that we think of as proper to religion—the existence of God, the purpose of human life, the nature of moral conduct—were in antiquity seen as the province of philosophy. This is illustrated by the fact that theology, dogma, and conversion were originally philosophical terms that were taken over by Christian theologians,[8] that Aristotle used the term 'theology' for the subject matter of the book we call the *Metaphysics*, that the Greeks, when they first acquired some knowledge of the Jews, described them as a 'philosophical race' on account of their concern with God, and that Josephus described the Pharisees, Sadducees, and Essenes as sects of philosophers—the term he thought best adapted to convey their religious concerns.

For the philosophical background, the place to begin is the attitude of ancient philosophers to belief acquired through testimony. As we have seen, the case for the non-reductionist view of testimony as an autonomous source of knowledge is strong, and fairly obvious. It is therefore surprising to find that this view was not only never accepted, but never even considered, in ancient philosophy. It is even more surprising when we realize that the non-reductive view was clearly expressed and argued for by Indian philosophers. The Nyāya school of philosophy held that testimony was one of the basic sources of knowledge, like perception and inference.[9] (Like Christian theologians, they divided testimony into two categories, divine and human.)

Part of the explanation for the lack of interest in testimony among ancient philosophers no doubt lies in historical circumstances; the principal relevant circumstance being the fundamental divide in Greek culture between philosophy and rhetoric. This divide reached its full flowering in the conflict between Plato and Isocrates, who consciously set up rhetoric in opposition to

---

[8] On this see Werner Jaeger, *Humanism and Theology* (Milwaukee: Marquette University Press, 1943), esp. pp. 46–53; 'dogma' was a term applied by Hellenistic philosophers to the important tenets of a philosophical school. The word 'theology' first occurs in Plato's *Republic* 2. 379a, and the idea of conversion comes from his Myth of the Cave—the philosopher turns from the shadows to the realities.

[9] On this see Matilal and Chakrabarti, *Knowing from Words*; Jonardon Ganeri, *Semantic Powers: Meaning and the Means of Knowing in Classical Indian Philosophy* (Oxford: OUP, 1999), and *Artha: Meaning* (Oxford: OUP, 2006); Bimal Krishna Matilal, *Epistemology, Logic, and Grammar in Indian Philosophical Analysis* (The Hague: Mouton 1971). Key Nyāya texts for this view are Gangesa's *Tattvacintāmani* and Jagadisa's *Śabdaśaktiprakāśikā*.

philosophy as a basis for education and human betterment. More people today have heard of Plato than of Isocrates, but it was Isocrates, rather than any of the Greek schools of philosophy, whose approach to education became standard in antiquity. The profound opposition between philosophy and rhetoric is expressed in Plato's *Gorgias* and *Protagoras,* and in Isocrates' *Helen, Against the Sophists,* and *Antidosis.* In these dialogues Plato attacks both the methods and the aims of rhetoricians and of their predecessors, the sophists. Isocrates, while distancing himself from the sophists, criticizes philosophical investigation of the fundamental principles of things as a useless waste of time. He allows a subordinate value to logic, science, and mathematics as helps to training the mind (*Antidosis* 261–6), but denies them any practical value. He presents the teaching of oratory as the best way to attain perfection of character (*Antidosis* 274–81), and the achieving of the highest end in human life, which he sees as promotion of the common good through public life. Isocrates exalts speech in an important passage:

They [who frown upon eloquence] are hostile to that power which of all the faculties belonging to the nature of man is the source of most of our blessings. For in the other powers which we possess we are in no respect superior to other living creatures; but, because there has been implanted in us the power to persuade each other and to make clear to each other whatever we desire, not only have we escaped the life of wild beasts, but we have come together and founded cities and made laws and invented arts; and, generally speaking, there is no institution devised by man which the power of speech has not helped us establish... if there is need to speak in brief summary of this power, we shall find that none of the things which are done with intelligence take the place of speech, but that in all of our actions as well as in all of our thoughts speech is our guide, and is most employed by those who have the most wisdom.[10]

Plato's claim that philosophy, rather than rhetoric, was the true guide to achieving the end of human life, did not lead him to totally dismiss rhetoric—just as Isocrates did not totally reject philosophical methods. In his *Phaedrus,* he allows a subordinate use for it—rather as Isocrates does for dialectic—and Aristotle taught rhetoric at the Academy. However, the focus of Aristotle's work is significant. In his *Rhetoric* Aristotle does consider the honesty of the speaker as a factor in rhetoric (1358a1), but it is not considered under the aspect of a feature that contributes to providing knowledge to a hearer. The discussion of rhetoric is conducted entirely from the point of view of the speaker, and the object of the speaker is considered to be success in persuading the hearers. This persuasion is supposed to consist in persuading them of the truth—that is what makes rhetoric an art that is not open to objection raised

---

[10] Isocrates, *Nicocles, or the Cyprians* 6–9, in Loeb Classical Library, *Isocrates* i, tr. George Norlin (Cambridge, Mass.: Harvard University Press, 1966), 79–91.

against sophistry, of being a means suited just as much to making the worse seem the better cause as vice versa—but acceptance of truth is the limit of the ambitions of rhetoric; it does not aspire to passing on knowledge (see *Rhetoric* 1355a20–1355b20). Communication of knowledge to the hearer, and the requirements for such communication to occur—the focus of contemporary discussion of testimony—do not even figure in Aristotle's discussion.

When reliance upon testimony is considered from the point of view of the hearer by ancient philosophers, it is not even clearly distinguished from other sources of belief but is lumped into the general category of opinion ($\delta\acute{o}\xi\alpha$). When Origen uses pagan philosophy to counter criticisms of the reasonableness of Christian faith, he gives the following:

> Why is it not more reasonable, seeing that all human life depends on faith, to believe in God rather than in them [the teachers of philosophical schools]? Who goes on a voyage, or marries, or begets children, or casts seeds into the ground, unless he believes that things will turn out for the better, although it is possible that the opposite may happen—as it sometimes does? But nevertheless the faith that things will turn out for the better and as they wish makes all men take risks, even when the result is not certain... (*CC* 1. 11)[11]

Henry Chadwick remarks that 'Origen's four examples...are commonplace, and go back to Clitomachus, leader of the New Academy. Cf. Cicero, *Lucullus*, 109.'[12] Arnobius, in his *Against the Pagans* (2. 8–9), cites the same examples. The significant thing about them is that these examples do not justify belief in testimony at all, but only claim to show that we should and must rely on probable belief—'probabilis' is the term Cicero uses in *Lucullus*. To defend acceptance of testimony using the resources of ancient philosophy, it was necessary for them to appeal to defences of this more general category of opinion that counts as probable belief, a category under which belief in testimony is presented as falling. This dismissal of belief based on testimony is found in pagan criticisms of Christianity. Galen remarks that 'They compare those who practice medicine without any scientific knowledge of it to Moses, who framed laws for the tribe of the Jews, since it is his way to write his books without demonstration, saying "God commanded, God spoke." '[13] Julian the Apostate claimed: 'Ours are the reasoned arguments (οἱ λόγοι) and the pagan tradition (τὸ ἑλληνίζειν) which comprehend at the same time due worship of the gods; yours are want of reason and rusticity, and all your wisdom can be summed up in the imperative "Believe".'[14]

---

[11] Origen, *Contra Celsum*, tr. Henry Chadwick (Cambridge: CUP, 1953), 14.
[12] Ibid. 14 n.
[13] Richard Walzer, *Galen on Jews and Christians* (Oxford: OUP, 1949), 18.
[14] Ibid. 54.

However, these historical influences do not suffice to explain why classical philosophers attached so little importance to belief in testimony, while Indian philosophers took a view of it that conforms more to the facts of human belief formation. In attempting to explain this difference, we can point to features of the Indian environment that were not present in classical antiquity. Indian philosophy grew up in a culture where the truth of sacred texts, the Vedas, was a basic religious tenet. Acceptance of the truth of such a text clearly motivates acceptance of testimony as a source of knowledge. (Curiously, acceptance of the truth of the Vedas was a more widely held doctrine than theism. Theists accounted for their truth by appealing to the knowledge and trustworthiness of God, rather along Christian lines, but atheists claimed that because the Vedas had no authors, the two possible sources of error in a text—ignorance and deceit—were necessarily lacking, and the text's assertions thus had to be true.) With the Nyāya philosophers in particular, it is significant that in response to sceptical challenges from other schools they took a reliabilist view of knowledge,[15] which permitted them to admit testimony as a basic source of knowledge without any difficulty.

The issue of the role of the notion of knowledge in an evaluation of belief from testimony leads to the heart of the account of faith held by the Greek fathers. The conception of knowledge held by ancient philosophers is the crucial determinant of those philosophers' position on testimony. This conception was not compatible with Isocrates' views, or with holding testimony to be a source of knowledge. The influence of this view of knowledge on Christian theologians discouraged their taking the straightforward line of Indian philosophers with respect to testimony, and led them to develop complex and subtle positions on the relation of knowledge to faith.

Plato, and Aristotle in a modified way, held the following views about knowledge:

(1) It excluded any possibility at all of error.

(2) It involved a grasp of *why* what was known was true.

(3) It involved a grasp of the causes or principles that account for what is known, since the causes or principles of a thing are what explain it.

(4) The principles of things are immaterial and divine, and hence knowledge, in its fullest realization, is knowledge of the divine.

(5) The ability to achieve knowledge is the highest power of human nature, and achievement of the fullest realization of knowledge constitutes happiness, or at least the principal part of happiness (cf. Aristotle, *Metaphysics* 983a5–10).

---

[15] On this see Stephen H. Phillips, *Classical Indian Metaphysics* (Chicago: Open Court Publishing, 1993), 51–7.

This notion of knowledge is one that developed in the absence of any belief in a sacred text containing a salvific message, and expresses the view, remarked on above, that it is the pursuit of philosophy itself that is the salvific enterprise. The Hellenistic philosophers lowered the requirements for knowledge somewhat, with some of them allowing for the possibility of knowledge of particulars through sense experience. However, they imposed upon this possibility a requirement that we would now call thoroughly internalist; an experience counts as knowledge only if it is marked by an experienced character that it is impossible for it to possess without its being veridical, and that is recognized as such. The disputes over knowledge between the Hellenistic schools did not concern the truth of this criterion, which all accepted, but rather the question of whether or not sense experience could satisfy it; sceptics claimed that this was impossible, and hence that sense experience could be no more than probable belief.[16] Clearly belief arising from testimony could not satisfy such a criterion, and hence was disqualified as knowledge.

The philosophical context of the Greek fathers was not restricted to the works of philosophers. Concepts of philosophical origin, or of philosophical import, were also to be found in the religious traditions that these fathers took to be authoritative. The exact nature of this philosophical influence on Jewish and Christian religion is an enormous, disputed, and difficult subject, and I can only touch upon two important elements of it. Their importance for our purposes lies in their implicit acceptance of elements (4) and (5) of the Platonic/Aristotelian conception of knowledge described above. These elements were mentioned by Pope Benedict XVI in an interesting address given to the University of Regensburg.

> We can see the profound harmony between what is Greek in the best sense of the word and the biblical understanding of faith in God. Modifying the first verse of the Book of Genesis, the first verse of the whole Bible, John began the prologue of his Gospel with the words: 'In the beginning was the λόγος... *Logos* means both reason and word—a reason which is creative and capable of self-communication, precisely as reason... The encounter between the Biblical message and Greek thought did not happen by chance... biblical faith, in the Hellenistic period, encountered the best of Greek thought at a deep level, resulting in a mutual enrichment evident especially in the later wisdom literature. Today we know that the Greek translation of the Old Testament produced at Alexandria—the Septuagint—is more than a simple (and in that sense really less than satisfactory) translation of the Hebrew text: it is an independent textual witness and a distinct and important step in the history of

---

[16] On this see e.g. A. A. Long and D. N. Sedley, *The Hellenistic Philosophers*, i (Cambridge: CUP, 1987), chs. 17, 40.

revelation, one which brought about this encounter in a way that was decisive for the birth and spread of Christianity. (Cf. A. Schenker, 'L'Écriture sainte subsiste en plusieurs formes canoniques simultanées', in *L'Interpretazione della Bibbia nella Chiesa. Atti del Simposio promosso dalla Congregazione per la Dottrina della Fede*, Vatican City 2001, pp. 178–186.)... The thesis that the critically purified Greek heritage forms an integral part of Christian faith has been countered by the call for a dehellenization of Christianity... The New Testament was written in Greek and bears the imprint of the Greek spirit, which had already come to maturity as the Old Testament developed. True, there are elements in the evolution of the early Church which do not have to be integrated into all cultures. Nonetheless, the fundamental decisions made about the relationship between faith and the use of human reason are part of the faith itself.[17]

The Pope did not exercise his magisterial authority in this address, which is presented simply as his personal view, but the picture he draws is an accurate one. Of especial importance for this picture is the thought of Philo of Alexandria, who was part of the Hellenizing Alexandrian Judaism that produced the Septuagint. Philo has been claimed to be a direct influence on the New Testament,[18] although it is very difficult to distinguish between concepts in the New Testament that originated directly in Philo from those that simply sprang from the general background of Alexandrian Judaism. The relations between the New Testament and Alexandrian Judaism of a Philonic sort are important enough, however, for us to be able to say with confidence that Benedict XVI is right in seeing acceptance of Greek thought as incorporated into the faith itself.

Benedict XVI's discussion of the importance of the notion of *logos* for Christianity addresses one of the two elements of Greek thought incorporated into the Christian faith that are especially important for our purposes. He also mentions, but does not really discuss, the second element, which is the description of God in the book of Exodus as 'he who is'. Étienne Gilson claimed that a 'metaphysics of Exodus' could emerge from this passage, with existence as its fundamental notion. Criticisms of Gilson's position that object that the original Hebrew of Exodus does not support this idea[19] do not really

---

[17] http://www.vatican.va/holy_father/benedict_xvi/speeches/2006/september/documents/hf_ben-xvi_spe_20060912_university-regensburg_en.html#_ftn9

[18] See David Runia, *Philo in Early Christian Literature: A Survey* (Minneapolis: Fortress Press, 1993), ch. 4, 'Philo and the New Testament'; Gregory E. Sterling, ' "Philo Has Not Been Used Half Enough": The Significance of Philo of Alexandria for the Study of the New Testament', *Perspectives in Religious Studies*, 30/3 (2003), 251–69; Roland Deines and Karl-Wilhelm Niebuhr (eds.), *Philo und das Neue Testament: Wechselseitige Wahrnehmungen* (Tübingen: Mohr Siebeck, 2004).

[19] For these criticisms, see É. Zum Brunn, 'La Philosophie chrétienne et l'exégèse d'Exode 3:14 selon M. Etienne Gilson', *Revue de Théologie et de Philosophie*, 102 (1969); P. Hadot and É. Zum Brunn (eds.), *Dieu et l'être: Exégèses d'Exode 3,13 et de Coran 20,11–24* (Paris: Études augustiniennes, 1978).

get to grips with the significance of this text, a significance that arises principally from the version of it given in the Septuagint and from the interpretation of the Septuagint text given by Hellenistic Jews and early Christians. This significance arises from the combination of the idea that God's existence is identical with his nature, the idea that the goal of the intellect is truth, and Aristotle's description of truth as to say (or think) of what is, that it is. For if these things are all true, it follows that it is through the intellect that one can grasp God, to the extent that that is possible. This in turn implies acceptance of the fourth component of the Platonic/Aristotelian conception of knowledge.

The significance of this understanding of God as being emerges from a comparison with the Neoplatonism of Plotinus, for whom the supreme hypostasis, the One, is above being. Consistently, Plotinus held that the One cannot be attained by the intellect; for him, 'another important feature of a putative mystical experience of the One is that, owing to what the One is and to the nature of all cognition, including the highest, this experience is trans-cognitional'.[20] Both Neoplatonism and the view that God is being itself have a negative theology, that denies that God's nature can be comprehended by humans, but the rationales for these negative theologies are different. For Neoplatonism, the One is not intelligible because it is above intellect. But for the position that God is being itself, God is excessively intelligible—only the divine intellect has the power to comprehend the divine nature; as Aristotle remarks (following Plato, *Republic* 8. 518), 'as the eyes of bats are to the blaze of day, so is the reason in our soul to the things which are by nature most evident of all'.[21] The notion of something being excessively intelligible is strange to us. To understand it, we need to realize that the starting point of this notion is not a definition of intelligibility as relative to the capacity for understanding of some intellect. Instead, it is a definition of intellect as a capacity to grasp reality. Being real—having being—as such therefore makes something intelligible, because reality as such is the proper object of the intellect; and thus, given the assumption that there are degrees of being, the more being a thing has, the more intelligible it is.

In distinguishing between Platonism and Neoplatonism on this subject, we should acknowledge that the Neoplatonist view elaborates some ideas found

---

[20] Lloyd P. Gerson, *Plotinus* (London: Routledge, 1994), 219. It is an interesting question whether or not Plotinus's One understands itself. Gerson claims that Plotinus holds the One to possess some sort of cognitive life, but he does not explain how this can be reconciled with Plotinus's 'rejecting Aristotle's identity of a first principle with Intellect or its activity' (p. 20). The inconsistency here may be Plotinus's rather than Gerson's.

[21] Aristotle, *Metaphysics* 2. 993b10, in *The Complete Works of Aristotle*, ii, ed. Jonathan Barnes (Princeton: Princeton University Press, 1984), 1570.

in Plato, in particular in the first hypothesis of the *Parmenides*. It is Aristotle who explicitly rejects the Neoplatonic view, arguing that the divine is existing and is intellectual (cf. *Metaphysics* 12. 7). One may speculate that the Supreme Pontiff, in endorsing the idea that God is accessible to reason, had in mind some current trends in which enthusiasm for Neoplatonism has become a scholar's form of apostasy from Christianity.[22] The fact that it is Aristotle who decisively chooses an option that later becomes central to Christian tradition, while Plato is not always of one mind on this question, is important for the later development of Thomism. It contradicts the often-held view that Plato's thought is somehow more friendly to Christianity than is Aristotle's.

It is interesting to note that Philo and the Greek fathers accepted the religious element of the Platonic/Aristotelian notion of truth, while the pagan Plotinus discarded it. The notion of the One as beyond being was not original to Plotinus; it was espoused by Speusippus, Plato's nephew and his successor as head of the Academy (and attacked by Aristotle, *Metaph.* 12. 7. 1072b30 ff.). Significantly, Speusippus also held that both pleasure and pain are evil, with the neutral state in between them being the good one.[23] The philosophy of Speusippus was thus a radical rejection of the view put forward by Plato in his most substantial dialogues; he teaches in the *Symposium* and the *Republic* that love and its supreme object the Form of the Good are the things of ultimate importance. This Platonic position is close to the view of love expressed in the New Testament; and Aristotle, while rejecting the Forms, agrees with the primacy of love and its directedness towards the good, a good which is identified with being. The disagreement between Speusippus on the one hand, and the Plato of these dialogues on the other, is not simply one between two historical schools. It is between different fundamental options that one can take to reality, options that are bound to arise for anyone who thinks deeply enough about the subject (consider the resemblances between elements of Speusippus's view and elements of Buddhism). While there probably are some Platonic influences on the New Testament, the resemblances between the two are more a matter of their having taken the same option than of historical links. This identity of fundamental approach

---

[22] For accounts of this trend, see Wayne J. Hankey, 'Neoplatonism and Contemporary French Philosophy', *Dionysius*, 23 (2005), 161–89. In describing 20th-century scholars of Neoplatonism, Hankey remarks that 'Pierre Hadot, Henry Duméry, Jean Pépin, and Michel Tardieu, started their scholarly careers as priests'. A. H. Armstrong is another, very eminent, scholar of Neoplatonism who used to be a Christian; see e.g. his 'Some Advantages of Polytheism', *Dionysius*, 5 (1981), 181–8, and John Peter Kenney, 'The Critical Value of Negative Theology', *Harvard Theological Review*, 86/4 (Oct. 1993), 439–53.

[23] John Dillon, *The Middle Platonists* (London: Duckworth, 1977), 19; see Aulus Gellius, *Noctes Atticae* 9. 5. 4.

between Plato and Christianity goes a long way towards explaining the eventual acceptance of Christianity by the Greeks.

Philo's teaching and influence are important for the presence of this Platonic/Aristotelian conception of the divine in Christianity. The Septuagint text of Exodus 3: 14 runs καὶ εἶπεν ὁ θεὸς πρὸς Μωυσῆν λέγων ἐγώ εἰμι ὁ ὤν· καὶ εἶπεν οὕτως ἐρεῖς τοῖς υἱοῖς Ἰσραὴλ ὁ ὤν ἀπέσταλκέ με πρὸς ὑμᾶς. In accordance with this text, Philo's preferred designation for God is ὁ ὤν, 'he who is'. He describes God as the self-existent (*De Agr.* 50–3) and as he who truly is (*De Decal.* 8), and asserts that God is the only being whose essence is his existence (*Det.* 160). He stresses both knowledge and love as the means by which we are united to God and become his adoptive sons (*De Post.* 69; *De Spec. Leg.* 1. 299–30), states that we ascend to God through reason (*De Praem.* 26), and describes the ultimate goal of human life as knowledge of the true and living God (*Decal.* 81; *Abr.* 58; *Praem.* 14). It is startling for the uninformed reader to come across these ideas, which one thinks of as characteristic of medieval scholasticism, in an author who was probably an influence on the New Testament. In fact, these positions were generally accepted by the Fathers of the Church—the preservation of Philo's works was due to Christians—and the medievals adopted them from patristic sources.

The degree to which Philo anticipated—or originated—scholastic ideas on the divine may go very far. Richard C. Taylor has pointed out that both Plato and Aristotle understood the divine being as a determinate kind of being, and thus as limited in a certain respect.[24] Taylor speculates that Porphyry revised Plotinus's view by accepting the Plotinian idea of the One as entirely unqualified, but rejecting the claim that the One is beyond being; thus producing the idea, espoused by Aquinas, that the divine being is being itself, and as such is not determined or limited in any way. However, Philo denies that God has parts or passions (*Quod Deus* 69), possesses qualities, or belongs to genus or species (in accordance with Aristotle's claim that being is not a genus). According to Wolfson,[25] Philo is the first Greek philosophical writer to claim that God is unnameable and ineffable; one may link this to the ideas of Speusippus, as David Winston suggests,[26] or more directly to the scriptural basis for this view. Philo's ascription of being to God, but denial to God of every way in which being can be determined (a denial endorsed by Clement in *Strom.* 5. 12), would seem to amount to an endorsement of the idea that God

---

[24] Richard C. Taylor, 'Aquinas, the Plotiniana Arabica, and the Metaphysics of Being and Actuality', *Journal of the History of Ideas*, 59 (1998), 218–19.

[25] H. A. Wolfson, *Philo*, vol. ii, rev. edn. (Cambridge, Mass.: Harvard University Press, 1948), 110–18. On this see also Dillon, *Middle Platonists*, 155.

[26] David Winston, introduction to *Philo of Alexandria* (New York: Paulist Press, 1981), 22.

is infinite unqualified being itself, long before Porphyry. It thus seems that there is something to Gilson's idea of a metaphysics of Exodus, at least as applied to the common understanding of the Septuagint version in Alexandrian Judaism.

Philo is also important as an influence on Christian ideas of the relationship between philosophy and theology. Greek philosophers had debated the question of the relation of encyclical studies (ἐγκύκλια) such as grammar and rhetoric to the study of philosophy, and Aristo of Chios had described encyclical studies as the handmaiden of philosophy, who is their mistress or queen.[27] Philo classified theology as belonging to ethics (*Mut.* 10. 75–6), and he described the rest of philosophy as the handmaiden of theology; knowledge of theology, which he describes as attainable through the Law of Moses, he calls wisdom, and he asserts that as encyclical studies are the handmaiden to philosophy generally, so the rest of philosophy is the handmaiden of theology (*Congr.* 14. 79). Clement follows him in this latter idea (*Strom.* 1. 5). Since these views describe philosophy as a preparation for theology, and a help in grasping it, rather than as its logical basis, they conform to the Thomist outlook.

To see how the Platonic/Aristotelian conception of knowledge can influence accounts of Christian faith, we can look at a view of faith proposed by St Thomas Aquinas in his earlier works—chiefly in the *Commentary on the Sentences of Peter Lombard* (henceforth *Sent.*), and the *Quaestiones disputatae de veritate* (henceforth *DV*). This account considers faith from the standpoint of what it is that is believed, the propositions that Aquinas calls the material object of faith. On this view, faith, considered as assent to the truths Christians believe on account of God's testimony, lies midway between *scientia* and *opinio*. *Scientia* is knowledge arrived at by logical deduction from *intellectus*, which is knowledge that arises from grasping the meaning of the terms of a proposition. *Opinio* is probable belief in a general proposition. Faith involves the same firmness of adherence by the intellect as *scientia* does, but it has the lack of evident truth in the propositions believed that belongs to *opinio*. (Aquinas thinks that if we acquire knowledge of an article of the faith, such as the existence of God, we cease to have faith in this article; see *Summa Theologiae*, 2a2ae, q. 1, a. 5.) Because of this lack of evident truth, faith is not an intellectual virtue. It attains the object of an intellectual virtue, which is truth, but it does not attain this object in the mode proper to an intellectual virtue, which is by seeing the truths believed as true in themselves (*3 Sent.*, d. 23 q. 2 a. 3 qc. 3 co). The firmness of assent in faith is provided not by the

---

[27] For debates see Diogenes Laertius 7. 32. 129: for Aristo see Diogenes Laertius 2. 79–80 and Stobaeus, *Florilegium* 4. 109.

intellect's grasp of the truth of what is believed, but by the will, which is motivated by the desire for eternal life—the life that is promised as a reward for belief. In formed faith, which justifies, the will is moved by charity, the love of God as he is in himself above all created things, to choose to believe (a choice that would be impossible for *scientia*, which is not voluntary). The desire for eternal life is compatible with a rejection of eternal life itself through sin, and that is why it is possible to have formless faith. Such faith is possessed by believers who do not have charity, and have not repented for sin; it does not justify. This account of faith covers the main properties of faith— its truth, its relation to choice, its relation to salvation—in a way that respects the claim that belief in testimony cannot be knowledge.

THE 'THOMISM' OF CLEMENT OF ALEXANDRIA AND HIS SUCCESSORS

This lengthy account of the intellectual context of the theology of faith of the Greek fathers puts us in a position to consider this theology itself. The principal elements of this theology are all to be found in Clement of Alexandria. Clement's irritatingly unsystematic exposition makes it hard to see the strength and depth of this theology, which uses the resources of Clement's thorough philosophical training. Clement clearly describes faith as belief in testimony—the testimony of God.

Now the disciples of the philosophers define knowledge as a state which cannot be overturned by reasoning. But does there exist elsewhere a situation as stable with respect to the truth as in a religion that has the Logos for her sole teacher? I do not think so... Therefore, he who has believed in the divine scriptures, with a firm judgement, receives as an irrefutable demonstration the voice of God who gave us those scriptures. So faith is no longer something that is confirmed by demonstration. 'Blessed then are they that have not seen, and yet have believed' [John 20: 29]. (*Strom.* 2. 2. 9[28])

We give to our adversaries this irrefutable argument; it is God who speaks and who, for each one of the points into which I am inquiring, offers answers in the scriptures. Who would be an atheist to the point of not believing God and requiring proofs from him, as one does from men? (*Strom.* 5. 1)

He denies that that Christian faith is based on signs (σημεῖον, a term that he probably takes from the Gospel of John). In *Strom.* 2. 6, he writes,

---

[28] Clement of Alexandria, *Stromate II*, Sources Chrétiennes, 38, tr. Cl. Mondésert (Paris: Éditions du Cerf, 1953), 39. I owe this translation to the help of Dr Angus Bowie.

'If "Abraham was believed and it was counted unto him for righteousness" [Rom. 4: 3], and we are the seed of Abraham from what we have heard, we too must believe. For we are the children of Israel who obey not because of signs but because of what they heard.'[29] He asserts that we should hear the word of truth purely and without malice, like the children who obey us; this is the interpretation he gives to the teaching of Matthew 18: 3, that those who do not become like children will never enter the kingdom of heaven (*Strom.* 5. 13). This belief is voluntary, which is necessary for it to be meritorious (*Strom.* 2. 3); he compares faith to a ball game, where it is necessary both for the thrower to throw the ball and for the catcher to catch it (*Strom.* 2. 6. 25).

Clement does not simply deny that faith is based on signs; he explicitly denies that it is inferred from evidence of any kind, by describing it as a preconception, a πρόληψις. Preconceptions were a standard notion in Hellenistic epistemology; they were understood as the fundamental judgements upon which all other judgements were based. Epicurus argued for the existence of such judgements, on the grounds that if we do not accept them as a starting point for reasoning, we will end up with an infinite regress. Clement quotes this argument with approval (*Strom.* 2. 4), and accepts Epicurus's definition of preconceptions (*Strom.* 1. 16. 3). He follows the Stoics in holding that in grasping preconceptions we have an awareness of their truth, because these preconceptions have a certain clarity that as it were declares their truth to us.[30] He applies this to faith, comparing it to the song of the Sirens, which exerted a superhuman power on its hearers, compelling them almost against their will to listen (*Strom.* 2. 9. 7). It is significant that Clement was a student of Pantaenus, who taught Christians in Alexandria, and was a Stoic.[31]

Clement thus accepts in essence the Thomistic view of the role of the motives of credibility for faith. What he does not do is to claim that testimony generally—as opposed to divine testimony in particular—is a basic source of knowledge. He gives knowledge a different, double, role, in his account of the Christian life.

The first role is a knowledge that can be possessed by believers in this life, a knowledge that builds on faith and that confers spiritual maturity on the Christian—that produces the 'Christian gnostic'; Clement's adoption of the term 'gnostic' was no doubt intended to counter the popularity of Gnosticism. In contrast to the Gnostics, he insists on the dependency of gnosis on faith; faith is necessary for gnosis (*Strom.* 2. 6. 31), it is the foundation on

---

[29] Ibid. 56; this passage was kindly translated for me by Dr Angus Bowie.
[30] See Eric Osborn, *Clement of Alexandria* (Cambridge: CUP, 2005), 172–5, 194–5, on this.
[31] On the question of Pantaenus as predecessor of Clement as head of the catechetical school of Alexandria (and the disputed existence of such a school at that time), see Osborn, *Clement*, 19–24, and the literature he cites.

which perfection is built (Strom 5. 4. 26. 1), and the Christian, who is always in the position of a child trusting his father, never leaves it behind (*Strom.* 4. 25). The Christian gnosis is for Clement a unity of knowledge, virtue that is an assimilation to the divine, and love of God. The knowledge is a knowledge of divine realities that is conferred by God. His conception of this gnosis is a Christological one—gnosis is a grace that comes from God through the Son (*Strom.* 5. 11).

The knowledge of the Christian gnostic in this life is in turn a preparation for the knowledge of God experienced in heaven (cf. *Strom.* 6. 14. 1). On the topic of knowledge of God Clement makes a significant alteration to Philo. Where Philo says that reason cannot attain to God, Clement, using almost the same words as Philo, says that it can.[32] He rejects the idea that there are any realities that are beyond comprehension:

Some claim that the wise man is persuaded that there are incomprehensible realities, while nonetheless having a certain comprehension of them, in that he grasps that the incomprehensible cannot be comprehended... but the gnostic of whom I am speaking understands, for his part, that which seems incomprehensible to others, because he believes that nothing is incomprehensible to the Son of God and that in consequence there is nothing that the Son cannot teach. (*Strom.* 6. 8. 70)

Of Christ, Clement says:

For he who hopes, as he who believes, sees intellectual objects and future things with the mind. If, then, we affirm that aught is just, and affirm it to be good, and we also say that truth is something, yet we have never seen any of such objects with our eyes, but with our mind alone. Now the Word of God says, 'I am the truth.' The Word is then to be contemplated by the mind. (*Strom.* 5. 3)[33]

This knowledge of God is not solely possessed by the Word (as it would have been if Clement had followed Philo, who claimed that what he understood by the Logos of God was graspable by the intellect, whereas the divine essence was not). Clement clearly states that the divine essence itself is graspable by the intellect:

For he who has not the knowledge of good is wicked: for there is one good, the Father; and to be ignorant of the Father is death, as to know Him is eternal life, through participation in the power of the incorrupt One.[34]... And meat is the mystic contemplation; for this is the flesh and the blood of the Word, that is,

---

[32] On this see A. van der Hoek, *Clement of Alexandria and his Use of Philo in the Stromateis* (Leiden: Brill, 1988), 176.

[33] Clement of Alexandria, *Stromata*, in *Library of the Ante-Nicene Fathers*, ii, ed. A. Cleveland Coxe (Grand Rapids, Mich.: Eerdmans, 1979), 448.

[34] Ibid. 459.

the comprehension of the divine power and essence. 'Taste and see that the Lord is Christ,' it is said. For so He imparts of Himself to those who partake of such food in a more spiritual manner; when now the soul nourishes itself, according to the truth-loving Plato. For the knowledge of the divine essence is the meat and drink of the divine Word.[35]

Clement thus makes a fundamental departure from Philo: while agreeing with him about the divine nature being beyond any category or determination, he agrees with Plato and Aristotle about the divine nature being graspable by the intellect. The Christological motivation for this innovation is evident in the quoted passages. The capacity to understand the divine essence cannot be denied to Christ. But Christ is a man; so the Incarnation requires us to accept that a man can grasp the divine essence. The unity of divinity and humanity in Christ, which permits a man to understand God, means that it is through Christ that other men can be brought to understand God.

It is very striking to contemplate the complexity and sophistication of Clement's account, and the extent to which it contains the positions later presented in a more systematic way by Aquinas. The surprise that may be prompted by these facts is liable to be due to a common mistake about early Christianity—the 'simple beginnings' idea, which holds that the original Christian message was a fairly straightforward one that got complicated in later centuries. This idea is no more than wishful thinking on the part of scholars who would like to simplify away parts of early Christianity that they find hard to accept. Christianity was the product of two complex and mature systems of thought (Jewish religion and Greek philosophy) both of which had reached a very high level centuries before the time of Christ. It was never simple, and given its origins could not have been simple. Clement, who lived c.150–c.215, was not only thoroughly conversant with those systems of thought as they existed in his time; he was also the beneficiary of a century of Christian reflection on their interconnections. It is therefore not surprising that he had a grasp of both the important questions that arise in connection with a philosophical account of Christian faith, and the possible answers to them that could be proposed.

A full discussion of the history of Clement's account of faith in the Greek fathers would take up volumes,[36] and we can only consider a few of the crucial aspects of it. Although Clement himself was not widely read by the other Greek fathers, his pupil Origen, who was read by everyone, accepted the basic

---

[35] Ibid. 460.
[36] A brief sketch is given in Lamont, *Divine Faith*, ch. 3; this chapter provides material that supplements that account.

outlines of his conception of faith.[37] Origen, in his apologetic defence of Christianity, devoted considerable effort to what would later be called the motives of credibility, but he is quite clear that these motives are not the basis for faith: 'I have no sympathy with anyone who had faith in Christ such that it could be shaken by Celsus...or by any plausibility of argument. I do not know in what category I ought to reckon one who needs written arguments in books to confirm and restore his faith after it has been shaken by the accusations of Celsus against the Christians' (*CC* 1. 4).[38]

An important follower of Origen on this issue is St John Chrysostom, who stated that in believing the scriptures, we are believing God, because he is their author (*in Gen.* 5. 1–2; *in 2a Tim.* 3. 15), and that the only reason we believe God's message is that God says it (*in 1a Cor.* 2. 5). Citing, like Clement, the example of the disciples of Pythagoras, Chrysostom says:

Mark how he disapproves of questioning. For where faith exists, there is no need of question. Where there is no room for curiosity, questions are superfluous. Questioning is the subversion of faith. For he that seeks has not yet found. He who questions cannot believe. Therefore it is his advice that we should not be occupied with questions, since if we question, it is not faith; for faith sets reasoning at rest... Let us not then give heed to questions. For we were called Faithful, that we might unhesitatingly believe what is delivered to us, and entertain no doubt. For if the things asserted were human, we ought to examine them; but since they are of God, they are only to be revered and believed... The knowledge of God is best shown by believing in Him without proofs and demonstrations... Even the Greeks know this; for they believed their Gods telling them, saith one, even without proof; and what?—That they were the offspring of the Gods. But why do I speak of the Gods? In the case of the man, a deceiver and sorcerer, (I speak of Pythagoras,) they acted in like manner, for of him it was said, He said it. (*in 1 Tim.* 1. 4[39])

Interesting evidence of the general acceptance of Clement's view, and of its connection to the philosophical position that he espoused, is found in Athanasius's *Life of Antony*. Antony is presented as encountering pagan philosophers who dispute with him about the truth of the Christian faith, and he argues with them as follows;

'Since, of course, you pin your faith on demonstrative proofs and this is an art in which you are masters, and you want us also to not worship God without demonstrative arguments—do you first tell me this. How does precise knowledge of things come about, especially knowledge about God? Is it by verbal proof or by an act of faith

---

[37] Ibid. 35–40.
[38] Origen, *Contra Celsum*, p. 5.
[39] St John Chrysostom, 'Homily on 1 Timothy 1:1, 2', in *Library of the Nicene and Post-Nicene Fathers*, 13, ed. Philip Schaff (Grand Rapids, Mich.: Eerdmans, 1976), 410.

($\grave{\epsilon}\nu\epsilon\rho\gamma\acute{\iota}as$ $\pi\acute{\iota}\sigma\tau\iota s$)? And which comes first, an active faith or verbal proof?' When they replied that an act of faith takes precedence and that this constitutes accurate knowledge, Antony said, 'Well said! Faith arises from the disposition of the soul, while dialectic comes from the skill of those who devise it. Accordingly, those who are equipped with an active faith have no need of verbal argument, and probably even find it superfluous. For what we apprehend by faith, that you attempt to construct by argument; and often you cannot even express what we perceive. The conclusion is that an active faith is better and stronger than your sophistic arguments. We Christians, therefore, possess religious truth, not on the basis of Greek philosophical reasoning, but founded on the power of a faith vouchsafed us by God through Jesus Christ.'[40]

Antony then goes on to work some miracles to convince the philosophers, which he cites as proof of the truth of the Christian faith, but he does not tell them to believe on the basis of this proof. The argument given clearly appeals to Hellenistic epistemological notions, and presents faith, as Clement does, as one of the basic starting points for knowledge. A significant feature of this passage is that the author of the *Life* (who was probably Athanasius[41]) was not engaged in apologetics, and was not a trained philosopher, but was nonetheless familiar with the idea of faith as a basic belief not derived from inference.

In describing this view as the characteristic position of the Greek fathers, it is not implied that the Latin fathers held a different position. The Latins seem to have agreed with this view insofar as they considered the question, but their focus was different. In accordance with the usual generalization about the Latins, with their Roman heritage, being more concerned with issues connected to law and the relation between God and man, and the Greeks with their more philosophical heritage being more concerned with the intellect and the nature of God in himself, the main issue in the Latin world was the connection between grace and faith. This issue was a principal concern in the debate over Pelagianism and Semi-Pelagianism, and was the subject of pronouncements by the Second Council of Orange:

Can. 5. If anyone says, that just as the increase [of faith] so also the beginning of faith and the very desire of credulity, by which we believe in Him who justifies the impious, and (by which) we arrive at the regeneration of holy baptism (is) not through the gift of grace, that is, through the inspiration of the Holy Spirit reforming our will from infidelity to faith, from impiety to piety, but is naturally in us, he is proved (to be) antagonistic to the doctrine of the Apostles... Can. 7. If anyone affirms that without the illumination and the inspiration of the Holy Spirit,—who gives to all sweetness in

---

[40] Athanasius, *The Life of Saint Antony*, 77–8, tr. Robert T. Meyer (London: Longmans, Green & Co., 1950), 82–4.

[41] On the question of the authorship of the *Life of Antony* I follow G. J. M. Bartelink's introduction to the *Sources Chrétiennes* edn. of *Vie d'Antoine* (Paris: Éditions du Cerf, 1994).

consenting to and believing in the truth,—through the strength of nature he can think anything good which pertains to the salvation of eternal life, as he should, or choose, or consent to salvation, that is to the evangelical proclamation, he is deceived by the heretical spirit...[42]

The canons of this council were lost during the Middle Ages, but they faithfully reflect the Augustinian view that dominated Western Europe, and after their rediscovery they were reaffirmed by the Roman Catholic Church (in the First Vatican Council, *Dei Filius*, ch. 3, and the Second Vatican Council, *Dei Verbum*, para. 5). Its position on the necessity of grace for faith was insistently taught by the original Protestants as well, and it will be assumed to be true. This clear and explicit teaching on the necessity of grace for faith has important implications for the Thomist position. The Greek fathers were content to say that we believe solely because we trust God's testimony, and that trust in this testimony is rational because it originates in God, who cannot lie or be mistaken. Although they also affirmed that faith is a gift of grace, their relative lack of focus on the nature of grace meant that they did not dwell on the question of why, if faith is rational, it requires grace for its existence, rather than simply the exercise of human reason. When the scholastics, with their philosophically systematized Augustinian theology of grace, came to consider the role of the motives of credibility in faith, this question became acute.

Clement's 'Thomist' view had no serious competitors until the time of Abelard. In his *Theologia 'Scholarium'*, Abelard objected that if we accept the faith simply on the basis of God's authority, we are guilty of credulity; if such faith is acceptable, it would be impossible to object to the religious beliefs of any people whatsoever, even those of idolaters. He proposed instead to prove the articles of faith using reason. This position was not found acceptable by the Church (the *Theologia 'Scholarium'* led to Abelard's excommunication by Innocent II), but his attack on the rationality of basic belief in God's testimony led to a change in the theology of faith in the Latin Church. Hugh of St Victor took the crucial step of explicitly asserting that faith falls short of knowledge in some respect: 'if any one wishes to note a full and general definition of faith, he can say that faith is a kind of certainty of the mind in things absent, established beyond opinion (*opinio*) and short of knowledge (*scientia*)'.[43] This is the position we saw in Aquinas's first account of knowledge, given above. The next important step was the introduction of the idea

---

[42] H. Denzinger, *The Sources of Catholic Dogma*, 30th edn., tr. Roy J. DeFerrari (St Louis: Herder, 1957), 176, 180, pp. 76–7.

[43] Hugh of St Victor, *On the Sacraments*, tr. Roy J. DeFerrari (Cambridge, Mass.: Medieval Academy of America, 1951), 168.

of acquired, as opposed to infused, faith. Acquired faith was belief that resulted from reasoning from the motives of credibility; it was termed 'acquired' because it was acquired by the exertion of unaided human reason, and hence was not held to merit salvation. Infused faith, on the other hand, is produced by grace, and is salvific. This distinction is made in the *Summa Theologica* attributed to the Franciscan theologian Alexander of Hales, which postulates the existence of both kinds of faith, and sees acquired faith as a preparation for infused faith. We can see this development as resulting from an incompleteness in Clement's position. With no articulated philosophical account of belief in testimony generally, it does not provide a philosophically grounded answer to Abelard's objection.

Explanation of belief in terms of both acquired and infused faith became the norm in Catholic theology after Alexander of Hales.[44] The exception to this norm is the second account of faith proposed by Aquinas. Where Aquinas's first view considers faith from the point of view of the propositions it leads us to accept (what he called its material object), his second view considers it from the point of view of the reason we have for believing. The rational motivation for faith Aquinas calls the formal object of faith, and he states that the formal object of faith is God's testimony. He asserts that the formal object of faith is First Truth as it is made known in Sacred Scripture, and the teachings of the Church, which proceeds from First Truth—that is, from God, who is truth itself (*2a2ae* 5. 3). It is not the word of man that we believe in having faith, but God (*In Ioan.* c. 5 l. 4 n. 5). The nature of faith is to believe someone, and assent not to what one can see one's self, but to what someone else testifies to; we believe God concerning things we do not see, as one would believe a good man concerning things which one does not see but which he does see.[45] Belief in humans as such is fallible, because men can deceive or be deceived, but this is not the case with believing God, for whom this is not the case (*In Heb.* c. 6 l. 1).

In discussing the motives of credibility, Aquinas states that the divine origin of the Christian revelation is shown by many evident proofs (cf. *SCG* 1. 4), but denies that these proofs are necessary or sufficient for faith (*2a2ae* 2. 10; *In Ioan.* c. 2 l. 3 n. 5). The things that are needed for faith are exterior preaching, and an interior call from God (*In Rom.* 10, l. 2). Without this call, even when miracles are present to provide evidence for faith, belief is impossible and

---

[44] See Lamont, *Divine Faith*, ch. 4, for a historical account.
[45] *3 Sent.* d. 23 q. 2 a. 2 qc. 2 co: 'Ratio enim quare voluntas inclinatur ad assentiendum his quae non videt, est quia Deus ea dicit: sicut homo in his quae non videt, credit testimonio alicujus boni viri qui videt quae ipse non videt.' St Thomas Aquinas, *Scriptum super sententiis Magistri Petri Lombardi*, ed. R. P. Mandonnet and M. F. Moos (Paris: P. Lethielleux, 1933), iii. 727.

unbelief is without fault (*In Ioan.* 15 l. 5 n. 4). The word of God is of such a power that as soon as it is heard it ought to be believed (*In Heb.* c. 4 l. 1).

I speak of two positions on faith in Aquinas, because of the incompatibility of his claim that faith is midway between knowledge and opinion and his claim that God's testimony is the formal object of faith. The trouble with reconciling these two views is that, as he points out, it is evidently impossible for God to deceive or be deceived. If we believed that God said something on the basis of merely probable motives of credibility, then it would make sense to say, as his first view does, that the degree of rational assent that is due to faith is less than that due to knowledge, and that faith has the strength of assent possessed by knowledge as a result of the will rather than as a result of the reason. However, Aquinas explicitly denies that we believe God on the basis of the motives of credibility, or that the trust due to God's assertions should be merely probable. In fact, he says that the light of faith is more capable of inducing assent than a grasp of self-evident first principles, because the light by which we assent to first principles can be impeded by bodily infirmity. The light of faith, on the other hand, which is like the seal of first truth in our minds, cannot fail, just as God can neither be deceived nor lie.[46]

The reason why this difficulty lets us speak of two positions on faith in Aquinas, rather than simply a lasting inconsistency, is that his second view of faith is virtually absent from his earlier works, but dominant in his later works, although his first view of faith is never explicitly renounced. The first view is found principally in his *Commentary on the Sentences and* the *De Veritate,* written in the period 1252–1256. In 1259 he moved from Paris to Rome. The libraries in Rome and Orvieto gave him much better opportunities to become acquainted with the works of the Greek fathers; his very extensive quotations from Chrysostom, for example, almost all date from after his departure to Italy. The discussions of faith in the works written after this departure—principally in the *Summa Theologiae* and the scriptural commentaries—present his second view of faith, and contain no proper exposition of his first view of faith. It is probable that his exposure to the Greek fathers, and to Chrysostom in particular, was responsible for this change. Aquinas and his followers, from this point onwards, are the heirs of the Greek fathers on the question of faith.

In his discussion of the relation of faith to knowledge, Aquinas develops the view of the Greek fathers in significant ways. He makes three main contributions to this aspect of their view. The first is his systematic argument for the beatific vision of God as the goal of the human intellect and the human

---

[46] St Thomas Aquinas, *Super Boetium de Trinitate,* ed. P.-M. J. Gils *et al.* in Leonine edn., vol. 50 (Rome, 1992), q. 3 a. 1 ad 4, p. 109.

person, achievement of which constitutes human happiness.[47] Drawing to a great extent on Aristotle, this argument benefits from his having to deal with well-developed scholastic positions that give a different account of human fulfilment, in particular with the view that happiness lies in the fulfilment of the will rather than the intellect (a view argued against in e.g. *1a2ae* q. 3 a. 4). His presentation of the real distinction between essence and existence is a decisive advantage for his defence of Clement's view of God as undetermined being but also as the ultimate goal of knowledge, because it made it much easier to make philosophical sense of this view. It means that the Clementine/Thomist view preserves the complete transcendence of the divine, but avoids the Neoplatonist dilemma of explaining how the ultimate principle has neither being nor the common or garden kind of non-existence attributed to it by the atheist. His characterization of God as infinite being enables him to fit the divine into the Aristotelian conception of truth and knowledge, since for this conception truth is intellectual grasp of being, and knowledge is possession of truth.

The second development is his integrating Clement's account of the different stages of Christian knowledge, through presenting Christ as a teacher, and describing what it is that a teacher does. (The theme of Christ as a teacher was a central theme for Clement as well, but Aquinas would not have derived it directly from Clement, whom he had not read—he would have received it from the general patristic heritage.)

The teacher does not at the beginning of his instruction at once hand on the reasons for the more subtle things concerning which he intends to teach; because then the student would have to have at the very beginning a perfect knowledge of what he is to be taught. Rather, he teaches the student things whose reasons the student cannot grasp when he is beginning to learn, but that the student will know afterwards when he is perfect in science. Hence it is said that it is necessary for the learner to believe (*oportet addiscentem credere*); the learner cannot attain the perfection of *scientia* otherwise than through accepting as true that which is first taught to him, the reasons for which he cannot then understand. The ultimate perfection to which man is ordered, however, is the knowledge of God; which no one can attain save through the activity and teaching of God, who is the perfect knower of himself. But man in the beginning is not capable of this perfect knowledge, so it is necessary that he accept,

---

[47] This view was the subject of a good deal of controversy in 20th-cent. Catholic theology, centring on its defence by Henri de Lubac; see his *Surnaturel: Etudes historiques* (Paris: Aubier, 1946); *Augustinisme et théologie moderne* (Paris: Aubier, 1965); *Le Mystère du Surnaturel* (Paris: Aubier-Montaigne, 1965). This controversy still goes on (for opposition to de Lubac see e.g. Lawrence Feingold, *The Natural Desire to See God According to St Thomas and his Interpreters* (Rome: Apollinare Studi, 2001)), but while not accepting every element of de Lubac's interpretation of Aquinas, I will take it that he is correct in attributing to Aquinas a single *telos* and a single kind of happiness for humans, which is the beatific vision.

through believing, things by which he is led to reach perfect knowledge. (*DV* 14. 10; my translation[48])

The third is Aquinas's systematizing and deepening of Clement's account of the knowledge held by the Christian Gnostic in this life, the knowledge that surpasses faith but falls short of the beatific vision. He does this in his account of the Gifts of the Holy Spirit;

> Faith, first and principally, is about the First Truth, secondarily, about certain considerations concerning creatures, and furthermore extends to the direction of human actions, in so far as it works through charity... Accordingly on the part of the things proposed to faith for belief, two things are requisite on our part: first that they be penetrated or grasped by the intellect, and this belongs to the gift of understanding. Secondly, it is necessary that man should judge these things aright, that he should esteem that he ought to adhere to these things, and to withdraw from their opposites: and this judgment, with regard to divine things, belongs to the gift of wisdom, but with regard to created things, belongs to the gift of knowledge, and as to its application to individual actions, belongs to the gift of counsel. (*2a2ae* q. 8 a. 6)

Aquinas distinguished between infused virtues, which are active powers given to the Christian by grace, and gifts, which are passive capacities to be acted upon by God. As the Christian advances spiritually, the role of God in his life increases, and hence the exercise of the gifts comes to predominate over that of the virtues. The passive reception of divine illumination of the intellect, in the form of contemplation, and its central role in the growth of holiness, becomes the main theme of the great Carmelite theologians, St Teresa and St John of the Cross.[49]

The only real weakness in Aquinas's presentation of the view of the Greek fathers (the difficulties that arise from the incompatibility of his two accounts of faith) is ultimately remedied by the thinker who brings this view to completion: the seventeenth-century Puritan theologian John Owen (1616–83). Owen's achievement is virtually unknown, because after Puritanism in England was discredited by the rule of Cromwell his audience was limited to Calvinist Dissenters and Evangelicals, who had little interest in his views on the Thomist account of faith—a position whose adherents were almost all to be found in the Dominican Order. Owen received an Aristotelian formation at university, and

---

[48] See also Aquinas, *In Heb.* c. 11 l. 1, and *Super Boet. de Tr.* 2, 2. The phrase 'oportet addiscentem credere', attributed by Aquinas to Aristotle in *De sophisticiis elenchis* c. 2, 165b3, seems actually to have originated with Alexander of Aphrodisias's commentary on the beginning of the *Posterior Analytics*.

[49] Their extension of the idea of Christian gnosis is expressed in terms of Aquinas's theology of the gifts by Reginald Garrigou-Lagrange, in an important work of 20th-cent. spiritual theology, *Perfection chrétienne et contemplation selon s. Thomas d'Aquin et s. Jean de la Croix* (Montreal: Milicia, 1952); see esp. vol. 1, ch. 4, arts. 4, 5.

clearly borrowed many of his arguments from Dominican writers (he mentions Melchior Cano OP), while understandably being shy about crediting them. He also, and significantly, cites Clement in defence of his view (Clement's works had been edited and published in 1550). His involvement in the Thomist controversy arose largely from a desire to attack the Quaker view of faith and inspiration. He offers four arguments against faith being based on the motives of credibility.

(1) If faith were based on the motives of credibility, the faith of the learned would be stronger than the faith of the simple: but it is not.

(2) Since the scriptures present the bare word of God, and not the motives of credibility, as the formal object of faith (Owen refers to Deut. 31: 11–13; Is. 8: 19–20; Jer. 23: 28–9; 2 Tim. 3: 16; and 2 Pet. 1: 16–21), it would be inconsistent to say that we believe the scriptures to be true on the basis of the motives of credibility.

(3) Granted that the motives of credibility can give us moral certainty of the divine origin of the scriptures, this will still not be sufficient for faith, which is infallibly certain; 'of faith divine and supernatural...no one will say that it can be effected by or resolved unto the best and most cogent of rational arguments and external testimonies which are absolutely human and fallible; for it doth imply a contradiction, to believe infallibly upon fallible evidence.'[50]

(4) Faith requires grace, but reasoning from the motives of credibility does not. 'The moral certainty treated of is a mere effect of reason. There is, therefore, on this supposition, no need of any work of the Holy Ghost to enable us to believe or to work faith in us; for no more is required herein but what necessarily ariseth from a naked exercise of the reason...Now this is not faith, nor can we be said in the scripture sense to believe hereby.'[51]

In giving a positive account of how God's bare word is the formal object of faith, and countering the accusation found in Abelard of exalting credulity, Owen makes a fundamental advance in European philosophy: he proposes a non-reductionist account of testimony. He lists three basic sources of knowledge: 'inbred principles of natural light', 'rational considerations of things externally proposed unto us', and 'faith'.

Of faith, he says,

This respects that power of our minds whereby we are able to assent unto any thing as true which we have no first principles concerning, no inbred notions of, nor can from more known principles make unto ourselves any certain rational grounds concerning

---

[50] John Owen, *The Reason of Faith*, in *The Works of John Owen, D.D.*, vol. iv, ed. Revd William H. Goold (Edinburgh: Johnstone & Hunter, 1852), 21.
[51] Ibid. 49.

them. This is our assent upon testimony, whereon we believe many things which no sense, inbred principles, nor reasonings of our own, could either give us an acquaintance with or assurance of.[52]

In what looks like a conscious borrowing from Isocrates, he asserts

this is the principal and most noble faculty and power of our nature. There is an instinct in brute creatures that hath some resemblance unto our inbred natural principles... but as unto the power or faculty of giving an assent unto things on witness or testimony, there is nothing in the nature of irrational creature, that hath the least shadow of it... And if our souls did want but this one faculty of assenting unto truth upon testimony, all that remains would not be sufficient to conduct us through the affairs of this natural life. This, therefore, being the most noble faculty of our minds is that whereunto the highest way of divine revelation is proposed.[53]

We thus find in Owen a union between the divided camps of Greek philosophy and Greek rhetoric, two millennia after their birth as opponents. He brings about this union by adding to Clement's claim that faith is rational and certain the further claim that it is knowledge, since it belongs to the category of knowledge acquired through testimony. In so doing he rejects the unitary conception of knowledge proposed by Plato and Aristotle, by splitting off the aspect of certainty that this conception accepts from the aspect of grasping the reason for the truth that is known that it insists on. He accepts a form of what would now be called externalism, by allowing that some forms of knowledge lack this second aspect.

This introduction of externalism is theologically relevant. The joining of certain knowledge of a truth to a grasp of the reason why that truth obtains was an understandable move on the part of Plato and Aristotle, because a grasp of the reason for a truth was the only guarantee of certainty of possession of truth that seemed available to them. What makes it possible for Owen to separate these aspects is his attributing the certainty of possession of truth through faith to the divine will. The role of the divine will goes deeper here on the Thomist view. In the epistemic order, faith will be rational because it is believing God's testimony. However, in the order of being, the capacity to acquire knowledge from testimony will ultimately exist because of faith. Such a capacity is one feature of human nature. However, human nature as a whole has as its goal attainment of the beatific vision. Capacities of human nature are subordinate to, and exist for the sake of, human nature as a whole; thus, the capacity to acquire knowledge through belief in testimony exists for the sake of believing the Word, which is the means to attain the beatific vision. If we attain that vision, though, we *will* grasp the 'why' of things: the divine

[52] Ibid. 83. [53] Ibid. 88.

nature (although as finite beings we will not have a complete understanding of it, something that is only possible for God). When it comes to ultimate happiness, therefore, the exigencies of the Platonic/Aristotelian conception of knowledge are satisfied.

Defending the rationality of faith simply by postulating an externalist account of knowledge from testimony would however seem insufficient on its own. We have seen that the Thomist view requires the non-reductionist view of testimony in order to be true. However, the non-reductionist view does not suffice by itself as a defence of the Thomist account. On the non-reductionist view, testimony gives knowledge when the speaker who is believed is honest and knowledgeable. In the case of God, there is no difficulty about the speaker's honesty and knowledge, since these are possessed necessarily. Instead, the difficulty lies in identifying divine speaking. In most of the Christian tradition this speaking is seen as being done by human instruments, or at least by human beings (Christ, as divine, not being an instrument of God), and as occurring at least in the scriptures, and for many Christians in the teaching of the Church as well. How are we to identify the assertions of these humans as God's assertions, without making appeal to the motives of credibility? Owen's answer is that it is the effect of divine speaking that enables us to identify it as coming from God. He asserts that there are two sorts of things that are self-evidencing, light and power; and that the scriptures bear both of these within themselves.

Without the Scripture all the world is in darkness...superstition, idolatry, lying vanities, wherein men know not at all what they do nor whither they go, fill the whole world, even as it is this day. And the minds of men are naturally in darkness; there is a blindness upon them that they cannot see nor discern spiritual things. With respect unto both these kinds of darkness the Scripture is a light... thereby evidencing itself to be a divine revelation; for what but divine truth could recall the minds of men from all their wandering in error, superstition, and other effects of darkness, which of themselves they love more than truth?[54]... The principal divine effect of the word of God is in the conversion of the souls of sinners unto God... of this great and glorious effect the word is the only instrumental cause, whereby the divine power operates and is expressive of itself... The work which is effected by it, in the regeneration, conversion, and sanctification of the souls of believers, doth evidence infallibly unto their consciences that it is not the word of man, but of God.[55]

Owen's answer serves the double purpose of giving a non-reductionist explanation of how we know the scriptures to be divinely revealed—explaining

---

[54] Ibid. 97.
[55] Ibid. 94–5. Note the crucial difference between this assertion and the claim made by Origen. Origen said that the redemptive effect of the Gospel shows to onlookers of this effect that the Gospel originates in God; Owen says that the redemptive effect shows to the *person who is redeemed by hearing* that the Gospel is spoken by God.

the 'siren's call' of faith postulated by Clement—and accounting for the salvific power of faith. Enlightenment of the mind, and conversion of the will, are jointly sufficient for salvation, at least on the Thomist view (when joined in the way Owen proposes, they constitute what Aquinas calls 'formed faith', which is salvific; see e.g. *2a2ae* q. 2 a. 9). It also explains how Christians can have faith and still sin (thus possessing what Aquinas calls 'formless faith'); it is because they experience the enlightenment of the mind, but refuse the conversion of the will.

No doubt the absence of philosophical support for non-reductionist views of testimony contributed to the oblivion into which Owen's ideas lapsed.[56] With the emergence of a strong case for these views in Western philosophy, we can see that this oblivion was undeserved. Owen's position completes the account of faith whose foundations were laid by Clement.

---

[56] That is not to say that they were without influence. Thomas Reid advanced a non-reductionist view, as noted above; and as a Presbyterian minister, it is quite likely that he had read Owen, although I have not been able to find any evidence of this.

5

'As Kant has Shown...'
Analytic Theology and the Critical Philosophy

Andrew Chignell

> The uniqueness of Kant's position can already be seen in the fact that it is a solitary one.... He stands by himself... a stumbling-block and rock of offence in the new age, someone determinedly pursuing his own course, more feared than loved, a prophet whom almost everyone—even those who want to go forward with him—must first re-interpret before they can do anything.
>
> (Karl Barth)

The goal of the present volume is to say something about what analytic theology might be, and about whether and why theologians and philosophers might want to engage in it. I can think of three general things that analytic theology might be, though I suspect that other contributors will have different ways of dividing up the territory. Analytic theology might be

(1) Good old-fashioned conceptual analysis (think: Moore, Ayer, Austin) applied to concepts of theological importance, especially the concept of God.

Few philosophers or theologians in the post-Quinean context are optimistic about the prospects of pure conceptual analysis all on its own, of course, and so analytic theology will need to go beyond (1) if it is to be more than a disappointing non-starter. Fortunately, there are at least two other candidates:

(2) The use of the characteristic tools of analytic philosophy[1] to generate arguments with theological content or import. These tools include: logical apparatuses of various sorts (deductive, probabilistic, epistemic, modal, etc.); abduction; rational intuition; thought-experiment;

---

[1] I do not mean to suggest that these tools are the sole possession of analytic philosophers of course. This is merely a sketch of some of the features that are responsible for the 'family resemblances' between works of 'analytic philosophy'. Michael Rea offers a more detailed account of these family resemblances in his introduction to the present volume.

reflective equilibrium; appeal to substantive theory-building constraints such as simplicity, elegance, and explanatory depth; stylistic rigor, clarity, and understatement; and, of course, necessary-and-sufficient-conditions analysis of our concepts, refined by appeal to counterexamples.

The problem with (2) is that it is hard to distinguish from what currently falls under the rubric of 'philosophy of religion' in analytic circles. So while (2) might be consistent with analytic theology, or even a part of analytic theology, it can't constitute the whole thing, for fear of losing our topic.

A third candidate is

> (3) The use of *explicitly principled* appeals to special religious sources—namely, scriptural revelation, testimony from the religious community, ecclesiastical tradition, and individual or corporate religious experience—in order to
>
> (a) supply topics (e.g. Creation, Fall, Trinity, etc.) and direct inquiry;
> (b) supply prima facie justification for claims with theological content or import; and
> (c) supply defeaters for claims that are prima facie justified on other grounds.

Note, first, that according to (3) these 'special religious sources' can both supply justification and defeat it. By way of example: suppose that the claim that the universe is the result of creation rather than emanation or chance is one for which Jim has little or no justification before he recognizes that the creation doctrine is a part of the scriptural and communal tradition in which he is theologizing. Other things being equal, that recognition supplies the doctrine with some (further) justification for him. Conversely, Sue may start out having plenty of prima facie justification for the common-sense claim that each person is a unique being or substance. But this justification is (at least partially) defeated when she realizes that a central, settled doctrine of the ecclesiastical tradition in which she is working is that at least one being comprises three different persons.[2]

---

[2] Justification comes in degrees, and I don't mean to take a position here regarding how much justification an appeal to such sources could supply or defeat. It's also worth pointing out that I'm speaking of claims, doctrines, and principles here, rather than of beliefs. That's because I do not want to presume that the propositions involved must be actual candidates for an analytic theologian's belief in order for her effectively to work with them. We could say, of course, that special religious sources give the analytic theologian prima facie justification for the belief that p even though she herself doesn't believe that p. But I think that this, too, is misleading, since it is natural to slip from talk of having justification for a belief that p to talk of having a justified belief that p. Analytic theologians can consider and weigh the justification a claim has within some broader system or set of assumptions, or within the context of some overarching narrative, or within a particular religious language-game, or etc., without being at all inclined to believe the claim themselves. Talking about having justification for claims, doctrines, and principles, rather than beliefs, helps keep all of this straight.

Second, note that (3) *does* clearly distinguish analytic theology from philosophy of religion, granting (as is customary) that the latter does not properly make justificatory appeals to any such special religious sources. Philosophy of religion involves arguments about religiously pertinent philosophical issues, of course, but these arguments are customarily constructed in such a way that, ideally, anyone will be able to feel their probative force on the basis of 'reason alone'. Analytic theology (3), by contrast, appeals to sources of topics and evidence that go well beyond our collective heritage as rational beings with the standard complement of cognitive faculties.

Third, note that (3) contains hints about how we might distinguish analytic theology from other species of revealed theology.[3] One paradigmatically 'analytic' feature of (3) is that appeals to special religious sources are governed by principles that are formulated as *explicitly* as possible by the theologian: making these principles explicit will presumably require the use of some of the tools of analytic philosophy listed in (2).[4] Another analytic feature of this practice is that the concepts involved in the claims that acquire or lose justification would have to be clarified, analyzed, and altered using some of the tools in (2). This means that (3) is not only compatible with, but also *entails* (2). And of course (2) entails (1), given that pure conceptual analysis (insofar as it is possible) is one of well-worn tools of analytic philosophy. The merging of our three candidates in this way is salutary, I think, since something in the neighborhood of the conjunction of (1)–(3) is what many (though perhaps not all) of the authors in this volume are likely to conceive as our collective topic.[5]

---

[3] There are of course further distinctions to be made between different kinds of 'revealed theology': biblical, liberation, ecclesiastical, womanist, historical, systematic, etc. I will pass over these distinctions in silence here, except to note that I suspect that 'systematic theology' is the closest cousin to analytic theology, although they may still differ in some of the ways described in this paragraph.

[4] I am not suggesting that non-analytic theologians do *not* make principled appeals to special religious sources, or that they make *un*principled appeals to such sources. The point is rather one of emphasis: my sense is that in analytic theology (3), a very high premium would be placed on making it explicit precisely how the deliverances of 'special religious sources' can e.g. justify a claim, and on carefully examining and explicating the claims that are so justified. It seems likely to turn out that the difference between analytic theology and other forms of revealed theology (and especially 'systematic theology') is a difference in emphasis or degree, rather than a difference in kind.

[5] I frankly have some trouble seeing a significant difference between analytic theology and what has recently been called 'philosophical theology' in the analytic tradition. As far as I can tell, the latter can and often does involve (1)–(3) above. Oliver Crisp suggests in correspondence that analytic theology uses the same *methods* as philosophical theology in the analytic tradition, but to somewhat different *ends*. He develops this idea in his contribution to the present volume, and so I will simply refer the reader to that chapter and set the question aside.

Immanuel Kant would not have been opposed to analytic theology conceived as (1) or (2)—he did a lot of it himself, as we will see. Nor would he have railed against the idea that (1) and (2) produce genuine a priori knowledge. He *would* have opposed the thought that (2) produces a priori knowledge of *synthetic* claims (i.e. claims that assert more than that some predicate is contained in some concept[6]). But it's not obvious that aspiring analytic theologians need to claim anything as strong as that. Instead, I will suggest, they might do better to follow Kant in holding that (1) produces analytic knowledge, and that (2) produces at most what Kant calls rational 'Belief' (*Glaube*) or 'Acceptance' (*Annehmung*)—i.e. a positive sort of propositional attitude which, even if it is justified and true, doesn't count as knowledge (*Wissen*). I'll say more about this suggestion, and about the Kantian notion of 'Belief/Acceptance', below.[7]

As for (3) and its various species, Kant himself recommends (3a) to readers of his works on religion, but he explicitly repudiates (3b) and (3c). For him, appeals to sacred texts, communal and ecclesiastical traditions, and individual religious experiences are acceptable only as signposts directing our inquiry to claims that are defensible from within the bounds of mere reason.[8] There are no principles, however explicit, which legitimize their use as sources of justification or defeat. So if a brand of analytic theology involves (3b) and (3c), it will find no friend in Kant.

Accordingly, in what follows, I'll try to lay out Kant's attitude towards analytic theology conceived as the conjunction of (1), (2), and (3a), and in particular his reasons for thinking that the results of such a practice will have the status of Belief. My goal here is not merely to provide a specific sort of analytic theology with the imprimatur of an eminent historical philosopher. Analytic theology (on this characterization or another) could certainly soldier on without the support of the Sage of Königsberg. My motive for focusing on Kant stems rather from the fact that his influence among people working in theology and religious studies is by all accounts *immense*, and that while many embrace that influence, others—especially those inclined towards analytic theology—find that influence deeply regrettable.

---

[6] I'm ignoring difficult questions regarding Kant's various notions of analyticity (and syntheticity) here. A rough intuitive grasp of the 'containment' notion of analyticity which he provides in the introduction to the first *Critique* will suffice for present purposes.

[7] For more on this, see my 'Belief in Kant', *Philosophical Review*, 116/3 (July 2007), 323–60. In general, I'll capitalize 'Belief' below when referring to Kant's notion of *Glaube*. There is unfortunately no good English translation of the German term: sometimes it means something like our words 'belief' or 'opinion', and sometimes it means something more like our words 'faith' or 'acceptance'.

[8] Kant writes in the *Religion* that 'any attempt like the present one to find a meaning in Scriptures that is in harmony with the *most holy* teachings of reason must be viewed not only as permissible but as a duty' (6: 83–4).

Let me explain this motive in somewhat more detail. Kant's influence is *embraced* by the many theologians, scholars, and religious thinkers who maintain that he taught something crucial about the limits of our cognitive, conceptual, and therefore epistemic access to supersensible objects ('things-in-themselves') and, by way of Hegel, about the cultural and historical sources of our conceptual schemes. As a result, one often encounters statements in theological circles that begin with the phrase 'as Kant has shown' and end with a claim about the inability of our concepts to apply to reality-in-itself in general—and to God in particular—and thus the impotence of all attempts at substantive theology in a traditional 'realist' mode. These statements are then used to motivate the shift to an anti-realist mode, or an allegorical mode, or an apophatic mode, or at the very least a practical mode in which doctrinal wrangling takes a back seat to concerns about liberation and social justice.

Kant's influence is typically *regretted* by would-be analytic theologians precisely because of this near-consensus picture and the philosophical and sociological obstacles it presents to those who wish to reflect in a traditional realist mode about substantive theological topics. As a result of 'what Kant has shown', questions regarding how we can even *begin* to engage in God-thought and God-talk dominate a great deal of theological discussion—questions which are often categorized, fittingly enough from a Kantian point of view, under the rubric of 'prolegomena'.[9] Those who regret Kant's influence regard this ongoing questioning as a kind of hand-wringing 'agony' or theoretical compulsion from which we should seek to 'recover'.[10] This does not mean that such people are not *also* interested in allegory, apophatic discourse, liberation, and social justice.[11] In many cases the contrary is true. Still, these thinkers wish that it were not true that Kant, for theologians, always plays the role of 'a stumbling-block and rock of offense...a prophet whom almost everyone, even among those who wanted to go forward with him, had first to re-interpret before they could do anything with him'.[12]

---

[9] Kant's own textbook summary of his theoretical philosophy, of course, was called *Prolegomena to any Future Metaphysics*. Citations from Kant's works are by 'volume: page' to the Akademie edn. of Kant's works (Berlin: de Gruyter, 1900–), except for citations from the *Critique of Pure Reason*, which will be by 'A-edition/B-edition'. I have consulted and typically followed the translations in the Cambridge edition of Kant's works, ed. Paul Guyer and Allen Wood (New York: Cambridge University Press, 1992–).

[10] Nicholas Wolterstorff, 'Is it Possible and Desirable for Theologians to Recover from Kant?', *Modern Theology*, 14/1 (Jan. 1998), 1–18.

[11] Wolterstorff, for instance, has written on every one of these topics, most recently producing an enormous book on justice considered from both philosophical and theological perspectives. Nicholas Wolterstorff, *Justice: Rights and Wrongs* (Princeton: Princeton University Press, 2007).

[12] Karl Barth, *Die protestantische Theologie im 19. Jahrhundert: Ihre Vorgeschichte und ihre Geschichte*, 3rd edn. (Zurich: Evangelischer Verlag, 1946). Partially translated as *Protestant Thought from Rousseau to Ritschl*, tr. Brian Cozens (New York: Simon & Schuster, 1969). This quotation is from p. 150. Gordon Michalson references this passage and also provides a more

I am not a professional theologian, and so I feel awkward doing what I just did—namely, discussing what members of another discipline do and don't do. My grounds are hardly scientific: they consist of personal observation, scattered reading and journal perusal, testimony from friends in the business, past participation in a weekly theology colloquium at a prominent Divinity School and, more recently, regular attendance at American Academy of Religion meetings. Even though these grounds are woefully unscientific, I propose for present purposes to take it as uncontroversial that modern theology has been immensely influenced by what 'Kant has shown', and that Kantian questions about the conditions of the possibility of speculative discourse have led to the ongoing prominence of 'agonizing' prolegomenal discussions.

I feel even more awkward saying anything about what people in another field *should* do and *shouldn't* do. So I won't do that at all. Rather, my goal in this chapter is to offer a few interpretive suggestions regarding Kant's own approach that might allow would-be analytic theologians to see him as an ally or even a forebear, rather than as a block over which to stumble or a disease from which to recover. In other words, I want to suggest that Kant doesn't really hold what 'Kant has shown'; in fact, he himself writes analytic theology *of a certain sort*, and he often goes beyond prolegomena with alacrity. The qualification 'of a certain sort' is crucial because, again, Kant is careful to note that the synthetic results of reflection about things-in-themselves can only be held as 'Belief' (*Glaube*) or 'Acceptance' (*Annehmung*), rather than what he calls knowledge (*Wissen*) or even what we *today* would call 'belief'. Belief is precisely the type of attitude for the sake of which Kant had to 'cancel' or 'set aside' (*aufheben*) knowledge, in the famous phrase from the preface to the first *Critique*.[13] And though Belief is *often* and most famously grounded in *practical* considerations (the 'moral proofs' for which Kant is well-known, for instance), Kant's under-noticed but official view is that *theoretical* considerations can sometimes justify Belief as well. My ultimate irenic suggestion here, then, is that if analytic theologians are willing to follow Kant in putting aside knowledge in order to aim at something like Belief, then they may not need to recover from him at all.[14]

---

elaborate description of the ways in which Kant has influenced modern theology in *Kant and the Problem of God* (Malden, Mass.: Basil Blackwell, 1999), ch. 1.

[13] 'Ich musste also das Wissen aufheben, um zum Glauben Platz zu bekommen' ('I thus had to put aside knowledge in order for there to be space for Belief' (Bxxx).

[14] It is worth emphasizing that it is also not part of my aim to endorse analytic theology here. My goal is rather to show that those who want to engage in analytic theology (at least construed as the conjunction of (1)–(3a) above) needn't regret Kant's influence in theological circles, though they might well regret the influence of 'what Kant has shown'.

ANALYTIC THEOLOGY AS CONCEPTUAL ANALYSIS

One of the first things one learns in an undergraduate survey on Kant is that he distinguishes, throughout his career, between analytic judgments that merely draw out what is already 'contained' in a concept, and synthetic judgments that 'amplify' or 'add something new to' the concept. Analytic judgments are always a priori for Kant: his usual example is 'All bodies are extended.' Such 'judgments do not really teach us anything more about the object than what the concept that we have of it already contains in itself, since they do not expand cognition beyond the concept of the subject, but only elucidate this concept' (A736/B764).

Kant is *modestly* worried about analyticity insofar as he thinks that knowingly generating *full* analyses or 'definitions' of the contents of our (non-mathematical) concepts is extremely difficult. We might think, while we're doing armchair conceptual analysis, that we've drawn out all the predicates of the concept of 'body' and laid them before us, when in fact there are some predicates concealed in the corners of the concept which our analysis hasn't yet brought to light. This should lead us to a kind of skepticism about full definition: 'the exhaustiveness of the analysis of my concept is always doubtful, and by many appropriate examples can only be made *probably* but never *apodictically* certain' (A728/B756).

Despite these modest worries, Kant never countenances the *radical* worries about analyticity that came to prominence 150 years later. It's true, of course, that we acquire most of the content of our concepts through empirical experience and testimony ('no concepts can arise analytically as far as content is concerned': A77/B103). But Kant assumes that once we possess a concept, we can normally keep our analyses of it from involving any *justificatory* appeals to experience. So his pessimism about full definition is tempered by optimism about our armchair sense of *when* we're doing conceptual analysis and when we're not. He never seriously worries that the synthetic judgments that we take to be 'adding something' to a concept might in fact be non-obvious, complex analytic truths, or vice versa.

Such modest optimism allows Kant to view conceptual analysis as a central component of intellectual life: 'a great part, perhaps the greatest part, of the business of our reason consists in analyses of the concepts that we already have of objects' (A5/B9). Such business allows us to achieve that 'distinctness of concepts which is requisite for a secure and extended synthesis as a really new acquisition' (A10/B14); moreover, these analyses themselves 'yield real a priori knowledge, which makes secure and useful progress' (A6/B10). This is as true in theology as elsewhere: analyses of our concepts of supersensibles (God, the soul, freedom, the afterlife, and so forth) are fully capable of giving us a priori knowledge. Again, however, the result is merely analytic knowledge of the contents of our concepts, and not synthetic knowledge that amplifies those concepts or, in particular, implies that something actually corresponds to them.

Kant himself engaged in analytic theology of something like type (1) throughout his career, often lecturing on theological topics and occasionally publishing in the field (at least when he wasn't barred from doing so by J. C. Wöllner, the Minister of Religion under Friedrich Wilhelm II, or the notorious ecclesiastical authority T. C. E. Woltersdorf, who in 1791 explicitly forbade Kant to write any further on religion[15]). This practice is by no means inconsistent with his objections to synthetic knowledge-claims in speculative metaphysics because, again, it merely involves type (1) analysis of what is contained in our theological concepts. With respect to the analysis of the concept of God, Kant follows his rationalist predecessors in taking a broadly Anselmian approach. He assumes that 'God' is the name we use for the most perfect or 'most real being' (*ens realissimum*), and then seeks to draw out and make explicit the predicates contained in our concept of such a being. These include the traditional 'omni-' predicates, as well as various other morally and ontologically superlative determinations. In his lectures on religion, Kant describes this method of 'natural' theologizing as a two-stage process: first, we remove all 'negativity' and 'lack' from our concepts of real predicates so as to focus only on the relevant 'reality' in them; second, we maximize that reality in order to arrive at a concept of a being with all and only the best or 'most real' predicates.[16] Thus, for example, the concept of *volitional power* as we acquire it introspectively is first *purified* by removing everything that makes reference to finite structures and agency, and then *maximized* in order to arrive at the predicate of *omnipotence*.

Kant is fundamentally opposed to one component of the Anselmian model, however: he doesn't think that we can squeeze *existence*-claims out of our concept of God. His career-long opposition to the a priori proof which he

---

[15] For discussion of this controversy, see Kant's correspondence at 11: 264 ff.

[16] Kant follows the scholastic/rationalist tradition in calling this method the *via eminentiae* (the way of eminence). Again, the method involves clarifying our concepts of the good-making predicates of finite beings, extrapolating to their most real or eminent versions (*all-powerful, all-knowing, infinitely extended*, etc.), and then ascribing the largest compossible set of the latter to God. See *Lectures on the Philosophical Doctrine of Religion*, 28: 999. Descartes famously opposes the *via eminentiae* in the Third Meditation and the Second Replies to Mersenne.

himself christened 'ontological' is based in his broader views in philosophical logic and often encapsulated in the dictum that 'Existence is not a real predicate.' The ontological proof says that there is an entity whose non-existence would produce a *logical* contradiction among its own predicates—namely, the entity which, by way of being maximally great, must by necessity possess the great-making predicate of existence. Kant repudiates this whole conception by arguing that a non-existence claim can never of itself generate a contradiction, because to say that a thing does or does not exist is not to predicate something further of *it*, but rather to say something about its concept—namely, that the concept does or does not have an instance (2: 73–4; A592–3/B620–1). So although we can and do *use* 'exists' casually as a predicate in natural language, it is not a *real* predicate of any object (relational predicates between concepts and their instances, then, are not 'real' predicates on Kant's view[17]). The attempt to smuggle it into the concept of a thing as just another predicate among many others, and then use armchair analysis to pull the actual thing out of a conceptual hat, is at best 'a mere novelty of scholastic wit', says Kant, and at worst 'nothing but a miserable tautology' (A597/B625; A603/B631).

This opposition to analytic existence-claims leads Kant to advocate what I will below describe as 'synthetic theology' (which despite its name is also a mode of analytic theology in the sense of (1)–(3a) above). But first let me note that what I have said so far is opposed by interpreters who insist that something about Kant's broader theoretical picture, and in particular his theory of object-reference, implies that we can't meaningfully think or talk about supersensible things-in-themselves at all. For ease of reference, I will call such commentators *Hardliners*.

Hardliners emphasize passages in which Kant says that in the absence of an appropriate connection to intuitional input from the senses, our concepts will remain 'empty' and such that we are not even able to judge whether it is *really possible* for them to have an instance. Consider, by way of example, the following passages:

For every concept there is requisite, first, the logical form of a concept (of thinking) in general, and then, second, the possibility of giving it an object to which it is to be

---

[17] We might well wonder why. Kant surely doesn't want to say that relational predicates are never 'real' predicates. It is more plausible to suggest that relations between concrete particulars and abstract objects are not real predicates. Thus, many contemporary philosophers think that predicates such as *being such that 2 + 2 = 4* is a predicate that can be applied to everything in every possible world, but that it doesn't express or pick out a real property. Kant's arguments, however, often make it sound as though his problem is not with relations to abstracta in general, but rather with the relation of instantiation in particular. Why that relation in particular is not 'real' is a puzzling feature of his account.

related. Without this latter it has no sense (*Sinn*), and is completely empty of content (*völlig leer an Inhalt*). (A239/B298)

If a cognition is to have objective reality, i.e., to be related to an object, and is to have significance and sense (*Bedeutung und Sinn*) in that object, the object must be able to be given in some way. Without that the concepts are empty and through them one has... merely played with representations... To give an object... is nothing other than to relate its representation to experience (whether this be actual or still possible). (A156/B195)[18]

Remarks such as these about the connection between 'giving an object' in experience, on the one hand, and conceptual *Sinn, Inhalt,* and *Bedeutung,* on the other, are taken by Hardliners to indicate that Kant holds (in a proto-verificationist fashion) that our concepts of supersensibilia are literally *Sinnlos*—senseless. Thus, an assertion that contains such a concept is, from a cognitive point of view, no more meaningful than a line from 'Jabberwocky': it may appear to be grammatically sound, but it ends up signifying nothing. Applying these principles to God-talk in particular, a prominent German Hardliner concludes that Kant's 'most radical claim in connection with natural theology is not that the existence of God cannot be proved theoretically but that theoretical reason cannot even legitimately *ask* whether or not God exists'.[19]

Unless one is aiming to write nonsense poetry, it is a monumental waste of time to string together long complicated sentences that fail to express coherent propositions. It seems downright absurd to publish those strings of sentences in journals and books, and to go to conferences and utter them before other people. Thus when it comes to our natural propensity to conjure ideas of the supersensible, Hardliners like Höffe tend to emphasize passages in which Kant enjoins us to take up our *Critiques* and resist. If we do manage to resist, Kant promises (in the vivid language of self-mortification) that we 'can be spared many difficult and nevertheless fruitless efforts, since [we] would not be attributing to reason anything which obviously exceeds its capacity, but would rather be subjecting reason, which does not gladly suffer constraint in the paroxysms of its lust for speculative expansion, to the discipline of abstinence' (A786/B814). This passage comes from the second half of the *Critique* which, for Hardliners, is basically an extended meditation on the various ways in which reason seduces us into the dark realm of things-in-themselves, and a therapeutic attempt to convince us that these illicit

---

[18] See also A146/B185; A485–8/B513–15; A493/B521.
[19] Otfried Höffe, *Immanuel Kant* (Munich: C. H. Beck, 1992). English translation by Marshall Farrier (Albany, NY: SUNY Press, 1994), 123.

inclinations of reason itself must be, to the best of our abilities, identified, 'disciplined', or extirpated.[20]

A closer reading of Kant's texts, however, suggests that the Hardline view is difficult to defend qua interpretation. For, first, there are countless passages in which Kant claims that human reason *is* able to think up (*denken*) concepts of the supersensible that are logically coherent and that *do* have some intelligible structure and content (Bxxx n.). Such ideas may indeed be *leer an Inhalt* and *ohne Sinn und Bedeutung*, but that does not mean for Kant what it does for Frege and the verificationists, or what it does for contemporary Germanophones. On the contrary, Kant uses *Sinn* and *Inhalt* as technical terms: they explicitly refer to the content that a concept gets *by way of relation to intuitional experience*. If a concept has *Sinn* or *Inhalt*, then its 'object must be able to be given in some way'—i.e. it must be possible for intuitions (pure or empirical) to be brought under it which would allow us to cognize an instance of it (A156/B195). 'Empty' is also a technical term in this context: being empty is the hallmark of the so-called 'problematic' concepts which may very well have a determinate, intelligible, and logically coherent structure, but which do not have a possible *sensory* content or *empirical* referent (A338–9/B396–7).[21] Similarly, an idea that lacks a *Bedeutung* in the technical sense is one that lacks a possible *empirical* referent (B149).[22] But clearly this does not entail that it does not or cannot have *any* referent whatsoever—it's quite possible that empty ideas, lacking a *Bedeutung*, still have non-empirical referents.[23] In effect, then, to say that a concept of the supersensible is 'empty' or 'without sense and reference' is very close to uttering a tautology (miserable or otherwise)—it's just to say that it's a concept of the supersensible. Hardliners go far beyond

---

[20] Some prominent Anglophone Hardliners are Norman Kemp Smith, Jonathan Bennett, and P. F. Strawson. See Kemp Smith, *Commentary to Kant's* Critique of Pure Reason (Atlantic Highland, NJ: Humanities Press, 1992; 1st edn. 1918), 398; Bennett, *Kant's Dialectic* (New York: Cambridge University Press, 1974), 52–3; and Strawson, *Bounds of Sense* (London: Methuen, 1966), 11–12.

[21] 'To represent a pure concept of the understanding as thinkable in an object of possible experience is to confer objective reality upon it, and in general to present it. Where we are unable to achieve this, the concept is empty, i.e., it suffices for no cognition' (20: 279).

[22] Cf. A240/B300 where Kant explicitly equates a concept's *Bedeutung* with the empirical object (*Objekt*) that serves as its referent.

[23] Kant himself *sometimes* uses a broader sense of *Bedeutung* which refers to the sort of logical significance that an idea of an uncognizable supersensible can enjoy. 'In fact, even after abstraction from all sensible condition, significance (*Bedeutung*), but only a logical significance of the mere unity of representations, is left to the pure concepts of the understanding, but no object (*Gegenstand*) and thus no significance is given to them *that could yield a cognition of the object* (*Objekt*)' (A147/B186). The word 'cognition' at the end of this passage was printed as 'concept' in the A-edn. *KrV*, but it is noteworthy that Kant himself changed it to 'cognition' in his copy of that edn. (Cf. Benno Erdmann's *Nachträge* transcriptions of the handwritten notes that Kant made in his own copy of the A-edn. of the *Critique* (23: 46).)

what the texts licence when they claim that, for Kant, a well-formed sentence in speculative metaphysics is no better than Jabberwockyan gibberish.

These points can help us make sense of the fact that in the *Critique* and the writings on religion, Kant develops a sophisticated theory of religious language according to which we *can* legitimately ascribe various predicates—predicates such as *having a will* or *being omniscient*—to the most real being after employing the *via eminentiae* in the manner discussed above. It is difficult to see why Kant would go to all of this trouble if he thinks that the resulting idea is without *any* possible referent whatsoever, or that the statements he entertains are complete nonsense which fail to express a coherent proposition. Clearly it is more charitable to see him as holding that, although we cannot *know* that the concept of a most real being has an actual or really possible referent (since we can't connect such a being via empirical laws to an object of possible experience), we also cannot *know* that it doesn't (A742/B770). In his lectures and writings on religion, he calls this position the 'minimum of theology'—the minimum commitment required in order rationally to practice theology. It is that God's existence is both logically possible (i.e. the concept of God is logically coherent), and epistemically possible (i.e. really possible as far as we know) (28: 1026; 6: 154 n.). And Kant himself, I have argued so far, is clearly committed to both of these claims.

ANALYTIC THEOLOGY AND MORAL BELIEF

Vestiges of Hardlinism can still be found in some interpretive circles, but most commentators nowadays reject it and claim that Kant thinks we *are* able, through speculative-theoretical reasoning, to develop logically coherent ideas of supersensible entities such as God, the world-whole, the free will, the future life, etc. and that we are able, further, to be aware that these ideas adequately reflect our best speculative conclusions about the issues in question. Let's call such commentators *Moderates*.

Unlike Hardliners, Moderates can make sense of how Kant's discussions of religious concepts and language fit into the critical project. Moderates join with Hardliners, however, in holding that any theoretical claims that affirm (or repudiate) the existence of these transcendent entities are out of line. In order legitimately to make claims with existential import about particular things-in-themselves, we have to turn to specifically *moral* considerations, i.e. to Kant's 'proofs' that underwrite moral Belief (*Glaube*) in God, freedom, and the immortality of the soul.

There are plenty of passages in the critical works in which Kant seems to advocate something like Moderation:

> Even though reason in its merely speculative use is far from adequate for such a great aim as this—namely, attaining to the existence of a supreme being—it still has in them a very great utility, that of *correcting* the cognition of this being by making it agree with itself... and by purifying it of everything that might be incompatible with the concept of an original being, and of all admixture of empirical limitations. (A639–40/B667–8)

This passage says that speculative/theoretical considerations lead us to generate the idea of God, and that the methods of analytic theology (1) and (2) above allows us to clean up the idea and make its contours more precise. But as far as theoretical reason is concerned, that sort of strictly analytical reflection can go no further. As a result,

> the highest being remains for the merely speculative use of reason a mere but nevertheless *faultless ideal*, a concept which concludes and crowns the whole of human cognition, whose objective reality cannot of course be proved on this path, but also cannot be refuted; and if there should be a moral theology that can make good this lack, then transcendental theology, up to now only problematic, will prove to be indispensable through determining its concept and by ceaselessly censoring a reason that is deceived often enough by sensibility and does not always agree with its own ideas. (A641/B669)

On the Moderate interpretation of passages like this, Kant is saying that speculative reason strives to reach out beyond the sensible with guidance not from experience but from rational principles of a sort.[24] But for complicated reasons based in Kant's criticism of rationalist metaphysics (the details of which I'll have to set aside here), these principles are not such as to underwrite *synthetic* knowledge-claims in a theoretical context; we can only accept synthetic claims about the existence of things-in-themselves or their other non-essential attributes when we have a sufficient *moral* basis for doing so. Moderates sum up their vision as follows:

> As far as theoretical/speculative reason is concerned, ideas are no more than thinkable possibilities beyond the reach of realizable knowledge. But practical reason shows that with such thinkable things 'the category as a mere form of thought is here not empty but obtains significance through an object which practical reason unquestionably provides through the conception of the good.' Practical reason can go where theoretical reason cannot tread.[25]

---

[24] Here I am thinking of the unschematized category of cause-effect (or, perhaps better, ground-consequence), for instance, as well as maxims of reason such as Ockham's razor.

[25] Nicholas Rescher, *Kant and the Reach of Reason* (New York: Cambridge University Press, 2000), 62–3. We don't need to reify different kinds or faculties of 'reason' in order to agree with

It should be clear that Moderates are effectively ascribing to Kant a practically oriented brand of analytic theology (2). Not only can we generate, analyze, and clarify concepts in accordance with (1), we can also form synthetic 'assents' or 'holdings-for-true' (*Fürwahrhalten*),[26] about the existence of various supersensibles on the basis of the intuitions, inferences to best explanation, demonstrative arguments, and so forth that are operative in the famous 'moral proofs'.[27] The result is moral Belief (*Glaube*) and not knowledge (*Wissen*), of course, but it is a substantive result all the same and one which should be of more than passing interest to theology.

ANALYTIC AND SYNTHETIC THEOLOGY

Those who take the approach that I propose to call *Liberalism* go one step further than Moderates in interpreting Kant's views about what we can think, say, believe, and know regarding things-in-themselves. It's true, Liberals will admit, that the operations of theoretical reason in its speculative capacity do not provide a demonstration of the existence of God, freedom, and the immortal soul: that's what Kant's criticism of the rationalists was supposed to show. And it's true that we can't have cognition of these things either, since we can't experience them or connect them to our experience in any of the appropriate ways: that's what Kant's criticism of the Swedenborgians and other enthusiasts was supposed to show. So Liberals are by no means full-blown *Libertines* about these matters—they don't think that we can have synthetic theological knowledge of either a demonstrative or an experiential sort. Still, theoretical inquiry *is* able in some contexts to identify grounds that underwrite rational synthetic assents involving these concepts. More

---

Kant's general point here. 'Practical reasoning' is just reasoning that appeals in some integral way to considerations regarding what we should do as practical agents, or to considerations regarding the necessary conditions of doing what we should do. Pure 'theoretical' reasoning, especially in the speculative metaphysical mode, doesn't make such appeals.

[26] For Kant, 'assent' or 'holding-for-true' is the general genus of positive attitudes that we take towards propositions. Its species include attitudes as weak as assuming for the sake of argument, and attitudes as strong as apodictic knowledge. 'Belief' or 'Acceptance' is a species of assent that is somewhere in between these two. For further discussion of this topic, as well as the various ways in which assents can be justified, see my 'Kant's Concepts of Justification', *Nous*, 41/1 (Mar. 2007), 33–63.

[27] For lengthy discussions of the moral proofs, see Allen Wood's now-classic treatment in *Kant's Moral Religion* (Ithaca, NY: Cornell University Press, 1970) as well as John Hare, *The Moral Gap* (Oxford: Clarendon Press, 1996), Gordon Michalson, *Kant and the Problem of God* (Malden, Mass.: Blackwell Publishers 1999), and Peter Byrne, *Kant on God* (Aldershot: Ashgate Press, 2007).

precisely, Liberals claim that for Kant some of our theoretical practices *require* as a hypothetically necessary condition of their rational performance the acceptance (*Annehmung, Annahme*) of the existence of various supersensibilia. Thus the realm of particular, concrete things about which we can form rational synthetic assents on *theoretical* grounds is wider than the realm of things about which we can have knowledge.[28]

I cannot develop this Liberal reading of Kant at any length here, but let me provide a sketch of how it would go with respect to one well-known theistic proof. The classical cosmological argument starts with a premise about some finite object or state in nature: the item in question could be as minimal as a state of self perceived in inner sense. From this premise—'something exists'—the argument employs what Kant calls the 'natural law of causality' to arrive at the 'unconditioned necessity of some being or other'—i.e. a First Cause. That is the 'first stage' of the cosmological argument: from experience of a conditioned, through the 'regress of causes', to a conclusion about an unconditioned (and thus necessary) First Cause (A584/B612).

Kant says that there is a 'second stage' to the cosmological argument—one which implicitly relies on a version of the ontological argument, and transforms the being that is delivered by it from a mere First Cause to the 'most real being' of classical theology. I'm going to set that portion of the argument aside here,[29] and note merely that Kant himself seems to think both that the first stage of the argument is an abject failure as a *demonstration* or ground of any sort of *knowledge* (*Wissen*) of the First Cause's existence (A606/B634), and yet that it is entirely natural and rational for us to have what he calls 'doctrinal' or 'theoretical' Belief (*Glaube*) in a First Cause on the basis of these considerations. But how is this supposed to work?

Note, first, that speculative inquiry not only *can* lead us to 'transcendental ideas' of supersensibles, but that it is somehow *natural* for it to do so. Here is a passage that is typical of many in the latter half of the *Critique*:

Reason is driven by a propensity of its nature (*einen Hang ihrer Natur getrieben*) to go beyond its use in experience, to venture to the outermost bounds of all cognition by means of mere ideas in a pure use, and to find peace only in the completion of its circle in a self-subsisting systematic whole. (A797/B825)

---

[28] Note that existence claims are synthetic because they say something about the *concept* of a thing—i.e. that it has an actual instance—which cannot be acquired through analysis of the concept of that concept. This way of putting the point avoids the charge that we're treating existence as a 'proper' or 'real' predicate.

[29] For discussion, see Bennett, *Kant's Dialectic*, 243–55; Wood, *Kant's Rational Theology* (Ithaca, NY: Cornell University Press, 1980), 123–30; William Vallicella, 'Does the Cosmological Argument Depend on the Ontological?', *Faith and Philosophy*, 17/4 (Oct. 2000); and Lawrence Pasternack, 'The *ens realissimum* and Necessary Being in *The Critique of Pure Reason*', *Religious Studies*, 37 (Dec. 2001), 467–74.

A 'systematic whole' (*systematische Ganze*) is, roughly, a fully explained and articulate account of a given subject matter, organized in accordance with explanatory principles like the causal rule that all states/events/objects have grounds/causes (cf. A616/B644). A metaphysical account, according to Kant, is complete and fully systematic only if every 'conditioned' entity within the universe of discourse is ultimately explained by something that is unconditioned (A832–3/B860–1; cf. 5: 110). A conditioned entity is just an entity that has a 'condition'—i.e. that cries out for an explanation, for a cause, for a subject of inherence, for a whole of which it is a part. An 'unconditioned' entity, on the other hand, is somehow self-grounding and self-explaining: it provides 'a therefore to every wherefore' (*zu allem Warum das Darum*) (A585/B613), and is as such a thing-in-itself.[30]

The application to cosmology is obvious: a 'complete' and 'systematic' metaphysical picture, organized according to the (unschematized) Causal Principle, will have every item in it either grounded by some other item or self-grounding. If the series of conditioned entities is finite, then there must be an unconditioned, self-grounding First Cause of at least the first item in the series. If the series of conditioneds is infinite, then the series as a whole must have a self-grounding Cause. Kant's contention, then, is that it is our natural inclination as inquiring beings to look for complete explanations (in order for reason to 'find rest'), and that it is this inclination or 'need' which leads us to generate ideas of unconditioned, supersensible things (A339/B397). As we have seen, he often employs this sort of erotic apostrophe to characterize the mental operations in question: reason is charged with having 'interests', 'needs', 'goals', 'concerns', 'ends', 'lust for expansion', 'drives', 'inclinations', and 'propensities'. By attributing these interests and needs to *reason* itself—our highest faculty—Kant makes it clear that the 'ideas' are not generated in a whimsical way by our passions, or in a mechanical way by our animal nature. On the contrary, reason 'has given birth to these ideas from its own womb alone, and is therefore liable to give account of either their validity or their dialectical illusion' (A763/B791).

So it is natural and perhaps even inevitable that many rational inquirers thinking about cosmological issues will both generate the idea of and also accept the existence of a First Cause (or, better, an Ultimate Ground) in order to satisfy the need that reason has to find a sufficient ground for everything. The resulting attitude would have the merit of responding to that need, but it

---

[30] I do not of course mean to suggest the converse—i.e. that all the things-in-themselves are self-grounders. Our minds have a noumenal component or correlate, but they are not presumably self-grounding. I won't try to say anything here about what a self-grounder is (or whether this is even a coherent notion).

would lack objective grounds (either experiential or inferential) that could allow it to count as knowledge.[31] Here is a lyrical passage in which Kant sums up his position:

> Everywhere we see a chain of effects and causes, of ends and means, regularity in coming to be and perishing, and because nothing has entered by itself into the state in which it finds itself, this state always refers further to another things as its cause, which makes necessary just the same further inquiry, so that in such a way the entire whole would have to sink into the abyss of nothingness (*Abgrunde des Nichts*) if one did not accept something (*nähme man nicht etwas an*) subsisting for itself originally and independently outside this infinite contingency, which supports it and at the same time, as the cause of its existence, secures its continuation. (A622/B650; cf. A677/B705)

But again, this Acceptance or Belief contains an empty concept: it is not based in cognition, and thus does not count as Knowledge. Speaking to metaphysicians and theologians who would like to employ, for instance, the Causal Principle to generate speculative knowledge of supersensibilia, Kant says *not* that they should give up their efforts but rather that they must redescribe the status of their conclusions: 'For enough remains left to you to speak the language, justified by the sharpest reason, of a firm Belief, even though you must surrender that of Knowledge' (A744–5/B772–3).

Having presented this brief on behalf of the Liberal interpretation, I should emphasize that Kant's concept of 'assent' is much broader than our contemporary concept of 'belief'. It is quite possible for a subject to form the assent that *p* in Kant's sense even if she doesn't believe that *p* in the contemporary sense. This is also true regarding the species of assent that Kant calls Belief or Acceptance: it seems quite possible for us to have the Belief that *p* without believing that *p* in the contemporary sense. In other words, the grounds the subject has for *p* might allow her rationally to act as if *p* is true, to assert that *p*, to appeal to *p* as a premise in an argument or a policy in deliberation—and together that will be sufficient for Kantian Belief. But just as with acceptances of firm hypotheses in natural science, all of this could be the case even though the subject doesn't really *believe* that *p*.

For this reason, I don't think we can regard what I've been calling Kant's 'synthetic theology' here as aiming at belief in the existence of supersensible, metaphysical entities. The arguments aim at something more like what some contemporary philosophers have called, in a witting or unwitting echo of Kant, 'acceptance' or 'holding-as-true'.[32] This sort of attitude is typically

---

[31] Again, for more of this story, see my 'Kant's Concepts of Justification'.
[32] L. Jonathan Cohen, *An Essay on Belief and Acceptance* (Oxford: Clarendon Press, 1992); Edna Ullman-Margalit and Avishai Margalit, 'Holding True and Holding-as-True', *Synthese*, 92/2 (Aug. 1992), 167–87. Michael Bratman, 'Practical Reasoning and Acceptance in a Context', *Mind*, 101/401 (1992), 1–16.

construed as voluntary, as lacking the characteristic phenomenology of occurrent belief—the 'feeling that the proposition is true'—and as being properly based on considerations—practical and theoretical—that go beyond our epistemic evidence. But it can still motivate our assertions, deliberations, inferences, and actions. The fact that Kantian Belief isn't even belief (in the ordinary sense) is another reason why contemporary epistemologists won't be inclined to regard it as a candidate for knowledge, even if it turns out to be true.

I want to suggest, finally, that analytic theologians who are looking for a compromise with those who embrace Kant's legacy might do well to characterize the goal of their practice as Kantian Belief rather than ordinary belief or knowledge. Kant's own vehement opposition to any justificatory appeals to special religious sources (i.e. analytic theology (3*b*) and (3*c*)), can safely be ignored in this context, because it is not that aspect of Kant, I am suggesting, that is the main stumbling block for analytic theology. Many contemporary theologians seem perfectly happy with principled appeals to special religious sources as providing a kind of justification and defeat, at least from within a tradition, and so making such appeals is unlikely to raise eyebrows or lead to invocations of what 'Kant has shown'. Rather, it is the practice of appealing to special religious sources to provide some of our subject matter (3*a*) and *then* using the characteristic tools of analytic philosophy (2) to refer to and make arguments about supersensible entities (God in particular) in a non-'agonized' way that leads to eyebrow-raised references to 'what Kant has shown'. But as we have seen above, Kant himself is not opposed to thinking that the results of such practice can be justified, even on *theoretical* grounds, so long as we are clear that the status of these results is Belief or Acceptance rather than belief or knowledge. I see no reason why analytic theologians could not accept this restriction, and then go on to engage in substantive speculation in a realist mode, free of all fear that lurking somewhere in the pages of the Kantian corpus is a devastating critique of their fundamental aspirations.[33] I further suspect that if analytic theologians were clear about the fact that their aim is mere Belief rather than belief or knowledge, other theorists in theological and religious circles would be less inclined to invoke what 'Kant has shown'—or any other such prolegomenal worries—against them.

---

[33] Indeed, I am skeptical that we have anything like belief (rather than Belief) regarding most of the metaphysical doctrines that we passionately assert and defend, though I can't provide my reasons for thinking that here. I also do not see that knowledge or belief (as opposed to Belief) is required or even clearly desirable from the point of view of *confessional* theology, or from a religious point of view generally.

CONCLUSION

Kant's writing is often obscure, and his legacy is hotly contested; indeed, the difficulty involved in grasping what he meant provides much of the fuel for the industry of Kant studies. The critique of speculative metaphysics is no different in this regard: what follows the phrase 'as Kant has shown' can range all the way from Hardlinism to Libertinism and almost any of the positions in between. I have noted that theologians and religious thinkers *tend* to take Kant to have shown something closer to the Hardline end of the spectrum, and thus that Kant has become a 'stumbling block' and a source of 'agony', especially for those who would go beyond prolegomenal reflection to substantive analytic theologizing.

Nothing in this chapter implies that what 'Kant has shown' is false or unimportant, or that our concepts do in fact apply to supersensibles, or that the methods of analytic theology (on some characterization thereof) are in fact a good guide to truth. My aims here were more modest: I hope to have raised doubts about whether the 'Kant' who has shown what 'Kant has shown' is really the historical Kant, and to make some suggestions about how the historical Kant's views (on my reading of them, anyway) might be appropriated in a different manner by those engaged in theological and religious reflection. In effect, then, this is an irenic suggestion: the proposal is that we *can* engage in substantive analytic theology, even by Kantian lights, as long as we are careful to deny the status of belief and knowledge to our results, and agree that Belief is enough. The suggestion is irenic because it is designed to appeal both to those who embrace what 'Kant has shown', and to those inclined to regret it.[34]

---

[34] Thanks to Oliver Crisp and Michael Rea for helpful discussion of this chapter, and to Dean Zimmerman, Daniel Garber, Kevin Hector, and Stephen Bush for a conversation that suggested the title. My debt to Nicholas Wolterstorff and Allen Wood for countless conversations is pervasive.

6

Schleiermacher's Theological Anti-Realism

Andrew Dole

INTRODUCTION

At the intersection of two of the observations offered by Oliver Crisp in Chapter 1 lies a problem which analytic theologians should take seriously. The first of these observations is that analytic theology is likely to be interested in a particular kind of metaphysical inquiry: one which attempts 'to give a correct account of what are the ultimate constituents of the world and how they interact', in the words of Richard Swinburne.[1] The second observation is that analytic philosophy of religion (to which Crisp anticipates analytic theology bearing a significant resemblance) is frequently accused, with some rectitude, of being 'ahistorical' and of failing to pay attention to 'the social and cultural factors that shape Christian doctrine'.[2] The problem at the intersection of these two observations is the fact that academic theology over the past several generations has, for broadly (intellectual-)historical reasons, largely shied away from the kind of metaphysical inquiry that Crisp describes in preference to examination of the social and cultural conditioning and impact of religious doctrines. That is to say, over the last two centuries or so of the field's development, the sort of metaphysical project described by Crisp has increasingly been regarded by theologians as simply not viable, and the view among theologians that this development represents a historically informed advance rather than a decline in collective wisdom has been common. Proponents of this view are likely to see those practicing analytic theology as described by Crisp as failing to realize that they are engaged in a fruitless endeavor precisely because of their 'ahistoricity'.[3]

---

[1] See p. 36 above.   [2] See p. 50 above.

[3] Some sort of antipathy between historical awareness and a willingness to engage in metaphysics is implied by Jean-Luc Marion's statement that '[i]f we understand by modernity the completed and therefore terminal figure of metaphysics, such as it develops from Descartes to Nietzsche, then "postmodernity" begins when, among other things, the metaphysical determination of God is called into question': *God Without Being*, tr. Thomas A. Carlson (Chicago: University of Chicago Press, 1991), p. xxi. The suggestion, I take it, is that those who assume that theological metaphysics is a viable undertaking have failed to keep pace with the movement of history itself.

One way of responding to this charge is to engage the history of theology with respect to the question of metaphysics. In the analytic mode, this means examining the work of those historical theologians who are reputed to have been responsible for shifting the emphasis of theological inquiry away from metaphysics—and, crucially, to ask whether the positions articulated and the arguments advanced have merit. Such engagement may produce results that diverge significantly from intellectual-historical narratives that have dominated the field—if, for example, those with analytical training come to the conclusion that such narratives are premised on faulty interpretations of the work of key figures, or that theologians have relied too heavily on those figures' own assessments of the merits of their arguments. Nicholas Wolterstorff's essay on Kant (cited by Crisp) is a case in point.[4]

This essay is an engagement of this sort with the 'father of modern theology', Friedrich Schleiermacher, who has frequently been accused of 'emptying' Christian faith of its (metaphysical) content and reducing it to a 'merely individual and subjective' phenomenon.[5] Indeed, Schleiermacher did articulate and demonstrate a model of the theological enterprise which set a concern for explicating the metaphysical content of religious doctrines and pursuing the question of their truth firmly to the side. But proper understanding of his position on the place of truth-claims in Christian theology has, it seems to me, generally eluded theological scholarship, and is both subtle and interesting.[6] Accordingly this chapter will focus on

---

[4] Nicholas Wolterstorff, "Is it Possible and Desirable for Theologians to Recover from Kant?', *Modern Theology*, 14 (1998), 1–18.

[5] Schleiermacher has been characterized as 'what today would be called an anti-realist' by Merold Westphal: 'Totality and Finitude in Schleiermacher's Hermeneutics', in *Overcoming Onto-Theology* (New York: Fordham University Press, 2001), 123. But the type of criticism I have in mind is better expressed in the words of Emil Brunner, who opined that '[Schleiermacher's] subjective interpretation of the faith of the Church, when closely examined, tends to empty it of content completely' and that '[w]hat of truth-content remains in his "interpretation" of Christian dogma is hard to say'. Brunner, *The Divine–Human Encounter*, tr. Amandus W. Loos (Philadelphia: Westminster Press, 1943), 34–5. Westphal draws his conclusion not from an examination of Schleiermacher's theology but from his writings on hermeneutics; roughly, he claims that Schleiermacher is an anti-realist (indeed, a Derridean) on the grounds that Schleiermacher denies that the process of interpretation can ever come to a definitive end, noting that drawing this conclusion requires 'extending [Schleiermacher's] hermeneutics beyond the realm of the textual' in line with the later continental tradition. But because Westphal notes explicitly (p. 118) that this view of the scope of hermeneutics is not Schleiermacher's but appears for the first time in Dilthey, it seems to me that he should have claimed instead that 'if Schleiermacher had extended his hermeneutics beyond the realm of the textual, he would have been what today would be called an anti-realist', or perhaps 'one who extends Schleiermacher's hermeneutics beyond the realm of the textual would be what today would be called an anti-realist'.

[6] My project, of getting clear on the extent to which Christian theology can and should incorporate claims to truth, should be distinguished from that of trying to get clear on the extent

exposition, although in closing I will state my position regarding just what contemporary theologians should 'learn from history' in this particular instance.

In my title I have promised to discuss Schleiermacher's *theological anti-realism*, and I will eventually attribute a position to Schleiermacher that fits plausibly under this heading. But to begin, let's look at a familiar form of anti-realism as a jumping-off point. As Michael Rea notes, one can be an anti-realist about *singular terms*, about *kind-terms*, about *claims*, or about *disciplines*.[7] Schleiermacher's anti-realism can be usefully compared to a form of anti-realism about *claims*. The position I have in mind is, to use Peter Byrne's terminology, a form of *contrastive* rather than *global* anti-realism,[8] and asserts that while members of a particular class of statements appear to make claims to truth about the entities which they name—in the sense that they have realist truth-conditions[9]—in reality they do not. To speak of *theological anti-realism* is thus to identify 'theological claims'—let us say, claims about the existence, nature and activities of God—as constituting a 'disputed class of statements',[10] and to assert that, while such statements appear to demand a realist interpretation, in fact they do not.

Now a variety of considerations can be advanced in favor of the conclusion that members of a disputed class of statements do not have realist truth-conditions. *Reductive* anti-realism models the crucial parts of Schleiermacher's *Glaubenslehre* quite well, however, so I will confine myself to that position. If whatever truth or falsity a claim enjoys can be established through examination of entities other than the ones putatively referred to, then one can argue that the claim in question cannot be interpreted realistically. In Bob Hale's words, the reductive anti-realist maintains about a particular class of statements, A-statements, 'that there are no distinctive A-facts: rather, A-truths can be translated or paraphrased without loss or residue into B-truths, truths of some other kind which enjoy an (at least relatively)

---

to which religion—or, perhaps, specifically Christian faith—puts human beings in cognitive contact with God or other extra-personal realities according to Schleiermacher. That project is pursued in exemplary fashion by Robert Adams in 'Faith and Religious Knowledge', in Jacqueline Mariña (ed.), *The Cambridge Companion to Schleiermacher* (Cambridge: Cambridge University Press, 2005), which makes a useful companion piece to the essay by Westphal cited in n. 5.

[7] Rea, 'Realism in Theology and Metaphysics', 323–45, in P. Candler and C. Cunningham (eds.), *Belief and Metaphysics* (London: SCM, 2007).

[8] Byrne, *God and Realism* (Aldershot: Ashgate, 2003), 6–8.

[9] As Rea puts it, a claim has realist truth-conditions 'only if realism about the xs and Fs [respectively, the singular and kind-terms] putatively referred to in the theory is true' (Rea, 'Realism', 324).

[10] Cf. Michael Dummett, 'Realism and Anti-Realism', in *The Seas of Language* (Oxford: Clarendon Press, 1996), 465.

unproblematic ontology and epistemology'.[11] It is the fact that A-truths can be translated 'without loss or residue' into B-truths that grounds the claim that the A-statements themselves make no claims to A-truth: if the truth of A-statements can be established without any reference to A-facts, then the question of realism or anti-realism regarding A-facts is irrelevant, and hence realism concerning A-statements is not warranted.

Reductive theological anti-realism, then, would be the position that theological statements can be translated into statements of another kind without loss or residue, and that therefore the question of whether the entities purportedly referred to by theological statements so much as exist is irrelevant to the truth or falsity of those statements—as, a fortiori, are questions regarding whether they have the properties or stand in the relations which those statements purportedly claim that they do. As we will see, in a crucial part of the introduction to *The Christian Faith* Schleiermacher presents an understanding of religious doctrines which at first blush looks like an unvarnished example of reductive theological anti-realism; on the basis of this passage alone one might reasonably regard him as a theological anti-realist full-stop. I will claim, however, that Schleiermacher conjoins to this view of religious doctrine additional convictions, and pragmatic considerations, which together yield a somewhat different picture.

THE NATURE OF DOGMATIC PROPOSITIONS

Dogmatic theology is, for Schleiermacher, concerned with the proper understanding of 'dogmatic propositions' (*dogmatische Sätze*).[12] These comprise a subset of the total set of Christian doctrines, distinguished by the fact that they aim at 'the highest possible degree of definiteness'.[13] In §30 Schleiermacher divides such propositions into three classes: descriptions of human states, claims about the constitution of the world, and conceptions of divine attributes or modes of action. Of the three forms, Schleiermacher famously

---

[11] Bob Hale, 'Realism and its Oppositions', in *A Companion to the Philosophy of Language* (Oxford: Blackwell, 1997), 286. The term 'reductive anti-realism' is originally Dummett's.

[12] In discussing passages from the 2nd edn. of the *Glaubenslehre*, I will provide references to both the *Schleiermacher Kritische Gesamtausgabe* (*KGA*) (Berlin: De Gruyter, 2003) and to the English translation by H. R. Mackintosh *et al.*, *The Christian Faith* (*CF*) (Edinburgh: T&T Clark, 1989). Translations will be my own.

[13] In particular, dogmatic propositions are distinguished from 'poetic' and 'rhetorical' religious doctrines by the fact that the former display 'the comprehension and appropriation of that which is originally given in these two forms, but bound to language and thereby made communicable'. *KGA* 1. 13. 1, §16.1, pp. 130–1; *CF*, pp. 78–9.

identifies the first, description of human states of mind, as the 'fundamental dogmatic form'; he holds that all dogmatic propositions first arose out of reflection upon pious emotions or states of consciousness,[14] and his stated preference is to work only with statements of this form and to understand statements of the second and third form in terms of statements of the first. Propositions about human states are simply closer to their point of origin than are statements about the world or about God; the latter, as we will see, are susceptible to 'contamination' by alien factors. Thus propositions of the second and third forms are to be retained 'only in so far as they can be developed out of propositions of the first form; for only on this condition can they be confidently regarded as expressions of pious emotions'.[15]

Schleiermacher goes further, however, than voicing a preference for working only with propositions which describe human states. He also makes a claim about how the content of these three types of propositions are related. In §31 he argues that the decision to privilege statements of the fundamental form over the others amounts to a preference for working 'first [with propositions] which come closest to being immediate expositions of emotional states, and then those which *express the same, in the form of* divine qualities and of properties of the world'.[16] This view leads him to propose that Christian theology might be able to eliminate claims about God and the world entirely by translating these into claims about human states: 'If, then, all propositions which belong to the system of Christian doctrine (*Glaubenslehre*) can indisputably be expressed in the fundamental form...then it seems that the Christian *Glaubenslehre* has only to carry through consistently that fundamental form in order to complete the analysis of Christian piety, and that the other two might be entirely set aside as superfluous.'[17] Schleiermacher even goes so far as to suggest that such a reductive treatment might be able to 'perfectly reproduce the content of Christian doctrine'.[18]

I take it that this passage can plausibly be interpreted as offering a reductively anti-realist account of such statements about the world or about God which are found within Christian theology: the dogmatic or theological content of statements of this class can be expressed entirely by statements about the human self and its states of consciousness. Nothing as regards content is lost when such statements are reduced to statements about human beings.

[14] CF §§15–16; see in particular §16 ps (81).
[15] *KGA* 1. 13. 1, §30.2, p. 195; *CF*, p. 126.
[16] *KGA* 1. 13. 1, §31.1, pp. 196–7; *CF*, p. 128, emphasis added.
[17] *KGA* 1. 13. 1, §30.3, p. 195; *CF*, p. 126.
[18] Ibid.

But in spite of the fact that this thoroughly reductive treatment of claims about God and the world is described and even advocated in the introduction, Schleiermacher's actual practice in the theological sections of the *Glaubenslehre* diverges from this model.[19] At crucial points of his treatment, what very much appear to be important claims about God and the world survive the reductive treatment more or less unscathed.

Here are two examples. First, in discussing the doctrine of creation in §40, Schleiermacher claims that

it is quite clear that our feeling of absolute dependence could not be referred to the general condition of all finite being if anything therein were, or had at any time been, independent of God. It is just as certain that if there were anything in all finite being as such which entered into it at its origin independently of God, then because it must exist in us as well, the feeling of absolute dependence could have no truth even in relation to ourselves.[20]

So the claim advanced is that *nothing finite came into existence, and nothing finite persists, independently of God's activity*; and the argument for this claim turns on the conditions for the possibility of the content of the feeling of absolute dependence (the feeling that not only we ourselves but in fact all finite being receives its existence and activity from an outside source) and of the *veridicality* of that feeling.

Second, in §93 Schleiermacher attributes to Christians the 'conviction' (*Überzeugung*) that 'no more perfect form of the God-consciousness stands before the human race' than that possessed by Jesus of Nazareth, 'and that any new one would be a step backwards'.[21] By the end of the section he has argued that the right thing to say is not simply that the pious self-consciousness of Jesus is the highest one of which we have evidence, but that there *could not be* a more perfect example of God-consciousness than that possessed by Jesus. If there could be a higher form of pious self-consciousness than that possessed by Jesus, Schleiermacher argues, then Christians would naturally hope that such a possibility will someday be realized, such that this truly perfect pious self-consciousness could then become the common possession of a truly redeemed community. But this idea is incompatible with the essence of Christian piety, according to which 'redemption is posited as something universally and completely accomplished through Jesus of Nazareth'.[22]

---

[19] I pass over the fact that in §30 Schleiermacher also voices reservations about the prospect of a completely reductive treatment because a project which followed this procedure would thereby largely cut itself off from the doctrinal tradition's history, and because it would lack a 'truly ecclesiastical character', would not be able to 'fulfil the real purpose of all dogmatics'.

[20] *KGA* 1. 13. 1, §40.3, pp. 234–5; *CF*, pp. 151–2.

[21] *KGA* 1. 13. 2, §93.2, p. 42; *CF*, p. 377.

[22] *KGA* 1. 13. 1, §11.3, p. 97; *CF*, p. 56.

In both of these cases, Schleiermacher appears to reach conclusions about mind-independent reality by means of a transcendental deduction from the contents of the Christian faith. That is to say, he appears to be operating on the principle that theologians can claim that whatever would have to be the case for the essential components of the Christian faith to be veridical is in fact the case. Schleiermacher's practice in the doctrinal sections of the *Glaubenslehre* would thus seem to allow theology to make substantive claims about God and world, the reductive treatment described in the Introduction notwithstanding. There is a tension, then, between Schleiermacher's stated preference for the fundamental form of dogmatic propositions and his practice of deriving claims about God and the world by transcendental deduction from the contents of Christian faith. I believe that this tension can be resolved, and the following sections of this essay will be dedicated to laying out an account of Schleiermacher's position on the place of truth-claims within the theological enterprise which accomplishes this. To anticipate my conclusion, it will turn out that there is a place for robust claims to truth about mind-independent reality within Schleiermacher's theology, but it is a far narrower place than most theological realists are likely to be happy with.

ELEMENTS OF THE SOLUTION

There are three components to the position which I will be attributing to Schleiermacher. The first component has to do with his desire to establish an 'eternal covenant' between theology and the sciences. The second is Schleiermacher's distinctive understanding of religion, and in particular of distinctly religious activity. And the third concerns his position in the *Glaubenslehre* on 'speculation'.

The 'eternal covenant'

Schleiermacher's mature idea of an 'eternal covenant' was his response to what he regarded as an increasingly broad and damaging separation between the life of religion and the life of the mind.[23] As early as the first edition of the

---

[23] A useful discussion of this aspect of Schleiermacher's thought is Gerhard Spiegler, *The Eternal Covenant: Schleiermacher's Experiment in Cultural Theology* (New York: Harper & Row, 1967). Spiegler's book is by now seriously dated, having been written under the shadow of Neo-Orthodoxy and its framing of Schleiermacher's thought in terms of the relationship between religion and 'culture'. A more recent treatment which reframes the issue (correctly, in my view) in terms of the relationship between religion and free inquiry is found in Brent Sockness, *Against*

Speeches on Religion Schleiermacher had been a vocal proponent of the view that the highest degree of intellectual acumen and creative activity coincide naturally with the highest degree of religiosity, and that only destructive cultural factors (above all, a deficient understanding of religion, whether held by the religious or by religion's 'despisers') are responsible for the separation of the two in actuality. But in spite of his lifelong efforts as a 'mediator', by the time of the composition of *The Christian Faith* powerful forces were arrayed against the liberal project of allowing advances in historical and scientific scholarship to inform Christianity's self-understanding. In the introduction to the third edition of the *Speeches,* whose publication coincided with that of the first edition of *The Christian Faith,* Schleiermacher worried openly about the rising tide of theological conservatism (one symptom of which had been the dismissal of his friend De Wette from his position at Berlin in 1819); in view of the changed times, now 'one might rather find it necessary to write speeches to the sanctimonious (*Frömmelnde*) and to the slaves of the letter, to those unknowing and unloving superstitious and hyperbelieving persons (*Aber- und Übergläubige*)' than to the *Speeches'* original audience, 'who seem no longer to be there at all'.[24] And the decade between the publication of the first and second editions of *The Christian Faith* saw the replacement of De Wette, after a long vacancy, with Ernst Wilhelm Hengstenberg, who had openly declared that matters of religion could not be 'penetrated' by 'philology, philosophy and human reason'.[25] Hengstenberg, who after 1827 edited the tremendously influential *Evangelische Kirchen-Zeitung,* became the center of a group of conservative neo-Pietists bent on restoring theological orthodoxy to Prussia's seminaries and universities; in 1830 he would orchestrate the publication of an article which accused prominent faculty members at Halle of 'rationalist unbelief' on the basis of students' lecture notes, which led to a public outcry and an investigation by the crown. The eventual outcome was a cabinet order by Frederick Wilhelm III that 'only theologians who accept the dogmas of our Evangelical Church [will] be appointed to new academic positions'.[26]

Thus when in 1829 Schleiermacher published two open letters to his friend Friedrich Lücke (who shared Schleiermacher's dismay at the goals and tactics of the *Partei Hengstenberg*[27]) as he prepared the second edition of *The*

False Apologetics: Wilhelm Hermann and Ernst Troeltsch in Conflict (Tübingen: Mohr Siebeck, 1998), particularly the concluding chapter, 'False Apologetics and Modernity: The Ambiguous Legacy of Schleiermacher's "Eternal Covenant"'.

[24] *KGA* 1. 12, p. 10. Cited in Robert Bigler, *The Politics of German Protestantism* (Berkeley, Calif.: University of California Press, 1972), 162.
[25] Bigler, *Politics,* 92.
[26] Ibid. 105–6.
[27] Ibid. 172.

Christian Faith, he devoted particular attention to the threat of reactionary hyper-orthodoxy.[28] 'Just think of the present state of the natural sciences as they increasingly develop into a comprehensive knowledge of the world', Schleiermacher requested. Such an advance would be bound to disprove many traditional Christian claims about the world and about God.

> What then do you suppose the future holds, not only for our theology, but for our evangelical Christianity?... Shall the tangle of history so unravel that Christianity becomes identified with barbarism and science with unbelief? To be sure, many will make it so. Preparations are already well underway, and already the ground heaves under our feet, as those gloomy creatures who regard as satanic all research beyond the confines of ancient literalism seek to creep forth from their religious enclaves.[29]

Schleiermacher was determined that the future of Christianity not belong to 'those who can hack away at science with a sword, fence themselves in with weapons at hand to withstand the assaults of sound research and behind this fence establish as binding a church doctrine that appears to everyone outside as an unreal ghost'.[30]

In Schleiermacher's own words, at the heart of the *Glaubenslehre* stands a vision of 'an eternal covenant between living Christian faith and completely free, independent scientific inquiry, so that faith does not hinder science and science does not exclude faith'.[31] Only the establishment of such a covenant, in his view, could forestall open warfare within the public sphere between advocates of religion and advocates of free inquiry. In order for the religious to participate in this 'covenant' Schleiermacher was convinced that 'we must learn to do without what many are still accustomed to regard as inseparably bound to the essence of Christianity'[32]—that is, learn to do without many of the claims upon which Christianity's validity had traditionally been thought to rest. The reductive treatment of religious doctrines in the *Glaubenslehre*, he explained, was intended to make this possible. 'I thought I should show as best I could', he explained to Lücke, 'that every dogma that truly represents an element of our Christian consciousness can be so formulated that it remains

---

[28] Schleiermacher, 'Über seine Glaubenslehre an Herrn Dr. Lücke, zwei Sendschreiben', *Theologische Studien und Kritiken*, 2 (1829), 255–84, 481–532. English tr.: *On the Glaubenslehre: Two Letters to Dr. Lücke*, tr. James Duke and Francis Fiorenza (Atlanta, Ga.: Scholars Press, 1981). Translations are those of Duke and Fiorenza.

[29] 'Sendschreiben', 489; *On the Glaubenslehre*, 60–1.

[30] 'Sendschreiben', 489; *On the Glaubenslehre*, 60. Hengstenberg did not respond well to this characterization of the movement which he championed; on his response in the *Evangelische Kirchen-Zeitung* and its consequences, see Kurt Nowak, *Schleiermacher: Leben, Werk und Wirkung* (Göttingen: Vanderhoek & Ruprecht, 2001), 412–13.

[31] 'Sendschreiben', 494; *On the Glaubenslehre*, 64.

[32] 'Sendschreiben', 489; *On the Glaubenslehre*, 60.

free from entanglements with science'.[33] The 'reduction' of dogmatic propositions to claims about human states removes them from those areas where the natural sciences claim authority, and allows theologians to abandon reliance on claims about God and the world as essential parts of Christian dogmatics.

So Schleiermacher thought that winnowing the traditional stock of theological claims about God and the world would forestall conflicts with the sciences. But even granting this, the question remains as to whether such claims are in fact 'optional' for a religion like Christianity, or whether on the contrary the abandonment of such claims would do irreparable harm. To understand why Schleiermacher thought that Christianity could withstand the abandonment of traditional claims about God and the world, we need to turn to a consideration of his understanding of religion, looking initially at his first published work on the subject.

Religion

In spite of the fact that Schleiermacher's first and most famous book purports to be 'on Religion', expositing his view of the subject is not a straightforward project. His pattern of usage of the term 'religion' in the *Speeches* is, to put it bluntly, unfortunate. Not only does he use the term in a profligate fashion— to denote 'religiosity, belief, piety, religious life, religious consciousness, the religious person, the religious precinct of *humanitas* as well as the religious realm of the spiritual world and the appearance of religion in history';[34] but the second speech in particular contains a number of 'religion is' statements which, taken in isolation, suggest that religion is restricted to the realm of the internal, the private, and the psychological (for example, 'religion is sense and taste for the infinite'). To do justice to the full sense of 'religion' for Schleiermacher we cannot be content with excerpting a few of these 'religion is' statements, but must attempt a reconstruction which takes into account the various ways in which he uses the term.[35]

Schleiermacher's account is centered around the notion of an 'essence' of religion. Considerable unhappiness attends the question of just what constitutes this 'essence', and here I propose to merely touch upon the subject in order to focus on the structural role of religion's essence within religion. The 'essence of religion' in the first edition of the *Speeches* is a matter of 'intuitions

---

[33] 'Sendschreiben', 495; *On the Glaubenslehre*, 64.

[34] Paul Seifert, *Die Theologie des jungen Schleiermachers* (Gütersloh: Gütersloher Verlagshaus, 1960), 88.

[35] A more complete version of this material is found in my *Schleiermacher on Religion and the Natural Order* (OUP, forthcoming), ch. 2.

and feelings' of the universe: very roughly, it is a matter of holding a view of the total organizational scheme of the universe, together with the strong emotions which seeing oneself and others in light of this view is supposed to generate. Knowing what religion's essence is, according to Schleiermacher, is supposed to enable one to discern what belongs to religion and what does not: the essence of religion is 'the highest and most universal formula of religion on the basis of which you should be able to find every place in religion'.[36] There is more to religion, for Schleiermacher, than simply intuitions and feelings: there are religious doctrines, religious artifacts, religious works of art and architecture, religious activities, religious communities and institutions, and so on.[37] But the way religion's essence is involved in making a particular activity, artifact, or community religious is not straightforward. Contemporary discussions of essentialism, which for the most part speak of identification as a member of a natural kind as a matter of possessing essential properties,[38] are thus not much help in interpreting Schleiermacher's 'essentialist' account of religion. Artifacts such as buildings, musical compositions, or texts cannot be religious by virtue of possessing intuitions or feelings as properties, and neither can hymns or sermons; for mental states cannot be predicated of any of these.

What I propose as a reconstruction of Schleiermacher's account of religion is the following. What distinguishes religion from non-religion is the *proper relationship* between a particular activity, community, or artifact and religion's essence. More specifically, an activity or artifact is religious to the extent that it serves the purpose of the *transmission* of religious intuitions from one person to another, the purpose of allowing individuals and communities to *arrange* and *refine* such intuitions, or the purpose of 'awakening' the ability to produce religious intuitions. A community, for example, is religious inasmuch as it is dedicated to the sort of communication activities which make such activities possible. It is not simply the *presence* of religious intuitions and feeling which makes for religion; it is the extent to which an activity serves the purpose of *propagating* them. The total field of the phenomenon of religion—which is what I understand by

---

[36] Schleiermacher, *On Religion: Speeches to its Cultured Despisers,* tr. Richard Crouter (Cambridge: CUP, 1988), 104.

[37] This claim runs counter to a significant amount of the secondary literature. What I have come to think of as the 'standard interpretation' of Schleiermacher effectively identifies religion with its essence, typically by treating a discussion of Schleiermacher's account of religion's essence as counting as a discussion of his account of religion. I argue more fully against the standard interpretation in *Schleiermacher on Religion and the Natural Order.*

[38] For a useful discussion of the varieties of contemporary essentialism in analytic philosophy, see Michael Della Rocca, 'Essentialists and Essentialism', *Journal of Philosophy,* 93/4 (1996), 186–202, and Mike Rea, *World Without Design* (Oxford: Clarendon Press, 2002), 101–2.

Schleiermacher's phrase 'the realm of religion' (*das Gebiet der Religion*)—is the sum total of those activities and objects which are instrumental in the propagation of religion's essence.

With a few modifications, Schleiermacher's mature view of religion remains consistent with that of the *Speeches*. In the *Glaubenslehre* Schleiermacher identifies the feeling of absolute dependence as the essence of all forms of *Frömmigkeit* or piety, which roughly constitutes what he calls 'inward religion'. 'Outward religion' he describes as 'the organization of the communicative expressions of piety in a community'.[39] So the *Glaubenslehre* identifies as part of the territory of 'religion' activities which serve what might be termed 'religious purposes'—in this case, communicating piety; and we can say that religion, in the final analysis, comprises *piety plus those activities which serve to develop, sustain, and communicate it.*

Now because religion is defined by a relationship to piety rather than by an external 'boundary', activities of the same type can be either religious or non-religious depending on whether they are related to piety in the right way. Religious speech acts, for example, are those which communicate piety; non-religious speech acts are those which do not. So too with musical compositions or works of architecture.[40] And because activities of the same type can be religious or non-religious according to their relationship to piety, religion is vulnerable to *contamination* by 'alien elements'. Such contamination occurs when religious individuals begin acting from an 'interest' in something other than religious communication—when a motivation which is alien to piety begins to inform purportedly religious activity.[41] Motivations will be alien to

---

[39] KGA 1. 13. 1, §6 ps, p. 59; CF, p. 30. It is important to note that the postscript to §6 contains Schleiermacher's decision *not* to use the term 'religion' in his exposition for the most part. Nevertheless this section offers us valuable information as to how Schleiermacher thinks various kinds of talk about religion could be translated into the terms of his account.

[40] Naturally, this proposal raises a host of questions: whether e.g. an activity is religious if it is intended to but fails to serve the purpose of the transmission of religion's essence, or if it does serve this purpose without anyone's intending that it do so. I do not propose to address these questions; Schleiermacher conflated, it seems to me, the matter of intent and the matter of efficacy, and so his account of religion leaves many questions unanswered. It does not seem to be a fatal defect of the basic idea that (if I am correct) structures Schleiermacher's account of religion that it yields substantial 'grey areas'—i.e. where it is not clear whether a thing should be considered religious or non-religious. If the respects in which a theory of religion fails to deliver a clear ruling correspond to areas of vagueness in our pretheoretical intuitions concerning what is religious and what is not, then at least the theory has the possibility of representing a formalization of those intuitions.

[41] In this connection Paul Capetz e.g. speaks of Schleiermacher as trying to keep 'speculative approaches' at arm's length from theology: Capetz, *Christian Faith as Religion: A Study in the Theologies of Calvin and Schleiermacher* (Lanham: University Press of America, 1988), 126. I prefer to speak of 'interests' rather than 'approaches', because it seems to me that Schleiermacher was in fact committed to the idea that religion, metaphysics, and morality are distinguished from each other by virtue of the *motivations* that drive each field of inquiry.

religion insofar as they aim at accomplishing something other than the development and transmission of piety.

So Schleiermacher's understanding of religion identifies some forms of activity as properly religious, to the extent that they serve religion's ends, and others as not properly religious. We are now interested in the question of where the activity of making claims about God and the world falls in relation to this division, since the question on the table is why Schleiermacher thinks that a legitimate theology can in principle set such claims aside.

'Speculation'

In a crucial passage from the *Speeches*, Schleiermacher describes the relationship between religion, ethics, and philosophy:

> [Religion] does not wish to determine and explain the universe according to its nature as does metaphysics; it does not desire to continue the universe's development and perfect it by the power of freedom and the divine free choice of a human being as does morals. . . . It wishes to intuit the universe, wishes devoutly to overhear the universe's own manifestations and actions, longs to be grasped and filled by the universe's immediate influences in childlike passivity.[42]

Here Schleiermacher describes two kinds of 'interests' which are alien to religion, and by which religion has often been contaminated. If one is motivated by a desire to understand and explain the universe, one is thereby engaged in metaphysics; if one is motivated by a desire to continue the universe's development through moral action, one is thereby engaged in morality. But inasmuch as one is acting from either of these two motivations, according to this passage, one is thereby *not* engaged in religion.

Once again, the terminology differs between the *Speeches* and the *Glaubenslehre*; and although the precise contents of the term 'speculation' in Schleiermacher's writings are a matter of debate, we can identify speculation roughly with philosophical reflection, and so as equivalent to the *Speeches'* 'metaphysics'.[43] For our purposes, what is important about 'speculation' in the *Glaubenslehre* is its relationship to the truth-value of dogmatic claims; and to see this relationship clearly, we will need to focus on the idea of a 'speculative interest'. In §17, Schleiermacher makes a claim about the Christian theological tradition which echoes the material from the *Speeches* cited above:

[42] Schleiermacher, *On Religion*, 22.

[43] So Thomas Curran: 'Schleiermacher's use of the word "speculative" does not lend itself to a single, absolute definition. In most cases, it probably indicates nothing more than a "higher" form of knowledge; "speculation" may then be used as a synonym for philosophy, or more specifically for that branch of philosophy commonly called metaphysics.' Curran, *Doctrine and Speculation in Schleiermacher's Glaubenslehre* (Berlin: De Gruyter, 1994), 75.

> The Evangelical church in particular bears within itself the unanimous consciousness that the formulation of dogmatic propositions which is proper to it does not depend on any specific philosophical form or school, nor in general has it arisen from a speculative interest, but rather only from an interest in the satisfaction of the immediate consciousness by means of the genuine and unfalsified foundation of Christ; and therefore it can only accept such propositions which are able to display the same lineage as dogmatic propositions which belong to it.[44]

In this passage Schleiermacher contrasts a 'speculative interest' with an interest, if I understand him correctly, in forming up in oneself, developing, and passing on Christian piety—which we can call simply a 'religious interest'. His point in this passage is that to produce church doctrine from a 'speculative interest' would represent a contamination of religion.

Drawing in part on the fact that Schleiermacher associates speculation with a 'purely scientific interest' in §17, I propose that we understand the phrase 'speculative interest' as an *autonomous interest in truth*. That is to say, I take Schleiermacher's position to be that, if one becomes interested in investigating a proposition's truth or entailments solely for the sake of pursuing knowledge, one is thereby acting from a 'speculative interest', and that however praiseworthy such an interest might be in other contexts, its introduction to the realm of religion results in a 'contamination' of that field. Indeed, Schleiermacher attributes the prominence of claims about God and the world within the Christian theological tradition to the influence of this interest, and in effect proposes that claims which have so resulted be excluded from consideration.

This answers the question raised above of why Schleiermacher thought that theology could afford to set aside an interest in truth-claims about God and the world without fundamentally betraying the interests of religion. Religion, in his view, does not incorporate an interest in truth for its own sake; religion's interest is in the upbuilding and communication of piety. Nothing essential to religion is lost when claims about God and the world are abandoned.

SCHLEIERMACHER'S THEOLOGICAL ANTI-REALISM

We now have the necessary material to assemble what I take to be an overall statement of Schleiermacher's position on the place of truth-claims within the theological enterprise. This assembly will require three steps.

---

[44] *KGA* 1. 13. 1, §16 ps, p. 135; *CF*, pp. 82–3.

First, we have seen that Schleiermacher does allow for the dogmatic theologian to affirm claims about God and the world in some cases. The theologian, on this view, may legitimately advance as the contents of dogmatic propositions claims as to what must be the case in order for the pious self-consciousness (and specifically, the feeling of absolute dependence which it contains) to be a veridical phenomenon. A form of realism about theological claims, then, would seem to occupy the core of Schleiermacher's theological method.

But second, given that Schleiermacher seems to hold that the theologian *may* advance such claims as the content of Christian doctrines, he also clearly indicates that the theologian should in general *avoid* doing so, in preference relying on the fundamental form of dogmatic propositions. Fairly clearly, Schleiermacher also thought that in general, the theologian should formulate her statements about God and the world as modestly as possible, in order to avoid 'entanglements with science'.

So far, this might seem like a chastened, but still vital, theological realism. But third, Schleiermacher's conception of the nature of distinctively religious activity and its separation from 'speculation' severely constrains the extent to which the truth-relevant content of such claims can be of interest to the theologian. If an autonomous interest in truth is truly alien to religion, then not only should the theologian strive to make as few and as modest claims as possible about God and the world; but once those claims have been deduced and their dogmatic value established, their truth-value and their entailments are supposed to be of no moment whatsoever to the theologian qua theologian. Once their suitability as expressions of the pious self-consciousness and their coherence with other doctrines has been established, the theologian's interest in these claims is supposed to be at an end.

So I offer the following as a statement of the content of 'Schleiermacher's theological anti-realism':

The dogmatic theologian should advance as few claims as possible about mind-independent reality as the results of her theological work. Such claims must be deducible from the contents of the pious self-consciousness under the supposition that this is veridical, and should be formulated so as to extend as little as possible into the domain of scientific inquiry. Furthermore, their theological value is restricted to their adequacy as expressions of pious self-consciousness and their mutual coherence; neither their truth-value nor their entailments are of independent interest to the theologian.

LEARNING FROM SCHLEIERMACHER

If I am correct in my interpretation of Schleiermacher, his position effectively excludes the kind of metaphysics described by Crisp from theology (although it says nothing about the prospects of metaphysics as such[45]). To engage in metaphysics within theology, for Schleiermacher, would be to contaminate religion by bringing an alien motivation—an interest in truth for its own sake—into the fold. The theologian should be interested primarily in religious doctrines as vehicles of piety, and should be concerned primarily with the ability of doctrines to serve this purpose; and while genuine truth-claims about mind-independent realities may be found among these doctrines, the theologian qua theologian should resist the temptation to use these as starting-points for metaphysical reflection.

In my view, awareness of Schleiermacher's theological anti-realism, as I have described it, should not prompt the analytic theologian to avoid metaphysical inquiry, but there is a lesson in his position for the metaphysically inclined theologian. I conclude with three brief sets of remarks on this topic.

First, I think the analytic theologian should be profoundly unmoved by Schleiermacher's contention that an interest in truth for its own sake is alien to religion. This claim rests on his belief that religion and the pursuit of truth for its own sake are mutually exclusive—not in the sense that a religious *person* cannot disinterestedly pursue truth, but in the sense that this pursuit can never count as a *distinctly religious activity*. I think this is one of Schleiermacher's least plausible and least well-supported assertions, and that the right attitude to take towards this claim is one of healthy skepticism. It was obvious to Schleiermacher, as it is to any casual observer of religious history, that an interest in the truth of religious ideas and doctrines is common within religion. Schleiermacher viewed this as a lamentable departure from 'ideal religion', one that both could and should be remedied; it does not seem to me that the contemporary theologian is under any obligation to agree with him on this point.[46]

---

[45] Indeed, in the 1st edn. of the *Speeches* Schleiermacher makes this clear. 'To present all events in the world as the actions of a god is religion; it expresses its connection to an infinite totality; but while brooding over the existence of this god before the world and outside the world *may be good and necessary in metaphysics*, in religion even that becomes only empty mythology.' *On Religion*, 105 (emphasis added).

[46] More specifically: such claims about what is proper to religion make sense only against the background of a definition which clearly demarcates the territory religion occupies (as, in a particular way, Schleiermacher's does) and sets the enterprise of pursuing truth firmly outside that territory. The problem such claims face at this point in history stems not principally from the fact that truth-seeking is, in historical perspective, plausibly seen as a 'natural' part of religion, but from the fact that the project of 'defining religion' such that clear boundaries of the requisite sort can be postulated (and such that the definition in question could be expected to command wide assent) is largely no longer regarded as a viable endeavor. This view is more prominent in the discipline of religious studies than philosophy; see e.g. Jonathan Z. Smith, 'Religion, Religions, Religious', in Mark C. Taylor (ed.), *Critical Terms for Religious Studies* (Chicago: University of Chicago Press, 1998), 269–84.

Second, I do not think that the theologian has an obligation to try to interpret traditional claims so that they extend as little as possible into the domain of scientific inquiry—so that, to put it differently, they no longer run the risk of being challenged by empirical investigation. The analytic theologian could, I think, see it as a wise policy to interpret traditional claims so that they are *not actually falsified* by what the natural sciences *have in fact* established. But that is not the same thing as trying to remove such claims altogether from the domain of the empirical. Schleiermacher's 'eternal covenant' was an attempt to establish a fixed and unchanging relationship between religion and the sciences, and called for the surrender (by Christian theologians in the first instance, but ultimately by the laity as well) of claims about God and the world *as a class, just in case they might* come into conflict with the deliverances of the sciences. His position thus represents a strategic decision, a counsel of prudence, or an ecclesiological experiment rather than being entailed by what analytical theologians are likely to recognize as philosophical convictions. The problematic cultural dynamic to which he was responding— the conflict between religious orthodoxies and free inquiry leading to the restriction of intellectual (and political) freedoms—persists today, and is one with which analytical theologians may well concern themselves (indeed, I wish that more would). But this does not generate an obligation on their part to adopt Schleiermacher's recommendations. If anything, 'learning from history' in this connection should involve an examination of the historical fortunes of Schleiermacher's particular kind of religious liberalism, and would require asking whether the anti-metaphysical strand of this tradition has in general had the results for which he hoped.

But third, and finally, I do think that there is a lasting lesson to be learnt from this investigation of Schleiermacher's theological program. In brief, Schleiermacher saw that religious doctrines do *more than* make truth-claims; they perform functions *beyond* the description of mundane and transcendent realities. I do not believe that he held the (confused) position that doctrines which serve other functions—such as the transmission of piety—cannot *also* serve as claims about what is the case regarding either mundane or transcendent realities. We can understand Schleiermacher as holding that the theologian should, quite simply, be more interested in the work that doctrines do among human beings than in their possible truth-content; the theologian, that is, should be concerned primarily with how particular religious doctrines affect the life of the church. This represents an important contribution to the history of Christian theology, and the fact that many contemporary theologians (among them, some cited in Randal Rauser's chapter in this volume) seem to be interested *exclusively* in this facet of religious doctrines is a testament to Schleiermacher's lasting influence.

Schleiermacher's Theological Anti-Realism 153

In my view those historically 'downstream' of Schleiermacher should be cognizant of this development in the history of theology—and should not only *agree* with Schleiermacher's basic point, but *develop* the insight it represents. Almost certainly, religious doctrines do more work than his account describes. They play an important role, for example, in the establishment and maintenance of religious group identity, of attitudes on political, racial and gender issues, and of overarching conceptions of human flourishing. Analytic theologians should concern themselves with these dynamics; indeed, in my view to ignore altogether this 'horizontal' dimension of religious discourse would in fact amount to a failure to attend sufficiently to the lessons of history.

It does not follow, however, that the theologian should be concerned *only* or even *primarily* with these dynamics. What analytical theologians should learn from Schleiermacher is that the task, to cite Crisp once again, of 'rightly deploy[ing] the doctrines concerned in the life of the church'[47] is not exhausted by metaphysical investigation, but also requires some grasp of the inner-worldly careers of those doctrines. The analytic theologian who acts from a serious interest in the truth-relevant content of religious doctrines without turning a blind eye to the other dimensions of religious discourse will, it seems to me, have learnt the lesson that Schleiermacher has to teach.[48]

But more than this, there is a sense in which a return to metaphysical reflection within theology might represent a capitalization on this particular lesson of history. Immediately after floating the possibility of a thoroughly reductive dogmatics—one that boiled all doctrines down to the 'fundamental form' of descriptions of human states—Schleiermacher distances himself somewhat from this project, declaring that such a work 'would have no link with the past, and just for that reason would be of little practical use'.[49] These words should weigh heavily upon the mind of any theologian concerned with what Van Harvey memorably described as the 'intellectual marginality' of theology during the contemporary period.[50] One of the causes of this marginality, according to Harvey, was the fact that following Kant theology increasingly set aside an interest in the truth-relevant dimensions of religious

---

[47] See p. 41 in the present volume.

[48] A recent essay in *Faith and Philosophy* displays the kind of dual attention which I have in mind here. Jerome Gellman argues that the institution of *creedal confession* does not necessarily simply serve as an expression of propositional attitudes that the confessor actually holds; rather, another purpose of such confession is 'creating the *impression*, among and for religious adherents, that religious devotees *believe* the doctrines ... rather than accept them, and that their belief has unrestricted scope, rather than merely grouply-scope'. Gellman, 'Beyond Belief: On the Uses of Creedal Confession', *Faith and Philosophy*, 23 (July 2006), 310.

[49] *CF*, §30.1, p. 127.

[50] Van Harvey, 'The Intellectual Marginality of American Theology', in *Religion and Twentieth-Century American Intellectual Life* (Cambridge: CUP, 1989), 172–92.

doctrines, and in so doing rendered itself largely irrelevant to the concerns of actual religious persons. In fostering an interest in the metaphysical truth-content of religious doctrines, an 'analytic theology' movement might prove to be more than just an umbrella under which academic careers could be forged: it might regain the ear of sectors of the religious population which long ago lost interest in the productions of academic theologians, and so actually serve the 'mediating' function between religion and the intellectual world which Schleiermacher himself considered the business of theology. It is conceivable that those affiliated with such a movement might, ironically, pursue metaphysical reflection for a deeply Schleiermacherian reason: in order to remain in continuity with the convictions, concerns, and curiosities of actual religious individuals and communities, and thus serve as an intellectual catalyst within the collective, historically extended process known as religion.[51]

[51] I received much useful feedback from two conference sessions where this material was presented. The first was an American Academy of Religion Philosophy of Religion panel in Nov. 2005; the second, an American Philosophical Association (Central Division) session in Apr. 2006. Thanks are due to participants in those sessions, and also to Oliver Crisp, Randal Rauser, and Michael Rea for their suggestions.

7

How Philosophical Theology Became Possible within the Analytic Tradition of Philosophy

Nicholas Wolterstorff

I

Never since the late Middle Ages has philosophical theology so flourished as it has during the past thirty years. There have been intensive and extensive discussions by philosophers on such topics as the relation of God to evil, the precise nature of God's omnipotence, whether God knows what persons will freely do, whether or not God is eternal, impassible, simple, and so forth.

This flourishing has occurred within the analytic tradition of philosophy; thus far there has been no counterpart flourishing within the continental tradition. Recently there has been a 'turn to religion', as some have called it, within certain quarters of continental philosophy;[1] some philosophical theology proper has even appeared—witness the work of Jean-Luc Marion. But philosophical theology has not flourished there.

Before roughly 1960, there was very little philosophical theology being done anywhere; and if someone had asked, at any time during the first two-thirds of the twentieth century, which tradition showed more promise of nurturing philosophical theology, the continental or the analytic, the reasonable answer would surely have been the former. One might have expected, within the analytic tradition, some philosophical discussion of the human phenomenon of religion, but not philosophical discussions concerning God.

That is not how it turned out. Something happened to bring about this unexpected flourishing of philosophical theology within the analytic tradition. My project in this chapter is to identify what that was. My proposals will lead, quite naturally, to some suggestions as to why philosophical theology has not similarly flourished within the continental tradition; but I will leave it to

---

[1] See esp. the discussion by Hent de Vries, *Philosophy and the Turn to Religion* (Baltimore, Md.: Johns Hopkins University Press, 1999). See also John Caputo, *The Prayers and Tears of Jacques Derrida: Religion without Religion* (Bloomington, Ind.: Indiana University Press, 1997).

those whose knowledge of continental philosophy is more detailed than mine to develop these suggestions in detail—or to propose other explanations.

There are some who deny any particular significance to the flourishing of philosophical theology within the analytic tradition. It is rather often said by members of the continental tradition that these philosophical theologians have failed to absorb the significance of the Husserl–Heidegger–Derrida dialectic—or, reaching back farther yet, that they have failed to learn from Kant. It is said by others that their concern is irrelevant to our times: religion is disappearing from modernized societies. Or it is said that they are religious fundamentalists, employing the techniques of philosophy for apologetic purposes without displaying anything of the critical spirit of the true philosopher.

On this occasion I do not propose responding directly to these attempts to belittle the significance of the development that I will try to explain, though what I say will prove relevant to the issue. My central thesis will be that the flowering of philosophical theology was made possible by the surrender, by analytic philosophers, of certain assumptions characteristic of philosophy in the modern period, and by the emergence of a new understanding of the task of philosophy and its role in culture—an understanding that I myself find compelling. It is my impression that behind attempts to belittle the significance of the flourishing of analytic philosophical theology is almost always a refusal to surrender those traditional assumptions, and resistance to accepting this new self-understanding of the task and role of the philosopher. The critic's accusations of traditionalism are inspired by his own traditionalism!

II

Let me begin my explanatory narrative with the late 1950s, when I myself entered the ranks of professional philosophers. As I mentioned, there was then almost no philosophical theology. Logical positivism was dominant within analytic philosophy; and logical positivism, to understate the matter, made philosophical theology difficult. A logical positivist can analyze God-talk; some did. A few positivists even suggested that such speech has a certain value. But if positivism were true, genuine talk about God could occur only under conditions that are most unlikely ever to be satisfied. Of course, though logical positivism appeared to be in its prime in those days, it was in fact near death.

We all know why logical positivism made philosophical theology difficult if not impossible; the positivist criterion of meaning was the culprit. The positivist criterion of meaning claimed that for an utterance to make a genuine assertion, the content of the utterance must be either analytically true or false, or empirically verifiable. Philosophical theology, if there were to be such a thing, could include some sentences offering an analysis of one and another concept; for the most part, however, it would have to consist of assertions about God. And the criterion of meaning implied that there could be such assertions only if they were empirically verifiable. It was hard to see how, even in principle, it could be empirically verified that God exists and is simple, eternal, impassible, and so forth.

As it turned out, however, the positivists found it impossible to articulate, even to their own satisfaction, the concept of *empirical verifiability*; that inability proved to be their downfall. The death of the movement meant that a formidable obstacle to the development of philosophical theology had been removed from the scene.

In retrospect there was another obstacle, more imposing than the positivist criterion of meaning, that was removed at the same time. A persistent theme in classical modern philosophy, from John Locke onwards, has been that of the limits of the thinkable and the assertible. A distinctive feature of Kant's treatment of the theme was his thesis that if we could understand the origin of concepts, we would be in a position to discern those limits. Thus it was that Kant's views on the origin of concepts became a central ingredient in his reflections on whether or not philosophical theology can satisfy the conditions of thought and judgment, and thus whether or not it is possible. Logical positivism, with its criterion of meaning, should be seen as taking up once again the traditional topic of limits, focusing this time on the limits of the assertible, and treating it in a distinctly new, non-Kantian, way.

A consequence of the demise of logical positivism has proved to be that the theme of limits on the thinkable and the assertible has lost virtually all interest for philosophers in the analytic tradition. Of course, analytic philosophers do still on occasion charge people with failing to think a genuine thought or make a genuine judgment. But the tacit assumption has come to be that such claims will always have to be defended on an individual, *ad hoc*, basis; deep skepticism reigns among analytic philosophers concerning all grand proposals for demarcating the thinkable from the unthinkable, the assertible from the non-assertible. I submit that one of the reasons that philosophical theology has not flourished in the continental tradition is that continental philosophers, unlike their analytic counterparts, are still preoccupied with that traditional question of the classical modern philosophers: the limits of thought and judgment.

III

The collapse of the logical positivist thesis concerning the limits of the assertible and the emergence of widespread skepticism concerning all grand attempts to demarcate the thinkable and assertible from the unthinkable and non-assertible were not by themselves sufficient to make possible the flourishing of philosophical theology. An additional constraint had to be removed.

In earlier essays of mine I developed the thesis that it was characteristic of the Enlightenment philosophers to hold that theistic belief, to be rationally held, must be grounded in evidence, and that such evidence must ultimately consist of that of which one is certain; in particular, I said that Locke, at the beginning of the Enlightenment, and Kant, at the end, were of the conviction that religious belief has to be rationally grounded in this way if it is to be rationally held. I need scarcely add that it was taken for granted that if a belief is not rationally held, then it is not responsibly held.

I then contrasted this view with that of the medieval philosophers who, though they certainly held that theistic belief must be rationally grounded if it is to belong to *scientia*, did not hold that it must be rationally grounded just to be rationally—and thus responsibly—held. The medievals, so I argued, were working with a clear distinction between *scientia*, on the one hand, and everyday life, on the other. The theistic beliefs of everyday life can be rational, and thus responsible, without being rationally grounded in certitudes; perhaps they do not have to be rationally grounded at all, either in certitudes or in anything else, to be rationally and responsibly held. From there I went on to tell the story of the spread of skepticism in the modern world concerning the possibility of rationally grounding theistic beliefs in a fashion that satisfies the demands of the (classical) foundationalist.[2]

Some recent studies of Kant have convinced me that this story must be slightly revised.[3] I still think the story is correct in what it says about Locke. And I still think that a prominent strand in the intellectual culture of post-Enlightenment modernity has been that theistic belief, to be rationally and responsibly held, must be rationally grounded, and that it is now widely assumed by intellectuals that such grounding is lacking. Theism is irrational, so it is widely thought. But I now think that Kant's view was different and more subtle.

Kant's reading of Rousseau led him to be far more respectful of the beliefs of the ordinary person and of everyday life than Locke was, including, then, theistic beliefs. It came to be Kant's view, so it seems, that for the most part such beliefs are acceptable as they are, but that it is the calling of the philosopher to determine their epistemic status by determining to what extent and in what way they can be given an articulate justification or

---

[2] I develop the above story in detail in my 'The Migration of the Theistic Arguments: From Natural Theology to Evidentialist Apologetics', in R. Audi and W. J. Wainwright (eds.), *Rationality, Religious Belief and Moral Commitment* (Ithaca, NY: Cornell University Press, 1986).

[3] See e.g. Ch. 5 of the present volume.

grounding—it being taken for granted that such grounding must satisfy the conditions of classical foundationalism. Of course, a common reading of Kant has been that he showed, and saw himself as having showed, that theistic beliefs cannot be rationally grounded. That interpretation, I now think, is also mistaken. It was Kant's view that though they do not have the epistemic status of *knowledge,* they do nonetheless have the status of acceptable *belief, Glaube.*

For our purposes here, what is important to note about this story concerning the Enlightenment and its influence is that, when the positivist strictures on the limits of the assertible fell by the way, there remained the conviction, widespread among the intelligentsia, that though theistic language might well express genuine assertions, those assertions were epistemically deficient—not rational, not responsible—because they were not adequately grounded.

But then, in the 1960s, a development took place within analytic philosophy that had the effect of radically changing our thinking about these matters. I have in mind the emergence of meta-epistemology. Instead of simply taking for granted some epistemological theory and plunging ahead to discuss, within that theory, one and another specific epistemological question, philosophers took a step backwards in order to survey the whole field of structurally distinct epistemological theories. It was this survey, this excursion into meta-epistemology, that yielded the sharp and clear identification of foundationalism, more specifically, of classical foundationalism, as just one among other epistemological theories.

Though I think that this emergence of meta-epistemology within analytic philosophy was an extremely important development, I concede that its novelty can be exaggerated. The idealists of the nineteenth century recognized that they were working with epistemological assumptions significantly different from those of their predecessors; rather than using the metaphor of a foundation, they spoke of coherence. And it is now clear that, farther back yet, the eighteenth-century Scottish philosopher, Thomas Reid, had both identified the fundamental assumptions of classical foundationalism and attacked them mercilessly—though without ever giving the title of 'foundationalism' to what he had identified; he spoke instead of 'the Way of Ideas'.[4] Nonetheless, I think it safe to say that never before in the history of philosophy had topics in meta-epistemology been so vigorously debated in their own right, and never before had what is now called 'classical foundationalism' been so clearly identified as just one among other theoretical options and its basic premises so carefully articulated.

Those working in analytic meta-epistemology rather quickly drew two conclusions that are important for our purposes here, one historical and

---

[4] See my *Thomas Reid and the Story of Epistemology* (Cambridge: CUP, 2001).

one systematic. Their historical conclusion was that the implicit epistemology of most philosophers of the modern period, idealists such as Hegel excepted, has been classical foundationalism; their systematic conclusion was that classical foundationalism is untenable as a theory either of knowledge or of rational (responsible) belief.

Though meta-epistemology never became a topic in its own right within continental philosophy to the extent that it became that within analytic philosophy, nonetheless continental philosophers have also, for some time now, been questioning the basic assumptions of classical foundationalism. The focus of their critique has been different, however, from that of analytic philosophers. Behind the conviction of a classical foundationalist, such as John Locke, that our beliefs, if they are to count as knowingly or rationally held, must be grounded in certitudes, was the assumption that one is truly certain of something when and only when it is directly present to one—when one 'perceives' it, to use Locke's metaphor. I am certain that I am dizzy when and only when the fact that I am dizzy is directly present to me; I am certain that $7 + 5 = 12$ when and only when the fact that $7 + 5 = 12$ is directly present to me; and so forth. Continental philosophers have tended to focus their attack on classical foundationalism on the assumption that facts can be directly present to a person; presence, be it of facts or of entities of some other sort, is said to be impossible. Prominent in the arguments offered for this conclusion are Kantian assumptions concerning the nature of concepts and their role in thought.

Some analytic philosophers have likewise questioned the assumptions of classical foundationalists concerning presence, Wilfred Sellars and his followers being prominent among these. However, the great majority of analytic critics of classical foundationalism have not contested the foundationalist's assumption that things are present to us; the fact that a certain awareness is an awareness under concepts is not seen as implying that that of which one is thus aware is not present to one. It is mainly other aspects of the theory that have drawn the fire of analytic philosophers. They have argued that the theory is self-referentially incoherent, in the sense that holding the theory is not acceptable by the criterion that the theory itself offers for acceptable belief; it is acceptable to hold the theory only if the theory is false. And they have argued that the theory simply gives the wrong results. For example, nobody has ever succeeded in grounding perceptual and inductive beliefs in the way the theory requires; the theory implies, thus, that perceptual and inductive beliefs are unacceptable. But that's a *reductio ad absurdum*![5]

---

[5] On both points, see Alvin Plantinga, 'Reason and Belief in God', in A. Plantinga and N. Wolterstorff (eds.), *Faith and Rationality* (Notre Dame, Ind.: Notre Dame University Press, 1983); and Alvin Plantinga, *Warrant: The Current Debate* (Oxford: OUP, 1993).

Now suppose that, with these results in hand, one turns one's attention to theistic beliefs of the everyday. These beliefs, for the most part if not entirely, are not rationally grounded in a way that meets the demands of the classical foundationalist. Probably some are not rationally grounded at all; rather than being produced by argumentation, they have been evoked immediately by some experience. The demise of classical foundationalism means that if one thinks that such theistic beliefs are nonetheless irrational, or in some other way unacceptable, one can no longer appeal to the theory of classical foundationalism in support of one's conviction.

Of course, the person who holds theistic beliefs that do not measure up to the demands of classical foundationalism might himself have launched an argument against foundationalism from those very beliefs. Presumably he holds that his theistic beliefs are acceptable. So rather than starting from perceptual beliefs, inductive beliefs, and so forth, and arguing that foundationalism should be rejected because it implies the unacceptability of such obviously acceptable beliefs as those, he might have argued that foundationalism should be rejected because it implies the unacceptability of his theistic beliefs. But though the theist might in principle have conducted the argument in this way, obviously it is much more effective dialectically to begin with perceptual and inductive beliefs, since while there are many in our society who doubt the acceptability of theistic beliefs and are willing to go along with what classical foundationalism implies about their non-acceptability, there are few who would be willing to concede that perceptual and inductive beliefs are all unacceptable.

In principle some other epistemological theory might have gained wide and rapid acceptance once classical foundationalism had fallen to enemy fire; and this alternative theory might likewise have carried the implication that most theistic beliefs of the everyday are unacceptable. Nothing of the sort happened. Our present situation is that of extraordinary epistemological pluralism. Perhaps some of the epistemological theories favored by one and another philosopher carry the implication that theistic beliefs of the everyday are irrational or in some other way unacceptable; and let me say here, lest I be misunderstood, that surely some theistic beliefs of the everyday are unacceptable in one way or another. But it is my impression that many if not most of the epistemological theories that have gained the allegiance of one or more philosophers do not carry that implication. In any case, I think it is now widely accepted that the charge of irrationality against theistic beliefs will have to be made on an individual *ad hoc* basis; if one were to defend the charge by appealing to some general epistemological theory, usually it will be at least as rational for the believer to retain her conviction concerning the acceptability of her theistic belief and reject the theory, as to accept the theory and give up that conviction.

IV

The main question I am addressing here is, to repeat: what happened within analytic philosophy to account for the flourishing of analytic philosophical theology over the past third of a century? Thus far I have called attention to two developments: the emergence of widespread skepticism concerning all attempts to specify general conditions for the thinkable and the assertible; and the collapse of consensus concerning epistemological theory, in particular, consensus concerning any theory which implies that theistic beliefs are rational only if they are rationally grounded in certitudes.

Though the lifting of these two constraints was necessary for the flourishing of philosophical theology in the analytic tradition, clearly it was not sufficient. Also required was the existence of a substantial number of philosophers who thought it important to capitalize on the opportunity offered by this lifting of constraints—to capitalize on it by actually developing philosophical theology. Opening a door has no effect if no one walks through the open door.

We are touching here on a fundamental cultural difference between the United States, on the one hand, and Europe and such European outposts as Australia, on the other. Up to this point in my account of how philosophical theology became possible I have referred to developments in analytic philosophy in general. What must now be noted is that the flowering of philosophical theology that I have been discussing has occurred mainly in the United States, this in spite of the fact that analytic philosophy is at least as dominant in such places as England, Scandinavia, and Australia as it is in North America. The reason for the difference is obvious: the United States is far more religious than these other parts of the world—in particular, far more *theistically* religious. This holds for American intellectuals as well as for ordinary people. No doubt American intellectuals are more secular than Americans generally; nonetheless they are much more religious than their European counterparts. In short, the sociological fact that a good many American philosophers are theists, Christian and Jewish especially, has been a decisive factor in the flourishing of philosophical theology.

V

I have been speaking of 'philosophical theology' without making any attempt to explain what this discipline is. My assumption has been, and will continue to be, that the reader already knows well enough for my purposes what the discipline is. Instead, let me move on to characterize the particular sort of philosophical theology that has flourished over the past third of a century within analytic philosophy. I will focus my attention on one of its most distinctive characteristics; toward the end of my chapter I will highlight a few additional ones.

Analytic philosophical theologians have shown relatively little interest in providing rational grounding for their fundamental theistic convictions; in that way they are strikingly different from their medieval forebears. A few have offered arguments for God's existence; a good many have analyzed traditional arguments. But the dominant attitude has quite clearly been that nothing of any great epistemological importance hangs on whether or not one can give arguments for God's existence—more specifically, arguments whose premises are certain, or if not that, arguments of a sort such that philosophers in general will concede that there are no cogent objections to the arguments.

A traditional philosopher, and also, so I would guess, most contemporary continental philosophers, would be strongly inclined to respond to this development along the following lines. Let it be granted, for the sake of the argument, that theistic beliefs of the everyday, whether held by a philosopher or not, do not in general have to be rationally grounded in certitudes or shared principles in order to be rationally held. Let it even be granted that, in general, they do not require rational grounding of any sort whatsoever to be rationally held; some may be rationally held even though evoked immediately by experience. It does not follow that those philosophers who hold theistic beliefs have a right, without further ado, to import those beliefs into their philosophizing. Philosophy is not to be blurred into the life of the everyday. Philosophy is a public communal activity, proper participation in which requires that one justify what one says—justify it to one's fellow philosophers. And though it is true that a good many American philosophers are theists—that is a peculiarity of the United States—it is important to keep in mind that many, perhaps most, are not. Accordingly, the philosopher who is a believer has to justify to those of his fellow philosophers *who are not believers* what he says.

One of the repercussions of the demise of classical foundationalism, and of the subsequent emergence of epistemological pluralism, has been that most analytic philosophers no longer accept the picture of philosophy that this objection presupposes. The objection assumes that philosophy requires shared foundations. Locke and Kant alike assumed that those shared foundations must be certitudes. Though Kant's reading of Rousseau may have led him to be less judgemental than Locke in what he said about the epistemic status of the beliefs of the everyday, there can be no doubt that he was at one with Locke in regarding philosophy itself as a classically foundationalist enterprise.

I have already brought Thomas Reid's attack on classical foundationalism into the picture. Reid saw that his attack on classical foundationalism implied that philosophy itself could no longer be understood as a classically foundationalist enterprise; a new understanding of philosophy was required. The understanding Reid advocated was that, in addition to whatever may be certain for him, the philosopher is entitled to accept in his philosophical work what Reid called *The Principles of Common Sense*, these being what we all do and must take for granted in our lives in the everyday.

In our lives in the everyday, for example, we all do and must take for granted that perception is a reliable source of information concerning the external world, and that memory is a reliable source of information about one's prior experience. The philosopher, in his philosophical work, is entitled to accept those principles; it is not required of him that, before accepting them, he first establish their truth by reference to the deliverances of introspection and rational intuition. And if he is entitled to accept that perception and memory are reliable sources of information, then he is also entitled, in his philosophical work, to accept the deliverances of those faculties. Not all deliverances, obviously; we are all sometimes careless in our employment of our belief-forming faculties. It's the deliverances one is *entitled* to hold that one may employ in one's philosophical work.[6] Already at the end of the eighteenth century, Reid had launched a powerful attack on the picture of philosophy as a classically foundationalist enterprise and proposed an alternative.

I suggest that what has emerged in analytic philosophy over the past third of a century is a yet more radical break with philosophy's traditional self-understanding as a classically foundationalist enterprise. The new view is largely implicit. Not only has this new understanding of the task of the philosopher not gained acceptance by way of analytic philosophers all gathering around some major figure who has spelt out this new understanding; most analytic philosophers have not bothered to articulate this new understanding for themselves. They have assumed it.

Readers of this chapter will be acquainted with John Rawls's concept of public reason. Rawls held that when citizens of a liberal democracy debate fundamental political issues, they ought to conduct their debates and make their decisions by reference to a body of principles that they all agree on. Rawls called that body of principles, *public reason*. He thought that the principles constituting public reason could be extracted from the 'idea' of liberal democracy.

The history of philosophy shows that it is tempting to think of philosophy along similar lines. It's tempting to think that there is a body of principles that all philosophers do or should accept, call it *public philosophical reason* in distinction from *public political reason*; and that philosophers should appeal to the contents of public philosophical reason in arriving at philosophical conclusions for themselves and in trying to persuade their fellow philosophers

---

[6] I explain Reid's thought on these matters in my *Thomas Reid and the Story of Epistemology*.

of those conclusions. The classical foundationalist picture of the philosophical enterprise regarded the content of public philosophical reason as limited to certitudes; though Reid regarded the content of public philosophical reason as considerably more expansive, he shared with his predecessors the picture of philosophy as an enterprise based on public philosophical reason.

Few if any analytic philosophers any longer think of philosophy this way. In developing a position on some philosophical issue, the philosopher employs whatever considerations he finds true and relevant; he doesn't so much as raise the question whether these considerations belong to the content of public philosophical reason. Suppose he is a physicalist in his worldview. Depending on the topic under discussion, in his arguments he may employ distinctly physicalist considerations. He knows very well that many of his fellow philosophers do not share his physicalist views; he does not assume that that's because they have failed to discern that these physicalist considerations are an implication of public philosophical reason.

When moving beyond developing his views to presenting them to his fellow philosophers, he cites the considerations that he has found true and relevant. He hopes that some of his fellow philosophers will find his arguments sound. If some do find them sound, that will be because he has succeeded in highlighting, and exhibiting the implications of, something that he and they both agree on, however that agreement came about. It will not be because he has seen to it that the premises of his arguments have all been drawn from the content of public philosophical reason.

He will not be surprised to learn, on the other hand, that a good many of his fellow philosophers do not find his arguments sound. Some may find them not valid. Others will find them valid but not sound; they do not accept the premises. When addressing them, he may try to show that his conclusion is an implication of views they hold but that he does not share. Often he will see no hope of doing that. Philosophy as a whole is an ineradicably pluralist enterprise. It operates without public philosophical reason. The dialogue that takes place is a pluralist dialogue.

If one is going to make a contribution to philosophy that at least some of one's fellow philosophers recognize as a contribution, there must, of course, be a good many things that all parties to the discussion agree on. But these agreements that make possible what is recognized as a contribution to the discussion are both shifting and situation-specific—nothing like public philosophical reason, which would be the relevant appeal for all philosophical topics from age to age. Not long ago, classical foundationalism was taken for granted by most philosophers who were not idealists as providing the right account of warrant; now everyone takes it for granted that that is not the right account. And the topics that I can profitably discuss with physicalists are very different from those that I can profitably discuss with Christian philosophers, since the convictions I have in common with physicalists are very different from those that I have in common with Christians.

For want of a better term, call the picture of the philosophical enterprise that I have just sketched, *dialogic pluralism.* Philosophy is now widely assumed, by analytic philosophers, to be a dialogical pluralist enterprise.

Had this new picture of philosophy not emerged, the flourishing of philosophical theology would not have been possible. Or more precisely, the flourishing of philosophical theology in the form it has actually taken would not have been possible. For as I have already mentioned, attempts at rationally grounding theistic belief have been a relatively minor part of recent philosophical theology.

I would say that the closest historical precedent to this way of understanding philosophy was the tacit self-understanding of late antiquity. In the discussions among the Stoics, the Neoplatonists, the Aristotelians, the Skeptics, the Christians, no one, so far as I can see, assumed that there was anything like public philosophical reason. The members of the contesting schools simply met each other in the public arena and started discussing and arguing, using whatever arguments they could think of that they thought might prove effective with the party they were addressing, trying to ward off the arguments addressed to them. And when they wearied of argument, each went back to his own school and there, with the assistance of his co-believers, tried both to articulate his view in more detail and to bolster his case against the others. Analytic philosophy today is like that. Philosophical theology is one component in the pluralist mix—one participant in the dialogue.

VI

Let me conclude with an additional word about the overall character of the philosophical theology that has emerged. Analytic philosophical theology has been heavily ontological in its overall character—which implies that, had analytic philosophy in general been hostile to ontology, analytic philosophical theology would not have flourished in its present form. There have, of course, been movements within analytic philosophy that were hostile to ontology, logical positivism and Oxford ordinary-language philosophy being prime examples. But analytic philosophy overall has been ontology-friendly, especially early in its career, and now again recently.

It should be noted, however, that though analytic philosophical theology is very ontological in its overall character, it is nevertheless not an example of what is nowadays called *onto-theology*. The idea of 'onto-theology' was introduced by Kant in his *Critique of Pure Reason,* A632 = B660. Three characteristics stand out in Kant's explanation of what he has in mind.

First, in onto-theology one makes no appeal to revelation or anything else of the sort; one's conclusions are 'based...solely upon reason' (A631 = B659). Second, onto-theology is distinguished from *natural theology*, which is also based solely upon reason, in that onto-theology 'thinks its object...through pure reason, solely by means of transcendental concepts (*ens originarium, realissimum, ens entium*)', whereas natural theology thinks its object through concepts 'borrowed from nature'—for example, 'from the nature of our soul'. The former, says Kant, is called *deism*; the latter, *theism*.

[Deists] grant that we can know the existence of an original being solely through reason, but maintain that our concept of it is transcendental only, namely, the concept of a being which possesses all reality, but which we are unable to determine in any more specific fashion. [Theists] assert that reason is capable of determining its object more precisely through analogy with nature, namely, as a being which, through understanding and freedom, contains in itself the ultimate ground of everything else. Thus the deist represents this being merely as a *cause of the world*..., the theist as the *Author of the world*. (A 631–2 = B 659–60)

In present-day usage, influenced especially by Heidegger, the term 'onto-theology' refers to what Kant here calls *deism*. Kant himself, however, explained onto-theology as just one species of deism. Deism, says Kant, comes in two forms, *cosmo-theology* and onto-theology. Cosmo-theology 'proposes to deduce the existence of an original being from an experience in general', being unlike natural theology in not 'determining in any more specific fashion the nature of the world to which the experience belongs'. Clearly what Kant has in mind is deism supported by so-called cosmological arguments. Onto-theology, by contrast, 'believes that it can know the existence of such a being through mere concepts, without the help of any experience whatsoever' (A 632 = B 660). Though he does not say so, clearly it is deism based on ontological arguments that Kant has in mind here.

As I said above, philosophical theology as practiced by present-day analytic philosophers is not onto-theology—and it makes no difference whether one thinks of onto-theology as Kant's onto-theology, or whether one thinks of it as Kant's deism, onto-theology plus cosmo-theology. Whichever of these meanings one employs, it is not onto-theology for two reasons. The analytic philosophical theologian enters the philosophical discussion already holding that God exists and already believing a good many things about God. Whatever it was that led him to believe these things—perhaps revelation, perhaps induction into an ecclesiastical tradition—certainly his convictions are not based 'solely upon reason'. Second, his understanding of God is not confined to the sorts of attributes that Kant's deist ascribes to God but includes the sorts of attributes that Kant's theist ascribes to God.

It is my impression that philosophers in the continental tradition are still seriously debating the Kant–Heidegger question, whether it is possible for there to be a version of philosophical theology that is not onto-theology, in either sense of the term. The analytic philosopher regards that question as decisively settled in the affirmative: yes, such a philosophical theology is possible. It is not only possible but actual. It's true that many of the questions discussed in traditional cosmo-theology and onto-theology are now once again under discussion in analytic philosophical theology: is God simple, is God eternal, is God impassible, and so forth. But that is because most analytic philosophical theology is Anselmian theology, not because it is onto-theology (in the broad sense).

In characterizing it as Anselmian theology, I have two things in mind. Analytic philosophical theology has been almost entirely kataphatic rather than apophatic; negative theology has been no more than a minor strand. Second, and more relevantly, Anselm entered the philosophical dialogue as who he was: believing what he did believe, loving what he did love. He began with a prayer, asking God to grant him what was necessary for the task ahead, that task being to understand *that* God is and *who* God is. His motto was *credo ut intelligam*—borrowed from Augustine, who in turn borrowed it from Clement of Alexandria. It is a fine motto for most analytic philosophical theology of the past thirty years. It is even a rather good motto for most recent analytic philosophy in general!

VII

But is it philosophy, some ask. What I have been calling *analytic philosophical theology*—is it not theology rather than philosophy? *Theological* theology, if you will.

I judge that here we touch on one last point of contrast between contemporary analytic and contemporary continental philosophy. It is my impression that continental philosophers remain very much concerned to preserve and protect the distinctness of philosophy as an academic discipline, a *Wissenschaft*. Kant's anxiety is alive and well: given the progress of the 'positive' sciences, what is left for philosophy to do? That anxiety has largely disappeared from present-day analytic philosophy.

'Is it philosophy or is it theology?' What difference does it make, now that analytic philosophers no longer believe that for some piece of discourse to be a specimen of philosophy, the writer must base all his arguments on public philosophical reason? Call it what you will.

III

On the Data for Theology

Scripture, Reason, and Experience

8

On Understanding Scripture as the Word of God

Thomas McCall

INTRODUCTION

The Second Vatican Council states 'that the books of both the Old and New Testaments in their entirety, with all their parts, are sacred and canonical because written under the inspiration of the Holy Spirit, they have God as their author and have been handed on as such to the Church herself'.[1] *Dei Verbum* goes on to say that Holy Scripture has dual authorship; God is truly the author, and 'God chose men and while employed by Him they made use of their powers and abilities, so that with Him acting in them and through them, they, as true authors, consigned to writing everything and only those things which He wanted'.[2] The document continues by affirming the trustworthiness of scripture, for 'since everything asserted by the inspired authors or sacred writers must be asserted by the Holy Spirit, it follows that the books of Scripture must be acknowledged as teaching solidly, faithfully and without error that truth which God wanted put into sacred writings'.[3] Thus 'the Sacred Scriptures contain the word of God and since they are inspired really are the word of God'.[4]

In saying that scripture really *is* the word of God, *Dei Verbum* reaffirms the traditional (or what we could call the 'classical') view of scripture.[5] Accordingly, scripture has what have been termed 'divine' properties (e.g. purity, holiness, perfection, truthfulness) in addition to those properties that

---

[1] *Dei Verbum: Dogmatic Constitution on Divine Revelation, Solemnly Promulgated by His Holiness, Pope Paul VI on November 18, 1965* (Boston: Pauline Books and Media, 1965), 9.
[2] Ibid.
[3] Ibid.
[4] Ibid. 16.
[5] I do not mean to flatten out or gloss over the real and important differences within the Christian tradition on issues of the nature and authority (not to mention interpretation) of scripture. Nor do I intend to pass judgment on the extent to which Vatican II modifies its heritage on the doctrine of scripture. Still, it seems clear enough to me that there is enough agreement on this to refer to it as the traditional or classical view.

it has in virtue of being a book written and edited by human authors.[6] Inspired by God, the Bible *is* the trustworthy revelation of God. It is *Holy Scripture* because it just *is* the Word of God.

Many modern theologians disagree, however, and Karl Barth's view has emerged as an important and influential alternative to the classical view. He does not endorse what is often loosely called a 'progressive' or 'liberal' view of scripture.[7] He does not think that the Bible *contains* or *reflects* the Word of God. And he surely does not think that it is merely the record of some important religious experiences! But nor does he endorse the traditional view, and indeed he is critical of it. Instead, he is convinced that scripture really *is* the Word of God—but only in the 'event' that it *becomes* so.

In this chapter I engage Barth's proposal. Although I sometimes find his arguments less than compelling and his own proposal less than satisfying, I offer these criticisms with a great deal of respect. I think that 'kerygmatic' theologians such as Barth have much to teach analytic theologians, and I hope that philosophical theologians will heed Barth's advice to listen to the Word of God. In this chapter, however, I work toward another goal: I seek to show how Barth's own concerns might be addressed by the use of analytic tools. Making use of recent developments in analytic philosophy of language, I argue throughout that the theologian who shares Barth's fundamental theological commitments can—and indeed should—hold to the classical view.

KARL BARTH ON THE NATURE OF HOLY SCRIPTURE

Barth's 'Actualist' Doctrine of the Word of God

George Hunsinger helpfully outlines six major motifs of Barth's theology.[8] These are particularism, objectivism, personalism, realism, rationalism, and

---

[6] On the 'divinity' of Scripture as understood by the Reformed scholastics (in the context of late medieval and Reformation understandings), see Richard A. Muller, *Post-Reformation Reformed Dogmatics: The Rise and Development of Reformed Orthodoxy, ca. 1520 to ca. 1725*, ii. *Holy Scripture: The Cognitive Foundation of Theology*, 2nd edn. (Grand Rapids, Mich.: Baker Academic, 2003), 295–370.

[7] I use the term 'liberal theology' in this context as does David Tracy, *Blessed Rage for Order: The New Pluralism in Theology* (San Francisco: Harper & Row, 1988), 25–7.

[8] Hunsinger sees these motifs 'as adjectival in force, not substantive': *How to Read Karl Barth: The Shape of his Theology* (Oxford: OUP, 1991), 31. He denies that Barth imports these as systematic principles around which theology must be structured; instead he thinks that Barth uses them 'because he thinks that they help to illuminate certain peculiar modes of thought implicit in the witness of Scripture'. 'Particularism' refers us to Barth's relentless focus on Jesus Christ; to his insistence that any knowledge we might have of God comes not from philosophical

actualism. 'Actualism' is what Hunsinger calls 'the most distinctive and difficult of the motifs'.[9] Although the concept is as slippery as it is important to Barth, perhaps a brief description will help us gain a conceptual foothold. As Hunsinger describes it, actualism 'at the most general level... means that (Barth) thinks primarily in terms of events and relationships rather than monadic or self-contained substances'.[10] Characteristic of Barth's theology is his repeated (and forceful) insistence that 'God's being is in his act and his act in his being.' At first blush, this might sound much like Thomas Aquinas's claims that God is *actus purus* and that God can be known according to the analogy of being, but in reality Barth means something quite different. For Barth does not seem to be attracted to—or even all that interested in—Aquinas's doctrine of divine simplicity; while on the other hand, he insists that the *analogia entis* is the 'invention of the Antichrist'.[11] For theology (proper), actualism is of decisive importance: there is no God other than or behind the back of the God revealed in the event of Jesus Christ, there is no substance called 'divinity'. God's being is his act, and his act is his being. There is no other God than the One revealed to us in the Christ-event.

And as with God, so of course it is also true with respect to God's act, God's 'event', and God's Word. Barth works to 'actualize' the doctrine of the Incarnation.[12] As Bruce L. McCormack explains it,

this emphasis on the 'becoming' of the hypostatic union... is intended to supplant a conception of the hypostatic union by means of a traditional ontology of being that is controlled by the category of 'substance.' It was attachment to the category of 'substance' that, historically, caused the terms brought into relation in Christology (viz., 'God' and the 'human') to be defined in static terms rather than in terms appropriate to the lived actuality of their union.[13]

inquiry but from and through the action of God in Jesus Christ. 'Objectivism' points us to Barth's break with theological liberalism and his resolute belief that our knowledge of God and our salvation come from beyond us. 'Personalism' is reflected in Barth's 'I–Thou' language, and it refers to his conviction that God is ultimately a 'Subject'—not *something* that we might treat as an object. Barth's 'Realism' is his belief that God exists in reality and can be referred to rightly in the *analogia fidei*, while his 'Rationalism' is his insistence that, in the miracle of the revelatory event, those who receive revelation are enabled to speak rationally of him. For further discussion of these issues (by an analytic theologian), see Jay Wesley Richards, *The Untamed God: A Philosophical Exploration of Divine Perfection, Simplicity, and Immutability* (Downers Grove, Ill.: InterVarsity Press, 2003), 115–16.

[9] Hunsinger, *How to Read Barth*, 30.
[10] Ibid. 31.
[11] Karl Barth, *Church Dogmatics: The Doctrine of the Word of God*, I/1, tr. G. W. Bromiley (Edinburgh: T&T Clark, 1975), p. xiii.
[12] Ibid. IV/2, 195–6.
[13] Bruce L. McCormack, 'The Being of Holy Scripture is in its Becoming: Karl Barth in Conversation with American Evangelical Criticism', in Vincent Bacote, Laura C. Miguelez, and Dennis E. Ockholm (eds.), *Evangelicals and Scripture: Tradition, Authority, and Hermeneutics* (Downers Grove, Ill.: InterVarsity Press, 2004), 64 n. 12.

Barth rejects such 'static' and 'abstract' essentialism in favor of a more 'dynamic' actualism.[14] He also extends this to scripture, and he wants an actualist account of the 'written' Word as well. Jesus Christ *is* the 'revealed' or 'living Word', and we are to understand the other modes or 'forms' of revelation (the Bible as the 'written' Word as well as the 'Word preached') as directly analogous to this revelation. Notably, the written Word is both human and divine, and the divinity and the humanity are never to be either separated or confused.

So Barth sees the Word of God (both living or 'revealed' as well as written) through the lens of his actualism.[15] Holy Scripture has its being only in its becoming. McCormack interprets Barth's position as entailing two important consequences:

first, what the Bible *is,* is defined by the will of God as expressed in his act of giving it to the church. And this means that where and when the Bible *becomes* the Word of God, it is only becoming what it already is. But, second, where and when the Bible does *not* become the Word of God, there God has chosen provisionally, for the time being, not to bear witness to himself in and through its witness *to this particular reader or set of readers of it.* This changes nothing whatsoever as to the true nature of the Bible as defined by the divine will which came to expression in the giving of the Bible to the church. It only means that God does not will, for the time being, that the Bible should *become* what it is for these readers.[16]

Now all of this is a mouthful, and its meaning is something less than obvious. What Barth is replacing and avoiding is fairly clear: he is rejecting a 'static' or essentialist doctrine of scripture in favor of an account that stresses the sovereignty of God and the particularity and actuality of God's revelation in a more radical way. But, as we shall see, what Barth is actually replacing the traditional 'static' and essentialist doctrine *with* is not quite so clear.

Barth's View: Puzzles and Problems

Barth insists that the Bible 'becomes God's Word in this event, and in the statement that the Bible is God's Word, the little word "is" refers to its being in becoming'.[17] McCormack understands Barth to be saying that

---

[14] This does not mean that Barth rejects all of the traditional terms; far less does it mean that he intentionally rejects Chalcedonian orthodoxy.

[15] McCormack states that, for Barth, his 'understanding of the being-in-becoming of Holy Scripture was a function of his commitment to the being-in-becoming of the God-human, his actualizing of the doctrine of the incarnation, which brought in its wake the necessity of affirming the being-in-becoming of the Trinity, of human beings, and, ultimately, of everything that is'. Ibid. 64.

[16] Ibid. 66; emphasis original.

[17] Barth, *Church Dogmatics*, I/1, 110.

the Bible must *become* what it is. And this is a becoming whose actualization rests solely on the divine discretion. The being-in-becoming of the Bible as the Word of God that took place *there* and *then* under the experience of inspiration must take place in the *here* and *now*, so that the being-in-becoming of the Bible here and now is made to correspond to the originating being-in-becoming.[18]

But what does it mean to say that 'Scripture really is the Word of God, but only so in the event where it continually becomes what it actually is'? What does it mean to say that 'where and when the Bible *becomes* the Word of God, it is only becoming what it already is'?[19] And what does it mean to say both that the Bible just *is* the Word of God while also saying that at particular times and places 'the Bible *for this person or set of persons* is not, in that moment, the Word of God'?[20] Barth is saying that scripture truly *is* the Word of God—irrespective of our reception or recognition of it—while also insisting that sometimes it is *not* the Word of God.[21]

But we have very little idea of what this really means. He could consistently claim that scripture potentially *contains* or *reflects* the Word of God (in the event of revelation); it seems clear enough that he could say in a loose sense that scripture sometimes becomes (and sometimes does not become) something that it previously was not. But Barth wants to say more. As Bernard Ramm puts it, 'Barth does believe that Holy Scripture is the Word of God in itself.'[22] Barth wants to say that scripture truly *is* the Word of God while still insisting on the primacy of divine action, but his actualism actually appears to hurt him here. Taken as a claim to the sober truth, it makes little sense to talk about scripture *becoming* what it already *is*, and it makes even less sense to speak of scripture *not being* or *not becoming* what it truly *is*. At best it is both mysterious and opaque.

One possible—albeit extreme—way of reading Barth is to see him as positing some sort of occasionalism. In offering this as a possible reading of Barth, I am not suggesting that he is in any way dependent on Malebranche, Berkeley, Edwards, or other prominent occasionalists (nor, for that matter, does what I say rest in any way on assumptions about influence). Instead, I am merely suggesting that Barth's heavy emphasis on divine sovereignty in the event of revelation leads him toward something that looks much like occasionalism. The thought that Barth holds an occasionalist doctrine of scripture may sound initially implausible, but it is a possible interpretation of his doctrine.

[18] McCormack, 'The Being of Holy Scripture', 71.
[19] Ibid. 66.
[20] Ibid. 70.
[21] On Barth's denial that the being of scripture as the Word of God depends in any way on our reception of it, see e.g. *Church Dogmatics*, I/1, 110.
[22] Bernard Ramm, *After Fundamentalism: The Future of Evangelical Theology* (San Francisco: Harper & Row, 1983), 120.

Following Alfred J. Freddoso's characterization of occasionalism, we can see that for our purposes it may be summarized as follows:

> (O1) For any state of affairs p and time t, if (i) there is any substance that causally contributes to p's obtaining at t and (ii) no created substance is a free cause of p at t, then God is a strong active cause of p at t.[23]
>
> (O2) No material substance has any active or passive causal power at all.[24]

Freddoso is clear about the theological motivation for this theory as it was put forth by Malebranche, Berkeley, and Biel: it is

> not any abstract metaphysical qualm about how one and the same effect might be immediately produced by both God and a creature; nor is it a relatively narrow worry about essentialism's ruling out a certain fairly small class of miracles. It is, instead, the sweeping and startling conviction that the attribution of *any* power at all (especially any active power) to *any* corporeal substance is not only unnecessary but blasphemous, not only philosophically confused but downright idolatrous.[25]

Freddoso is describing the views of Malebranche, Berkeley, and Biel, but his characterization of their theological motivation resonates with Barth's concerns about divine revelation. Barth is also exercised to deny that, apart from the action of God in Christ, there could be *any* human contribution to divine revelation, and he is resolutely opposed to the idea that any causal power rests in the Bible itself (or, to use Barth's characteristic phrase, 'in itself and as such'). Barth may not care about just 'any' power being attributed to just 'any' substance, but when he talks about scripture and the Word of God he certainly seems to think that *the Bible* has absolutely no causal power. For Barth, the Bible as such certainly has no *active* causal power (at least none worth talking about). Nor does it have any *passive* causal power, for its finitude does not pose a barrier to or impose limitations upon the divine revelatory act. Furthermore, Barth seems to be insisting that God indeed *is* the strong active cause of the written Word in the event of revelation. The Bible as such surely has nothing to do with it—for God could just as easily have used 'Russian Communism, a flute concerto, a blossoming shrub, or a dead dog'.[26]

---

[23] Alfred J. Freddoso, 'Medieval Aristotelianism and the Case Against Secondary Causation in Nature', in Thomas V. Morris (ed.), *Divine and Human Action: Essays in the Metaphysics of Theism* (Ithaca, NY: Cornell University Press, 1988), 83. Freddoso defines 'a strong active cause' thus: 'S is a strong active cause of p at $t =$ df (i) S is an active cause of p at t, and (ii) no substance distinct from S is an active cause of p at t' and he further defines 'an active cause' as one in which: '(i) S causally contributes to p's obtaining at t, and (ii) S's causal contribution to p's obtaining at t is at least in part active' (p. 80).

[24] Ibid. 97.

[25] Ibid.; emphasis original.

[26] Barth, *Church Dogmatics*, I/1, 55.

Barth does not deny the reality of secondary causality generally.[27] So if he is an occasionalist, then surely he is an occasionalist only at this point. Thus he would be what we might call an 'Impure Occasionalist' (his occasionalism would extend only to his doctrine of the Word). But if Barth endorses occasionalism only at this point, then it is hard to see how it might be true that Barth thinks of all of revelation, and indeed *all of reality*, 'out of a center in Christology'. If so, then his account of the threefold-form of the Word of God would be in jeopardy, for his doctrine of scripture would be at odds with what he says about the 'revealed Word' (Christ). Or suppose that his occasionalism does extend to Christology; then we are faced with the accompanying worries about Christology. For according to occasionalism there is no mundane causation, thus—if Barth were to be understood as endorsing occasionalism with respect to Christology—the human nature of Christ would have no causal powers. This would threaten to make his Christology at least functionally docetic, and surely Barth is no docetist!

Furthermore, and more importantly, occasionalism does not seem very promising for Barth's theology. For on his doctrine of revelation, the revealed Word is never *logos asarkos*. The revealed Word is never without flesh, it is never separated from the humanity of the man Jesus. But, on Barth's account, the written Word sometimes *is* separated from the humanity of the Bible, for sometimes the Bible does not 'become' what it 'is'. If this is so, then Barth again loses his ability to appeal to the 'threefold form of the Word'. Moreover, according to Barth's own Christology, in Jesus Christ the revealed Word the human nature indeed *is* causally active, for the Word of God is seen in the 'humanity of God'.[28] If the humanity of the God-man is *not* causally active, then Barth loses his claim to 'Chalcedonian' Christology.[29] On the other hand, if the humanity of the God-man *is* causally active while the humanity of scripture is not, then Barth loses traction in his argument for the threefold form of the Word. Neither way looks all that promising as a way ahead for Barth.

A Speech-Act Reading of Barth

But perhaps there is another way of understanding Barth's claim that 'the being of Scripture is in its becoming'. Maybe he means nothing so drastic as

---

[27] e.g. ibid. II/2. *The Doctrine of God*, 99–100.

[28] Karl Barth, *The Humanity of God* (Philadelphia: John Knox Press, 1960).

[29] On this see George Hunsinger, 'Karl Barth's Christology: Its Basic Chalcedonian Character', in his *Disruptive Grace: Studies in the Theology of Karl Barth* (Grand Rapids, Mich.: William B. Eerdmans Publishing Co., 2000), 131–47.

the ontological revolution ascribed to him by McCormack; perhaps Kevin J. Vanhoozer is right that analytic philosophy of language (especially speech-act theory) can help us make sense of Barth's view.[30] According to Vanhoozer, Barth can be understood as claiming that

> the Bible *is* the Word of God insofar as its inspired witnesses—which is to say the inspired locutions and illocutions—really do present Jesus Christ. Yet the Bible also *becomes* the Word of God when its illumined readers receive and grasp the subject matter by grace through faith, which is to say, when the Spirit enables what we might call illocutionary uptake and perlocutionary efficacy. The full measure of Scripture as a communicative act of God, then, involves the-Spirit-testifying-about-Jesus-through-Scripture-to-the-church.[31]

On this reading of Barth, scripture just *is* God's Word (at least with respect to locution and illocution), but the divine speech act is incomplete without the perlocutionary work of the Holy Spirit.

If Vanhoozer's reading of Barth—which strikes me as both charitable and sensible—is viable, then what Barth says might well be compatible with the classical view. If so, then we are to understand that Barth's language, provocative as it is, really refers to what traditionally has been called the Holy Spirit's work of illumination. Barth is not, on this reading, so much making startling claims about the ontology of Holy Scripture as much as he is reminding us that revelation is the work of the triune God. His point is that revelation is the action of the God who is sovereign, and we can never presume upon it; we can never take it for granted, as if it simply waits for us to accept or reject it at our leisure and according to our whims. Vanhoozer recognizes that 'whether Barth would in fact be happy to view the Word of God as *bound* to the text is, of course, ultimately beyond our ability to say', nevertheless, he argues 'that, thanks to the speech act concepts, he *could* do so consistently'.[32]

I do not claim to know whether or not Vanhoozer's proposal would have been acceptable to Barth. I surely hope so, for I think that the puzzles and problems that attach themselves to the other interpretations are both obvious enough and severe enough that we should opt for a charitable reading such as this one. On this reading, Barth's account seems compatible with the classical doctrine; indeed, it seems to fit well. If so, then his distinctive contribution

---

[30] Kevin J. Vanhoozer, 'A Person of the Book? Barth on Biblical Authority and Interpretation', in Sung Wook Chung (ed.), *Karl Barth and Evangelical Theology: Convergences and Divergences* (Grand Rapids, Mich.: Baker Academic, 2006), 26–59.

[31] Ibid. 57. On speech-act theory, see esp. J. L. Austin, *How to Do Things with Words*, 2nd edn. (Cambridge, Mass.: Harvard University Press, 1975); John Searle, *Speech Acts: An Essay in the Philosophy of Language* (Cambridge: CUP, 1969).

[32] Vanhoozer, 'A Person of the Book?', 58.

would be a strong emphasis on what traditionally has been referred to as 'illumination'. There is an important sense in which the Bible *is*—'in itself and as such'—the Word of God, but there is also an important sense in which it takes a divine act for the Bible to *become* the Word of God. Divine revelation is always *God's* action, even given the existence of the written Word, and it is ultimately up to him whether or not he reveals himself to human persons. Christians can, on this reading, accept with gratitude Barth's timely reminders of the sheer gratuity of revelation.

Unfortunately, however, I am dubious about the prospects for reception of any reading of Barth that brings it in line with the traditional view without taking into account the criticisms raised by Barth. I do not have much confidence that those theologians attracted to Barth's account will find this proposal attractive (at least initially), for it raises again the worries of Barth about the classical view. So unless there is some way to meet Barth's objections, I doubt very much that a speech-act reading of Barth will be congenial to Barth's admirers and defenders.

BARTH AND THE CLASSICAL VIEW AGAIN

Barth Against the Classical View

Barth's principal objection to the classical view seems to be this: it compromises the sovereignty of the Word of God. As Barth sees it, to call scripture the Word of God—to say that the Bible *has* essential 'divine' properties and thus *is* the Word of God—is to say that the Word of God is in a position where it is in the possession of men and women. But for Barth this simply cannot be— the Word is, after all, *God's* Word, and surely *God* can never be in the possession of men and women:

> that the Bible is the Word of God cannot mean that with other attributes the Bible has the attribute of being the Word of God. To say that would be to violate the Word of God which is God Himself—to violate the freedom and sovereignty of God. God is not an attribute of something else, even if this something else is the Bible.[33]

As McCormack says, Barth's refusal to ever speak of revelation as in any sense the possession of men and women is at least partially motivated by his desire to 'locate revelation in a "place" that would make it immune from domestication by humans (with all the terrible consequences, political and otherwise, that such domestication brought in its wake)'.[34]

[33] Barth, *Church Dogmatics*, I/2, 513.
[34] McCormack, 'The Being of Holy Scripture', 62.

The Word is not, for Barth, something in our possession or at our disposal. It is not, nor can it be, something that we can either decide to recognize or to ignore. As the Word of God—*because* it is the Word of *God*—it cannot be something that we can handle or mishandle, something that we either can accept or reject at will. The Word of *God* is sovereign over us, and *God* decides when, how, and if the Bible will become his Word: 'the fact that God's own address becomes an event in the human word of the Bible is, however, God's affair and not ours'.[35] It comes to us as God's address—if it comes at all—when God decides that it will do so. Thus scripture *becomes* the Word of God in the event of revelation, and when it does 'the Word which was spoken and will be spoken again by God stands over against it afresh in strict sovereignty'.[36]

And when, in the event of revelation, scripture becomes the Word at the sovereign command of God, it does so by 'claiming and commandeering' humanity.[37] When this happens, 'neutrality towards the Word of God is impossible'; we are not at liberty to accept or reject, to coolly weigh the options before deciding if we will accept or reject, obey or disobey.[38] No, when God makes scripture God's Word in the event of revelation, God does so in a sovereign way. God leaves us with 'only one possibility: the possibility of obedience'.[39] McCormack insists that there is 'nothing defensive about the move he was making in the least'.[40] As McCormack sees things, it is not as if Barth is cowering before the results of two centuries of biblical criticism and desperately trying to recover a 'safe' place for the Bible. Rather, Barth's insistence that the scripture can only be said to *be* the Word of God in the event of its *becoming* so is grounded in a fundamental theological commitment. When Barth insists that we give 'the Bible poor and unwelcome honor if we equate it directly with this other, with revelation itself', he is moving forward with boldness, not mounting a rearguard apologetic action from a position of retreat.[41]

Vanhoozer points out that Barth's stance here is 'not that of the skeptic, but (that) of the prophet'.[42] Barth is convinced that the traditional doctrine of scripture makes the Word out to be an object; more precisely, the classical view reduces scripture to an object *at our disposal*. Identifying scripture with the Word of God (in the traditional sense) reduces the Word of God to a

---

[35] Barth, *Church Dogmatics*, I/1, 109.
[36] Ibid. I/1, 141, cf. p. 206.
[37] Ibid. I/1, 152.
[38] Karl Barth, 'The Christian Understanding of Revelation', in Barth, *Against the Stream: Shorter Postwar Writings 1946–1952* (New York: Philosophical Library, 1954), 215.
[39] Ibid.
[40] McCormack, 'The Being of Holy Scripture', 64.
[41] Barth, *Church Dogmatics*, I/1, 112.
[42] Vanhoozer, 'A Person of the Book?', 41.

thing—it portrays the Word of God as a thing that can be either picked up or put down, something that can be either taken or left, accepted or rejected, handled or mishandled, revered and cherished or desecrated and destroyed. But this simply cannot be, for the Word of God is, well, *God's* Word. Rather, God's sovereign appropriation of scripture in the event where God makes it God's own Word is always *God's* action. Thus Barth sees his doctrine as

> an absolute barrier against reducing its wording to a human system or using its wording to construct a human system. (For) it would not be God's faithfulness but His unfaithfulness to us if he allowed us to use His Word in this way. This would mean His allowing us to gain control over His Word, to fit it into our designs, and thus to shut up ourselves against Him to our own ruin.[43]

And since the classical doctrine takes just this fatal step in identifying scripture with the Word of God, it must be rejected for a better alternative.

The speech-act reading of Barth runs squarely into this objection. I cannot see how appeal to speech-act theory helps at all on this point. For the locution and illocution in fact *do remain* in our hands. The locution and illocution *are* in our hands as an object at our disposal. Even though the perlocutionary effects are ultimately out of our hands and beyond us, the very Word of God (God's own locution and illocution) is ours, it is in our possession to do with as we please. It can be picked up or thrown down, received and cherished or rejected and destroyed. For Barth, surely this is not acceptable. So the sovereignty objection must be faced.

Why Barth Should Embrace the Classical View

Barth is in his most prophetic form here, and, for many Christians, there is an undeniable appeal in his position. Much of the appeal dissipates, however, when we take seriously Barth's insistence that we formulate and understand our doctrine of the written Word in light of our understanding of the 'revealed' and living Word. As Nicholas Wolterstorff points out, 'If it is indeed a limitation on God's freedom that God would commission a human being to speak "in the name of" God, then perhaps we have to take seriously the possibility that God is willing on occasion to limit God's freedom in that way—or alternatively, consider the possibility that we are working with an alien and inapplicable concept of freedom'.[44] Wolterstorff's point is well taken; if God wants to limit his freedom in such a way, who are we to say that this is

---

[43] Barth, *Church Dogmatics*, I/1, 139.
[44] Nicholas Wolterstorff, *Divine Discourse: Philosophical Reflections on the Claim that God Speaks* (Cambridge: CUP, 1995), 74.

not either possible or appropriate? Indeed, on Barth's own advice—that we should look to the Incarnation of the 'revealed' Word to better understand divine intent and action—it seems that this is exactly what God has done.

For what Barth fears to say about the written Word is exactly what the Christian believer must say about the *living* Word.[45] Central to the orthodox Christian belief in Jesus is the conviction that, in the Incarnation, the living Word gave himself over to humanity. The living Word put himself at our disposal. The action of the living Word is surely *God's* action, as such it is right to affirm with Barth that it is a sovereign action. But—on Barth's own doctrine of the Incarnation—the Word became flesh and allowed himself to be either taken or left, accepted or rejected, handled or mishandled. Did not the incarnate Word—for Barth the last, ultimate, and 'only' Word of God—allow himself to be either revered and cherished or desecrated and destroyed? Indeed he did. This is—on Barth's own account—what God incarnate reveals to us about the being and actions (or, if we prefer the Barthian language, the being-in-act and act-in-being) of God.

We are, according to Barth's own theology, to affirm that it is in Christ that we see the revelation of God. We are, on Barth's own dictum, to understand all other forms or modes of revelation in this light. Thus we are, in McCormack's words, to 'start with Christology' and allow 'the conclusions drawn there to control what can and should be said subsequently about Holy Scripture as the second form of the one Word of God'.[46] And, in affirming the doctrine of the Incarnation, orthodox Christians—Barthian and otherwise—express the conviction that the person Jesus Christ *is* the Word of God. They confess that the 'Word *became* flesh'. They say that, given the Incarnation, the Word *is* the man Jesus—and not so just on state occasions![47] Orthodox Christians actually *deny* that Jesus Christ sometimes *becomes*—but sometimes does *not become*—the living Word. Given this, orthodox Christians thus say that Christ put himself at our disposal—they affirm that he allowed himself to be objectified and finally rejected.[48] If we can (and should) affirm this of the 'revealed', living, and incarnate Word, why would we insist on refraining from affirming it also of the written Word? It seems to me that, on Barth's own theological principles, we not only can affirm that scripture *is* the written Word of God but also *should* do so. If this is the extent of Barth's objection from divine sovereignty, then there seems to be little reason to find it persuasive. It should

---

[45] I am grateful to J. Mark Beach for helpful dialogue on this point.

[46] McCormack, 'The Being of Holy Scripture', 63.

[47] It seems that Barth, with his denial of the *logos asarkos*, would have all the more reason to make this affirmation.

[48] For a helpful discussion of Barth's insistence on the 'vulnerability' of the Word to rejection, see Hunsinger, *How to Read Barth,* 84–5.

CONFUSING THE NATURES? CHRISTOLOGY REVISITED

But perhaps this is too quick. Maybe what I've said here misses some important aspects of Barth's project. More specifically, perhaps it overlooks some important Christological issues. Maybe there is another objection in the area.

Another Objection?

McCormack states that on Barth's view 'Holy Scripture is like the unity of God and man in Jesus Christ. It is neither divine only or human only. Nor is it a mixture of the two nor a *tertium quid* between them.'[49] He goes on to say that 'the "union" of the divine and the human in Scripture does not result in the divinization of the human element any more than it does in the case of Christ's humanity. If Christ's humanity is true humanity—and it is—then the hypostatic union may not be thought to result in a divinization of the human nature.'[50] And as in Christology, so also with respect to scripture.

The lesson drawn by McCormack is this:

at this point it has to be frankly acknowledged that Barth's denial that the Bible has either an intrinsic or permanently bestowed capacity to be an adequate bearer of the Word of God is, in large measure, simply a function of the Reformed character of his Christology. If there was a constant in Reformed treatments of the person of Christ, it was that the divine and human natures of Christ remain distinct and unimpaired in their original integrity *after* their union in one Person.[51]

And since 'the human nature of Christ is not divinized through the hypostatic union, how much less are the human words of the prophets and apostles divinized through the sacramental union by which God joins them to the Word of God'.[52]

The precise nature of this objection is far from clear, but the general worry seems to be that an important Christological norm is violated by equating scripture with the written Word of God. It appears to be something like this:

---

[49] McCormack, 'The Being of Holy Scripture', 68.   [50] Ibid.
[51] Ibid. 70.   [52] Ibid.

(1) To confuse either the divinity of Christ with the humanity of Christ or the 'divinity' of scripture with the 'humanity' of scripture is to commit a grave theological error.

(2) The classical view confuses the 'divinity' of scripture with the 'humanity' of scripture.

(3) Therefore, the classical view commits a grave theological error.

Or in other words, an orthodox Christology (at least a 'Reformed' account) demands something like Barth's view of scripture. But I think that there is reason to doubt that this argument (even if it could be adequately clarified) is successful: the defender of the classical view can quite easily deny (2).

Meeting the Objection

For according to classical Christology, the properties of the distinct natures are to be predicated of the *Person*. And, on Barth's own view, the Person is directly analogous to the Bible. So even though the natures remain distinct, the properties of each nature are rightly attributed to the person—and, in the case of scripture, to the book. Assuming (with Barth) that 'Reformed' Christology is in line with classical, Chalcedonian orthodoxy, it is not hard to see this illustrated.[53] As Thomas Aquinas puts it, 'those things that belong to the divine nature are predicated of Christ in His Divine Nature, and those that belong to the human nature truly are predicated of Christ in His human nature'.[54] So the two natures remain distinct, but the properties of both natures are predicated *of Christ*. While we do not say that the divine nature of Christ was vulnerable, we *do affirm* that the *person* of the Son—*the Word*—indeed was vulnerable.[55] And if we do not hesitate to say this about the

---

[53] I take this to be a safe assumption. See David Willis-Watkins, *Calvin's Catholic Christology: The Function of the So-Called* Extra Calvinisticum *in Calvin's Christology* (Leiden: E. J. Brill, 1966).

[54] Thomas Aquinas, *Summa Theologica*, III. 16. 4, tr. the Fathers of the English Dominican Province, rev. edn., 3 volumes (New York: Benziger, 1948). Thomas appears to adopt a position that would be in disagreement with Barth, however, in insisting that the human nature is deified (not by essence, nor by being converted into divinity, but by union with the divine nature in the hypostasis), *Summa Theologica*, III. 16. 3.

[55] Of course this raises all sorts of fascinating issues related to contradiction, characterization, and identity (whether or not the natures are understood as abstract or concrete). But since discussion of such issues is not of immediate concern, I shall not focus on them. On the difference between concrete and abstract natures in incarnation doctrine, see the discussion by Alvin Plantinga, 'On Heresy, Mind, and Truth', *Faith and Philosophy* (1999), 183–5. Two major options are open to the 'abstractists': they can adopt either some version of 'two minds' Christology or some form of kenotic Christology. On the former, see esp. Thomas V. Morris, *The Logic of God Incarnate* (Ithaca, NY: Cornell University Press, 1986); on the latter, esp. C. Stephen Evans (ed.), *Exploring Kenotic Christology: The Self-Emptying of God*

'revealed' or 'living' Word, then—according to Barth's own dictum—we should not hesitate to affirm it of the written Word either.

CONCLUSION

In this chapter I have looked at Barth's doctrine of scripture. I have noted that, as it stands, it is beset with puzzles and plagued by problems. Endorsing the suggestion that insights from contemporary philosophy of language (speech-act theory) can bring coherence to Barth's view, I have argued that the theologian who shares Barth's fundamental theological commitments both can and should understand scripture as the written Word of God.

Although I disagree with him on some important theological issues, let me be clear that I do not regard Barth as 'a joke in several volumes'.[56] To the contrary, I think that contemporary theologians, analytic and otherwise, have a good deal to gain from interaction with 'kerygmatic' theologians such as Barth. Analytic philosophy of religion and philosophical theology is sometimes criticized—and occasionally rightly criticized, by my lights—for being detached from the multiple genres and speech acts of scripture, for ignoring vast tracts of the Christian tradition and proceeding in an ahistorical manner, for being unconcerned with what Thomas V. Morris helpfully calls 'revelational control', and for sheer disrespect and perhaps even arrogance in the face of the biblical portrayal of God.[57] On all of these matters, as well as many others, analytic theologians might benefit from engagement with Karl Barth. They would do well to hear his insistent reminders that Jesus Christ is *the* final and ultimate revelation of God, that God is the Triune One who 'loves in freedom', that all theology—philosophical or otherwise—involves the whole person and is not detachable from the affections, and that

---

(Oxford: OUP, 2006). Marilyn McCord Adams provides a helpful discussion of several medieval 'concretist' strategies, and she argues that the Scotist strategy of 'qualifying the predicate term' (e.g. 'the Divine Word is *F-qua*-divine and not-*F-qua*-human') is a way both to 'keep characterization and avoid contradiction': *Christ and Horrors: The Coherence of Christology* (Cambridge: CUP, 2006), 133. But for a dissenting opinion, see Richard Cross, *The Metaphysics of the Incarnation: Thomas Aquinas to Duns Scotus* (Oxford: OUP, 2002), 203–5.

[56] John Webster, 'Response to "What Wondrous Love is This?" ', in George Hunsinger (ed.), *For the Sake of the World: Karl Barth and the Future of Ecclesial Theology* (Grand Rapids, Mich.: William B. Eerdmans Publishing Co., 2004), 159.

[57] Thomas V. Morris, *Our Idea of God: An Introduction to Philosophical Theology* (Downers Grove, Ill.: InterVarsity Press, 1991), 43; idem, *Anselmian Explorations: Essays in Philosophical Theology* (Notre Dame, Ind.: University of Notre Dame Press, 1987), 2–3, 25.

the theologian's vocation is to listen for and bear witness to the voice of God. In all of these ways, and more, Barth's theological witness can be of great help. Where Barth helps us most, I'm sure, is where he points us to the Word of God.[58]

[58] Thanks to many friends and colleagues (perhaps most notably, though not exhaustively: David Luy, Scott Manetsch, James R. A. Merrick, Randal Rauser, Michael Rea, Doug Sweeney, Kevin Vanhoozer, and John Woodbridge) for their insightful and constructive criticisms of earlier drafts of this chapter.

9

On Believing that the Scriptures are Divinely Inspired

Thomas M. Crisp

This chapter will investigate the epistemology of belief that the Bible is divinely inspired. Christians believe that it is; many take it that, furthermore, their belief is justified—that it is appropriate or proper from the epistemic point of view. Suppose they're right on both counts. Then there's this question: what makes Christian belief in the divine inspiration of the Bible justified? What is the source of justification for this belief?

Does it come by way of historical argument? Call the proposition that the Bible is divinely inspired 'IB'. Is it, then, that there is some group of propositions such that (*a*) the probability of their conjunction C on our knowledge of history is high, and (*b*) the probability of IB on C is high? Or is it rather that the source of justification for belief that IB is testimony, testimony that traces back to some authoritative source—the Synods of Carthage or Athanasius perhaps? (Suppose the latter. Then what was the source of justification for *his* belief that IB?) Or is it rather that the Holy Spirit, perhaps by way of a process like Calvin's 'internal witness of the Holy Spirit', produces in each Christian belief that IB, thereby conferring justification on the belief? Or something else yet?

In what follows I look into these and connected questions.

PRELIMINARIES

I begin with a few comments about (*a*) what I shall mean by talk of a belief's being 'justified', (*b*) what I shall mean by the claim that the Bible is 'divinely inspired', and (*c*) what I shall mean by talk of 'the Bible'.

First, justification. I'm thinking here clearly enough about *epistemic* justification—the sort that attaches to beliefs or believings when they are epistemically proper, proper from the intellectual point of view. Given the history of recent epistemology, of course, this isn't to say anything very informative: disagreement runs riot in contemporary epistemology about what exactly epistemic justification is, whether one property deserves the label 'epistemic justification' or many, and much more besides. I have my own view about what deserves the label but won't be able to argue for it here. I shall simply presuppose that a belief B is epistemically justified for a human being S iff B is *properly basic* for S or *properly based* for S, where the key terms here are to be understood as follows:

> B is properly basic for a human being S iff B is the output of a properly functioning, truth-aimed, belief-independent belief-forming process in S. B is properly based for a human being S iff B is the output of a properly functioning, truth-aimed, belief-dependent belief-forming process in S whose inputs are either properly basic for S or properly based for S.

So for those who follow these things, I'm plumping for a Plantinga-style 'proper functionalist' approach to justification.[1] A belief-forming process is any cognitive process whose output is belief. A belief-forming process functions *properly* iff it functions, well, the way it's *supposed* to, the way God designed it to function. A belief-dependent process is a belief-forming process whose inputs are *inter alia* other beliefs. A belief-independent process is a belief-forming process that isn't belief-dependent. Finally, a belief-forming process is *truth-aimed* iff its function is to produce true belief (as opposed to, say, belief that conduces to survival or emotional well-being).[2] *Much* more could said, of course, to fill this in, but we've enough on board, I think, to proceed.

Secondly, as to what I shall mean by the claim that the Bible is 'divinely inspired': I assume that to say of the Bible that it is divinely inspired is to say, among other things, that it has been *authored* by God and that, by way of its sentences, God asserts various propositions. (There's more to it, of course. He asserts propositions by way of its sentences, true enough, but he also heals our affections, warns us against sin, encourages us, directs us, comforts us, and more.[3] I assume though that inspiration of the scriptures is *at least* a matter of God's communicating various propositions by way of its sentences.) This raises many questions. In what *sense* was the Bible 'authored' by God? Can we really make sense of the idea that God asserts propositions by way of the

---

[1] See e.g. Plantinga 1993a, 1993b, 2000. For a close cousin of the approach to justification I favor, see Bergmann 2006. My approach is also indebted to Goldman 1979.
[2] For more on what's involved in a belief-forming process's being truth-aimed, see Plantinga 1993b: ch. 2.
[3] Thanks to Al Plantinga for helpful feedback here.

sentences of the Bible? Isn't that way of thinking passé, fundamentalist, or otherwise suspect? To *whom* does God assert these propositions? Who's the audience here?

I haven't much to say about these questions. I take it that God authored the Bible in the sense that he arranged for the inscription of its sentences and that he intends to assert various propositions to us by way of these sentences. As to *how* he arranged for their inscription, I've nothing to say here other than that he seems to have employed a multitude of methods. As to whether we can really make sense of the idea that God asserts propositions by way of the sentences of the Bible, it seems to me that we clearly *can* and that arguments to the contrary are underwhelming. And finally, his audience, I take it, is either the whole human family (or perhaps the larger family of rational creatures), or that part of the human family comprising the Church. I'm not sure which; I don't think it much matters for present purposes.

Thirdly, as to what I shall mean by talk of 'the Bible': as is well known, no single book uncontroversially answers to that title. There's the Catholic Bible, the Greek Orthodox Bible, the Ethiopian Orthodox Bible, the Protestant Bible, and so forth. Which do I propose to refer to when talking of 'the Bible'? For now, let me hold off on answering this question. It'll be clear by the end of the chapter that not much hangs on it.

Now to the main question of the chapter, which again is this: assuming that Christian belief that the Bible is divinely inspired is justified, how does it come by way of justification? Put differently, what is the *source* of justification for this belief? Call this the Main Question.

What I want to do next is sketch what I take to be the principal options for answering the Main Question and suggest along the way reasons for dissatisfaction with each. Then I'll propose an amendment to one of those options that avoids my objections to its unamended compeer and close by considering several questions about my proposal.

THE PRINCIPAL OPTIONS

The principal options for answering the Main Question, I think, are these. First, there's the Lockean suggestion—developed in recent years with subtlety and sophistication by Richard Swinburne[4]—that belief that the scriptures are divinely inspired is justified on the basis of argument from 'natural theology',

---

[4] See e.g. Swinburne 1992, 2003.

where the idea here is that one starts with an evidence base that intelligent, reasonably well-educated people would think of as epistemically above board—a set of propositions that intelligent, reasonably well-educated people would think of as *known*—and tries to show that the likelihood or probability that the scriptures are divinely inspired is high or reasonably high on the relevant evidence base.

Secondly, there's the suggestion that justification for belief that the scriptures are divinely inspired comes by way of testimony. Much that we justifiedly believe is believed on the basis of testimony—the say-so of others. So too with belief that the Bible is divinely inspired. The Church teaches that it is, and when we accept the Church's testimony, we get justified belief, just as I got justified belief when I accepted testimony, for example, that there is a place called 'China', that my name is 'Thomas Crisp', and that Caesar crossed the Rubicon.

Thirdly, there's the suggestion mooted by the Belgic Confession, one of the central confessions of the Reformed branch of Protestantism:

...we believe without a doubt all things contained in [the Bible]—not so much because the church receives them and approves them as such, but above all because the Holy Spirit testifies in our hearts that they are from God, and also because they prove themselves to be from God. (Belgic Confession, Article 5)

The idea here is that something like Plantinga's 'internal instigation of the Holy Spirit' (Plantinga 2000) operates in the minds and hearts of believers, producing in them either belief that the Bible is divinely inspired or something in the near neighborhood. Since, you might think, belief so produced is epistemically justified, we get an answer here to the Main Question.

There are problems with each of these suggestions, problems I now turn to.

NATURAL THEOLOGY AND 'DWINDLING PROBABILITIES'

Plantinga has argued that attempts to argue for 'the great things of the gospel' (i.e. incarnation, atonement, Jesus's resurrection) on the basis of natural theology and historical argument suffer from a problem he dubs the 'Principle of Dwindling Probabilities'.[5]

The Principle of Dwindling Probabilities afflicts arguments with a certain structure. Suppose you want to show some proposition P probable on our

---

[5] See Plantinga 2000: 270–80. For response and counter-response, see Swinburne 2004; McGrew 2004; Plantinga 2006; McGrew 2006.

background knowledge K. You might do that by producing some other proposition A, showing that P(A/K) and P(P/A&K) are high, and concluding that, by the probability calculus, it follows that P(P/K) is high.

You might, however, try to show that P(P/K) is high by iterating the above procedure, arguing that some proposition A is probable on K, that some other proposition B is probable on A&K, and that P is probable on A&B&K, concluding that, therefore, P is probable on K. But such an argument is subject to Plantinga's Principle. If all you've said is that P(A/K), P(B/A&K), and P(P/A&B&K) are high, say around .8 each, then, so far, all that follows from the probability calculus is that P(P/K) is greater than or equal to .8 × .8 × .8, a tad higher than .5. Though the conditional probabilities P(A/K), P(B/A&K), and P(P/A&B&K) are each high, the probabilities 'dwindle' when you multiply them through.

This Principle of Dwindling Probabilities (PDP), then, makes trouble for arguments with the foregoing iterative structure, arguments that attempt to motivate the claim that P(P/K) is high for some P by arguing, for some $Q_1 \ldots Q_n$, that $P(Q_1/K)$, $P(Q_2/Q_1 \& K)$, ..., $P(Q_n/Q_1 \& \ldots Q_{n-1} \& K)$, and $P(P/Q_1 \& \ldots \& Q_n \& K)$ are high.

Plantinga's PDP, notice, will afflict just those arguments with the relevant iterative structure. There's a problem closely connected to PDP though that can arise for *any* historical or natural theological argument, whether it displays that structure or not. I shall now argue that this close cousin of PDP will afflict any attempt to argue for the divine inspiration of the Bible on historical or natural theological grounds and that, therefore, we need to look elsewhere for an answer to the Main Question.

The point of any historical or natural theological argument, I take it, is to show of some conclusion C that it is probable—or more exactly, that it is probable with respect to what we know or take for granted (K)—by putting forward certain premises $P_1, \ldots P_n$, and urging, roughly, that (*a*) $P_1, \ldots P_n$ are probable given K, and (*b*) $P_1, \ldots P_n$ make it probable, given K, that C.

Let us look into this more carefully. Suppose you propose to argue from premises P_1 and P_2 that P(C/K) is high. What you'll need to do, then, roughly, is show that P_1 and P_2 are probable given K and that P_1 and P_2 make it probable (given K) that C. Less roughly, what you'll need to do may be seen by reflecting on the 'lattice' diagram shown in Figure 9.1.[6]

The four pathways from K to C correspond to four jointly exhaustive and mutually exclusive ways for C to be true given K. The probability of C given K is equal to the sum of the probabilities (on K) of the conjunctions of C and the propositions along each path, that is:

[6] I borrow this way of representing probabilistic arguments from McGrew 2004.

```
        C
      /|\ \
    P₁ ~P₁ P₁ ~P₁
     \/     \/
     P₂    ~P₂
       \  /
        K
```

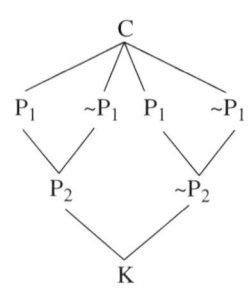

Figure 9.1

$$P(C/K) = P(C\&P_1\&P_2/K) + P(C\&\sim P_1\&P_2/K) +$$
$$P(C\&P_1\&\sim P_2/K) + P(C\&\sim P_1\&\sim P_2/K).$$

To each path, then, corresponds a probability (the probability (on K) of the conjunction of C and the propositions along that path); P(C/K) is equal to the sum of the probabilities corresponding to each path.

We can see, then, what you must do if you're to argue from P_1 and P_2 that P(C/K) is high: show that the sum of the probabilities corresponding to the leftmost three pathways of the above lattice is high. (What if you can't show that the sum of the probabilities corresponding to the leftmost three pathways is high, but *can* show that the probability corresponding to the rightmost pathway is high? Then you've got an argument to C alright, but not an argument from P_1 and P_2: more an argument from their denials.)

So: you have a good argument to C from P_1 and P_2 only if you can show that the sum of the probabilities corresponding to the leftmost three pathways of the above lattice is high. Reflection on this point suggests some ways of objecting to your argument from P_1 and P_2 to C. First, I could show that the sum of the probabilities corresponding to the leftmost three pathways is low on account of the sort of 'dwindling' discussed by Plantinga. Since, by the probability calculus, the probability corresponding to each pathway (or more simply: the probability *along* each pathway) is equal to the product of various conditional probabilities, Plantinga-style dwindling can arise. So, for example, the probability calculus gives us that the probability along the leftmost pathway ($P(C\&P_1\&P_2/K)$) is equal to

$$P(C/P_1\&P_2\&K) \times P(P_1/P_2\&K) \times P(P_2/K)$$

Even if the values of the three multiplicands are high, the product of the three might be low. If the probabilities along each of the three leftmost pathways is low enough, their sum might be low as well.

Secondly, I could show that the sum of the probabilities along the leftmost three pathways is, to borrow Plantinga's language, 'inscrutable'—such that one can't tell what it is.

And thirdly, I could show that the sum of the probabilities along the leftmost three pathways lies in an interval with a low lower bound and inscrutable upper bound. That'd be to show that the sum of the probabilities along the leftmost three pathways is greater than or equal to some smallish number but that we don't know how *much* greater (if it's greater).

There's trouble for your argument if I can show any of these. Each constitutes reason to either withhold or deny the proposition that the sum of the probabilities along the leftmost three pathways of the above lattice is high. And reason to withhold or deny that proposition is reason for thinking your argument from P_1 and P_2 to C no good. As we might put it, it undermines the evidential value of your premises *vis-à-vis* your conclusion. Let us say that objecting to your argument from P_1 and P_2 to C by giving one of the above reasons for withholding or denying the proposition that the sum of the probabilities along the leftmost three pathways of the above lattice is high is to put against your argument an *undermining* objection.[7]

Below I shall suggest that the strongest argument from history and natural theology to IB is compromised by an undermining objection. I shall there need a notion of undermining objection that is more general than the one described in the previous paragraph, which applies just to two-premise arguments. A few remarks, then, about how to make that notion more general: Note that the three leftmost pathways through the above lattice are pathways in which one or more of P_1 and P_2, the premises of the argument, are true. We might say that those pathways are *favorable with respect to* P_1 and P_2, where a pathway through the lattice is favorable with respect to P_1 and P_2 iff one or more of P_1 and P_2 are true in that pathway. Now, corresponding to any argument A from premises $P_1, \ldots, P_n$ for the claim that P(C/K) is high, for some proposition C and body of background belief K, will be various lattices like that considered above. You have an undermining objection to A, let us say, iff for at least one of these lattices L, you have reason to withhold or deny the proposition that the sum of the probabilities along the pathways through L favorable to $P_1, \ldots, P_n$ is high.

This generalized notion of an undermining objection in hand, let us return to natural theology and the Main Question. I suggested above that a close cousin of PDP will afflict any attempt to argue for the divine inspiration of the Bible on historical or natural theological grounds and that, therefore, we need

---

[7] Here I have in mind John Pollock's well-known distinction between rebutting and undermining defeaters (Pollock 1986).

to look elsewhere for an explanation how belief that IB (where 'IB', again, denotes the proposition that the Bible is divinely inspired) comes by way of justification. I can now spell that suggestion out in more detail.

To argue for the divine inspiration of the Bible on historical or natural theological grounds, I take it, is to argue that it is probable that the Bible is divinely inspired given some body of background knowledge K comprising propositions from history and/or the data of natural theology, propositions that all or most of us would think of as known. I think any such argument will be subject to an undermining objection. This is because I suspect the strongest case from the deliverances of history and natural theology for the claim that P(IB/K) is high will rely, if not on these precise premises, then on premises in the near vicinity of these:[8]

> T: God exists.
> A: God intervenes in history to provide a propositional revelation about himself.
> B: Jesus's teachings were such that they could be plausibly interpreted as implying that he intended to found a church that would function for a long period time as an authoritative source of information about him.
> C: Jesus rose from the dead.
> D: In raising Jesus from the dead, God declared his approval of Jesus's teachings.
> E: The Church that, by the start of the fifth century, had pronounced on which books were divinely inspired, is a legitimate successor—the 'closest continuer'—of the church founded by Jesus.

If so, then the strongest case for IB will be compromised by an undermining objection. Let me try to indicate why. The probability lattices from these premises are intricate, but we get a feel for whether an argument of this sort is compromised by an undermining objection by considering a partial lattice for the argument, one that omits pathways running through ~T and ~A since, plausibly, the probabilities along those pathways will be 0: see Figure 9.2.

Other pathways through the lattice that 'zero out', arguably, are those running through ~C. The resurrection is central to the message of the Christian scriptures; if it didn't occur, then, one thinks, the probability that those scriptures are divinely inspired is small indeed.

---

[8] This way of thinking about arguing to IB is inspired by Swinburne's (1992) argument for the central claims of Christianity. Plantinga (2000) argued that Swinburne's argument is compromised by PDP. Swinburne then denied this on grounds that his argument lacks the iterative structure relevant to PDP (2004). I am not attempting to adjudicate their dispute here. I am merely arguing that any attempt to argue for IB on the above Swinburne-inspired premises will be subject to what I am calling an undermining objection, an objection that is closely related to but not identical with Plantinga's PDP.

Believing the Scriptures Divinely Inspired

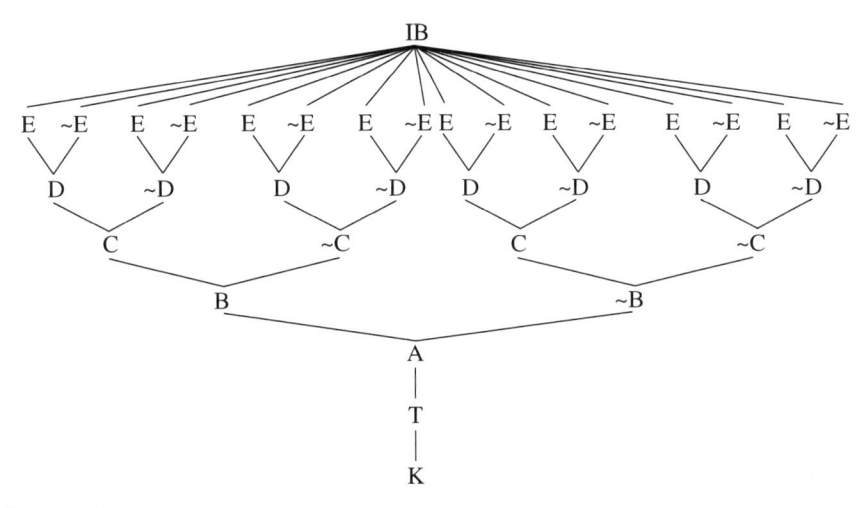

Figure 9.2

Other pathways, while not obviously such as to 'zero out', are such that, so it seems to me, we don't know what their probabilities are.[9] The pathways running through ~B are like this. So consider the K&T&A&~B&C&D&E&IB pathway. The probability along it is equal to

$$P(IB/T\&A\&\sim B\&C\&D\&E\&K) \times P(T\&A\&\sim B\&C\&D\&E/K).$$

Consider the left multiplicand, the probability of IB given that God exists, he intervenes in history to provide us a propositional revelation about himself, Jesus's message *couldn't* be interpreted as implying that he intended to found a church that would be an authoritative source of information about him, he rose from the dead, and so forth. What is this probability? Hard to say. If God exists, provides a propositional revelation about himself, and raised Jesus from the dead thereby endorsing his teachings, then it seems likely he'd provide us with propositional revelation about Jesus and his teachings. But what's the probability that revelation would be the one identified by the Church of the first few centuries, the one specified by IB, given that Jesus never claimed to be founding a group that would function as an authoritative source of information about him? Perhaps the Church got it wrong: perhaps God left us a propositional revelation about Jesus, alright, but it's much smaller than we suppose, comprising for example, just the gospel of Luke, or just the book of Romans. What's the probability (again, given ~B) that the Church got it right here? I think we've no way of saying; we can't tell. The probability along this pathway, so it seems to me, is inscrutable.

[9] Here I am indebted to Plantinga 2006: 10–12.

Similar reasoning applies to the other ~B pathways. And to the ~D pathways. Think about the K&T&A&B&C&~D&E&IB pathway. The probability along it is equal to

$$P(IB/T\&A\&B\&C\&\sim D\&E\&K) \times P(T\&A\&B\&C\&\sim D\&E/K)$$

What to say, then, about the probability of IB given that God exists, intervenes in history to make a propositional revelation of himself to us, Jesus's message could be sensibly extrapolated to the relevant claims, he rose from the dead, the church that was the closest continuer of the church founded by Jesus pronounced on the books of the Bible, *but* Jesus's resurrection did not constitute a divine declaration of approval of Jesus's teachings. I'm not sure. One possibility here is that God's raising Jesus from the dead wasn't a declaration of approval of his teachings because in fact he did not approve of them—or some of them at least. So perhaps he disapproved of teaching to the effect that Jesus was the Messiah, but approved teaching to the effect that Israel would soon be judged for its flirtation with armed resistance to the Romans. Perhaps then he raised Jesus from the dead as an endorsement of just that part of Jesus's message. What's the probability of IB on that scenario? About zero: if God disapproved of Jesus's claim to be the Messiah, then Jesus presumably wasn't the Messiah, and IB, one thinks, is false. Another possibility: in raising Jesus from the dead, God was not declaring his approval of Jesus's teachings, though in fact he did approve of them. What's the probability of IB on that scenario? High, I guess. We've two possibilities, then, each consistent with T&A&B&C&~D&E&K. IB is extremely *improbable* on the first, and fairly *probable* on the second. Which possibility is more likely on T&A&B&C&~D&E&K? I have no idea: no answer seems more defensible than another here. As best I can tell, we've no way of answering this question. As best I can tell, then, we've no way of knowing the probability of IB on T&A&B&C&~D&E&K. Likewise with the other ~D pathways.

Next the ~E pathways. So consider the K&T&A&B&C&D&~E&IB pathway. Its probability:

$$P(IB/T\&A\&B\&C\&D\&\sim E\&K) \times P(T\&A\&B\&C\&D\&\sim E/K).$$

What then of the probability of IB given that God exists, he intervenes in history to make a propositional revelation of himself, Jesus rose from the dead, etc., but the church that pronounced on IB wasn't the legitimate successor—the 'closest continuer'—of the church founded by Jesus? Same point here: hard to tell.

This leaves the leftmost pathway. The probability along it:

$$P(IB/T\&A\&B\&C\&D\&E\&K) \times P(T\&A\&B\&C\&D\&E/K),$$

which is equal to

$$P(IB/T\&A\&B\&C\&D\&E\&K) \times P(T/K) \times P(A/T\&K)$$
$$\times P(B/T\&A\&K) \times P(C/T\&A\&B\&K) \times P(D/T\&A\&B\&C\&K)$$
$$\times P(E/T\&A\&B\&C\&D\&K).$$

What to say about it? Well, consider P(T/K), the probability of theism on K. How high is it? Much depends, clearly, on how we construe K. McGrew (2004) suggests that P(T/K) will be high indeed if we think of K as including historical evidence for the resurrection. If I'm understanding him aright, the thought is that P(C/K)—where C, again, is the proposition that Jesus rose from the dead and K is thought of as including the historical evidence for the resurrection—is *extremely* high, that P(T/C&K) is also extremely high, and that, therefore, P(T/K) is extremely high as well (since, by the probability calculus, P(T/K) ≥ P(T/C&K) × P(C/K)).

I am not so sure. I grant there are powerful historical arguments for the resurrection. Arguments by *inter alia* N.T. Wright, William Lane Craig, Stephen T. Davis, and Gary Habermas are quite strong.[10] But they don't, I think, show P(C/K) (or P(T/K)) anywhere near 1. Here's why. Let K− be the evidence relevant to natural theological arguments for the existence of God, evidence regarding the big bang, fine tuning of the fundamental constants of physics, and so forth. And let R be the detailed historical evidence we possess for the resurrection: the evidence for the empty tomb, the disciple's post-crucifixion experiences of what seemed to be the risen Jesus, their subsequent martyrdoms, and so forth. K, we can suppose, is the conjunction of K− and R.

The question, then: how to think about P(C/R&K−)? It's a theorem of the probability calculus that

$$P(C/R\&K-) = P(C/T-\&R\&K-) \times P(T-/R\&K-) +$$
$$P(C/\sim T-\&R\&K-) \times P(\sim T-/R\&K-),$$

where T−, let us say, is the doctrine of minimal theism, the doctrine that there exists some god or other: some powerful, non-physical person capable of interacting causally with the physical world. Start with the rightmost addend (P(C/∼T&R&K−) × P(∼T/R&K−)). What sort of value can we sensibly assign it? Not a very high one, I should think, for as Wright and others have pointed out, the early Christian claim that Jesus had been resurrected was not a claim to the effect that he had been somehow resuscitated, but something much more dramatic: that his body had been transformed into something utterly new, something incorruptible, something not bound by the ordinary

[10] See e.g. Wright 2003; Craig 1989; Davis 1993; Habermas 1987.

operation of the laws of physics and chemistry. The probability that that's what happened, given the denial of minimal theism, is not far from zero, I should think. Therefore:

$$P(C/R\&K-) \approx P(C/T-\&R\&K-) \times P(T-/R\&K-).$$

What to say then about $P(C/T-\&R\&K-)$ and $P(T-/R\&K-)$? Treat them in order. First, how probable is the resurrection given the evidence of natural theology, minimal theism, and the historical evidence for the empty tomb, the post-mortem appearances, and so forth? Here there'll be disagreement, but it's not unreasonable to think it high. Given that we're conditionalizing on an evidence base that includes minimal theism, I think Wright *et al.* make a strong case that C is highly likely. Suppose so and see what happens.

Next, $P(T-/R\&K-)$. Bayes' Theorem gives us that

$$P(T-/R\&K-) = \frac{P(R/T-\&K-) \times P(T-/K-)}{P(R/K-)}$$

Start with $P(R/K-)$: the probability, given the evidence of natural theology, that there'd be evidence of the sort we have for the empty tomb, the post-mortem appearances, and so forth. How high is that? Low, I should think. Given merely the evidence of natural theology (the cosmos came about by way of the big bang, its fundamental constants are fine tuned, etc.), it isn't particularly probable that there'd be evidence for the empty tomb, the post-mortem appearances, and so forth. Now enrich our evidence base by T−. Does the probability of R go up? Is it more probable that there'd be evidence of the sort we have for the empty tomb, etc., on T−&K− than on just K−? That depends on the likelihood ratio

$$\frac{P(R/T-\&K-)}{P(R/\sim T-\&K-)}.$$

If it's 'top heavy', the probability of R (on K−) goes up when we add T−; if it's not, it doesn't. (Well, this iff $P(T-/K-)$ isn't 1. And surely it isn't.) So is it top heavy? Hard to say. Minimal theism says there is some god or other, some powerful non-physical person, but tells us almost nothing about this being. Hard to see then why minimal theism should generate any *expectation* that we'd see something like R, something we'd expect not to see given the denial of minimal theism. I'd think the above ratio either inscrutable (who knows *what* $P(R/T-\&K-)$ is) or not too far above 1. If it's inscrutable, then McGrew's suggestion that $P(C/R\&K-)$ is extremely high is in trouble: If the above ratio is inscrutable, then, I should think, so is P(T−/R&K−). But if so, then since

$$P(C/R\&K-) \approx P(C/T-\&R\&K-) \times P(T-/R\&K-),$$

P(C/R&K−) looks to be inscrutable as well. If the above ratio is near 1, then

$$P(R/T-\&K-) \approx P(R/K-).$$

But if so, then

$$P(T-/R\&K-) \approx P(T-/K-).$$

And since, as we've seen,

$$P(C/R\&K-) \approx P(C/T-\&R\&K-) \times P(T-/R\&K-).$$

we get that the probability of minimal theism on K− puts an upper bound on the probability of C on R&K−. Here again, there's trouble for the suggestion that P(C/R&K−) is extremely high. The evidence for theism—minimal or otherwise—from natural theology is strong but not knockdown.

One possibility here is that I've mischaracterized the above likelihood ratio. I said I thought it was either inscrutable or somewhere near 1. Perhaps it's higher than 1. Suppose it's as high as two: that it's twice as likely that R given T−&K− than given ∼T−&K−. Then assuming that P(T−/K−) isn't much higher than .5 and plugging in the numbers, we get that

$$P(T-/R\&K-) \approx .67,$$

and that

$$P(C/R\&K-) \approx P(C/T-\&R\&K-) \times .67.$$

Assuming that P(C/T−&R&K−) is extremely high, .99 say, it turns out that P(C/R&K−) isn't much higher than around .66. Therefore, even if it's twice as likely that R given T−&K− than given ∼T−&K−, the probability of C on R&K− isn't much higher than the probability of T− on K−.

Perhaps you'll reply that our above ratio is considerably higher than 2, and that P(C/R&K−) is, accordingly, considerably greater than .66. I'd wonder, though, what grounds you could have for thinking the ratio that high. I can't see what they'd be.

(A likelihood ratio closely connected to the one presently under discussion plays a key role in Swinburne's recent argument for the resurrection (Swinburne 2003; see especially pp. 212–15). His argument turns on the ratio of (*a*) the probability we'd find historical evidence of the sort and strength we have for Jesus's life and resurrection given the evidence of natural theology and the proposition that God incarnates himself at some time to (*b*) the probability we'd find historical evidence of that sort and strength given the evidence of natural theology and the proposition that it is not the case that God incarnates himself at some time. Swinburne thinks that ratio quite high: about 100:1. If he's right, then, given plausible assumptions, the ratio I discuss above is much higher than 2:1. But is he right? Hard to say. It's not implausible to think his ratio greater than 1:1, but why think it 100:1? Why not think it more like, say, 5:1 or 2:1? I don't know, and Swinburne doesn't say much that would help us decide. He proposes that it is somewhat unlikely, though not very unlikely, we'd have the sort and strength of evidence we do for Jesus's life and resurrection if God had incarnated himself, suggesting that the relevant probability is something in the neighborhood of .1 (2003: 212). He then proposes that it is 'very unlikely indeed' we'd have that sort and strength of evidence if God hadn't incarnated himself, suggesting a probability here of .001 (2003: 213). Take the first probability. Swinburne has argued in various places (e.g. 2003: 173–4), plausibly to my mind, that we should expect a certain amount of divine hiddenness, a certain amount of 'epistemic distance' between us and God, so as to leave us free to choose for and against him. How much distance should we expect? Should we expect the distance on display in the sort and strength of evidence we have for Jesus's life and resurrection? Should we expect more distance than that? Less? I have no idea. I think we have no principled way of answering such questions. Consequently, I think we have no principled way of assigning a number like .1 to the above probability, and thus no principled reason for thinking Swinburne's ratio nearer 100:1 than, say, 2:1 or 5:1. But if his ratio is nearer the latter numbers than the former, it'll follow given plausible assumptions that our focal ratio, the one under discussion in the last several paragraphs, is low. I tentatively conclude that Swinburne's arguments shed little light on the question how to think about that ratio.)

Pace McGrew, then, I think we have no good reason for thinking P(C/R&K−) extremely high. Arguments for the resurrection by Wright *et al.* are powerful, but they don't show P(C/R&K−) near 1.

To recapitulate: we are presently considering the probability along the leftmost pathway of our above lattice

$$P(IB/T\&A\&B\&C\&D\&E\&K) \times P(T/K) \times P(A/T\&K) \\ \times P(B/T\&A\&K) \times P(C/T\&A\&B\&K) \times P(D/T\&A\&B\&C\&K) \\ \times P(E/T\&A\&B\&C\&D\&K)$$

and wondering about P(T/K). McGrew suggests it's extremely high if K includes historical evidence for the resurrection. I think he's wrong. I can't see any reason for thinking it much higher than the probability of T on K−, the evidence of natural theology. And as I read that evidence, it's good but not knockdown: it shows theism more probable than not, but not that it's certain. The most we can say about P(T/K), I think, is that falls somewhere in an interval like [.7 − .9]. Likewise with P(A/T&K). That God would intervene in history to provide us with propositional revelation about himself seems likely but not certain. The most we can say about P(A/T&K), I should think, is that it too is somewhere in an interval like [.7 − .9]. But if so, then even if the other of the above multiplicands are extremely high, each .99 say, the most we can say for the probability along the leftmost pathway is that it's greater than .47 or so.

As I read the evidence, then, there's reason to withhold the proposition that the sum of the probabilities along the pathways of the above lattice favorable to T and A–E is high. If I'm right to think the strongest case for IB from history and natural theology will rely on premises in the near vicinity of T and A–E, we get that the strongest case for IB from history and natural theology is vitiated by an undermining objection.

I conclude we have good reason to look elsewhere for an answer to the Main Question.

THE MAIN QUESTION AND TESTIMONY

The second principal option for answering the Main Question—the question whence comes justification for belief that IB—is that justification for such belief comes by way of testimony. Perception, memory, and rational intuition are sources of justified belief; so too is testimony. Much, perhaps most, of what we justifiedly believe we believe on the basis of testimony. Likewise, you might think, with belief that IB. The Church teaches that IB; when I accepted its testimony, I *eo ipso* got justified belief, just as I got justified belief when I accepted my parents' testimony that my name is 'Crisp', my teachers' testimony that Caesar crossed the Rubicon, and so forth. Ultimately, I think something like this is right, but it needs some fleshing out before it can be sensibly accepted.

True enough, testimony is a source of justification for many of our beliefs. In the ordinary case, though, if one's *only* evidence for belief that P is testimony that P, then, one thinks, one's evidence for belief that P is *defeated* if one comes across testimony that ∼P and has no reason for thinking the one bit of testimony more trustworthy than the other. So suppose you form a belief that it's half-past-four on the basis of testimony from me. (Say too my testimony is your only evidence that it's half-past-four.) You thereupon overhear testimony to the effect that it's half-past-*five* and have no reason for trusting my testimony over this latest bit of testimony. Then, one thinks, your original testimonial evidence has been defeated and you've reason to be agnostic about the time.

If belief that IB is justified by way of ordinary testimony, therefore, and your only justification for belief that IB is testimonial, then you'll get a defeater for your belief that IB if you run across testimony that ~IB and have no good reason for trusting one bit of testimony over the other. Most of us, clearly enough, *have* run across testimony that ~IB. There's testimony from various other religions that *their* holy books are inspired and that the Bible isn't, testimony from skeptical practitioners of historical biblical criticism that the Bible is a mishmash of error, and more besides. So most of us have plenty of testimonial evidence that ~IB, suggesting that absent good reason for preferring the Church's testimony to these other sources—absent good reason for crediting the Church's authority on these matters over its competitors'—testimonial evidence from the Church that IB isn't good reason for belief that IB.

All this, of course, *absent good reason to prefer the Church's testimony to its competitors*. If we'd good reason to trust the Church over alternative sources of testimony on IB, then testimonial evidence provided by the Church's teaching that IB might well justify our belief that IB.

The crucial question, then: *is* there good reason for trusting the Church over alternative sources of testimony on IB? Well, if there *were*, it'd presumably comprise some combination of the following. First, it might comprise an argument from history and natural theology that the Church is a divinely backed source of information about matters of faith. Secondly, it could consist of arguments from history and natural theology impugning the credibility of competitors to the Church—arguments impugning the credibility of historical biblical criticism, other religious traditions, and so forth. And thirdly, it could consist of argument from propositions known not by way of history and natural theology, but in some other way, for example, Plantinga's 'internal instigation of the Holy Spirit' (IIHS).

I doubt it would consist of the first; I doubt, that is, it would consist of argument from history and natural theology that the Church is a divinely backed source of information about IB. Note here that there is non-trivial dispute among the various branches of Christendom about what the Bible *is*—that is, about *which* books comprise the Bible. There's the Catholic view, on which the list of the divinely inspired books comprises the standard twenty-seven New Testament books and the Alexandrian canon of the Greek Septuagint, including the so-called deuterocanonical books; there's the Greek Orthodox canon comprising the foregoing books plus five books of the Septuagint not found in the Catholic canon; there's the Slavonic Orthodox canon comprising all of the foregoing less three; there's the Protestant canon which comprises only the standard twenty-seven New Testament books and the standard Hebrew canon; there are the Ethiopian and Armenian Orthodox canons, which differ in further ways yet on the limits of both the Old and New Testament canons; and there are more canons besides.

So there's disagreement between the major branches of Christendom about what the Bible comprises. All this suggests that talk thus far about the proposition I've been calling 'IB', the proposition that the Bible is divinely inspired, has been a tad imprecise. It looks as if no one proposition uncontroversially answers to the definite description 'the proposition that the Bible is divinely inspired' on account of the fact that no one book uncontroversially answers to the name 'the Bible'. There isn't one Bible; there are many. For each, then, there is the proposition that it is inspired: IB_i, IB_j, ...

Well, suppose so, and suppose you accept some one of the IBs, IB_x, on the basis of testimony from the teachers of your branch of Christendom. If your reason for trusting your branch of Christendom over alternative sources of testimony on IB_x is some argument from history and natural theology, then, I suggest, you'll have undermining troubles like those explored above. For any argument you give from history and natural theology to the effect that your branch of Christendom is to be trusted on IB_x over other branches of Christendom and other non-Christian religious traditions will, I suspect, invoke at least these premises (or premises in the near neighborhood):

> T: God exists.
> A: God intervenes in history to provide a propositional revelation about himself.
> B: Jesus's teachings were such that they could be plausibly interpreted as implying that he intended to found a church that would function for a long period of time as an authoritative source of information about him.
> C: Jesus rose from the dead.
> D: In raising Jesus from the dead, God declared his approval of Jesus's teachings.
> E': The Church that pronounced on IB_x is a legitimate successor—the 'closest continuer'—of the church founded by Jesus.

And for reasons given above, any such argument will be subject to an undermining objection.

Perhaps, then, your reason for trusting your branch of the Church over alternative sources of testimony on IB_x is that you have arguments that undermine the credibility of those sources, reasons for thinking that other branches of the Church, non-Christian religions, semi-Christian religions, and skeptical practitioners of historical biblical criticism aren't to be trusted on IB_x. Perhaps, but you'd be unusual. Most of us don't have much at all by way of decent argument against the credibility of other branches of the Church, non-Christian religions, and so forth. Most of us, then, lack this sort of reason for trusting the testimony of our branch of Christendom on its version of IB over competitors. Of course, it could be that only those who have this sort of reason are justified in accepting their church's teaching on IB,[11] and that, consequently, relatively few Christians are justified in believing the Bible to be divinely inspired. It could be, but I'm assuming it's not. It's a working assumption of this chapter that most Christians justifiedly believe that the scriptures are divinely inspired. The question is, how does this belief (or these beliefs) come by way of justification? I'll assume, then, that for most, it's not because they have serious objections to the credibility of traditions other than their own.

Finally, there's the possibility that your reason for trusting the testimony of your branch of Christendom on IB_x over the testimony of competitors comprises argument from propositions known not by way of history and natural theology, but in some other way, perhaps via something like Plantinga's IIHS. This suggestion connects up neatly with our third principal option for answering the Main Question, on which belief that IB or something in the near neighborhood arises via IIHS. Let us look into this option then.

THE MAIN QUESTION AND IIHS

The central suggestion here is that the Holy Spirit directly produces in us certain beliefs. On Plantinga's view, the Holy Spirit directly produces in us belief in the 'great things of the gospel': sin, incarnation, atonement, resurrection, and so forth (Plantinga 2000). The process works something like this: one hears the gospel preached, evinces an openness to the leading of the Holy Spirit and thereupon has belief in the great things of the gospel produced in one by the Holy Spirit. Belief thus arrived at is, says Plantinga, perfectly reasonable, perfectly respectable from the epistemic point of view. In our terms, such belief is justified.

Suppose all this is right: various of our Christian beliefs arise via IIHS and belief so produced is justified. The idea we're exploring, then, is that your reason for trusting the testimony of your community on IB_x over the testi-

---

[11] Here and below, I use an unmarked 'IB' when precision about which version of IB is at issue is unnecessary.

mony of competitors comprises argument from premises that are deliverances of this process—deliverances of IIHS. This could happen in various ways.

So, for example, perhaps it's a deliverance of IIHS for you that your specific branch of the Church has been guided by the Spirit and preserved from error on important matters of faith, including matters pertaining to the extent of the scriptures. So suppose you're an Ethiopian Orthodox Christian. The idea, then, is that the Holy Spirit is directly producing and sustaining belief in you to the effect that the Ethiopian Orthodox Church has been protected from error on important matters of faith, including matters pertaining to the extent of the scriptures. Clearly enough, if the Holy Spirit is producing this belief in you, then you have the makings of an excellent argument for trusting the testimony of your community on its version of IB ('IB$_x$' as we're calling it) over that of competitors.

Two worries though. First, once again, it's a working assumption of the chapter that most Christians justifiedly believe that the scriptures are divinely inspired. Hard to see, though, how to turn the above suggestion into an account of how most Christians get justified belief that the scriptures are inspired.

And secondly, the suggestion carries a theoretical cost. The idea is that the Holy Spirit directly produces belief in some to the effect that their branch of the Church has been preserved from error on the question what the extent of the scriptures is. Since, one thinks, the Holy Spirit *isn't* producing the analogous belief in members of other Christian communities (lest the Holy Spirit be in the business of producing false belief in many of us), we get the following explanatory asymmetry. Though *your* belief that the teachings of your branch of the Church on IB$_x$ are true is to be explained by the inspiration of the Holy Spirit, *my* belief that the teachings of my branch of the Church on IB$_y$ (for some distinct IB$_y$ among the IBs) are true is to be explained in some other way (the instigation of unholy spirits, 'group think', perhaps some other psychological mechanism). Now, though it's hard to be sure, I would suspect that our beliefs are quite similar in terms of phenomenology, that 'downstream of experience', to borrow Plantinga's phrase, they're pretty similar. But then the present suggestion displays this inelegance: it postulates diverse explanations of what would seem to be very similar phenomena. This costs. Better to give a unified explanation of similar phenomena; theories that don't pay a theoretical price. It could be, of course, that the cost here is small and that it's worth paying when all is said and done. It could be. That'll depend on what other theories are on offer. Let us look further into that, then.

The basic idea we're exploring is that your reason for trusting the testimony of your community on IB$_x$ over the testimony of competitors comprises argument from premises some of which are deliverances of IIHS. Maybe it works like this. Maybe Christians of all stripes get belief in the great things of the gospel (incarnation, atonement, resurrection) via IIHS. These beliefs, combined with premises like

> B: Jesus's teachings were such that they could be plausibly interpreted as implying that he intended to found a church that would function for a long period of time as an authoritative source of information about him,

and

> E′: The Church that pronounced on IB_x is a legitimate successor—the 'closest continuer'—of the church founded by Jesus,

might, then, provide the makings of a good argument for trusting your community on IB_x over the testimony of competitors.

They might. But it'd be a small minority of Christians that come to justified belief that IB by this sort of argument. Clearly most of us aren't in possession of historical argument robust enough to underwrite such reasoning. But, again, I am assuming that most Christians have justified belief that IB. If so, then for most of us anyway, it's not by way of the above sort of argument.

The foregoing ways of deploying the IIHS model leave it a mystery how it could be that most Christians get justified belief that IB. There are ways of deploying the model that avoid this. So recall the Belgic Confession: 'we believe without a doubt all things contained in [the Bible]—not so much because the church receives them and approves them as such, but above all because the Holy Spirit testifies in our hearts that they are from God, and also because they prove themselves to be from God'. The basic idea: we believe what the Bible teaches because the Holy Spirit testifies in our hearts that its books are from God—that is, that they're divinely inspired. Maybe it works like this. There is some core list of biblical books endorsed by all or most major branches of Christendom such that belief in their inspiration is a deliverance of IIHS. Belief in the inspiration of these books is nearly universal across Christianity and is justified by dint of being a deliverance of IIHS. Such is the sense in which most Christians get justified belief that IB.

What to say, though, about belief in the inspiration of those books that aren't endorsed across Christendom, for example, Catholic and Orthodox belief in the inspiration of the deuterocanonical books? Whence come those beliefs? Looks like we'll need some story other than IIHS to account for them, at the above-discussed cost in unity of theory. (Though it's hard to be sure, one suspects that, 'downstream of experience', belief in the inspiration of the deuterocanonical books is quite similar to belief in the inspiration of, say, the Gospel of Matthew. So we've dissimilar explanations of what would seem to be very similar phenomena and consequent theoretical cost.)

The obvious ways of deploying the IIHS model face this difficulty: either it's not clear on them how it could be that most Christians are justified in belief that IB or we get diverse explanations of similar phenomena and consequent theoretical cost. In the next section, I'll sketch a model for thinking about the epistemology of belief that IB not subject to this difficulty, a model that, so I'll claim, is more satisfying than the options so far considered.

MORE ON AUTHORITY

I argued above that if justification for belief that IB comes by way of ordinary testimony, we get a defeater for belief that IB when we run across testimony that ~IB and lack good reason for preferring one source of testimony to the other. I said this makes trouble for the idea that justification for belief that IB arises by way of ordinary testimony since most of us have run across plenty of testimony that ~IB. I want to propose now a model that gets round this worry, a model on which justification for belief that IB *does* come by way of testimony, but not by way of ordinary testimony.

Peter Van Inwagen's point here is surely correct:

Each of us accepts certain authorities and certain traditions. You may think that you are an epistemic engine that takes sensory input (that 'fancifully fanciless medium of unvarnished news') and generates assignments of probabilities to propositions by means of a set of rules that yields the most useful (useful for dealing with the future stream of sensory input) probability assignments in most possible worlds. In fact, however, you trust a lot of people and groups of people and—within very broad limits—believe what they tell you. And this is not because the epistemic engine that is yourself has processed a lot of sensory data and, in consequence, assigned high probabilities to propositions like 'Dixy Lee Ray is a reliable source of information on ecological matters' or 'Most things that the *Boston Globe* says about the homeless are true.' You may have done some of that, but you haven't had time to do very much of it. (1994: 48)

The central suggestion: we accept the testimony of certain authorities, oftentimes without much by way of argument that we should. Typically this is a matter of accepting the testimony of those deemed authoritative or expert by our social group. When I was young, my social group was my family and the experts were my parents. I accepted much that they told me, usually in the basic way (where to accept a belief in the 'basic way' here, is to accept it without having *inferred* it from argument or evidence—it's to hold the belief *non-inferentially*). Nowadays, my social group is much wider and its experts more diverse. I accept quite a bit of testimony from, for example, physics, often in the basic way: it's not as if I've much by way of decent, non-circular argument that the methods of physics are truth-conducive.

Note that we'll often accept the testimony of those deemed expert by our social group in the face of conflicting testimony. So when I was young, I'd occasionally run across testimony that conflicted with that of my parents but would go on believing my parents nonetheless. (I remember hearing much testimony on the playground to the effect that there was no Santa Claus; I didn't believe it for a minute.) Not that I had much by way of argument for thinking my parents should be trusted over these other sources. I didn't. But confronted with conflicting testimony, without much by way of argument that my parents should be trusted over conflicting sources of information, I'd go on believing my parents.

I still do this sort of thing. So, for example, science assures us there is overwhelming evidence for the claim that the cosmos is considerably older than 10,000 years. I believe there is. I know of people, though, who claim there isn't. They think the idea that there is powerful evidence for this claim is based on enormous confusion in the scientific community. I think they're mistaken, but pressed for argument why we should trust the deliverances of mainstream science here and not these people, I'm not sure what to say. I've only a halting grip on the relevant science.

Of course I'm not alone here. We all do this sort of thing. We trust those deemed expert by our social groups, often in the face of conflicting testimony, often without much by way of argument for preferring the experts to the non-experts. As I'll put it, we *defer* to those deemed expert by our social group, where, let us say, you defer to an expert in your social group iff (*a*) you accept her testimony in the basic way, and (*b*) you'd continue to do so if apprised of conflicting testimony by those your community deems non-expert, whether or not you had good argument for preferring the expert's testimony to the non-expert's.

We do this sort of thing, but why? Why do we engage in this doxastic practice?[12] I conjecture that it's hard-wired into us. Deferring to experts is, I conjecture, a matter of proper cognitive function. More, I conjecture that God's intention in hard-wiring the practice into us had to do with his desire

---

[12] Where a *doxastic practice*, for present purposes, is a way of forming belief, a mode of belief formation; e.g., forming belief on the basis of testimony, forming belief on the basis of perceptual experience, forming belief on the basis of deductive reasoning—all are ways of forming belief and doxastic practices in my sense. I borrow the expression 'doxastic practice' from Alston (see e.g. Alston 1989). He develops a sophisticated epistemology around the notion of a doxastic practice—his so-called doxastic practice approach to epistemology (see e.g. Alston 1989). I am borrowing his expression, but not his epistemology, which differs in important ways from the proper-functionalist approach to epistemology I assume at the chapter's outset.

that we have true belief about the world. He designed us to come to know much about the world, but his intention was that we do it cooperatively. We're built for cooperative knowledge acquisition and the hard-wired tendency to defer to those deemed expert by our social group is plausibly thought of as conducive to that.

Suppose all this right. Then the practice of deferring to those deemed expert by one's social group evinces proper cognitive function. Plausibly, many of the deliverances of this practice are outputs of a properly functioning, truth-aimed, belief-producing process. Therefore, given the view of justification presupposed at the outset of the chapter, many of the deliverances of the practice are justified. (I don't say all deliverances of the practice are justified. No doubt there are situations in which deference to your community's experts would be unreasonable. I'll say a bit about this below.)

Call this practice of deferring to those your social group deems expert the *authoritative testimonial* doxastic practice: 'AT' for short. Interesting questions about AT clamor for attention. What is it, exactly, to be an 'expert'? What counts as one's 'social group'? What if one is a member of several social groups with conflicting experts? What if you yourself are an expert and disagree with other experts? And more besides. I propose to set these aside and turn instead to a sketch of the bearing of our discussion of AT on the Main Question, the question, again, how it is that Christian belief that the Bible is divinely inspired comes by way of epistemic justification.

AT AND THE MAIN QUESTION

So: Suppose you are a serious Roman Catholic Christian and consider the Roman Catholic Church your primary social group. That Church deems certain of its teachers authoritative on matters of faith and practice—it deems certain of them *experts* on these matters. These teachers claim that certain books are divinely inspired. Suppose, aware of all of this, you accept their testimony in the basic way; you defer, in the above sense, to those deemed expert by your social group. Then, so I say, your belief is a deliverance of AT and *ipso facto* justified.

Suppose you then come across testimony that conflicts with the Church's teaching about the inspiration of the Bible and have no powerful argument for preferring the Church's testimony. Still, you reflect on it and find yourself firmly convinced that the Church's teaching is true. I said above that if justification for belief that the Bible is divinely inspired comes by way of ordinary testimony, then you get a defeater for that belief if you run across conflicting testimony and have no good argument for preferring one source of testimony to the other. That's as may be given what we might call our *ordinary testimonial* doxastic practice (OT): the kind that's operative when you accept testimony on some matter from someone your social group deems non-expert on the matter. (The kind that's operative in the usual case of accepting someone's testimony about what time it is, say.) But if you're a serious Catholic, then your belief that the books of the Catholic Bible are inspired isn't a deliverance of OT but of AT, and conflicting testimony from those deemed non-expert by the Church makes no epistemic trouble for your belief. (What if you got conflicting testimony from those deemed expert by the Church? Then you'd have trouble, but I'm assuming that's not what's going on here.)

I conjecture that for many Christians, perhaps most, something in the near vicinity of the above story characterizes their belief that the Bible is divinely inspired. For many Christians, perhaps most, belief that IB is a deliverance of AT. If so, then we have an answer to the Main Question: Christian belief that IB is justified by dint of being a deliverance of AT.

I take this to be a more satisfying answer to the Main Question than the options explored above. The natural theological option is vitiated, I think, by undermining worries. The testimonial option considered above is basically right, but needs nuancing in the direction of our recent discussion of AT. The IIHS options either leave it unclear how it could be that most Christians are justified in belief that IB or postulate diverse explanations of similar phenomena at the above-discussed theoretical cost. The AT model explains how it is that most Christians are justified in belief that IB but doesn't incur this cost, since, for the ATer, belief in the various versions of IB arises via the same cognitive process. Wherefore, I take it, the AT model has a slight edge over the IIHS option.

I close by considering a few questions about the model.

A FEW QUESTIONS ABOUT THE AT MODEL

First. What if you come across extremely powerful evidence that the experts in your tradition are wrong about IB. So suppose you learn of extremely powerful evidence that claims by Jesus's early followers that he'd risen from the dead were part of an elaborate hoax. Then, one thinks, you should give up your belief that IB: if Jesus didn't rise from the dead and the disciples deceived the world into thinking he did, it is implausible in the extreme that the Christian scriptures are inspired. But doesn't the AT model imply otherwise?

Doesn't it imply, that is, that one could go on blithely accepting IB despite such evidence to the contrary (cf. Plantinga 2000: 420–1)?

No, it doesn't. The model suggests you can reasonably believe the deliverances of your community's experts in the face of conflicting testimony, but it doesn't imply that testimony from your community's experts is indefeasible. It's consistent with the model that one could acquire sufficiently strong evidence against the claims of your community's experts to warrant your rejecting their testimony.

Second. It's a consequence of the AT model that Christians of a variety of stripes can be justified in accepting the version of IB indexed to their tradition. So it looks to follow from the model that Protestants are justified in accepting IB_P, Catholics are justified in accepting IB_C, Greek Orthodox are justified in accepting IB_G, and so forth. More, it looks to be a consequence of the model that many Muslims are justified in thinking the Quran divinely inspired, that many Jews are justified in thinking the Talmud and Mishnah divinely inspired, that many Latter Day Saints are justified in thinking the Book of Mormon divinely inspired, and so forth. But isn't there something untoward about this? Isn't there something infelicitous about the suggestion that such conflicting beliefs could all be justified?

No, I don't see that there is. It's no part of my claim that all these beliefs are *true*. *That* would be infelicitous. I say only that adherents to these various traditions can be justified in accepting the teachings of those deemed authoritative by their traditions. This doesn't strike me as objectionable at all; quite the reverse: it strikes me as obviously right.

Third, suppose you're a Greek Orthodox Christian and accept the deliverances of certain authorities in your tradition on IB_G—the version of IB indexed to your tradition. There's this question about those authorities though: whence comes *their* justification for belief that IB_G? Perhaps some accept their belief on the basis of further authorities yet, but this can't go back indefinitely. Eventually, we reach authorities whose beliefs that IB_G aren't based on expert testimony. So where does their justification for belief that IB_G come from? If the above arguments are on target, not by the arguments of history and natural theology and not by IIHS. If not by those, though, and not by expert testimony, it's hard to see how their beliefs could be justified. But if their beliefs that IB_G aren't justified, how could *your* belief that IB_G, based as it is on their testimony, be justified? Similar problems arise, of course, for those of us accepting other versions of IB.

Two points in reply. First, the objection suggests that, given my arguments, we should doubt the Church fathers' beliefs on IB were deliverances of IIHS. I deny that. Nothing I've said suggests the fathers' beliefs weren't products of IIHS. I said: better to postulate similar explanations of similar phenomena, and, so I suspect, belief in the inspiration of the scriptures across the major branches of Christendom is, by and large, pretty similar. Who's to say, though, whether the fathers' beliefs on IB were relevantly similar to ours? Perhaps they weren't; perhaps they were accompanied by powerful religious experiences, signs and wonders, or some such thing. I don't know. Nothing I say above suggests one way or another about it. So nothing I say above casts doubt on the suggestion that some of the fathers' beliefs that IB were products of IIHS.

Secondly, the objection assumes that belief that P held on the basis of a chain of testimony tracing back to someone your social group deems expert is justified only if the expert in question was justified in believing that P.[13] I deny that. Suppose an unscrupulous high school physics teacher knowingly foists various subtly false claims about physics on his students. Provided his sophistry is sufficiently subtle and that his students had no reason for suspicion, wouldn't they be justified in accepting his testimony? I think so.[14]

To be sure, there's epistemic trouble for my testimonial belief B if I come to think that the initial link in the testimonial chain subtending B isn't likely to be true. But in the case of belief that IB, few Christians would think that. Most of us, I suspect, think that God providently guided the development of the Church fathers' beliefs on IB in such a way as to protect them from error.[15] Perhaps their beliefs were also justified, maybe via IIHS. Not much hangs on it. If like most Christians, you think the beliefs of the fathers on IB a product of provident guidance and protection from error, the justificatory status of those beliefs isn't very relevant to the justificatory status of your belief that IB.[16,17]

---

[13] Cf. Plantinga 1993*b*: 82–8.

[14] Cf. Lackey 1999: 480–1. For a recent, full-length treatment of related issues, see Lackey 2008.

[15] Where 'provident guidance', as I'm thinking of it here, may or may not involve the sort of direct production of belief by the Holy Spirit postulated by the IIHS model. God could providently arrange for someone to hold a certain belief by directly causing it in her, but I assume he could do it in less direct ways too.

[16] Objection: 'Surely the justificatory status of the fathers' beliefs on IB *is* relevant to the justificatory status of present-day belief that IB. For if the Fathers weren't justified in belief that IB, we shouldn't deem them experts on IB. And if we shouldn't deem them experts on IB, we shouldn't think present-day belief that IB a deliverance of expert testimony. And if we shouldn't think belief that IB a deliverance of expert testimony, then given your earlier arguments, it seems we shouldn't think present-day belief that IB justified at all.' By way of reply, why think the fathers' status as experts on IB thus dependent on whether they were epistemically justified in belief that IB? So long as their beliefs regarding IB resulted from divine guidance and protection from error, I should think them experts in the relevant sense, even if they lacked what we would think of as justified belief that IB (and as I say above, I don't see any reason for thinking they did). Thanks to Mike Rea for helpful feedback here.

[17] Thanks to Nathan Ballantyne, Daniel Howard-Snyder, Alvin Plantinga, Ted Poston, Michael Rea, Donald Smith, and Gregg Ten Elshof for helpful comments and conversation.

REFERENCES

Alston, William P. (1989) 'A "Doxastic Practice" Approach to Epistemology', in Marjorie Clay and Keith Lehrer (eds.), *Knowledge and Skepticism*, pp. 1–29. Boulder, Colo.: Westview Press.

Bergmann, Michael (2006) *Justification Without Awareness: A Defense of Epistemic Externalism.* Oxford: OUP.

Craig, William Lane (1989) *Assessing the New Testament Evidence for the Historicity of the Resurrection of Jesus.* Edwin Mellon Press.

Davis, Stephen T. (1993) *Risen Indeed: Making Sense of the Resurrection.* Grand Rapids, Mich.: Eerdmans.

Goldman, Alvin I. (1979) 'What is Justified Belief?', in G. S. Pappas (ed.), *Justification and Knowledge*, pp. 1–23. Dordrecht: D. Reidel.

Habermas, Gary, and Antony Flew (1987) *Did Jesus Rise from the Dead? The Resurrection Debate*, ed. Terry L. Miethe. San Francisco: Harper & Row.

Lackey, Jennifer (1999) 'Testimonial Knowledge and Transmission', *Philosophical Quarterly*, 49: 471–90.

—— (2008) *Learning from Words: Testimony as a Source of Knowledge.* Oxford: OUP.

McGrew, Timothy (2004) 'Has Plantinga Refuted the Historical Argument?', *Philosophia Christi*, 6: 7–26.

—— and Lydia McGrew (2006) 'On the Historical Argument: A Rejoinder to Plantinga', *Philosophia Christi*, 8: 23–38.

Plantinga, Alvin (1993a) *Warrant: The Current Debate.* Oxford: OUP.

—— (1993b) *Warrant and Proper Function.* Oxford: OUP.

—— (2000) *Warranted Christian Belief.* Oxford: OUP.

—— (2006) 'Historical Arguments and Dwindling Probabilities: A Response to Timothy McGrew', *Philosophia Christi*, 8: 12–21.

Pollock, John (1986) *Contemporary Theories of Knowledge.* Totowa, NJ: Rowman & Littlefield.

Swinburne, Richard (1992) *Revelation: From Metaphor to Analogy.* Oxford: OUP.

—— (2003) *The Resurrection of God Incarnate.* Oxford: OUP.

—— (2004) 'Natural Theology, its "Dwindling Probabilities" and "Lack of Rapport"', *Faith and Philosophy*, 21: 533–46.

Van Inwagen, Peter (1994) 'Quam Dilecta', in Thomas V. Morris (ed.), *God and the Philosophers: The Reconciliation of Faith and Reason*, pp. 31–60. Oxford: OUP.

Wright, N. T. (2003) *The Resurrection of the Son of God: Christian Origins and the Question of God*, iii. Minneapolis: Fortress Press.

10

The Contribution of Religious Experience to Dogmatic Theology

Michael Sudduth

INTRODUCTION

Scripture is typically regarded as the primary if not exclusive source for Christian theology. Tradition, though, has often been considered a supplemental source for theological beliefs, or at least as constituting an important framework for the interpretation of the text of scripture, for example by imposing various constraints on its interpretation. While the phrase 'systematic theology' has traditionally been used to designate systematic reflection on the content of scripture, 'dogmatic theology' situates this reflection in the context of tradition, in organic connection with the life of the Church. Dogmatic theology refers to the examination and systematic development of dogmas, ecclesiastically formulated and sanctioned core theological beliefs ostensibly based on scripture.[1] In this way, dogmatic theology includes and makes explicit what might in principle otherwise be excluded from Christian theology, namely the present and past work of an ecclesiastical tradition.

In addition to divinely revealed truth about God provided in scripture and formalized in the creedal and confessional traditions of the Church, there are two other putative grounds for beliefs about God.[2] First, there is *natural theology*. Catholics and Protestants have traditionally recognized that there are some truths about God that may be known by the light of natural reason. Most Catholic theologians and many Protestant theologians have regarded

---

[1] The Council of Trent (1545–63) recognized both written (scriptural) and unwritten revelation, so some dogmas in post-Tridentine Catholic theology need not be based on scripture, though they must be compatible with the teachings of scripture. By contrast, Protestants have emphasized that scripture is the exclusive basis for Christian beliefs that have the status of dogma. Tradition functions in an ancillary fashion.

[2] In speaking of different grounds for beliefs about God, I don't intend to make the stronger claim that these grounds function *independently* of each other, much less that they ought to so function. Indeed, it is one of the important claims of this chapter that these grounds are inextricably linked to each other.

this natural knowledge of God as inferential and so as codified in various classical arguments for the existence and attributes of God. Secondly, there is *religious experience*. The theistic beliefs of many people are based on experiences in which it seems to them that God is present. They directly or indirectly perceive God or God's actions, rather than draw inferences about God from their experience. While such experiences may in turn provide material for natural theological reasoning, we should nonetheless distinguish between the two. Theistic beliefs based directly on religious experience are non-inferential or non-discursive, not the product of reasoning or argument.

In contemporary analytic philosophy of religion there has been considerable work on both natural theology and religious experience as epistemic grounds for beliefs about God, that is, as grounds capable of conferring justification or warrant on various beliefs about God. There has been less attention paid to how natural theology and religious experience relate to dogmatic theology. However, an analytic approach to theology should be able to relate these issues in the epistemology of belief in God to dogmatics, at least to assess their relevance to the project of dogmatic theology. I'll do precisely this in the present chapter. I will argue that natural theology, contrary to what we might initially suppose, has an important role to play within the system and discourse of dogmatic theology. We need not conceive of natural theology solely as a rational propaedeutic to the system of revealed theology, a kind of pre-dogmatic foundation for the faith. Rather, natural theology can contribute to goals internal to dogmatics itself, for example, the desiderata of systematicity and the explication of biblical doctrines. However, I will also argue that natural theology and religious experience are intertwined at different levels, so religious experience is also inextricably linked to dogmatic theology. I'll outline several of these links, some of which parallel the relationship between natural and dogmatic theology. My focus will be on dogmatic theology in the Protestant tradition, but several of my observations can be adopted by dogmatic theology in the Catholic and Greek Orthodox traditions.

NATURAL THEOLOGY AND DOGMATIC THEOLOGY

One of the goals of dogmatic theology is the development of a systematic doctrine of God and God's relation to the world. Natural theology, rational arguments for the existence and attributes of God, enters this picture in at least three, related ways. First, if God can be naturally known, this fact should be brought into dialogue with the knowledge of God given by way of scriptural revelation. If God is naturally knowable, this presupposes a more general kind of revelation in the natural order of things and accessible in principle to human reason. A systematic account of God and God's relation to the world must consider the totality of the modes by which God reveals himself. Secondly, the text of scripture itself raises the possibility, if not actuality, of a natural knowledge of God based on a general revelation of God in the created order (Romans 1: 19–21; Psalm 19; Acts 14, 17). If so, the project of natural theology has biblical warrant at least indirectly,[3] and natural theology may be construed as an attempt to clarify and develop the scriptural testimony to general revelation and the natural knowledge of God. Finally, the development of a natural theology allows the Church to relate its confession and witness to the broader range of human life and society. It can thereby articulate how God relates himself to the world independent of the particularities of the Church's witness, as well as establish the unique value of the Church's witness in clarifying the nature and limits of general revelation. So natural theology would seem to be a necessary element within dogmatic theology by virtue of the latter's need for systematicity, explication of biblical doctrines, and Church–world dialogue.

While some Protestant theologians have rejected natural theology,[4] there has been a deeply entrenched and widespread endorsement of natural theology in the Protestant tradition, stretching back at least to the latter part of the sixteenth century. One of the interesting features of this endorsement has been its pluralism. Protestant theologians have endorsed different models of natural theology, different ways of thinking about the nature and function of theistic proofs, especially in relation to dogmatics. This is particularly true in the Reformed or Calvinistic streams of the Protestant tradition, where objections to natural theology have been prominent since the latter part of the nineteenth century. These so-called 'Reformed objections' to natural theology must be interpreted in the larger context of the tradition's pluralistic dialogue on natural theology.[5] For our present purposes, this pluralism provides

---

[3] For a detailed development of this argument, see James Barr, *Biblical Faith and Natural Theology* (Oxford: Clarendon Press, 1993).

[4] e.g. Friedrich Schleiermacher, Karl Barth, G. C. Berkouwer, and conservative Calvinists such as Herman Hoeksema and Gordon Clark. In the seventeenth and eighteenth centuries, the rejection of natural theology was typically linked to pietism or reactions to the 'natural religion' of the deists. For the latter, see John Ellis, *The Knowledge of Divine Things from Revelation not from Reason or Nature* (London, 1743) and William Irons, *On the Whole Doctrine of Final Causes* (London, 1836). In the 19th and 20th centuries it has been philosophically motivated primarily by the influence of Immanuel Kant's critique of natural theology and theologically inspired by Catholic–Protestant polemics. See Berkouwer, *General Revelation* (Grand Rapids, Mich.: Eerdmans, 1955), chs. 2 and 3.

[5] Viewed in this light, many so-called Reformed objections to natural theology turn out to be more modest than they first appear, typically targeting particular models of natural theology rather than the project of natural theology itself. I argue this in detail in my *Reformed Objection to Natural Theology* (forthcoming, Ashgate).

insight into different ways of developing the preliminary suggestions above and thereby showing the necessity of natural theology to dogmatic theology.

Conceptions of Natural Theology in the Protestant Tradition

It is now widely accepted that the presentation of arguments for the existence and nature of God first unambiguously appear in the Protestant tradition in Philip Melanchthon's *Loci Communes* (1535, 1543–4) and *Commentary on Romans* (1532, 1540). In the latter they appear as an elaboration and development of Romans 1: 19–21: 'For what can be known about God is plain to them, because God has shown it to them. Ever since the creation of the world his eternal power and divine nature, invisible though they are, have been understood and seen through the things he has made. So they are without excuse' (NRSV). In the former they appear under the heading *de creatione*, a biblically based discussion of creation. In each case, it is clear that theistic arguments are directed to the Christian as a means of rationally reflecting on the data of biblical revelation. Melanchthon develops theistic arguments in the course of articulating aspects of revealed or biblical theology, with the stated goal of strengthening the Christian's knowledge of God.[6] There is a natural theology here embedded in the larger context of revealed theology, but no attempt to construct a theology of God based solely on reason and then use it as a gateway to dogmatic theology.

In sixteenth- and many seventeenth-century Protestant dogmatic systems theistic arguments were typically presented under theological prolegomena or the *locus de Deo*,[7] the former being a discussion of the principles and presuppositions of dogmatic theology and the latter being a discussion of the existence and attributes of God. Within the setting of early Protestant scholasticism, neither theological prolegomena nor the *locus de Deo* was pre-dogmatic in nature. Each exhibited a dependence on and integration with scripture and the correlated Christian doctrine of God, even where the dogmatic system begins with the *locus de Deo*. This explains the reliance on scripture in the *locus de Deo*, as is illustrated in the use of the 'divine names' derived from scripture as a point of departure for articulating and systematizing the divine attributes.[8] It also explains the inclusion of the doctrine of

---

[6] See John Platt, *Reformed Thought and Scholasticism: The Arguments for the Existence of God in Dutch Theology, 1575–1650* (Leiden: E. J. Brill, 1982), ch. 2.

[7] For a detailed discussion of theistic proofs in Reformed scholasticism, see Richard Muller, *Post-Reformation Reformed Dogmatics*, 4 vols. (Grand Rapids, Mich.: Baker Academic, 2003), iii. 48–52, 153–95. See also my *Reformed Objection to Natural Theology* (forthcoming, Ashgate), ch. 1.

[8] Ibid. 254–72.

the Trinity under the *locus de Deo*,[9] even though the Trinity is not an aspect of natural theology for these Protestant thinkers. In some instances the *locus de scriptura* is prior to the *locus de Deo*[10] so it is clear that the doctrine of God rests on scriptural revelation as its foundation, not reason. In these early dogmatic systems, we find no independent *locus* on natural theology, either within or prefaced to the theological system. Rational arguments for the existence and nature of God are situated in the larger context of the exposition of the contents of revealed theology.

By contrast, when we examine theistic proofs in many of the Protestant dogmatic systems of the late seventeenth and eighteenth centuries, we find natural theology presented as a pre-dogmatic, rational foundation for the faith.[11] Under the influence of Cartesianism and Wolffian rationalism, natural theology was transformed into a purely rational discourse on the divine existence and attributes, separated from scripture and designed to prepare the way for the system of revealed theology. The nineteenth century inherited this pre-dogmatic conception of natural theology, which arguably reached its culmination in the famous Gifford Lectures established by Lord Gifford in 1888. Gifford's goal was to provide a platform for a purely scientific or rational treatment of the existence and nature of God, independent of any claims originating from an ostensible divine revelation. This pre-dogmatic conception of natural theology represents a significant departure from the earlier Protestant scholastics.

To be sure, we do find an apologetic use of theistic arguments among the earlier Protestant scholastics, ostensibly an illustration of the Church–world dialogue I mentioned above. However, in this context theistic arguments are not used to *establish* either theism or the Christian faith but simply to *refute* atheists and remove objections to the faith within the larger logical architecture of revealed theology. Francis Turretin and Edward Leigh, for example, both used theistic proofs to refute atheists, but these arguments appear subsequent to the doctrine of scripture under a biblically informed doctrine of God. This is, of course, entirely consistent with the instrumental use of reason in dogmatic theology.[12] There is a reasoned defense of the faith *within*

---

[9] e.g. Hyperius, *Methodus theologiae* (1568); Musculus, *Loci communes* (1560); Daneau, *Christianae isogoges* (1583); Turretin, *Institutio theologiae elencticae* (Geneva, 1679–85).

[10] e.g. Polansdorf, *Syntagma theologiae christianae* (Geneva, 1617), Edward Leigh, *Body of Divinity* (London, 1654), and Turretin, *Institutio theologiae elencticae* (Geneva, 1679–85).

[11] e.g. Salomon van Til, *Theologiae utriusque compendium* (Leiden, 1704, 1719), I. i–iii, II. i–iii; Johann Friedrich Stapfer, *Institutiones theologiae polemicae universae, ordine scientifico dispositae*, 4th edn., 5 vols. (Zurich, 1756–7); Daniel Wyttenbach, *Tentamen theologiae dogmaticae methodo scientifico pertractatae*, 3 vols. (Frankfurt, 1747–9). For further discussion, see Muller, *Post-Reformation*, i. 305–8, iii. 121–9, 141–50, 193–5.

[12] What I'm designating the 'instrumental' use of reason is roughly equivalent to what Oliver Crisp, in Chapter 1, refers to as the 'procedural' use of reason.

the system of dogmatic theology but no apologetically motivated theological prolegomenon in which natural theology is used to lay the foundations for subsequent claims about God derived from scripture. The scientific or reflective elaboration of the faith may require the refutation of various objections to the faith, but the *principium* of dogmatics remains scripture, not reason.

The Justification of the Instrumental Role of Reason

There are interesting parallels between the Protestant dogmatic conception of natural theology and Thomas Aquinas's demonstrations of the existence of God as they occur in Thomas's *Summa Theologiae*.[13] In neither do we find natural theology functioning as a rational foundation for revealed theology. The *Summa* does not begin with the Five Ways. The proofs are actually placed subsequent to Aquinas's initial discussion on the nature and domain of sacred doctrine. When the proofs occur (in the *prima pars*, question 2), they actually presuppose scripture, in much the same way that the theistic proofs do in many Protestant dogmatic systems. There is no attempt to begin with any natural theology, nor does Thomas move from a purely rational knowledge of God based on reason to a revealed knowledge of God based on scripture. Like the earlier Protestant scholastics, Aquinas's doctrine of God is biblically informed.[14] Of course, Aquinas's concern in the *prima pars*, question 2 of the *Summa* is not to prove the existence of God over against atheist denials of the existence of God, but to prove the demonstrability of the existence of God over against *religious* denials that God's existence can be demonstrated. The proofs are an answer to fideistic tendencies internal to the Christian tradition.

The use of the proofs to refute fideism is closely tied to Aquinas's prior concern in the *prima pars* (question 1, article 8) whether sacred doctrine is argumentative. From this vantage point we can see the demonstration of the existence of God as a way of exploring the nature of our knowledge of God and the possibility of a theological discourse in which there is a reasoned exploration and elucidation of the articles of faith. But this is for the sake of the Christian. The proofs provide reason to believe that reason itself can enter into the theological realm and elucidate the articles of faith.

---

[13] See Muller, *Post-Reformation*, iii. 153–9; Muller, 'The Dogmatic Function of the St. Thomas' "Proofs": A Protestant Appreciation', *Fides et Historia*, 24/2 (Summer 1992), 15–29. I am indebted to Muller for much of the argument in this section of the chapter.

[14] Stanley Hauerwas has recently emphasized the faith-context of Aquinas's five ways. See Hauerwas, *With the Grain of the Universe: The Church's Witness and Natural Theology* (Grand Rapids, Mich.: Brazos Press, 2001), ch. 1. See also G. de Broglie, 'La Vraie Notion thomiste des "praeambula fidei"', *Gregorianum*, 34 (1953), 349–89.

There is no need to establish the existence of God within the framework of the dogmatic system, for dogmatics already presupposes the existence of God. There *is* a need, however, to establish the instrumental validity of reason for theology, to show that it is fit for the task of being the handmaiden of sacred doctrine. Viewed in this light, while the proofs are intended as genuine logical demonstrations of God's existence, they are not foundations upon which revealed theology is built. They provide the Christian with a justification of the instrumental role of reason for the sake of the dogmatic elaboration of the articles of faith.[15]

While the apologetic and pre-dogmatic conceptions of natural theology may be legitimate ways of thinking about natural theology and its connection to dogmatic theology, it is equally important to see natural theology as a project internal to the discourse of dogmatics itself, as an intellectual activity arising from conceptual needs internal to dogmatics and the more general desideratum of faith seeking understanding. From this vantage point, the development of a systematic doctrine of God based on scripture and the rational justification of reason's ability to accomplish this task become deeply intertwined, but they do so as elements within not foundational to dogmatics.

NATURAL THEOLOGY AND RELIGIOUS EXPERIENCE

Where does religious experience factor into this picture and how does it ultimately relate to dogmatic theology? One of the connections here is indirect and depends on a particular relationship between natural theology and religious experience. We must examine this first and then consider its implications for relating religious experience to dogmatic theology.

The Nature of Religious Experience

One tendency, particularly prominent in post-Kantian liberal Protestant thought, has been to construe religious experience as non-cognitive in nature. On this view, religious experience does not place the cognizer in possession of any truth about God. Hence, religious experience isn't a source of knowledge of God. It is a feeling or some other affective state of the subject. On this view, religious experience stands in sharp contrast to natural theology. Whereas natural theology ostensibly informs us about the ultimate metaphysical

---

[15] Muller, 'Dogmatic Function', 24.

furniture of the world, religious experience functions as a source of moral and spiritual transformation. The reflective examination of religious experience informs us about theological doctrines, not as true or false, but as vehicles of piety and personal transformation.[16] If, on this view, we see religious experience as a ground for truths of any sort, it is solely truths about human nature and experience, not divine realities.[17] The psychology of human belief in God replaces theology. It is this understanding of religious experience that has been responsible for the widespread skepticism among conservative Protestants towards the integration of religious experience and dogmatic theology. The fear has been that dogmatic theology may turn out to be neither dogmatic nor theology.[18]

Of course, plenty of theologians and philosophers have maintained that religious experience is cognitive, that it can inform us about divine realities. Cognitive accounts of religious experience have been one of the important developments in contemporary philosophy of religion since the second half of the twentieth century. Some thinkers have held that religious experience involves an intuitive perception of God's presence that generically resembles our intuitive perception of other minds.[19] Others have focused on a class of religious experiences characterized as non-sensory perceptual experiences of God, generically resembling our sensory perceptual experiences of the physical world.[20] Some have taken religious experience to be a perceptual experience in a fairly broad sense: it seeming to the person that God is present, where this may or may not be mediated by something sensory.[21] Of course,

---

[16] See Ch. 6 above, by Andrew Dole.

[17] See T. R. Miles, *Religious Experience* (London: Macmillan, 1972).

[18] e.g. the Reformed theologian Herman Bavinck wrote: 'In many schools of theology, there is a tendency to replace all transcendent-metaphysical statements about God, his essence and attributes, his words and works, with descriptions of Christian experience and its content.' Bavinck, *Reformed Dogmatics; Prolegomena*, ed. John Bolt, tr. John Vriend (Grand Rapids, Mich.: Baker Book House, 2003), i. 48; cf. pp. 106–7, 165–6. See also Louis Berkhof, *Systematic Theology*, 4th edn. (Grand Rapids, Mich.: Eerdmans, 1984), 19–20, and B. B. Warfield, 'The Idea of Systematic Theology', in *The Works of Benjamin B. Warfield*, 10 vols. (1932; repr., Grand Rapids, Mich.: Baker Book House, 2000), ix. 55–8.

[19] John Baillie, *Our Knowledge of God* (New York: Charles Scribner's Sons, 1939), 166–77, 207–18.

[20] See John Hick, *Arguments for the Existence of God* (New York: Herder & Herder, 1971), ch. 7; William Wainwright, 'Mysticism and Sense Perception', *Religious Studies*, 9 (1973), 257–78; Gary Gutting, *Religious Belief and Religious Skepticism* (Notre Dame, Ind.: University of Notre Dame Press, 1982); William Alston, *Perceiving God* (Ithaca, NY: Cornell University Press, 1991).

[21] Richard Swinburne, *The Existence of God* (Oxford: Clarendon Press, 1979), ch. 13. Two clarifications. First, 'seems' here is epistemic and refers to what the cognizer is inclined to believe on the basis of her present experience. This is usually contrasted with the non-epistemic use of 'seems' that involves a comparison of an object with other objects. It seems to me (in the comparative sense) that the stick in the water is bent because it looks the way bent things look, but it won't seem bent to me (in the epistemic sense) if I'm not inclined to believe that the stick

others have regarded religious experience as an experience the subject interprets as religious, that is, a mundane experience the subject merely takes to be caused by God.[22] On the perceptual views, religious experience can directly be a source of warranted beliefs about God, so at least some theistic beliefs can be immediately warranted. Their warrant does not (entirely) depend on the subject's other warranted beliefs. On the interpretive view, religious experience can be epistemically efficacious only if the subject's interpretive beliefs about the cause of her experience are warranted. In this case, religious experience cannot directly confer warrant on beliefs about God.

For our present purposes, I'll adopt the view that at least some religious experiences ground immediately warranted beliefs about God, so that the interpretive view of religious experience is at best only part of the story of the nature of religious experience. I will, however, note the implications of the interpretive view for aspects of my argument in what follows. Furthermore, I take the perceptual model to provide an account of a broad range of experiences from extra-ordinary mystical experiences of union with God to the more regular perception of God in the workings of nature and in one's daily devotional life. In some of these experiences God is directly perceived, whereas in others he is indirectly perceived through the perception of something else (e.g. the beauties of nature, the hearing of the words of scripture, miraculous events).

Natural theology and perceptual models of religious experience have an important common ground. They are both cognitive models. Each proposes a source of beliefs about God that potentially gives us knowledge of the ultimate metaphysical furniture of the universe. Nonetheless, an important difference remains. Religious experience would be a source of *immediately* warranted beliefs (or knowledge) about God, whereas natural theology would be a source of *inferentially* warranted beliefs (or knowledge) about God. The distinction is analogous to the difference between forming the belief that it is raining outside because one sees the rain falling, and forming the belief that it is raining outside because one has inferred this from other bits of knowledge (e.g. the weather channel predicted rain today, the sound of pitter-patter on the roof, and someone has just walked in the house with a dripping wet

---

is bent. I might lack this inclination, for example, because I know the appearance is an optical illusion. Secondly, where religious experience is mediated by something sensory, Swinburne distinguishes between religious experiences mediated by publicly observable phenomena and those that are mediated by sensations private to the individual. In the former, the phenomena may be ordinary or extra-ordinary. In the latter, the sensory states private to the individual may or may not be describable by ordinary vocabulary.

[22] Wayne Proudfoot, *Religious Experience* (Berkeley, Calif.: University of California Press, 1985).

umbrella). This distinction naturally raises the question as to how, if at all, these two putative sources of warranted theistic belief positively interact with each other.

The Positive Interface between Natural Theology and Religious Experience

Despite their distinctness, there is an important positive interface between religious experience and natural theology, which will in turn be important to assessing the relationship between religious experience and dogmatic theology.

First, we need not suppose that religious experience confers maximal warrant on theistic belief, so inference can always, at least in principle, *add* warrant to theistic beliefs that receive some warrant directly from religious experience. This may be particularly important in cases where the warrant provided by religious experience isn't sufficient to transform true belief into knowledge. Inference can make the difference between warranted true beliefs and knowledge.[23] Moreover, even where theistic beliefs grounded in religious experience have an initially high degree of warrant (enough for knowledge) this degree of warrant may be subsequently reduced, for instance as the result of acquiring a defeater against theistic belief.[24] The positive epistemic status of religious beliefs is defeasible. It is subject to being overridden by reasons for supposing that God doesn't exist or reasons for supposing that some ground of theistic belief is unreliable. The warrant of theistic belief based on religious experience could be defeated in either way, but independent reasons for supposing that God exists could defeat defeaters in these circumstances and allow theistic belief to remain warranted, even to continue receiving warrant from religious experience.

Secondly, it seems implausible to suppose that just *any* kind of belief about God could be directly warranted by religious experience. In that case, perhaps inference can confer warrant on theistic beliefs that are not supported by

---

[23] I assume that knowledge entails a strongly warranted true belief, even if knowledge requires the satisfaction of some further condition, e.g. to handle so-called Gettier counter-examples.

[24] I am thinking of defeaters here as items internal to the cognizer (in the form of the cognizer's experiences or other beliefs) that eliminate warrant or reduce a belief's degree of warrant. In some epistemological theories, defeaters are conditions external to the cognizer (e.g. in the form of some true proposition) that prevent a sufficiently justified true belief from counting as knowledge. For further discussion on defeaters in connection with religious belief, see my 'Proper Basicality and the Evidential Significance of Internalist Defeat: A Proposal for Revising Classical Evidentialism', in Godehard Bruntrup and Ronald Tacelli (eds.), *The Rationality of Theism* (Dordrecht: Kluwer Academic Publishers, 1999), 215–36.

religious experience. Granted, it is difficult to spell out limits on how God may be experienced, but particular conceptions of religious experience would seem to suggest boundaries of some sort. For example, if we suppose that religious experience involves a direct presentation of God to our experience, it is doubtful that God will present himself in the totality of his being at any given time. And even where God presents himself to us as φ (some particular divine attribute), theism may wish to say more about φ than is underwritten by the experience. God may present himself to our experience as good or powerful, but not as a being with *unlimited* goodness or power. However, these kinds of beliefs can be the product of rational inferences. In fact, they are typically part of the package of natural theology. So inference may help fill out the content of experientially grounded theistic beliefs. Also, ostensible perceptions of God (indirect and direct) would seem to depend on a set of background beliefs that allow the individual to identify what is being experienced as God. These background beliefs may at least in part be built up from the resources of natural theology.[25]

These first two points highlight ways in which inference can make contributions to the natural knowledge of God even if religious experience is epistemically efficacious. But religious experience seems capable of making its own important contributions here.

First, while religious experience may be a source of immediately warranted beliefs about God, the fact that people have religious experiences can function as a datum for the arguments of natural theology. This is precisely what has been done in the so-called argument from religious experience, roughly, arguments that contend that the facts of religious experience constitute at least prima facie evidence for certain theistic beliefs.[26] The argument from religious experience has often been combined with other arguments for the existence of God in a cumulative case approach to proving God's existence. On this view, religious experience functions as an empirical datum along with the existence of the universe, its temporal and spatial regularities, and so forth. It is then argued that the existence of God (understood in a robust theistic sense) provides the best explanation for these empirical data taken collectively. The data of religious experience are arguably of considerable importance in supporting divine attributes established by other theistic arguments (e.g. divine power, goodness) and those not so obviously established (e.g. divine love). Considerations from religious experience could also

---

[25] William Alston develops the points raised in the prior two paragraphs in some detail: *Perceiving God*, ch. 8.

[26] C. D. Broad, *Religion, Philosophy, and Psychical Research* (London: Routledge & Kegan Paul, 1930); Swinburne, *Existence of God*, ch. 13; Gutting, *Religious Belief*; Carolyn Franks Davis, *The Evidential Force of Religious Experience* (New York: OUP, 1989).

provide support for other theistic doctrines (e.g. sanctification) some of which have traditionally been linked to the domain of natural religion and rational argument (e.g. an afterlife).[27] So this particular use of religious experience would seem to be of considerable importance to a well-developed natural theology.

Secondly, religious experience, if a source of warranted belief in God, would provide warrant for very different kinds of theistic beliefs than the kind of theistic beliefs that are underwritten by the arguments of natural theology. Religious experience often functions as a ground for the formation of beliefs about specific divine actions towards oneself at a particular time, for example, that God is now forgiving me (for some wrong doing), God is guiding me (in some particular decision-making process), or that God comforting me (in the aftermath of some particular tragedy). These are not the kinds of claims natural theology establishes, even where natural theology incorporates material from the data of religious experience. It is one thing to appeal to the religious experiences of other people as evidence that God exists and is active in the lives of people, quite another to be aware of God's presence and activity in one's *own* life at some particular time.[28] So religious experience can make a unique contribution to the knowledge of God, even where we grant inference an epistemically significant role.

Finally, one of the common criticisms of theistic arguments is that these arguments are not strong and so do not confer a significant degree of warrant on theistic beliefs. However, the consequences of this for the epistemology of belief in God are less dire if we recognize that theistic belief receives significant warrant from religious experience, for in that case inference need not bear a heavy epistemic burden. The proper role of inference will be to add weight to and fill out theistic beliefs warranted on grounds other than inference. Rather than being an attempt at proving the existence of God *de novo*, natural theology will be a way in which religious persons confirm and reflectively develop an antecedent belief in God. Perhaps more controversially, the actual force of theistic arguments may be affected by the presence or absence of a background of religious experience. The force of inductive theistic arguments depends in part on the antecedent probability of theism, but this probability is affected by the totality of our experience. It would seem to be higher for those who have experienced God than for those who have not. Arguably then religious experience not only strengthens the conclusions of natural theology,

---

[27] Near death experiences, e.g., if they involve a perception of some divine reality (as many do) count as religious experiences, but they potentially provide evidence for post-mortem survival.

[28] With the assistance of tradition or scripture, one may *infer* that God is at work in one's life, or more specific propositions such as God loves me or God forgives me. See below for a further discussion.

but it might make possible whatever epistemic efficacy the arguments of natural theology possess.

DOGMATIC THEOLOGY AND RELIGIOUS EXPERIENCE

Religious experience and rational inference, then, appear to be interdependent sources of knowledge of God. However, here I wish to emphasize one facet of this interdependence suggested above, namely that religious experience seems to be necessary to the project of natural theology in at least two related ways. (i) The data of religious experience, though not necessary to the content and structure of some particular theistic arguments, is essential to the overall project of natural theology. A robust or sufficiently developed natural theology will, in the interest of systematicity, integrate all aspects of general revelation. Moreover, as argued above, natural theology without the data of religious experience is likely to lose something in the way of the cumulative force of its arguments, its ability to suitably establish particular divine attributes, and its ability to integrate other theistic doctrines. (ii) Theistic arguments (with or without integrating data from religious experience) are epistemically efficacious for some people only because they have had some religious experience(s). According to (ii) it is the *fact* of religious experience that is necessary for the epistemic efficacy of natural theology for some persons, whereas according to (i) it is the *reflective use* of the facts of religious experience that is necessary for a robust form of natural theology.

In the first section I argued that natural theology is necessary to dogmatic theology, but the implication of the argument in the second section is—as just outlined—that religious experience is necessary to natural theology. It follows that religious experience is necessary to dogmatic theology. If dogmatic theology were to make use of the resources of natural theology, for any of the reasons noted earlier, it will invariably find itself making use of the resources of religious experience in the ways suggested by (i) or (ii). The argument here is of course indirect. It can be supplemented with a more direct engagement of the relationship between religious experience and dogmatic theology.

The Contribution of Dogmatic Theology to Religious Experience

From the perspective of the subject having a religious experience, the precise character of a religious experience is strongly dependent on the subject's broader set of beliefs about God, many of which will be derived from dogmatic theology. This is obviously true in the case of interpretive accounts of religious experience, but it is equally true in the case of perceptual models of religious experience. As in the case of sensory perceptual beliefs, object identification and property attribution are shaped by our background beliefs. The point was made earlier in connection with natural theology, but it would seem to be of greater significance here for two reasons.

First, dogmatic theology is likely to exert a greater influence on the beliefs of ordinary believers than natural theology. The content of dogmatic theology is communicated to ordinary believers through the communal life of the Church, its creeds and catechisms, and pulpit sermons, all of wider appeal to the practice of religion than works devoted to the philosophical elucidation of the faith. Where natural theology has influence, it tends to be through the fairly indirect route of its influence on dogmatic theology. Consider, for example, the influence of Greek natural theology on the concept of God in various systems of dogmatic theology and their articulation in the confessions of the Church. To take a Calvinistic example, the Westminster Confession of Faith claims 'there is but one only living and true God, who is infinite in being and perfection, a most pure spirit, invisible, without body, parts, or passions, immutable, immense, eternal, incomprehensible, almighty, most wise, most holy, most free, most absolute'.[29] While the confession provides scriptural references for each of these attributions, the confession reflects a tradition of natural theological reflection embodied in Protestant scholasticism and which stretches back to medieval philosophy.

Secondly, unlike the traditional arguments of natural theology, dogmatic theology provides a detailed narrative of God's interactions with humans. It thereby informs us about the conditions under which people have genuinely experienced God (e.g. conversion, prayer, meditation), the character of these experiences, how they may be induced, and an account of their moral and spiritual fruits. While this is far from giving us a recipe of experiencing God, it is relevant to certain expectations about God's interaction with humans. Moreover, it at least provides criteria for distinguishing genuine religious experiences from spurious ones. Most religious traditions recognize that there are 'counterfeit' religious experiences,[30] whether induced by cognitive disorders or malevolent spiritual forces at work in the world. Consequently, claims to perceiving God have historically been tested for consistency with Christian doctrine and paradigmatic religious experiences of saints and other

---

[29] *Westminster Confession of Faith*, 2: 1.
[30] An excellent Protestant illustration of this is found in Jonathan Edwards's discussion of religious experience in his *Treatise on the Religious Affections* (1746).

believers in the history of the Church. So the practice of forming beliefs about God on the basis of religious experience operates with distinctive testing and checking procedures.[31]

It is important to add here that the presence of testing and checking procedures for religious experience is an important point of similarity between sense perception and religious experience. This similarity strengthens the case for supposing that religious experience can be a source of warranted religious belief, for we might suppose that sense perception is a source of warranted beliefs about physical objects only if specific sensory perceptual experiences and the beliefs they engender are subject to various testing and checking procedures, as in fact they are. At any rate, the alleged absence of any testing procedures for religious experiences is often raised as an objection to treating religious experience as sufficiently like sensory perceptual experience. However, the point here is that dogmatic theology (along with natural theology) provides significant input to the larger belief framework in which religious experiences are situated and over against which their deliverances may be tested. In that case, though, dogmatic theology makes an important contribution to the epistemology of religious experience.

The argument from religious experience is, if evidence for the existence of God, evidence of divine–human interaction. So there is a sense in which natural theology can provide us with a generic narrative of the sort I have attributed to dogmatic theology above. But the raw data from ostensible religious experiences makes up a very large collection of experiences, many of which engender incompatible beliefs about the divine, even within the same religious tradition. If reason alone must navigate these waters, it is usually at the expense of the particularities of many of the experiences or the ramified nature of the beliefs allegedly grounded in such experiences. The evidential value of such experiences (outside the context of dogmatic theology) usually requires trimming away many of the details that render these experiences most significant for the believer.[32] Arguably, then, there is a need for a tradition-specific normative guide to religious experience, and dogmatic theology provides this, and in such a way that it is easily accessible to ordinary believers.

---

[31] For further discussion of the nature and ramifications of testing and checking procedures for religious experience, see Alston, *Perceiving God*, 209–22, Wainwright, 'Mysticism', and Davis, *Evidential Force*, 70–7.

[32] Carolyn Franks Davis argues that the 'conflicting claims challenge' cannot defeat the evidential force of religious experience if the latter is taken only to support theistic beliefs of a very low level of ramification. While Davis says that the introduction of evidential considerations beyond religious experience can result in evidential support for more highly ramified theistic beliefs, it is doubtful this can be effective in the absence of a reliance on tradition-specific doctrines. See Davis, *Evidential Force*, chs. 7 and 9.

The Contribution of Religious Experience to Dogmatic Theology

As with natural theology, dogmatic theology not only shapes but is also shaped by religious experience. Here I'll consider four salient contributions of religious experience to dogmatic theology.

There is first what we might designate the *genesis factor*. Historically, religious experiences have made dogmatic theology possible. Dogmatic theology involves a systematic reflection on the data of scripture, but scripture is in large part a record of religious experiences ostensibly involving the communication of divine truths. In this way, much of the content of dogmatic theology originates ultimately from the religious experiences of central figures in biblical history. What would dogmatic theology be without the voice of God calling to Abraham in Ur of the Chaldees, God speaking to Moses from the burning bush, or Saul of Tarsus's encounter with the risen Christ on the road to Damascus? Not only would we be missing testimony to particular interactions between the human and divine but we would be missing the distinctive doctrines that have emerged historically from such interactions. We would also be missing the vitality of religious consciousness that inspires the rise of theological doctrines and formulae. As William James said: 'In one sense at least the personal religion will prove itself more fundamental than either theology or ecclesiasticism. Churches, when once established, live second-hand upon tradition; but the founders of every church owed their power originally to the fact of their direct personal communion with the divine.'[33]

Second, there is the *confirmation factor*. Religious experience and its data confirm some of the essential content of dogmatic theology, most generally the personal nature of the divine being and the fact of divine–human interaction. While the traditional arguments of natural theology confirm some essential features of dogmatic theology (e.g. the existence and natural attributes of God), the appeal to religious experience permits a confirmation of the fact that God reveals himself in concrete historical events and individual human lives, which is precisely what dogmatic theology affirms and would lead us to expect. While dogmatic theology does not lead us to expect that every purported experience of God will be genuine, it does lead us to expect that there would be experiences of the sort that humans have reported throughout history.[34]

---

[33] William James, *The Varieties of Religious Experience* (New York: Modern Library, 2002), 35.

[34] Arguably, some systems of dogmatic theology would also lead us to expect counterfeits of such experiences, whether as the product of the noetic effects of sin or the activity of some malevolent spiritual agents. These systems would lead us to expect conflicting claims arising from ostensible religious experiences.

Third, there is the *explication* factor. Reflection on the phenomenon of religious experience within dogmatic theology is not merely an activity of rational confirmation of elements of the dogmatic system but it is, perhaps more importantly, a means of rationally explicating the content of biblical theology itself. Earlier I argued that natural theology is important to dogmatic theology since it helps explicate and develop the biblical testimony to general revelation and the natural knowledge of God. But many kinds of religious experiences arguably ground a natural knowledge of God. At any rate, this is true within the Protestant tradition, where theologians have recognized that, in addition to the knowledge of God that can be acquired inferentially from features of the natural world, there is an intuitive knowledge of God that arises spontaneously with mental maturation and experience of the world. The intuitive knowledge of God includes the more ordinary kinds of religious experiences, for example, the experience of God in the beauties or providences of nature. Both kinds of knowledge of God (inferential and intuitive) are natural and testify to God's general revelation of himself in the created order and natural constitution of the human person. The relevant point here is that reflection on some religious experiences constitutes reflection on the intuitive natural knowledge of God. Religious experience and natural theology are once again intertwined.

Of course many religious experiences transcend the natural order of things, and so do not amount to natural grounds for belief in God. This seems to be the case with certain paradigm cases of extra-ordinary religious experiences provided in the biblical narrative, for instance, Moses' experiences at the burning bush and the receiving of the law on Mt Sinai, or Saul of Tarsus's experience of the risen Christ on the road to Damascus. Scripture recognizes more extra-ordinary modes of self-revelation that appear to be supernatural (e.g. by way of dreams, visions, theophanies, angelic manifestations). Protestants of course disagree about whether such modes of revelation continue in the present day, and if so the extent and centrality of such revelations. However, Protestants agree about the continuing indwelling and testimony of the Holy Spirit in the lives of individual believers. The internal testimony of the Holy Spirit brings conviction of sin, sense of forgiveness, awareness of conversion, and persuasion of the truth of the Christian gospel. These are religious experiences that produce convictions about God and the human person's relation to God, but they are supernaturally induced experiences according to Protestant dogmatics. Hence, reflection on some religious experiences, while not an aspect of natural theology, would amount to an explication of God's more extra-ordinary ways of revealing himself in the economy of individual salvation.

Finally, there is the *reality factor*. On a realist conception of perceptual experience, it is God himself who is directly known in the perceptual experience of God, in much the same way that physical objects are directly known by way of sensory perceptual experience. Now physical science surely shapes many of the details of our experience of the physical world, but science emerges and is sustained as a reflective activity on the realities given to us by way of sense perception. In much the same way, while dogmatic theology shapes the experience of God in the ways I earlier suggested, the experience of God gives the fundamental realities about which dogmatic theology reflects and speaks. Dogmatic theology is rational discourse about God that is dependent on personal contact and interaction with the divine being, both in the collective and individual sense.

We can of course *infer* the personal presence and activity of God in our lives from criteria of this presence and activity given by dogmatic theology. I can infer that God forgives me by perceiving the satisfaction of certain conditions of forgiveness in my life. I can infer that God is sanctifying me from divine promises in scripture and my experiential awareness of spiritual fruit in my life. I can infer that God loves me from what scripture says about God and God's relationship to the world. But inferring that God forgives or loves me is fundamentally different than experiencing divine forgiveness or love itself. In much the same way, I can infer that my friend loves or forgives me, but I can also experience this love and forgiveness through our personal interactions, an experience through which the bonds of friendship are strengthened. Something similar needs to be said about the human–divine relationship. The experiential awareness of God is arguably essential to the personal relationship between God and individual human persons, a relationship about which dogmatic theology speaks. The absence of this experiential dimension would certainly change the theologian's approach to dogmatic theology itself. Perhaps it would degenerate into a deistic system of rational theology or a theology disconnected from the interests and experiences of the Church.

As in the case of natural theology, the dogmatic goals of systematicity and the explication of the biblical doctrine of general revelation play an important role in justifying the integration of religious experience and dogmatic theology. In this regard, it is important to note the position of the great conservative Princeton theologian B. B. Warfield. According to Warfield, although we cannot construct any complete system of theology from the data of Christian religious experience, it is quite legitimate for the dogmatician to draw inferences from Christian experience and to incorporate these into dogmatic theology. He said, 'the data of the theology of the feelings, no less than of natural theology, when their results are validly obtained and sufficiently authenticated as trustworthy, as divinely revealed facts... must be wrought into our system'.[35] However, these inferences must be subject to the doctrinal constraints of scripture, as well as confirmed and supplemented by the teachings of scripture. Warfield understood that the aim of systematicity requires the dogmatic treatment of religious experience, but we can only avoid subjectivist and rationalist distortions of this treatment if scripture remains the *principium* of theological inquiry.

SUMMARY

In this chapter I have explored the interrelated contributions of natural theology and religious experience to dogmatic theology. I examined the functional diversity of natural theology, which I argued gives us good reason to view natural theology as an essential part of the discourse of dogmatic theology itself as the latter reaches toward the desiderata of systematicity, explication of biblical motifs concerning general revelation, and Church–world dialogue. I subsequently argued, though, that natural theology and religious experience are conceptually and epistemically intertwined to such a degree that any attempt to integrate natural and dogmatic theology forces the dogmatician to consider the nature and deliverances of religious experience. The more conservative streams of Protestant theology have tended to look at religious experience with a high degree of suspicion for fear of dogmatic theology degenerating into subjectivism or a psychology of religion in which the metaphysical claims of Christianity are lost or substantially trimmed down. However, cognitive accounts of religious experience would seem to help avoid this pitfall, especially if (like natural theology) reflections on religious experience take place within the system of dogmatic theology, not as an autonomous system of rational thought prefaced to dogmatic theology.[36]

[35] Warfield, 'Idea of Systematic Theology', 62–3.
[36] I wish to thank Michael Rea for his helpful comments on an earlier draft of this chapter.

11

Science and Religion in Constructive Engagement

Michael J. Murray

In his *Summa Contra Gentiles* Thomas Aquinas characterized faith as consisting of beliefs held on the basis of authority rather than on the basis of the evidence of the senses and what can be inferred from that evidence.[1] This view of faith was not new to Christian theology, nor was it the predominant position it later became. However, in demarcating the domains of faith and reason in this way, St Thomas set the stage for establishing the possibility of genuine conflicts between them. And since authoritative religious teaching pronounces on so many things, the emergence of conflict was nearly inevitable.

Of course, St Thomas was convinced that the God who created the world and inspired the Bible would not permit the authoritative teachings to conflict with a proper understanding of the empirical data. For him,

The natural dictates of reason must certainly be quite true: it is impossible to think of their being otherwise. Nor is it permissible to believe that the tenets of faith are false, being so evidently confirmed by God. Since therefore falsehood is contrary to truth, it is impossible for the truth of faith to be contrary to principles known by natural reason.[2]

Nonetheless, even if Thomas and his followers were convinced that, at the end of the day, the 'dictates of reason' and the 'tenets of faith' would be consistent, it was not at all clear, as later disputes between science and religion would show, when the end of the day had been reached. If and when conflict arises, which should yield?

Most academic theologians and philosophers interested in the historical relationship between science and religion are well aware of a few celebrated incidents in which, so we have been told, seemingly bull-headed theologians resisted the clear light of scientific reason and evidence and clung fast to theological 'orthodoxy', only later to be embarrassed when the evidence against them became painfully inescapable. What these incidents are supposed to

---

[1] Bk 1, c. 3.   [2] Bk 1, c. 7.

show us is that, when religious folks dig in their heels against the orthodoxies of science, religion tends to fare rather badly. And this is supposed to provide us with a morality tale: cross science only at your peril!

The two illustrative examples that most readily come to mind are the Galileo Affair and the Scopes Trial. We now know that the folk accounts of these historical episodes are by and large scams foisted on us by early historians of science, many of whom regarded themselves as victims of the charge of religious heterodoxy. Andrew Dixon White, the nineteenth-century historian and president of Cornell University, was, for example, the originator of the cultural mythology that most now erroneously believe concerning Galileo. In his vitriolic *History of the Warfare of Science and Theology*, White provides the first detailed account of the Galileo story in English, characterizing the religious authorities who resisted Galileo's arguments as a 'seething, squabbling, screaming mass of priests, bishops, archbishops, and cardinals'.[3] Unfortunately, the anti-religious tone of the work was inspired in large measure by what White perceived as the apparent injustice of being denied a much coveted post at Yale because of his own unorthodox religious beliefs. The 'clear light of reason and evidence' that theologians were resisting in these cases—especially in the case of Galileo—were far less clear than we have oftentimes been led to believe.[4]

Nonetheless, these historical tales leave many theologians and lay religious believers nervous about how to negotiate the relationship between science and religion. Such worries have became more urgent over the last couple of decades as academic and social forces have conspired to bring issues at the crossroads of science and religion to the forefront of our cultural consciousness. All of this attention has served to render theologians skittish at the prospect of finding themselves once again on the sharp end of these engagements unless they are willing to quickly abandon theological positions which are seemingly at odds with contemporary scientific currents. In some cases, the abandonment has come, as we will see, in dramatic form, resulting in a radically altered theological landscape.

In proceeding in this way, many theologians seem to assume that in the marriage of science and religion, theological dogma owes a fidelity to the deliverances of empirical data that is unyielding. Any other relationship will only insure that the marriage of science and religion will end in science

---

[3] *History of the Warfare of Science with Theology in Christendom* (New York: D. Appleton & Co., 1898).

[4] For an excellent, objective, and concise treatment of the Galileo Affair one can consult Jerome Langford's *Galileo, Science and the Church* (South Bend, Ind.: St Augustine's Press, 1998).

becoming a premature widow. Is that right? Is the only way to keep the marriage of science and religion intact to subjugate one to the other? That is the question that will occupy the remainder of this chapter.

SCIENCE AND RELIGION

Before we proceed we need to be clear about exactly who the potential marriage partners are. Let's begin with science. As in most other topics treated by philosophers, defining science is an enormously contentious topic. But since we need to start somewhere, we can begin with a very minimalist characterization: *science is the collective judgment of professional scholars who aim to explain the workings of the natural world through empirically testable theories*. Of course, science could as easily (and appropriately) be characterized as a certain sort of activity, or practice, or discipline; and a variety of other characterizations might do as well. But for present purposes let's think of science primarily as a (perhaps rather loosely defined) body of belief or doctrine, since the most significant points of contact between science and religion will lie in the domain of belief and doctrine.

Similarly, we can take religion to consist in *the collective judgment of theologians who aim to interpret written revelation and theological tradition*. As with 'science', there are many other ways to characterize 'religion'. But since we are looking for potential points of conflict and concord between the two, it will be most suitable to think of religion here in terms of judgments: claims held or beliefs endorsed. Of course, the 'collective judgment of theologians' will be a much more fragmented affair than the corresponding collective judgment of scientists. On this way of characterizing religion we will not even be able to speak in broad terms such as 'the Christian faith' or 'the Islamic faith'; instead we will rather have to look for smaller subsets of convergent belief where a certain doctrinal unity can be found ('Reformed Christianity' or 'Sunni Islam').

WAYS TO AVOID WIDOWHOOD

There are a number of ways to avoid making science a widow in the science–religion relationship. We will first consider a most extreme way, and then turn to increasingly moderate proposals.

Celibacy

Some have argued that the best (if not only) way to maintain harmony between science and religion is to abandon the notion of marriage altogether. That is, this model counsels celibacy. On this view, science and religion can live in a state of peaceful coexistence because they are independent of one another in ways that make marriage, and thus marital conflict, impossible. There are different ways of developing the claim that science and religion are independent in this way. One is to argue that science and religion cannot overlap because they treat *distinct domains of objects*. For example, one might hold that religion concerns only supernatural reality while science is confined to describing and explaining the natural world. On this view, religion relies on revelation or religious experience to inform us about *the existence of God or of angels or of an afterlife*, while science, relying on sense experience, informs us about *what the natural world contains and why natural things behave as they do*. Alternatively, one might argue that religion concerns only the objects of one's *religious experiences* while science concerns the objects of our *sense experience*.

A second way to develop this model is to argue that science and religion differ not with respect to their *objects* but with respect to their *methods or aims*. For example, one adopting this model might argue that the job of science is to use the method of empirical hypothesis testing to determine what things the natural world contains and how those things behave. The task of religion, on the other hand, is to rely on revelation or other normative claims to explain how God's providential purposes play out through the workings of the natural world.

This second version of the Celibacy model has been defended by the notable evolutionary theorist Stephen Jay Gould. According to Gould, science and religion represent distinct 'magisteria' (i.e. sources of teaching authority) such that 'science covers the empirical realm, answering questions like: what is the universe made of (fact) and why does it work that way (theory). The magisterium of religion, on the other hand, extends over questions of ultimate meaning and moral value.'[5] Thus science uses theory construction and experimentation to determine, for example, how cloning works. Religion uses philosophical theorizing or appeals to authority to determine the moral boundaries in our use of cloning technology. As a result, science and religion are, for Gould, 'Non-Overlapping Magisteria' (NOMA). Gould's position rests on two central yet ultimately implausible claims:

---

[5] Stephen Jay Gould, *Rocks of Ages* (New York: Ballantine Books, 1999), 6.

(1) Religion makes no natural or empirical claims (even if religious texts do).
(2) Science can make no claims concerning supernatural reality or morality.

The first claim holds that religion makes no claims either about the natural world or indeed about anything else that is subject to empirical discovery. However, when a Muslim affirms that Muhammad ascended bodily into heaven, or the Christian affirms that Jesus rose from the dead, they are indeed making just such claims. Likewise, any time a religious believer affirms that something happens in the world as a result of direct divine intervention (turning water into wine, parting Red Seas), they are claiming to explain why things in the world behaved in a certain way. But for Gould, claims about what the world contains and why it behaves as it does lie outside the magisterium of religion. Thus, if Gould is right, we are forced to say that Muslims and Christians are not entitled to hold beliefs of this sort at all, or at least that they are not entitled to hold these beliefs as 'religious beliefs'. Unfortunately, Gould has given us no reason to accept either of these claims aside from his own definitions of what counts as religion.

Some theologians nonetheless warm to the idea that revelation does not make any empirical claims. On this view, claims that have apparent empirical content should be reinterpreted so that they affirm only some abstract, spiritual message. Indeed, it is not uncommon to find theologians taking refuge in the remarks of Galileo himself at this point. In his famous letter to the Grand Duchess of Tuscany in which he defends both his scientific and theological views, Galileo wrote the following oft-cited (though rarely correctly quoted) words:

Since the Holy Ghost did not intend to teach us whether heaven moves or stands still, whether its shape is spherical or like a discus or extended in a plane, nor whether the earth is located at its center or off to one side, then so much the less was it intended to settle for us any other conclusion of the same kind... I would say here something that was heard from an ecclesiastic of the most eminent degree: 'That the intention of the Holy Ghost is to teach us how one goes to heaven, not how heaven goes.'[6]

Many take this to be a tacit endorsement of something like Gould's NOMA. But it is nothing of the sort. In other instances Galileo is quite clear that natural science can be of great value in helping us determine when a passage of scripture intends to teach us truths about the empirical world and when it does not. Galileo was convinced, for instance, that his astronomical observations demonstrated that biblical passages that proclaimed the 'fixity' of the earth were to be understood only metaphorically. Yet he was equally

---

[6] 'Letter to Grand Duchess Christina of Tuscany', http://www.fordham.edu/halsall/mod/galileo-tuscany.html (accessed May 2007).

convinced that Jesus of Nazareth was bodily raised from the dead. The resurrection is, by his lights, an empirical fact that, at least in principle, is open to confirmation (and disconfirmation) by empirical evidence.

The second claim holds that empirical observations of the natural world can tell us nothing about the domain of morality or the supernatural. Even if this claim is right concerning morality (something that is not uncontroversial), there is no reason to think it true when it comes to the supernatural. Many arguments for and against the existence of God take as their starting point facts that we come to know through empirical observations. If, for example, we discover that the universe exhibits a sort of fine-tuning that is best explained by appeal to a non-natural intelligent designer, then empirical evidence has direct implications for religious belief. Furthermore, many of the arguments for atheism take as their starting points apparently empirical observations. One version of the atheistic argument from evil holds that the fact that pain and suffering are not distributed in ways that are proportionate to their biological value shows that the universe is not designed by an all-good, all-powerful being.[7]

'Self-Serving Love'

So perhaps celibacy is no option after all. Reasonably construed, science and religion can, in principle, stand in mutual conflict or mutual support. If that's right, how can the marriage of science and religion be kept alive if not always harmonious? Some theologians adopt a model practiced in some dysfunctional marriages. On this model, one spouse views the marriage in a way that is utterly self-serving. As long as the husband, let's say, engages in pursuits that please or accord with the wife's, she is happy to join in. However, in cases of where their interests diverge, she is nowhere to be found.

Such is the marriage relationship between science and religion in the eyes and minds of many (typically fundamentalist) theologians. The most extreme contemporary example of this can be found among young earth creationists such as those associated with fundamentalist organizations such as the Institute for Creation Research or Answers in Genesis. They proclaim that their organizations maintain 'that God's infallible Word, the Bible, must be our ultimate authority', and that this entails, for example, that in the case of the controversy over the age of the earth '*Scripture must judge man's fallible*

---

[7] Paul Draper, 'Pleasure and Pain: An Evidential Problem for Theists', in Daniel Howard-Snyder (ed.), *The Evidential Argument from Evil* (Bloomington, Ind.: Indiana University Press, 1996).

theories about the past, not vice versa.[8] Theologians of this stripe are happy to embrace science when its deliverances accord with or support whatever claims religion already trumpets. But when neuroscience seems to indicate that belief in immaterial human souls is superfluous and so should be abandoned, the results aren't contested, they are just simply ignored. This is the self-serving love model of marriage brought to the domain of science and religion.

Unfortunately, as in marriage, such a relationship in the domain of science and religion is unstable. No doubt, ignoring science when its deliverances are at odds with one's favored understanding of the teaching of authority insures that one's religious beliefs are never undermined by science. But at the same time, theologians adopting this stance don't ever stand to learn anything of significance to their faith from science. Initially, fundamentalist theologians who adopt this model might not be troubled by this. But they should be. Religious believers are forced on pain of contradiction to acknowledge that, at least in some cases, written revelation is ambiguous, and that empirical discoveries have served to show religious believers what the proper disambiguation is. If such negotiation between science and religion were not allowed, Christians, both Roman Catholic and Protestant, would still endorse the geocentrism so ardently defended by both against Galileo in the seventeenth century.

Doormat Love

The model of science and religion discussed above is not one that is attractive to many mainstream academic theologians, scientists, or philosophers. More popular is a model we might call 'doormat love'. Doormat lovers allow themselves to be run over by the whims of the beloved, no matter how unreasonable (or whimsical) the demand might be. As long as the doormat lover is willing to play along, we have a recipe for preserving the marriage. But the price is high.

Some theologians, tired of what they perceive to be the relentless, unyielding encroachment of science on former occupied territory of religion have internalized a form of learned helplessness that compels them to embrace every turn of scientific fancy. There might be a temptation to think that this sort of accomodationism is of recent vintage. There are, however, numerous historical instances of doormat love.

---

[8] Original emphasis. Jonathan Sarfati, *Refuting Compromise* (Green Forest, Ark.: Master Books, 2004), 17. Sarfati is one of the most widely read and cited critics of standard cosmology and evolutionary biology among Christian fundamentalists.

The Roman Catholic eucharistic doctrine of transubstantiation, declared to be a matter of faith at the Fourth Lateran Council in 1215, was given its definitive expression later in the third part of St Thomas's *Summa Theologica*. There Thomas argued that, although the substance of the bread and wine are replaced by the substance of the body and blood of Christ, it is nonetheless true that the accidental qualities of the bread and wine remain. But what it is that *has* these qualities? In what do they *inhere*? With others, St Thomas argued that the accidents of the bread and wine couldn't properly be thought to inhere in the substance of the body of Christ. But since no other substance was present, the accidents must inhere in something else—something non-substantial. Thomas's solution was to argue that God miraculously permitted the qualities we associate with the pre-transubstantiated bread and wine to inhere in the 'dimensive quantity' of the body of Christ. In other words, on this view, these qualities are 'had by' or inhere in *another property*—that one in virtue of which the substance in question *takes up space*, and takes up the particular space that it does. We can, as later philosophers did, call that property 'extension'. Extension cannot, Thomas claimed, ordinarily serve as the substratum for other qualities. But in this case, God miraculously allows it to play this role. One important consequence of this view, then, is that the properties of a substance are not merely reducible to the property of extension; some properties inhere in, and are thus superadded to, extension.[9]

In the seventeenth century, the Roman Catholic philosopher Descartes defended a metaphysics of substance that was radically anti-Thomistic. On Descartes's view, *all* of the properties of material substance are ultimately reducible to extension and motion. Like many corpuscularian scientists of his day, Descartes was perfectly happy to admit that the properties of distinct substances can be explained in terms of those substances being composed of particles of various shapes and sizes. But Descartes took corpuscles or particles to be nothing more than regions of extension that are in a certain type of (vortical) motion. Thus, at the metaphysical ground floor, material substance consists of micro-level 'tornadoes of extension'—nothing more than extension in motion.

Descartes's Roman Catholic friends (most notably Antoine Arnauld) immediately sensed trouble for this view, and for obvious reasons. The view Descartes defended was *the very one* that undermined the possibility of St Thomas's explanation of transubstantiation. Since Cartesian material substances are nothing more than the extension that constitutes them, there is no

---

[9] This is so since, on this view, while the same extension remains, the substantial nature changes.

way to change the substance while retaining the same extension, as Thomas's theory demanded. Aristotelian critics (and the Church) took this to be a fatal blow to Cartesian science. Descartes and his defenders, however, argued that the science was sound.[10] If accommodation was required, it was theology that would have to give way. Descartes and the new scientists were wrong. The science was not in the end sound.

If the lesson of the Galileo Affair is that theologians must be willing to explore the possibility that cherished interpretations of authoritative teachings are in error, the lesson of the Cartesian Affair is that theologians ought not to be too quick to accommodate scientific fashion. While the former makes theologians appear immune to evidence, the latter makes them appear to have theological convictions that are so fluid or malleable as to lack content altogether.

Unfortunately, accommodationism of this Cartesian sort is becoming quite fashionable. While numerous examples could be cited I will focus on just one. Theologian John Haught has gone to some lengths to construct a theological framework that centrally incorporates an evolutionary cosmology and biology. While big bang cosmology and Darwinism seem to present Christians with substantial theological obstacles, Haught argues that they are part of a broader teleological framework that fits in quite naturally with theism in general, and Christianity in particular. Once this framework is articulated, it provides the theist with resources for explaining numerous puzzling aspects of the universe such as the pervasiveness of evil prior to the advent of human choice and sin.

Haught describes the apparent theological problem of biological evolution as follows:

What is so theologically challenging...about the [Darwinian] account of life?... First, as we have already seen, the variations that lead to differentiation of species are said to be purely *random*, in the sense of being 'undirected'.... In the second place, the fact that individuals have to struggle for survival, and that most of them suffer and lose out in the contest, points to the underlying *indifference* of natural selection, the mechanism that so mercilessly eliminates the weaker organisms. Finally, as a third ingredient in the recipe of evolution, life's experiments have required an almost unimaginably extensive amount of *time* for the diversity of species to come about. That the origin of life would take so many billions of years to bring about intelligent beings seems...to be clear evidence that neither life nor mind is the consequence of an intelligent divine plan for the universe. We humans...could have done a much quicker and more competent job of it.[11]

---

[10] *The Philosophical Works of Descartes*, tr. Elizabeth Haldane and G. R. T. Ross (Cambridge: CUP, 1911–12), ii. 120.
[11] *Deeper than Darwin* (Boulder, Colo.: Westview Press, 2003), 70.

Appearances notwithstanding, Haught argues that those features of the natural world which make it seem to be an endless, random, indifferent cascade of events are instead conditions that are necessary for creating a world capable of fully manifesting divine glory and grace. Haught claims that a universe which moves from chaos to order by lawlike means is necessary for securing a world that is (1) truly distinct from God, (2) capable of supporting a 'narrative structure', and (3) filled with *promise*. Let's consider these in turn.

Distinct creation

In order for the creation to give genuine expression to divine goodness and love, it must be *distinct* from the being of God and have a sufficient degree of *independence* from God. Haught explains as follows:

if there is truth in the Biblical conviction that God really cares for this world as something other than God, then the universe must always have had some degree of autonomy, even during its long prehuman evolution. Otherwise, it would have been nothing more than an extension of God's own being, an appendage of deity. In that case, it could never have become genuinely other than God.[12]

The 'autonomy' necessary for the creation to be 'something other than God' precludes the possibility that God can bring about the creation in the fully formed way envisioned by, for example, the 'young universe' creationist:

For God's love of creation to be actualized, the beloved world must be truly 'other' than God. And in an instantaneously finished universe, one from which our present condition of historical becoming and existential ambiguity could be envisaged as a subsequent estrangement, would in principle have been only an emanation or appendage of deity and not something truly other than God.[13]

Narrative structure

Not only is progress toward order via lawlike means required for a world to be distinct and sufficiently independent, it is also necessary for a world to be capable of supporting a *narrative structure and ultimate promise*. It is these two features which allow the creation to be the recipient of both divine love and grace. In fact, Haught goes so far as to say that, 'At its very foundations, the universe appears to have been shaped by what I would like to call the "narrative cosmological principle."'[14]

This narrative capacity in turn requires three features: *contingency, lawlikeness*, and sufficient *time*.

[12] Ibid. 78. [13] Ibid. 168. [14] Ibid. 60.

Contingency, as we have just seen, renders nature open to *novelty*, an essential element in evolution. The consistency embedded in physical laws and natural selection endows the evolutionary process with a *coherence* that gives organizational unity and continuity to life across time. And nature's irreversible temporality, in conjunction with the elements of contingency and consistency, marks the universe with sharp *historicity*. After Darwin—and even more so after Einstein—nature has revealed itself, beneath previous impressions of it, as being an immense story. And the significance of the three features we have just isolated is that they make it possible for a universe to have a narrative disposition.[15]

Promise

Finally, Haught claims that contingency, lawlikeness, and time are further required for the universe to be a place of *promise*. The contingency is required in order to make real the possibility that things might go astray. Lawlikeness provides a way for God to insure that there are limits on how far nature can wander. Time is required in order to give the universe and its inhabitants the ability to bring the potential of the universe to fruition. Evolutionary cosmology, in other words, 'invites us to complete the biblical vision of life based on hope for surprise rather than allowing us to wax nostalgic for what we imagine once was'.[16]

Among other things, Haught claims that this picture helps us solve the problem of evil that pre-exists the advent of sin in the universe:

Evolution... means that the world is unfinished. But if it is unfinished, then we cannot justifiably expect it to be perfect. It *inevitably* has a dark side. Redemption... must mean... the healing of *tragedy*... that accompanies a universe *in via*.... It would be callous indeed on the part of theologians to perpetuate the one-sidedly anthropocentric and retributive notions of pain and redemption that used to fit so comfortably into pre-evolutionary pictures of the world.[17]

However, in his rush to accommodate contemporary science, Haught has left us with a picture that is underdefended and deeply problematic. Haught first argues that a universe that is not appropriately 'self-actualizing' cannot possibly be *distinct* from God. But the underlying argument here is invalid. Agents can be fully distinct from states of affairs to which they give rise directly. Our paintings and sculptures are not parts of us even though they are non-self-actualizing. Furthermore, if the initial state of the universe is directly created by God, it too would be a mere 'appendage of deity'. Yet in that case, how could any of the subsequent stages of the universe be any more distinct from the divine being?

[15] Ibid. 58–60. [16] Ibid. 173–4. [17] Ibid. 169.

Leaving aside these less serious philosophical concerns, there is a further and perhaps more serious worry. Haught's condition for a universe that is a suitable object of divine creation seems so unabashedly *ad hoc*. Haught gives the illusion of specifying the characteristics that a divinely created world would have, and then explaining how the actual world fits the specifications. But it is hard to avoid the impression that he has rather looked at the apparently bumbling, random, indifferent course of natural history as specified by contemporary evolutionary cosmology and concocted a story that keeps reality from slipping from the theist's grasp. One gets a sense that theists like Haught could retrodict the existence of almost any world, no matter how bleak. We can almost imagine a solitary Haught, sitting in a bunker in the wake of a nuclear holocaust that has annihilated every other living thing on the planet, arguing that this is just what we would expect of a God who creates a world characterized by the cycle of seasons: new life in the spring followed by death and dormancy in the fall. Undoubtedly we can tell such stories. But given their *ad hoc* character, they are simply not credible.

Haught attempts to integrate the deliverances of evolutionary cosmology and theology in an attempt to accommodate contemporary science and to solve certain crucial theological challenges to which it gives rise. But in doing so he forces the Christian to embrace a poorly defended, *ad hoc* theological framework.

A FOURTH WAY

In *Rocks of Ages* Stephen Jay Gould lauds the twentieth-century Roman pontiff Pius XII as a defender of his NOMA principle. As evidence, Gould cites the Pope's 1950 encyclical letter *Humani Generis* in which he argues that faithful Catholics can accept the claim that the human organism arose as a product of natural, evolutionary forces (an empirical, scientific matter), while the human soul was infused directly by God (a non-empirical, religious matter).

Unfortunately for Gould, Pius was no fan of NOMA-like principles, and the encyclical is no evidence to the contrary. What Pius meant to affirm is not that scripture and tradition cannot pronounce on empirical matters, but rather that the authoritative pronouncements on biological matters leave open the possibility that something like Darwinism is correct as an explanation for the origin of the human organism. Gould was a fan of Pius XII because of his apparent willingness to embrace evolution on behalf of the Roman Catholic Church and, as Gould saw it, to demarcate science and religion into domains that cannot falsify one another. What Gould does not seem to know is that one year later, Pius XII delivered an address to the Pontifical Academy of Sciences, the content of which flies squarely in the face of NOMA. Taking inspiration from early versions of big bang cosmology, Pius argued that science clearly proves the existence of a creator:

> Indeed, it would seem that present-day science, with one sweep back across the centuries, has succeeded in bearing witness to the august instant of the primordial *Fiat Lux*, when, along with matter, there burst forth from nothing a sea of light and radiation, and the elements split and churned and formed into millions of galaxies...
>
> What, then, is the importance of modern science in the argument for the existence of God based on change in the universe? By means of exact and detailed research into the large-scale and small-scale works it has considerably broadened and deepened the empirical foundation on which the argument rests, and from which it concludes to the existence of an *Ens a se*, immutable by His very nature.... Thus, with that concreteness which is characteristic of physical proofs, it has confirmed the contingency of the universe and also the well-founded deduction as to the epoch when the world came forth from the hands of the Creator. Hence creation took place. We say: therefore, there is a Creator. Therefore, God exists![18]

Pius's remarks on cosmology both emboldened religious leaders, anxious to embrace big bang cosmology, and struck fear into the hearts of those naturalist cosmologists who wanted to use science only as a bludgeon against religion. What we see in the thought and writing of Pius then is a mature, balanced stance on the interplay between science and religion. He was willing to accept that established science could lead to revised theological opinions (e.g. in biology), while also seeing ways in which science can confirm dogma (in cosmology).

There are a number of contemporary scientists and theologians who aim to negotiate the relation of science and religion in similar fashion. But rather than taking sides among the current disputants, let me once again appeal to a less well-known historical episode as a model for a healthy marriage between science and religion.

In the early twentieth century, when cosmology was still in its infancy, scientists who addressed cosmological questions often did so more as a hobby, with an understanding that the available data were extraordinarily limited and ambiguous. Those who are familiar with the historical interplay between science and religion are often well aware of the fact that by the middle of the twentieth century two cosmological models were taken most seriously; the first was a version of the (later to be dubbed) big bang model, developed by

---

[18] Excerpts from the papal address 'Un Ora', tr. in P. J. McLaughlin, *The Church and Modern Science* (New York: Philosophical Library, 1957), 137–47.

Georges Lemaître in the 1920s, the second was the (again, later to be dubbed) 'steady state' model on which the universe is eternal and expanding. Because the former model hypothesizes a first moment, it was often taken, by critics and defenders alike, to be especially congenial to Western theistic religions which suppose that God created the universe *ex nihilo* in the finite past. In fact, it is clear that in the middle of the century the chief defenders of the rival steady state model took no small pleasure in the fact that their view could get on without making any appeal either to a first moment of creation or to a creator.[19] Neither of these models was worked out in any detail until the late 1940s and neither was predominant until the mid-1960s. Still, even before the 1940s, scientists and theologians were aware of the two models and their theological implications.

Those familiar with the debate only from the mid-century onwards would be surprised to know that in the early part of the century the theological lines were not as clearly drawn as they became later. While later theists and atheists often lined up on opposite sides of the big bang/steady state debate respectively, theologians earlier in the century found choosing sides a more ambiguous matter. A notable example of this is the Cambridge theologian William Ralph Inge. While Inge recognized that a universe that came to be in the finite past seemed to require a creator—a congenial corollary for theists—Inge pointed out that Lemaître's model had other consequences that were theologically troubling. Most troubling to Inge was that the model entailed that the universe that began in the finite past would continue to expand forever, ultimately flickering out in a cold and distant heat death. 'The astronomers tell us as a certain fact—Eddington says it is the most certain truth of science—that the whole universe is steadily and irreversibly running down like a clock... That is the doom of all that exists—annihilation, from which there can be no recovery.'[20]

Almost as troubling in the big bang cosmology was what Inge saw as an implicit deism. Since steady state theories hypothesized the eternity of the universe they were forced to incorporate some mechanism which continually infuses usable energy (or matter) into the universe. Were there no such mechanism, the universe would have reached entropic heat death in the infinite past. Steady state theories thus invited theists like Inge to see God's involvement with the universe as one of continual creation. To the contrary, Inge remarked that the big bang model 'seems to be a naïve deistic doctrine

---

[19] Helge Kragh, *Cosmology and Controversy: The Historical Development of Two Theories of the Universe* (Princeton: Princeton University Press, 1996), 253.

[20] *God and the Astronomers* (London: Longmans, Green & Co., 1933), 8.

that some billions of years ago God would up the material universe, and has left it to run down of itself ever since'.[21]

Finally, in light of the apparent fate of the universe on the big bang model, there seemed to be no hope for either the material creation itself or our place in it. If it was doomed ultimately to 'run down' the only hope for us would be in some extra-natural heavenly sphere: 'The question is asked, and must be faced, whether Christianity is optimistic about the world in which we have to live, or only about that other world which we cannot see, and which often seems to us, "the land very far off.". . . Our religion, I know, has been grievously secularized; but we are not willing to banish Hope altogether from this earth.'[22]

Like the Cartesians, Inge turned out to be on the wrong side of history. The steady state model was not the most widely endorsed model of his time and it was, in the end, ultimately rejected. Still, unlike the Cartesians, Inge was not willing simply to be a theological doormat to the scientific currents of his day. Although big bang models had theological implications that many theists welcomed, he carefully and reflectively noted that the model had other implications which were deeply troubling.

In these episodes, Pius XII and William Inge embody and illustrate a model for the marriage of science and religion. On this model of *constructive engagement*, religious believers must take seriously the fact that authoritative religious teaching can and does have consequences for the natural world, consequences which yield empirically testable conclusions. However, as the Galileo Affair shows, and as Pius reaffirmed in his *Humani Generis*, religious believers can misunderstand that authoritative teaching. Subjecting that teaching to the standards of empirical science provides one way of figuring out whether or not our understanding is correct. Religious believers can thus learn deep theological lessons from the scientists, *pace* the self-serving marriage model.

On the other hand, unlike the doormat marriage model, these two theological figures were not willing to twist theological doctrine in just any old direction in response to the demands of scientific fancy. While evolutionary theorists might be adamant that every facet of human nature is ultimately amenable to explanation by appeal to the forces of natural selection operating in the ancestral environment, Pius XII was not. For him, authoritative teaching ultimately demands that what is most central to human nature is created directly by God. Thus constructive engagement requires that religious believers display a willingness to look with a clear head at all of the theological implications of a scientific position and not simply adopt the most passionately defended scientific claim.

[21] Ibid. 34.   [22] Ibid. 171.

IV

Analytic Approaches Reconsidered

12

The Problem of Evil
Analytic Philosophy and Narrative

Eleonore Stump

ANALYTIC PHILOSOPHY AND ITS LIMITS

The contemporary debate in Anglo-American philosophy over the problem of evil has become complicated and technical; for example, intricate questions of probability have played an important role in some of the philosophical literature on the subject. The analytic precision in such debate is a good thing; and I, along with many others, welcome it. But this turn in the discussion has the vices of its virtues. In its focus on such philosophical technicalities as the appropriate patterns of probabilistic reasoning, it seems simply to sidestep much that has been at the heart of the problem of evil for many reflective thinkers. And so, to many people, there has also been something heartily unsatisfying about the direction of this contemporary debate.

This vague, unfocused complaint is reminiscent of the sort of criticism often leveled against the whole field of analytic philosophy by its opponents, within philosophy and in other disciplines as well. Philosophy as it is commonly practiced in the Anglo-American tradition (a tradition to which I count myself an adherent) prizes lucidity, analysis, careful distinction, and rigorous argument—all unquestionably worth prizing. Nonetheless, those more sympathetic to other traditions in philosophy have regularly complained about what they call 'the narrowness' of Anglo-American philosophy. This reproach is not altogether unjustified. To the extent to which one prizes rigor, one will eschew or even disdain breadth, since it is obviously easier to achieve rigor if one limits one's focus. And so Anglo-American philosophy sometimes looks like a species of the lapidary's art. But simply encouraging philosophers in this tradition to broaden their focus would not yield satisfactory results. This trouble with the gauge of vision is, I think, a symptom of something deeper, which is both the strength and the weakness of this style of philosophizing.

Anglo-American philosophy has typically been concerned with analysis, to such an extent that its other common name is 'analytic philosophy'. It has been preoccupied with precise definitions of terms, fine distinctions among concepts, and complex arguments for philosophical claims. (It is in consequence also marked by a hunt for counterexamples to someone else's definition, further distinctions lying between things someone else has already distinguished, and even more complex arguments showing the invalidity of someone else's complex arguments.)

These practices of Anglo-American philosophy, characterized by an attention to analytic detail and a predilection for precision, can be conveniently thought of as mediated by left-brain skills (to use amateur but accurate neurobiological concepts). Such practices and skills are certainly important to any careful thinking in general and to philosophy in particular. Without them, philosophy is in some danger of turning into what can be (and often is) practiced by anyone at all over a couple of beers. But there is also no reason to suppose that left-brain skills alone will reveal to us all that is philosophically interesting about the world. The narrowness for which Anglo-American philosophy is reproached is thus a concomitant of the analytic strengths that characterize it. Breadth of focus is a right-brain skill. So are many abilities useful in interpersonal relations. As one contemporary neurobiological text puts it, those who are impaired with respect to right-hemisphere functions have an 'inability to give an overview or extract a moral from a story, . . . or to assess properly social situations'.[1]

In his recent book *The Empirical Stance,* Bas van Fraassen, who is a paradigmatic analytic philosopher, frames a related charge that he levels against a part of his own discipline, namely, analytic metaphysics. He says: '[analytic] metaphysicians interpret what we initially understand into something hardly anyone understands, and then insist that we cannot do without that. To any incredulous listener they'll say: Construct a better alternative! But that just signals their invincible presumption that [analytic] metaphysics is the sine qua non of understanding.'[2]

---

[1] Larry Benowitz, Seth Finkelstein, David Levine, and Kenneth Moya, 'The Role of the Right Cerebral Hemisphere in Evaluating Configurations', in Colywyn Trevarthen (ed.), *Brain Circuits and Functions of the Mind: Essays in Honor of Roger W. Sperry* (Cambridge: CUP, 1990), 320–33. For some interesting recent work on the differences between the two halves of the cerebrum, see e.g. Norman Geschwind and Albert M. Galaburda, *Cerebral Lateralization* (Cambridge, Mass.: MIT Press, 1989). I am using the distinction between left-brain and right-brain skills here primarily as an heuristic device. Nothing in the claims I want to defend would be undermined even if it turned out (*per improbabile*) that all our cognitive capacities were processed on the left; and all the claims I make using the distinction between left-brain and right-brain skills can be rephrased without it.

[2] Bas van Fraassen, *The Empirical Stance* (New Haven: Yale University Press, 2001), 3.

I would put the point, or my version of what I take his point to be, in this way. At its best, the style of philosophy practiced by analytic philosophy can be very good even at large and important problems. Aquinas's analytic analysis of the nature of free will is an example. Alvin Plantinga's work on the modal logic of ontological arguments for the existence of God (or any of a host of other issues) is another. (Van Fraassen's own analysis of the shortcomings of analytic philosophy is, ironically enough, yet another.) But left to itself, because it values intricate, technically expert argument, the analytic approach has a tendency to focus more and more on less and less; and so, at its worst, it can become plodding, pedestrian, sterile, and inadequate to its task.

In particular, in its emphasis on left-brain mediated pattern-processing, philosophy in the Anglo-American tradition has tended to leave to one side the messy and complicated issues involved in relations among persons. When analytic philosophers need to think about human interactions, they tend not to turn to complex cases drawn from real life or from the world's great literature; rather they make up short, thin stories of their own, involving the philosophical crash-dummies Smith and Jones. Bernard Williams, himself an analytic philosopher, considers the question why philosophers shouldn't simply attempt to make up their own examples, drawn from life, as philosophers see it; and he says 'what philosophers will lay before themselves and their readers as an alternative to literature will not be life, but bad literature [in the form of their own philosophical examples]'.[3]

It is therefore misleadingly imprecise, I think, to diagnose the weakness of analytic philosophy as its narrowness. Its cognitive *hemianopia* is its problem. Its intellectual vision is occluded or obscured for the right half of the cognitive field,[4] especially for the part of reality that includes the complex, nuanced thought, behavior, and relations of persons. The deficit will perhaps be undetectable in work on modal logic or philosophy of mathematics, but in any issues where the interactions of persons makes a difference it is more likely to be in evidence.[5]

---

[3] Bernard Williams, *Shame and Necessity* (Berkeley, Calif.: University of California Press, 1993), 13.

[4] To attribute a weakness to a field is not the same as attributing a weakness to every thinker or every piece of research in the field. There are lots of examples of analytic philosophy which show all the strengths of the discipline without what I've characterized here as its weakness. To take just one example among a number that come to mind, Alvin Plantinga's books, *Warrant: The Current Debate* (New York: OUP, 1993), *Warrant and Proper Function* (New York: OUP, 1993), and *Warranted Christian Belief* (New York: OUP, 2000) exemplify the care for detail and accuracy distinctive of analytic philosophy while ranging broadly, with depth and insight, over the whole tradition of epistemology in the modern period.

[5] And, of course, if the major Western monotheisms are right, then ultimate reality itself is irreducibly personal as well as patterned. On these views of the nature of reality, the Grand Unified Theory of Everything will have at its foundation both persons and patterns.

But personal relations are at the heart of certain philosophical problems. Central to the problem of evil in all its forms, for example, is a question to which a consideration of interpersonal relations is maximally relevant. Could a person who is omnipotent, omniscient, and perfectly good allow human persons to suffer as they do?

ANALYTIC PHILOSOPHY AND NARRATIVE

Expertise regarding persons and personal relations can be found with psychologists and anthropologists, among others, but it seems to me to manifest itself most helpfully among the creators of literature, especially the storytellers.[6] One idea, then, for addressing the shortcomings of analytic philosophy while preserving its characteristic excellences is to marry it to the study of narrative.[7] As this chapter shows, analytic philosophy can use its strengths to diagnose its own weaknesses. Analytic reason can see what analytic reason cannot see; and, having seen it, it can correct for its defects and limitations by bolstering itself with the cognitive virtues embodied in other intellectual endeavors. So one way to compensate for the limitations of analytic philosophy as regards philosophical problems such as the problem of evil is to reflect on them by drawing on the insights of narratives as well as the results of contemporary analytic discussions.

I am hardly the first philosopher to whom it has occurred that analytic philosophy would benefit by some attention to literature. Others have also advocated this approach. Different proponents of it explain it in different ways; but the person who has perhaps done the most to make it familiar is Martha Nussbaum. (The occasional acidulous complaints by critics that Nussbaum's work involving literature is not really philosophy seem to me an indictment of analytic philosophy, revealing the very defects I have just canvassed, rather than a criticism of the methods Nussbaum employs.[8]) To

---

[6] I am here in effect claiming that what narrative has to contribute to philosophy is not just some affective influence on its readers, by engaging their emotions and imaginations as well as their intellects, but rather some cognitive content which is explicable less well or not at all by non-narrative philosophical prose.

[7] Certain uses of bits of narratives have been common in some areas of Anglo-American philosophy at certain periods. For a discussion of the use of literary examples in 20th-cent. Wittgensteinian ethics, see Onora O'Neill, 'The Power of Example', *Philosophy*, 61 (1986), 5–29. As O'Neill explains the use of narrative in this sort of ethics, it consists largely just in prompting ethical reflection on particular ethical cases.

[8] For an example of such criticism, see Jenny Teichman, 'Henry James among the Philosophers', Review of *Love's Knowledge: Essays on Philosophy and Literature* by Martha Nussbaum, *New York Times Book Review* (10 Feb. 1991), 24. I doubt whether anyone can give necessary and

take just one example from her work, in examining Aeschylus's *Agamemnon*, Nussbaum focuses on the way circumstances trap Agamemnon in a moral dilemma and on the emotions with which Agamemnon confronts that dilemma; and she also calls our attention to the repugnance we feel for the attitude Agamemnon adopts in making the choice he does. These considerations then illuminate her examination of the role of luck in moral choice and in the formation of moral character.[9]

My own reasons for valuing a turn to literature, however, are somewhat different from those that have been given by Nussbaum and others.[10] To me, it seems that there are things to know which can be known through narrative but which cannot be known as well, if at all, through the methods of analytic philosophy.

THE KNOWLEDGE OF PERSONS

It is almost axiomatic in analytic philosophy that all knowledge is knowledge *that* something or other is the case. Some philosophers have gone so far as to argue that even knowing how to do something is reducible to knowledge *that* of some sort.[11] But this position is hard to maintain, in my view, in the face of recent developments in developmental psychology and neurobiology.

These disciplines have produced a wealth of data in recent years having to do with the knowledge of persons. For example, they have shown that a pre-linguistic infant can know her primary caregiver as a person and can, as it were, read the mind of her caregiver, in ways which only increase in sophistication as the infant develops.[12] But infants who know their primary caregiver as a person and who are able to know (some of) the mental states of their primary caregiver do not have this knowledge as knowledge *that*

---

sufficient conditions for something's counting as philosophy, but surely *the search for truth, by means which especially include arguments, about matters of importance* is roughly the genus within which philosophy will be found. If that is right, and I think it is, then clearly Nussbaum's work counts as philosophy.

[9] See Martha Nussbaum, *The Fragility of Goodness: Luck and Ethics in Greek Tragedy and Philosophy* (Cambridge: CUP, 1986), 33–8.

[10] Nussbaum, for example, tends to talk in terms of knowing through emotion and imagination, and she argues that there are some kinds of knowledge which can't be grasped by the intellect. (See Nussbaum, *Fragility*, 45–7.)

[11] See e.g. Jason Stanley and Timothy Williamson, 'Knowing How', *Journal of Philosophy*, 98 (2001), 411–44.

[12] See e.g. Naomi Eilan, Christoph Hoerl, Teresa McCormack, and Johannes Roessler, *Joint Attention: Communication and Other Minds* (Oxford: Clarendon Press, 2005).

something or other is the case. As one developmental psychologist, Peter Hobson, puts it, in reaction to a common position which attributes to such children a theory of mind consisting of knowledge *that*,

> Developmental psychologists [and, he might have added, philosophers] have taken to calling a child's growing understanding of people's mental life a 'theory of mind'. In many ways this is a daft expression because it suggests that a child theorizes about the nature of feelings, wishes, beliefs, intentions, and so on. This is not what happens at all. The child comes to know about such aspects of mental life, and the way the child comes to know is mostly very *un*like theorizing.[13]

Hobson cites Wittgenstein to help him explain the kind of cognition which he himself thinks is at issue for infants: '"We *see* emotion"—As opposed to what?—We do not see facial contortions and *make the inference* that he is feeling joy, grief, boredom.'[14] For Hobson, we cognize the mental states of others not as knowledge *that* but more nearly by direct awareness, in the manner of perception.

It has become clear that a pre-linguistic infant's knowledge of a person as a person is foundational to the infant's ability to learn a language or to develop normal cognitive abilities in many areas. In fact, one currently promising approach to autism is to take it as something gone wrong in an infant's ability to know the mind of another person.[15] The knowledge missing for an autistic child, however, cannot be taken as knowledge *that* something or other is the case. An autistic child can know *that* a particular macroscopic object is a human person or *that* the person in question is sad. The autistic child might know that the person whose face he is seeing is sad just because some authority reliable for the child has told him so; but this is not the same as the child's knowing the sadness in the face of the person he is looking at.[16] What is apparently impaired in the cognition of an autistic child is the ability to know a person or to know the mental states of that person.

---

[13] Peter Hobson, *The Cradle of Thought* (Oxford: OUP, 2004), 143.

[14] Ibid. 243.

[15] There is some dispute about whether the primary deficit is cognitive or affective, but, whichever one is primary, there is ample evidence for a very early cognitive deficit. As one researcher puts it, 'There is another reason why this issue might be unresolved, and it concerns the assumed separateness of cognition and affect. The extent to which cognition and affect are separate domains, especially early in development, is debatable. An argument for a combined cognitive and affective impairment in autism would be supported by recent neurological and brain imaging studies showing that there are reciprocal connections between parts of the brain that predominantly serve either emotional functions or cognitive functions...': Sue Leekam, 'Autism and Joint Attention Impairment', in Eilan et al., *Joint Attention*, 208.

[16] See Derek Moore, Peter Hobson, and Anthony Lee, 'Components of Person Perception: An Investigation with Autistic, Non-Autistic Retarded and Typically Developing Children and Adolescents', *British Journal of Developmental Psychology*, 15 (1997), 401–23.

As far as that goes, information about mental states is conveyed not only by facial expression, but also by gesture, body language (as we say), and inarticulate vocal sound; but the information conveyed by these means is not always, or entirely, accessible as or translatable into knowledge *that*. As one pair of researchers puts the point about gesture, 'because gesture is less codified than speech and has the potential to convey information imagistically..., meanings not easily encoded into speech can be conveyed in the accompanying gestural stream'.[17] Congenitally blind children, who have never seen the gesture of another, tend themselves to develop patterns of gesture and use them as a means of aiding communication.[18]

It is also not surprising to learn from neurobiology that the production and interpretation of inarticulate vocal sound is subserved by a different brain system from that responsible for language. What is it that we know when we hear a person groan or giggle? What is the difference between a groan and a giggle? Or between a chuckle and a giggle? How would we translate what we know when we hear a person giggle into knowledge *that*? That the person giggling is amused? Is nervous? Is trying to be flirtatious? Or that the person has a conjunction of some but not all of these attitudes? And how would those attitudes have had to be different if the person had chuckled instead of giggling?

These results from psychology and neuroscience should prompt us to reflect more broadly about knowledge which is not knowledge *that*. Not all such knowledge has to do with persons. It is also the case that an infant knows a ball as a ball before the infant is in a position to know that *this* is a ball. And even for adults, there is a difference between knowing something as a thing of a kind and knowing *that* this is a thing of that kind. A person who has a visual agnosia might not be able to know a glove as a glove, but he might still be able to know *that* this is a glove, say, because his physician has told him so. In fact, it seems as if knowledge which is not knowledge *that* must be primary. Without *any* knowledge of a thing as a thing, it is hard to see how anyone could have knowledge *that* this something-or-other has certain properties or stands in certain relations to something else. Aquinas makes this point by saying that the primary act of the intellect is the knowledge of the quiddity of a thing, that is, the knowledge of a thing as a thing; on his view, this sort of cognition is prior to the intellect's having knowledge expressible in propositional form.[19]

This is, of course, a contentious claim, which cannot be adequately supported or assessed in passing here. But whatever the truth of that claim, the

---

[17] Jana Iverson and Susan Goldin-Meadow, 'What's Communication Got to Do with it? Gesture in Children Blind from Birth', *Developmental Psychology*, 33 (1997), 453.
[18] Ibid. 453–67.
[19] See my *Aquinas* (London: Routledge, 2003), 264–6.

work of contemporary psychologists and neurobiologists has made us aware that there is a kind of knowledge which is central to human cognitive capacities and cognitive development, but which is not knowledge *that*. If it is like anything in the currently accepted philosophical pantheon, it is more nearly like knowledge by acquaintance than it is like knowledge *that*. Whatever knowledge by acquaintance is (and this is controversial too), it constitutes a broad array of knowledge which is commonly had by human beings and which cannot be formulated adequately or at all as knowledge *that*. Some instances of such knowledge are provided by first-person experiences, especially those in which the qualia of the experience are among the salient parts of the knowledge. Another important species of such knowledge is acquired in direct interaction with other people. In what follows, I will call such interaction among persons 'second-person experiences'.[20]

While we cannot express the distinctive knowledge we gain in such an experience as a matter of knowing *that*, we can do something to re-present the experience itself in such a way that we can share it with others who were not part of it, so that the knowledge of persons garnered from the experience is also available to them.[21] This is generally what we do when we tell a story.[22] A story takes a real or imagined second-person experience and makes it available to a wider audience to share.[23] It does so by making it possible, to one degree or another, for a reader or listener to experience what it would have been like for her if she had been a bystander in the second-person experience represented in the story.[24] That is, a story gives its reader some

---

[20] For a detailed discussion of second-person experiences, see my *Wandering in Darkness: Narrative and the Problem of Suffering* (Oxford, forthcoming).

[21] In this respect, a second-person experience differs from a first-person experience of the sort we have in perception. There is no way at all for me to convey to someone who has never seen colors what I know when I know what it is like to see red.

[22] I am not here implying that the only function, or even the main function, of narratives (in one medium or another) is to convey real or imagined second-person experiences. My claim is just that much less is lost of a second-person experience in a narrative account than in a non-narrative account, ceteris paribus.

[23] Someone might object here that any information which could be captured and conveyed by a story could also be conveyed by an account consisting only of expository prose. I have no good argument against this claim, for the very reasons I have been urging, namely, that we can't give an expository description of what *else* is contained in a story; but I think the claim is clearly false. Consider, to take just one example, some excellent and current biography of Samuel Johnson, such as Robert DeMaria's *The Life of Samuel Johnson: A Critical Biography* (Oxford: Blackwell, 1993), and compare it to the pastiche of stories in Boswell's *Life of Johnson*, and you see the point. There is a great deal to be learnt about Johnson from DeMaria's *The Life of Samuel Johnson*, but Boswell's stories give you the man as the biography can't.

[24] On the role of simulation in audience reaction to fiction, see e.g. Kenneth Walton, 'Spelunking, Simulation, and Slime: On Being Moved by Fiction', in Mette Jhorte and Sue Laver (eds.), *Emotion and the Arts* (New York: OUP, 1997). On simulation theory in general, see e.g. Martin Davies and Tony Stone, *Mental Simulation* (Oxford: Blackwell, 1995).

of what she would have had if she had had unmediated personal interaction with the characters in the story while they were conscious and interacting with each other, without actually making her part of the story itself.[25] We can call the re-presenting of a second-person experience in a story 'a second-person account'. It is a report of a second-person experience which does not lose (at least does not lose entirely) the distinctively second-person character of the experience.

Experience of other persons and stories thus plays a role with regard to the knowledge of persons analogous to the role played by postulates and arguments with regard to knowledge *that*. Each—experience and stories or postulates and arguments—is a means of the acquisition and transfer of knowledge, although the kind of knowledge acquired or transferred and the sort of acquisition or transfer involved differ.

And so, in my view, stories transmit a kind of knowledge of persons which is not reducible to knowledge *that*. We can put the point the other way around by noticing what we lose if we try to reduce a narrative to expository (that is, non-narrative) prose. If we boil a story down to non-narrative propositions, so that all the knowledge it conveys is knowledge *that*,[26] then we lose the knowledge that the story distinctively provides just because we cannot convey by means of expository prose alone even a simulacrum of a second-person experience.[27] A real story cannot be captured in a set of non-narrative propositions designed to summarize it; Cliff Notes are no substitute for the literary work itself. A Cliff Notes summary of *The Brothers Karamazov* would lose what is best about the novel itself.

How much of what can be known in a second-person experience is made available to others to learn by means of a story depends in part on the artistry of the story-teller. Harlequin romances no doubt give us something; the world's great literature, drama, and film give us much more. It is, of course, clear that the degree of transmission of knowledge through stories is also a

---

[25] I do not mean to say that the story-teller or artist does not contribute something of her own in the narrative presentation. On the contrary, part of the importance of narrative is that its artistry enables us to see what we might well have missed without the help of the narrative even if we had been present as bystanders in the events recounted. It is for this reason that the quality of the artistry in a narrative makes a difference to what there is to know on the basis of it.

[26] Someone might suppose that we could turn any story into expository propositional form just by prefixing to the story the words 'It is true in this story that' and then filling out the remainder of the sentence with a conjunction formed from all the sentences in the story. But this swollen sentence would not constitute an example of expository prose since it would contain a story within it. And, in any case, it would not be true that all the knowledge in the story was conveyed by means of propositions *that*. The story would be embedded in a proposition *that*, but the distinctive kind of knowledge of the story would be conveyed by the story itself.

[27] I can't, of course, specify what that knowledge is, since to do so would be to translate it into terms of knowledge *that*.

function of the sensitivity of the story reader (or listener or watcher). Some people are more natively gifted than others in their ability to learn from second-person experiences and from narratives. Furthermore, sensitivity of this sort, like perceptual sensitivity, can be trained. The ability to hear a key change in a piece of music is a function not just of native aural acuity but also of musical training. An untrained ear will take in the sounds of Lutoslawski's Cello Concerto but not hear it.[28] In the same way, native sensibility and training each make a difference to one's ability to understand and learn from narratives.

NARRATIVES AND THE PRECISION OF ANALYTIC PHILOSOPHY

One general concern which a proposal to include narrative in philosophical discussion will raise in some people has to do with order and structure. Philosophical work in the analytic tradition commonly has a certain sort of tight order to it because it is typically structured around arguments. There is a thesis that is the conclusion of an argument, and that argument consists of premises, which themselves are argued for or at least elucidated. And so the discussion proceeds in an orderly way designed to try to command agreement. For philosophers, the structure of the argument is a kind of exoskeleton for the discussion, immediately visible and effective for defense.

Now one might suppose that this sort of structure can be preserved even with the inclusion of narrative in the discussion. One just has to let a narrative be brought in at the appropriate point where it supports or illustrates a premise. But to weave narrative into philosophy in this way is to demean the role of narrative, so that the narrative becomes little more than a picture put next to the text for those who find books without pictures boring. If we use literary texts in this way, just to illustrate premises in a philosophical argument, we are in effect dragging the literature in gratuitously, like anecdotes in an after-dinner speech, added to give entertainment to the proceedings without advancing the thought. But a real story cannot be reduced to an illustration for a premise or two. Unless the literary texts in question are like Aesop's fables, designed on purpose to teach one philosophical lesson, what is philosophically interesting about a text will illustrate or illuminate philosophical reflection in a much messier way.

[28] I am grateful to John Foley, who taught me to hear it.

How, then, is narrative to be brought into philosophical discussion? Antiphonally, I think. A narrative has to be considered in its disorderly richness. But once it has been allowed into the discussion on its own terms, philosophical reflection enlightened by the narrative can proceed in its customary way.

In this choice of methodology, there is therefore a sacrifice of sharp and visible orderliness. By comparison with a philosophical work which moves in a disciplined way through argument to the demonstration of a thesis, philosophical examination including narratives will look—will tend to be—softer and more rambling, with the bones of the thought beneath the surface. Something is lost as well as gained in right-brain approaches. Furthermore, there will ineluctably be some loss of the crisp, clean order of thought favored in philosophy even in the exposition of the narratives themselves. Interpretations of texts—for that matter, interpretations of people and their actions—do not admit of rigorous argument. We can definitively rule some interpretations out, but it is hard to make a compelling argument that only *this* interpretation is right. Even a carefully supported interpretation of narratives is, in effect, only a recommendation to look at a text in a certain way. It invites readers to consider that text and ask themselves whether after all they do not see the text in the way the interpretation recommends. Interpretations present, suggest, offer, and invite; unlike philosophical arguments, they cannot attempt to command.

On the other hand, part of what is useful about this methodology is that it helps us to remember that precise, compelling arguments are not everything. If we insist on rigor above everything else, we are in danger of getting it above everything else: a fossilized view of the world, unable to account for the richness of the reality in which we live our lives. Van Fraassen seems to me right when he says, 'The world we live in is a precious thing; the world of the philosophers is well lost for love of it.'[29]

PHILOSOPHICAL EXAMINATION OF NARRATIVES

What, then, would the combination of philosophy and literature as I am recommending it look like? Any attempt to characterize a methodology (and especially an interdisciplinary one) in a few lines invites trouble, of course, but I can begin cautiously enough by describing the approach I am recommending as a method that involves asking philosophical questions of literary texts. This method will necessarily involve techniques used in literary criticism, in

[29] Van Fraassen, *Empirical Stance*, ch. 1.

order to avail ourselves of the narrative, but those techniques will also incorporate philosophical concerns and interests. So, for example, while both literary and philosophical examinations of a narrative might engage in character analysis, a philosophical study is more likely to ask whether the character in the narrative is violating moral standards in doing what she does or whether the worldview ascribed to her is coherent. Similarly, while both literary and philosophical examinations may look for philosophical or theological themes in a literary work—providence in *Hamlet* or nature in *Lear*—focused consideration of the concept of providence or the concept of nature is more likely to be found in the philosophical examination.

On the other hand, if the methodology involved in a philosopher's examination of a literary text came to no more than asking philosophical questions of literary texts, then philosophical examination of narratives would hardly count as new and should not need to be argued for. Many of the influential figures in the history of Christianity, for example, brought philosophical skill to bear on biblical narratives; and there is still much to be learnt which is philosophically interesting from, for example, Chrysostom and Augustine on John, Jerome on Daniel, Aquinas on Job, Luther on Galatians, Calvin on Romans, Kierkegaard on Genesis, and hosts of other authors and biblical stories. (I know just enough of the history of Judaism to be sure that a similar list could be compiled for that tradition, including, for example, Saadya Gaon and Moses Maimonides on Job.) And, of course, philosophy has its own literary texts, such as Plato's dialogues, Augustine's *Confessions*, and Boethius's *Consolation of Philosophy*, in which philosophers present their positions through the literary devices of the literary texts they themselves construct, rather than expound.

Now it is possible to ask philosophical questions of literary texts in blissful disregard of their literary character, as some scholarship on Plato's dialogues, for example, makes clear.[30] The patristic, medieval, and Reformation thinkers who asked philosophical questions of biblical narratives often had as their purpose just the analysis, as directly as possible, of the philosophical or theological lesson in the text. Sometimes that approach prompted a deep, sensitive interpretation of the texts, as we can see in Augustine's *De Genesi ad litteram*, for example. On other occasions, however, it yielded a superficial reading of a text precisely because it was ignoring the narrative's literary character, and in particular the human interplay in the narrative. Stories presenting some human drama worth reflecting on were sometimes treated as if the human details were disposable wrapping around the far more

---

[30] For a recent treatment of Plato's dialogues which takes the opposite tack and uses their literary character as a key to the interpretative analysis of the dialogues' philosophical content, see James Alexander Arieti, *Interpreting Plato: The Dialogues as Drama* (Savage, Md.: Rowman & Littlefield, 1991).

interesting philosophical or theological lesson. Augustine, for example, uses the biblical text describing the exchange between Jesus and Mary at the wedding at Cana as an occasion to give a theology lesson on the nature of the incarnate Christ, but he leaves the human side of that exchange and all that it implies virtually unexplored.

And so the methodology I am recommending has more to it than simply asking philosophical questions about literary texts. Rather, it is an attempt to combine the techniques of philosophy and literary criticism in order to achieve something neither set of techniques would accomplish on its own. Its purpose is thus to give us access to a side of reality that can be captured better in narratives than in philosophical prose but to give us access to it as philosophers.

Finally, I want to recommend philosophical attention to biblical narratives, and especially in connection with such philosophical problems as the problem of evil. Those philosophers willing to engage narratives have tended to consider literary works devised by single authors who were the creators of that literature. But narrative comes in many forms, from the highly self-conscious artistry of Aeschylean tragedy to the communally produced narratives of folklore. Whatever their authorship, whether they are more like single-authored works or more like folklore, biblical stories embody the reflections of communities signally concerned with both the insights and the problems of religion, and the narratives are also at least partially constitutive of the religions under attack in arguments from evil.[31] Furthermore, in a number of biblical narratives, not only is God a character in the narrative but he is also the character who manifestly allows or even brings about the suffering highlighted in the story. The biblical stories are therefore specially pertinent to reflections on the problem of evil. So it seems clearly appropriate to incorporate biblical narratives in any attempt to meld literature and philosophy in reflection on the problem of evil. To my mind, there is therefore a certain commonsensical obviousness about bringing biblical narratives into the discussion of certain philosophical problems, and particularly those in the philosophy of religion, such as the problem of evil.

CONCLUSION

The appropriate conclusion to the argument for any methodology ought to be the employment of it. But showing the use of the methodology I have just

---

[31] This is true even for Islam, part of whose self-understanding depends on certain interpretations of narratives in the Hebrew Bible.

argued for would require another chapter at least as long as this one; no useful exemplar of the method could be tucked into the end of this brief chapter. And so I will content myself with pointing out what just one glance at the biblical text most often associated with the problem of evil can show us when we look at it in the light of the considerations adduced here. The Book of Job is commonly taken by theologians and philosophers as having the problem of evil as its central concern. What commentators generally say about the book is that, although in the book Job cries out for an explanation of his suffering, the book gives us no help with the problem of evil. The Anchor Bible commentary on the book puts that view this way:

> It has been generally assumed that the purpose of the book [of Job] is to give an answer to the issue with which it deals, the problem of divine justice or theodicy. This question is raised inevitably by any and every instance of seemingly unmerited or purposeless suffering, and especially the suffering of a righteous man. Job's case... poses the problem in the most striking possible way. A man of exemplary rectitude and piety is suddenly overwhelmed with disasters and loathsome disease. How can such a situation be reconciled with divine justice and benevolent providence? It must be admitted first and last that the Book of Job fails to give a clear and definitive answer to this question [footnote omitted].[32]

What this view fails to notice, however, is that the book concludes with the lengthiest face-to-face discourse between God and a human being anywhere in the biblical texts. One way to read the book, then, is to see it as recommending second-person experience as a solution to the problem of evil. On this way of understanding the book, knowledge of a person is also an efficacious way to satisfy the desire to know generated by reflection on suffering.

Elsewhere I explore the book of Job and its approach to the problem of evil in great detail.[33] For now, it is enough for me to have gestured toward the counter-(analytic)cultural approach to the problem of evil suggested by the biblical narrative and to have argued for a methodology that lets us bring the book of Job as a story into our philosophical reflections.[34]

---

[32] Marvin Pope, *Job*, The Anchor Bible (New York: Doubleday, 1965), p. lxxiii.
[33] See my *Wandering in Darkness*.
[34] I am grateful to Jeff Brower, Frank Burch Brown, John Foley, John Kavanaugh, Scott MacDonald, Mike Murray, Mike Rea, and Ted Vitali for helpful comments on earlier drafts of this material.

13

Hermeneutics and Holiness

Merold Westphal

PROLOGUE ON EARTH

There is probably no such thing as *the* analytic tradition or *the* continental tradition in philosophy; but there are recognizably analytic traditions and continental traditions. They are different in their vocabularies, their canons, and their methods or styles of 'argument'.[1] Philosophers primarily at home on one side of this divide may well feel discomfort or even disorientation when crossing over to the other.

But the differences are not absolute by any means. Thus, for example, the analytic philosophers on whom Rorty draws, especially Sellars, Quine, and Kuhn, have recognizable affinities with such continental philosophers as Heidegger, Gadamer, and Derrida, on whom he also draws;[2] and Nancey Murphy evokes similar overlaps when speaking about 'Anglo-American Postmodernity'.[3]

In this chapter I have not tried to draw a comprehensive comparison between analytic and continental modes of thought, nor to argue for the superiority of the latter. I have rather tried to give a sense of how discourse to and about God (God-talk), especially the discourse of believers, whether academic or lay, can be understood in the light of two overlapping continental traditions, phenomenology and hermeneutics. I leave it to the reader to draw comparisons and conclusions.

PHENOMENOLOGY AND THEOLOGY

Heav'n above is softer blue, Earth around is sweeter green!
Something lives in every hue Christless eyes have never seen:
Birds with gladder songs o'er flow, Flow'rs with deeper beauties shine,
Since I know, as now I know, I am His and He is mine.

---

[1] Thus e.g. deductive arguments play a significantly larger role in analytic traditions than in their continental cousins.

[2] Richard Rorty, *Philosophy and the Mirror of Nature* (Princeton: Princeton University Press, 1979).

[3] *Anglo-American Postmodernity: Philosophical Perspectives on Science, Religion, and Ethics* (Boulder: Westview, 1997).

The phenomenologist tells us, 'True philosophy consists in re-learning to look at the world.'[4] The hymn-writer cited above[5] might be understood to be saying the same thing about theological discourse, whether scholarly, catechetical, liturgical (for example, his own hymn, which makes him also a theologian), kerygmatic, prayerful, or contemplative (for example, one's meditation in *lectio divina*).

The phenomenologist thinks that this relearning involves both cognitive and transcognitive dimensions. So he continues, 'We take our fate in our hands, we become responsible for our history through *reflection*, but equally by a *decision* on which we stake our life...'[6] The hymn-writer might well agree and speak of our God-talk not merely as having conversion and sanctification as their goal but as *consisting* in such transformation of our being-in-the-world. In other words, absent such relearning to see, either it is not really we who are speaking (or listening) or it is not God but some idol about which we converse. God-talk is rightly scary because whenever it really happens we are in play, we are being challenged and changed. With or without the Lutheran formula, Law and Gospel, our God-talk always implies commands and promises that deny our autonomy in relation to the agendas of our lives. We are rather responsible to and dependent on Another. To state the obvious, this is scary, because most of the time, already as Sunday School children, we are more interested in having God on our side than on being ourselves on God's side.

The phenomenologist hammers away at the existential significance (decision, transformation) of the phenomenological concern for the essential structures of experience in its various modes.[7] Its eidetic nature

means that we cannot subject our perception of the world to philosophical scrutiny [reflection] without ceasing to be identified with that act of positing the world, with that *interest* in it which delimits us, without drawing back from our *commitment* which is itself thus made to appear as a spectacle, without passing from the *fact* of our existence to its *nature*, from the Dasein to the Wesen. But it is clear that the essence is here *not the end, but a means*... The need to proceed by way of essences does not mean that philosophy takes them as its object, but, on the contrary, that our existence is too tightly held in the world to be able to know itself as such in the moment of its *involvement*, and that it requires the field of ideality in order to become acquainted with [cognitive goal] and prevail over [trans-cognitive goal] its facticity.[8]

---

[4] M. Merleau-Ponty, *Phenomenology of Perception*, tr. Colin Smith (London: Routledge & Kegan Paul, 1962), p. xx.

[5] George W. Robinson. The hymn is known both as 'I am His, and He is Mine' and by its first line, 'Loved with Everlasting Love'.

[6] Emphasis added.

[7] Phenomenology's concern for essences is not unlike analytic concern for propositions.

[8] Merleau-Ponty, *Phenomenology of Perception*, pp. xiv–xv; emphases added. To 'prevail over our facticity' means to preside over the givens of our life, to be an agent and not merely a function of impersonal forces within us and without.

The hymn-writer will once again feel a certain kinship, but this time with a significant difference. He will agree that theological discourse, whether we speak or listen, write or read, is always preceded by interests, commitments, and involvements that shape our 'seeings', both perceptual and conceptual, both empirical and a priori;[9] and he will agree with the general thrust of the idea that the point of it all is not to enjoy a spectacle but to 'prevail' over our facticity in the sense of altering those interests, commitments, and involvements for the better. But we are not the primary agents of such change; so the hymn-writer introduces a whole dimension of which the phenomenologist, as such, knows nothing: Christ.

The phenomenologist hopes to renew ' "wonder" in the face of the world ... to watch the forms of transcendence fly up like sparks from a fire'[10] by performing the phenomenological and eidetic reductions. The theologian cries out, 'Help me, O Lord ... Let me be reborn in you and *see through you* the world in the right way, so that all my actions, words, and thought can become a hymn of praise to you.'[11] This difference between the phenomenologist and the theologian can be spelt out in at least four contrasts.

(1) The phenomenologist speaks of possibilities, the theologian of actualities.

Thus Jean-Luc Marion writes, 'Between phenomenology and theology the frontier passes between revelation as possibility and revelation as historicity.'[12] The phenomenologist says, in effect, 'The realm of possible experience includes this sort of experience—relearning to see, conversion, sanctification. It could happen.' Kant speaks as a phenomenologist when he says, about acting 'not from inclination, but from duty', that 'reason unrelentingly commands actions of which the world has perhaps hitherto never provided an example ... for instance, even though there might never yet have been a sincere friend, still pure sincerity in

---

[9] For Merleau-Ponty the most basic a priori is what he calls the 'ante-predicative life of consciousness' in which we find ourselves 'before any thematization'. Ibid., pp. xv, xviii. To insist that we are always somewhere and never nowhere in this way is not to deny that our pre-predicative being-in-the-world has been shaped in various degrees and manners by the language-games into which we have been socialized. It is often said e.g. that we have to be taught to be racists. But if we have been, our racism is not in the first instance a set of beliefs but a congeries of seeings, not a matter of self-evident propositions but of automatic perceptions and attitudes.

[10] Ibid., p. xiii.

[11] Henry Nouwen, *A Cry for Mercy: Prayers from the Genesee* (Garden City, NY: Doubleday, 1983), 45–6; emphasis added.

[12] 'Metaphysics and Phenomenology: A Summary for Theologians', in Graham Ward (ed.), *The Postmodern God: A Theological Reader* (Oxford: Blackwell, 1997), 293. This is Marion's repeated reply to the charge from Dominique Janicaud that he sneaks theology into phenomenology through the back door. Cf. Marion's *Being Given*, tr. Jeffrey L. Kosky (Stanford, Calif.: Stanford University Press, 2002), 234–6, 242, and my discussion in 'The Importance of Overcoming Metaphysics for the Life of Faith', *Modern Theology*, 23/2 (Apr. 2007), 266–7.

friendship is nonetheless required of every man'.[13] The philosophical task is to describe this possibility.

By contrast, the hymn-writer[14] speaks as a theologian, with reference to John 9: 25, when singing,

> Once I was blind, but now I can see:
> The light of the world is Jesus.

He here affirms two actualities, one concerning Jesus and one concerning himself. The latter point does not imply that theology is confessional in the autobiographical sense, as in confessional poetry. But it does imply that the theologian identifies, at least to some degree, the actual faith perspective from which (in this case) he speaks. He does not pretend to occupy 'the view from nowhere', to be the voice of 'pure' reason.[15]

The phenomenologist makes a similar point when he says, 'The most important lesson which the reduction teaches us is the impossibility of a complete reduction.'[16] But while disclaiming any presuppositionless or perspective-free location, Merleau-Ponty does not identify his location; he just acknowledges that he and every other phenomenologist occupies some actual space of interests, commitments, and involvements, is always somewhere and never nowhere even during reflection.[17] This last point, together with the hymn-writers' references to Christ and to Jesus, signifies another aspect of the difference between the two practices.

> (2) The phenomenologist speaks of universal structures (essences), the theologian of particular events or persons.[18]

Perhaps this is why the *name* of God is so important in the Bible.[19] Thus 'God', which could be a generic name for deity, is specified so that it comes to function as a proper name and to identify this very God: the God of Abraham,

---

[13] *Grounding for the Metaphysics of Morals*, tr. James W. Ellington (Indianapolis, Ind.: Hackett, 1981), 12, 20. Academy edn., 4: 399, 408.

[14] P. P. Bliss. The hymn is 'The Light of the World is Jesus'.

[15] This may well be the boundary line between religious studies and theology. For the latter, 'religion' does not signify the object that the scholar studies but the way of life (language-game, life world) into which the speaker or writer has been caught up and within which reflection takes place under the rubric 'faith seeking understanding'.

[16] *Phenomenology of Perception*, p. xiv.

[17] Thus the phenomenologist stands between the theologian and the religious studies scholar as described in n. 15 above.

[18] At least within the framework of the Abrahamic monotheisms, a theologian whose metaphysical interests in abstract concepts and impersonal structures loses contact with the historical revelation that gives rise to the community of faith might be seen more as the enemy than as the friend of faith.

[19] And in Islam and devotional forms of Hinduism and Buddhism.

Isaac, and Jacob; the God and Father of our Lord Jesus Christ; the God who raised Jesus Christ from the dead; and so forth. Similarly, names that are titles come to function as proper names. Reference to 'our Lord Jesus Christ' includes two titles and one proper name. But both 'Lord' and 'Christ' become proper names and, following New Testament usage, we say Jesus Christ far more often than Jesus, the Christ. Even the Tetragrammaton, usually rendered as perhaps the only truly proper name for God in the Old Testament, is further specified to distinguish this God from any other. Thus the Ten Commandments do not come from pure practical reason or from the moral wisdom of the human race but rather,

> I am Yahweh your God who brought you out of Egypt, where you lived as slaves
> You shall have no other gods to rival me... (Ex. 20: 2–3; NJB)

and

> our help is in the name of Yahweh,
> who made heaven and earth. (Ps. 124: 8; NJB)

Of course, the theologian risks, indeed may be said to invite, the 'scandal of particularity' at just this point. Kierkegaard is especially clear about this in *Philosophical Fragments*, and in *Practice in Christianity* we are told that the incarnate Christ has to be 'the sign of offense *in order to be* the object of faith'.[20] For in the Incarnation God becomes very particular indeed and, quite apart from any specific content, the mere fact of this radical singularity may be a 'stone of stumbling and a rock of offense' (1 Pet. 2: 8; KJV; cf. Isa. 8: 14).

(3) The phenomenologist speaks in the name of reason, the theologian in the name of faith.

Phenomenology presents itself as the latest and most adequate form of critical reason, fulfilling the projects of Descartes, Kant, and even Hume![21] Husserl makes a stronger claim in this respect than subsequent phenomenologists.[22] But

---

[20] *Philosophical Fragments/Johannes Climacus*, tr. Howard V. Hong and Edna H. Hong (Princeton: Princeton University Press, 1985); *Practice in Christianity*, tr. Howard V. Hong and Edna H. Hong (Princeton: Princeton University Press, 1991), 98. See my commentary, 'Kenosis and Offense: A Kierkegaardian Look at Divine Transcendence', in Robert L. Perkins (ed.), *International Kierkegaard Commentary: Practice in Christianity* (Macon, Ga.: Mercer University Press, 2004), 19–46.

[21] Hume? Yes, because phenomenology purports to be the true empiricism, giving a much more faithful account of experience than classical British empiricism. See Edmund Husserl, *Ideas Pertaining to a Pure Phenomenology and to Phenomenological Philosophy, First Book*, tr. F. Kersten (The Hague: Martinus Nijhoff, 1982), 142.

[22] See esp. 'Philosophy as Rigorous Science', in *Husserl: Shorter Works*, ed. Peter McCormick and Frederick Elliston (Notre Dame, Ind.: University of Notre Dame Press, 1981), 161–97. The concluding part 4 of *Ideas*, i, is titled 'Reason and Actuality'. Also see Maurice Natanson,

even for Merleau-Ponty, our phenomenological guide and tutor, who does not claim the status of 'rigorous science' for phenomenology, it remains a description of general structures that is not a response to anything particular enough to bear a proper name. It is not a response to revelation but an act of revealing. It articulates what human understanding can *discover* and *validate* on its own on the basis of its *experience* of the *world*.[23]

By contrast, the theologian speaks from the standpoint of faith about (1) what cannot be discovered and validated by unaided human powers and (2) what is essentially tied to specific events and persons. In this way both the autonomy and the universality that phenomenology takes over from a long philosophical history are compromised, and deliberately so.[24] Of course, this does not mean that the theologian makes no universal claims; but such claims are made about the universal significance of particular events and persons.

(4) The phenomenologist speaks of law, the theologian of law and gospel.

This is not to say that phenomenology is legalistic and theology always Lutheran. It is rather to say that whatever conversion or transformation phenomenology may point us to is to be effected only by our own decision, by performing the reductions. We might say that the phenomenologist is a kind of Pelagian who knows as little of the need and reality of gracious help in the transcognitive dimension of life as in the cognitive.

By contrast, the theologian knows that it is Jesus who opens our blinded eyes, that it is Yahweh who delivers us from the slaveries into which we fall, and that, in general, our help is in the name of Yahweh.

These differences are not trivial. There is surely a point to Heidegger's claim that the relation of the two practices 'includes the fact that *faith* [and therefore theology which grounds itself in faith], as a specific possibility of existence, is in its innermost core the mortal enemy of the *form of existence* that is an essential part of *philosophy* [clearly identified here as phenomenology]'.[25] This is a useful reminder that from ancient times philosophy has not been merely a (putative) science but a way of life[26] and that the life of faith, including its reflective mode as theology, needs to be on guard against attempts by philosophy if not to conquer it outright at least to colonize it.

Edmund Husserl: Philosopher of Infinite Tasks (Evanston, Ill.: Northwestern University Press, 1973), esp. ch. 9.

[23] For Merleau-Ponty's account of how phenomenology is the answer to the philosophical question of reason and rationality, see *Phenomenology of Perception*, pp. xix–xx.

[24] Martin Heidegger emphasizes this difference between phenomenology and theology. See 'Phenomenology and Theology', in *Pathmarks*, ed. William McNeill (New York: CUP, 1998), 43–54, if only to give to phenomenology the task of 'correcting' theological discourse.

[25] Ibid. 53.

[26] See Pierre Hadot, *Philosophy as a Way of Life*, tr. Michael Chase (Oxford: Blackwell, 1995).

Is it possible that because of these convergences and in spite of these divergences, phenomenology might be helpful to theology, in some sense an *ancilla theologiae*? I believe so, especially after phenomenology takes the hermeneutical turn. But before we turn to that turn, let us note one possibility of this sort. Two general comments about phenomenology as a partner to theology. First, I am obviously writing, as I was asked to do, about continental philosophy in a volume about the relation of analytic philosophy to Christian theology. The suggestions I offer about a possible positive relation between phenomenology and theology are meant more as an alternative to than as a critique of analytic theology. There are divergences, which I shall not try to paper over. But apart from the fact that neither 'analytic philosophy' nor 'continental philosophy' is one single, univocal practice, I do not see the two generically different approaches as mutually exclusive but rather as supplementary to each other. Each can do things that the other cannot, and each is prey to perils and pitfalls that can pervert the life of faith rather than nourish it.

Second, the points of possibly fruitful intersection are perhaps better seen as methodological than as substantive. By method I do not mean anything like an algorithm for cranking out theorems, *more geometrico*, but rather the self-conscious reminder of (1) what one is doing, (2) how one goes about it, (3) within what limits, and (4) to what end. I think when we talk about 'scientific method', for example, we are thinking about possible answers to all of these questions.

No sooner did Husserl seek to found phenomenology as the fulfillment of the Cartesian aspiration for certainty presented in clear and distinct ideas than his followers replaced the idea of phenomenology as 'rigorous science' with notions such as 'existential' and 'hermeneutical' phenomenology. We will soon turn our attention to the latter, but we have already seen a glimpse of the former in Merleau-Ponty's existentialism.[27] How might it be helpful to the theologian?

By describing the goal of reflection as relearning to see the world, existential phenomenology reminds the theologian that, while 'seeing is believing', according to a familiar adage, believing is not necessarily seeing. I can sincerely believe, for example, that the lives of the homeless poor of New York and Calcutta and the shanty-town poor of Africa and Latin America are of equal value to the lives of highly educated, highly affluent suburban Americans without seeing the former and myself in these terms. I can sincerely believe that my sins are forgiven by the grace of God and that

---

[27] It hardly needs to be mentioned that the phenomenological ontologies of Heidegger in *Being and Time* and Sartre in *Being and Nothingness* are classics of existential phenomenology, with (in the case of Sartre) or without (in the case of Heidegger) the authors' approval.

justification is a gift and not a form of wages and still see myself as carrying a load of guilt that I must work off with pious practices.

That this is problematic does not mean that what I believe is unimportant, but rather that having my doxastic house in order is not the ultimate goal of theological discourse. It is rather *to bring my seeings (and thereby feelings and actions, since these arise more from my seeings than from my believings) into conformity with my best judgments about what is true.* This reminder is an important prophylactic against what I sometimes call the King Midas theory of truth: that the goal is to have my barns filled with the largest possible piles of true propositions, or at least warranted beliefs, so as to find my *security* (and my *superiority*) in these possessions. 'Lord, I thank Thee that I am not like those who err.' Both the analytic preoccupation with the truth, justification, or warrant of propositions and the phenomenological goal of intuiting essences (*Wesensschauen*) can give aid and comfort to the Midas tendencies. Of course, theology doesn't need any philosophical help to develop the notion that 'we' are the repositories of the Gold Standard in Truth and possess all the rights and privileges, often violent, pertaining to 'our' role as possessors and dispensers of Absolute Truth. Quite possibly in stark contrast to what we say about God, we end up seeing ourselves as God's owners, since we have captured God in our conceptual apparatus. But Merleau-Ponty's reminder that the goal is conversion rather than certainty can warn the theologian against these tendencies as temptations to be resisted. In a similar vein, Heidegger insists that all theology is practical theology. 'Theology is systematic only when it is historical and practical. It is historical only when it is systematic and practical. And it is practical only when it is systematic and historical.'[28] Theoretical truth (orthodoxy) always has its *telos* in practice (ethics, politics, spirituality). Theology doesn't need to learn this from existential phenomenology, but often enough it does need to be reminded.

THE HERMENEUTICAL TURN

With Heidegger, and then with Gadamer and Ricoeur, phenomenology turns hermeneutical. In doing so it comes closer to theology in two ways (without abolishing the differences cited above). First, it becomes a theory of interpretation. With Heidegger all human understanding has the form of interpretation, but with Gadamer and Ricoeur the focus returns largely to the interpretation of texts, and this is utterly central to the theologian's practice.

---

[28] 'Phenomenology and Theology', 48.

Second, the hermeneutical turn takes philosophical reflection on a detour through textual material. Rather than try to go directly to phenomena, 'to the things themselves', hermeneutical phenomenology takes 'the detour through the contingency of cultures, through an incurably equivocal language, and through the conflict of interpretations'.[29] It travels 'the long detour of the signs of humanity deposited in cultural works' and 'the detour of understanding the cultural signs in which the self documents and forms itself... [so that] reflection is nothing without the mediation of signs and works'.[30]

Paul Ricoeur's own work, *The Symbolism of Evil*,[31] is an example of what he means. In order to get a handle on the phenomena of evil, defilement, sin, guilt, and confession, he explores four different narratives of the origin and overcoming of evil found in the ancient world. In other words, he is interpreting texts which are already interpretations of the phenomena that interest him. In the same way theologians interpret texts that are already interpretations, for example, the four gospels as four interpretations of the Christ event.

When hermeneutical phenomenology turns from the theory of interpretation to its actual practice in relation to texts with a specific cultural provenance, it closes somewhat the gap cited above between phenomenology's concern for universal structures and theology's interest in particular events and persons. Especially when the texts are of religious import, the phenomenologist looks a good bit more like the theologian than before. Attention is directed to something historically and culturally specific.

Hermeneutical phenomenology can be understood as an extended meditation on two biblical themes. As the hermeneutics of finitude, it can be a meditation on creation, a reminder that, in our attempts to understand by interpreting, we are but creatures. As the hermeneutics of suspicion, it can be a meditation on the fall, a reminder that, biblically speaking, sin is an epistemic category. In 'ungodliness and wickedness' we 'suppress the truth' (Rom. 1: 18; RSV). Because I have written at length about the hermeneutics of suspicion and its importance for theology,[32] I shall focus here on the hermeneutics of finitude.

Hermeneutically speaking, finitude is not understood in Cartesian fashion merely as the equation of finitude with fallibilism, an equation alive and well

---

[29] Paul Ricoeur, *Freud and Philosophy*, tr. Denis Savage (New Haven: Yale University Press, 1970), 42.
[30] Paul Ricoeur, *Hermeneutics and the Human Sciences*, ed. and tr. John B. Thompson (New York: CUP, 1981), 143, 158–9.
[31] Tr. Emerson Buchanan (New York: Harper & Row, 1967).
[32] See *Suspicion and Faith: The Religious Uses of Modern Atheism* (New York: Fordham University Press, 1998).

in some modes of analytic philosophy and theology. On this view all facts or true propositions are divided into three groups: the ones of which we are simply ignorant, the ones we think we know but don't because we've gotten them wrong, and the ones we really know. These latter we know as well as they can be known; there is a complete *adequatio intellectus et rei* and our mind is the perfect mirror of the real.[33] However we get to this point, once we arrive we just see things as they are. We are in the land of clear and distinct intuitions, where no interpretation is needed.

Proposition talk encourages this viewpoint. Since 'I love you', 'Ich liebe dich', and 'Je t'aime' are said to express the same proposition, it would seem, and is sometimes asserted, that propositions do not belong to any natural language and the cultural particularity embodied therein, but are like Platonic forms, populating some transhistorical, transcultural, even transhuman ether. Thus I recall a major philosopher of religion telling me that when he and God understand and know the same proposition, he understands and knows at least that proposition as well as God does.[34] When we actually achieve knowledge, its finitude is only quantitative: there are many true propositions we don't know.

Over against this quantitative understanding of finitude and its clean either/or between what we know and what we don't know, hermeneutics thinks in qualitative terms. Understanding approximates more or less closely to its object, and the real is in some degree revealed and in some degree remains concealed. To begin with, hermeneutics understands understanding as interpretation rather than as intuition, as construal and seeing-as rather than as simply seeing. The object underdetermines our perception or understanding in the way that Wittgenstein's duck-rabbit figure does.[35] More than one construal is quite legitimate, and to see it as a duck does not mean that to see it as a rabbit is a mistake. Understanding interpretation in this way, Gadamer says that 'understanding is not merely a reproductive but always a productive activity as well'.[36] Derrida agrees, and writes

[33] Rorty derives the hermeneutical turn from Sellars and Quine as well as from Heidegger and Dewey and sees it as the denial that the mind is the mirror of nature. See *Philosophy and the Mirror of Nature*.

[34] For my critique of proposition talk, see 'Taking Plantinga Seriously: Advice to Christian Philosophers', *Faith and Philosophy*, 16/2 (Apr. 1999), 173–81.

[35] Actually it is Jastrow's, cited by Wittgenstein in *Philosophical Investigations*, tr. G. E. M. Anscombe (Oxford: Basil Blackwell, 1958), 194.

[36] *Truth and Method*, 2nd edn., tr. Joel Weinsheimer and Donald G. Marshall (New York: Crossroad, 1989), 296 (same page in 2004 edn.). 'Daher ist Verstehen kein nur reproduktives, sondern stets auch ein produktives Verhalten.' In his eagerness to make Gadamer look dangerous, E. D. Hirsch, Jr. misquotes this passage, leaving out the *nur* and the *auch*, 'Understanding is not a reproductive but always a productive activity', and he takes this to be a denial 'that the text has *any* determinate meaning'. *Validity in Interpretation* (New Haven: Yale University Press, 1967), 249. As if it would be all right to construe the duck-rabbit as a railroad locomotive or a copy of Homer's *Iliad*!

This moment of doubling commentary [the reproductive moment of interpretation] should no doubt have its place in a critical reading. To recognize and respect all its classical exigencies is not easy and requires all the instruments of traditional criticism. Without this recognition and this respect, critical production would risk developing in any direction at all and authorize itself to say almost anything. But this indispensable guardrail has always only *protected*, it has never *opened*, a reading.[37]

In this spirit we are told that Luther, for example, 'always takes the Decalogue and the New Testament writings as his starting point, but he never simply repeats them'.[38]

This hermeneutical version of Gestalt psychology and the Kantian dialectic of receptivity and spontaneity is embedded in the theory of the hermeneutic circle.[39] In other words, we always see more than is 'given' in the narrowest sense of the term, and we always do so on the basis of a priori assumptions or expectations. Here hermeneutics develops the perspectivism implicit in the phenomenological insight that interpretation is like physical vision: we are always somewhere and never nowhere. In other words, our interpretations are always relative to the location—linguistic, historical, cultural—from which they are made.

Many theologians will be afraid of this relativism, but they need not be. After all, is it not the case that only God is absolute and we creatures are always relative? Do we not see 'through a glass, darkly' (1 Cor. 13: 12; KJV), 'in a mirror, dimly' (NRSV), 'puzzling reflections in a mirror' (REB)? Does not God tell us

> For my thoughts are not your thoughts,
> nor are your ways my ways, says the LORD.
> For as the heavens are higher than the earth,
> so are my ways higher than your ways
> and my thoughts than your thoughts. (Isa. 55: 8–9)

Just as we don't have to be purple to think about pansies, so we don't have to be absolute in our knowing to think rightly about the God who alone is absolute. If the chief end of our theological discourse is 'to glorify God, and to enjoy him for ever',[40] does it not stand to reason that in this life we can achieve

---

[37] *Of Grammatology*, tr. Gayatri Chakravorty Spivak (Baltimore, Md.: Johns Hopkins University Press, 1976), 158. So much for the myth that deconstruction is a philosophy of 'anything goes'.

[38] Jens Zimmermann, *Recovering Theological Hermeneutics* (Grand Rapids, Mich.: Baker Academic, 2004), 74.

[39] For the Kantian dimension, see my quarrel with Al Plantinga, 'Christian Philosophers and the Copernican Revolution', in my *Overcoming Onto-Theology* (New York: Fordham University Press, 2001), 89–105. For the hermeneutical circle, see below.

[40] From question 1 of the Westminster Shorter Catechism.

this goal only within the limits of our bodily and cultural finitude? Nor need we assume that the purpose of divine revelation is to elevate us above the human condition. Does not Calvin, for example, say that 'as nurses commonly do with infants, God is wont in a measure to "lisp" in speaking. Thus such forms of speaking do not so much express clearly what God is like as accommodate the knowledge to our slight capacity. To do this he must descend far beneath his loftiness.'[41]

With these reminders, let us turn to the hermeneutical circle. The basic idea is that we always come to the task of interpreting guided by presuppositions, anticipations of experience that function as the a priori conditions of possible understanding.[42] But whereas for Kant the a priori is fixed and permanent, within the hermeneutical circle it can be revised or even replaced.[43] The circular movement is from twelve o'clock to six o'clock as our presuppositions guide our interpretations, and then back from six to twelve as we revise or replace our presuppositions in the light of the interpretations to which they have led us. This circle is at work in science when paradigms guide normal science but anomalies also lead to paradigm shifts. We are dealing with a threefold perspectivism: tradition as prejudice, hermeneutical holism, and practices as presuppositions.

Tradition as Prejudice

Gadamer's distinctive contribution to the theory of the hermeneutical circle is the notion of tradition as prejudice in the etymological sense of pre-judgment, pre-understanding, presupposition. Tradition embodies the a priori in contingent, particular, revisable forms. Whereas Plato understands reason as the reflective escape from the body and the senses, modern philosophy, especially in Descartes and Locke, understands reason as the reflective escape from tradition as prejudice. Thus 'the fundamental prejudice [NB] of the Enlightenment is the prejudice against prejudice itself, which denies tradition its power'.[44]

---

[41] *Institutes*, 1. 13. 1. See Ford Lewis Battles, 'God was Accommodating Himself to Human Capacity', in Donald K. McKim (ed.), *Readings in Calvin's Theology* (Grand Rapids, Mich.: Baker Book House, 1984), 21–42. Aquinas's doctrine of analogy seems to me on this same wavelength.

[42] See Heidegger, *Being and Time*, tr. John Macquarrie and Edward Robinson (New York: Harper & Row, 1962), §§32–3. 'An interpretation is never a presuppositionless apprehending of something presented to us' (pp. 191–2).

[43] See Gadamer, *Truth and Method*, 267/269. The double pagination signifies the two versions of the 2nd edn.

[44] Ibid. 270/273. The power of tradition is both *de facto* and *de jure*. As a matter of fact it has shaped and continues to shape us in ways of which we are never fully aware. As a matter of right, just as we ought to learn from our parents and teachers, so the wisdom of our cultural-historical predecessors has a right to be taken seriously, though this entails no infallibility. Like ourselves and our contemporaries, our predecessors were human, all too human.

Of course, this denial promises what it cannot deliver, and histories of the Enlightenment show its dependence on particular traditions just as it becomes a tradition itself,[45] the 'modernity' that is revised and replaced by a variety of paradigms which thereby get called 'postmodern'.

For Gadamer our cognitive finitude consists largely in our concrete historicity, 'being situated within traditions... In fact history does not belong to us; we belong to it. Long before we understand ourselves through the process of self-examination, we understand ourselves in a self-evident way in the family, society, and the state in which we live... *That is why the prejudices of the individual, far more than his judgments, constitute the historical reality of his being.*'[46] Of course, pre-judgments can deafen us to the voice of the other, the voice of the text, but 'legitimate' prejudices play an 'enabling' role without which we would not be able to understand at all.[47]

Theologians can be reminded here (1) that throughout Christian history biblical interpretation has been shaped by and relative to a rich variety of traditions, and (2) that getting the most reliable look at things, the goal of objectivity, is often achieved by multiplying perspectives rather than by the (futile) flight from perspective.

Hermeneutical Holism

Schleiermacher's account of the hermeneutical circle is primarily a matter of whole and parts. Our interpretation of the parts is guided by our pre-understanding of the whole, which, in turn, is revised in light of our ongoing interpretation of the parts.[48] Analogs of this holism can be found in Hegel, in structuralism, in deconstruction, and in Quine, who famously tells us that 'our statements about the external world face the tribunal of sense experience not individually but only as a corporate body'.[49] For Hegel and Quine holism is primarily a matter of truth, whereas for structuralism, deconstruction, and hermeneutical phenomenology, it is primarily about meaning and a fortiori about truth. The point is that neither words, nor sentences, nor paragraphs, nor chapters, nor even books have either meaning or truth by themselves; they

---

[45] See esp. Peter Gay, *The Enlightenment: An Interpretation*, i. *The Rise of Modern Paganism* (New York: Random House, 1966).
[46] *Truth and Method*, 276–7/278.
[47] Ibid. 277/278 and 295/295.
[48] See my 'Totality and Finitude in Schleiermacher's Hermeneutics', in *Overcoming Onto-Theology*, 106–27.
[49] Willard Van Orman Quine, *From a Logical Point of View*, 2nd edn. rev. (New York: Harper & Row, 1961), 41. Holism is an important theme for both Rorty and Murphy as cited above.

are relative to the whole in which they occur. That old homiletical adage that a text without a context is a pretext has real bite.

And here's the rub for both philosophy and theology. Hegel thinks there is a meaningful sense in which we can possess the whole and bring the process of interpretation to a definitive conclusion. But for hermeneutical phenomenology (and Schleiermacher and deconstruction) finitude denies us this totality. Within the hermeneutical circle we always project a whole in terms of which we understand such parts as pericopes, parables, psalms, prophecies, apocalypses, and epistles. But this whole is always penultimate, only a work in progress, less than fully determinate, and subject to revision and even replacement. That means, of course, that all my interpretations will be relative to one whole among many possible wholes, my systematic theology or my theological tradition. It might seem that there is more than a little arrogance in the assumption that my system is *the* system or that my tradition has a monopoly of meaning and truth. Hermeneutical phenomenology requires that theology be ecumenical and dialogical. The assumption is that each perspective *may* open an important dimension of the truth but that no one perspective *can* encompass it all.

Practices as Presuppositions

Heidegger does not merely reaffirm Schleiermacher's hermeneutical circle;[50] he radicalizes it by taking it beyond the cognitive realm. The circle within which our knowing, believing, representing, and predicating take place is part of a larger circle of practices. It is not only that all statements are theory-laden, but both statements and theories are shaped by practices that precede them and in turn are modified by them.[51] To think just in terms of the 'propositional content' of statements is to think abstractly twice over. It is to abstract statements from the entire cognitive horizon within which they function and it is to abstract that whole domain from the practices (language-*games*) in which it is embedded. But, to paraphrase Spinoza, the abstract is that which can neither be nor be understood by itself.

This 'pragmatic turn' has implications not only for the input of theological thinking but also for its output. Understanding does not only arise out of our practices but strengthens, or weakens, or alters them as well. For Gadamer,

---

[50] See nn. 42 and 48 above.
[51] For a helpful analysis of Heidegger's 'pragmatism', see Hubert Dreyfus, 'Holism and Hermeneutics', *Review of Metaphysics*, 34/1 (1980–1), 3–23. See also my analysis, 'Hermeneutics as Epistemology', in *Overcoming Onto-Theology*, 47–74, where both theory and practice are embedded in a further circle of affect, which I'll not try to develop here.

texts address us, and the claims they make are not merely cognitive. So understanding essentially involves application and Aristotle's *phronesis* or practical wisdom is a hermeneutical paradigm. He acknowledges pietism as the source of this insight,[52] and might well have been thinking of the four questions Luther suggests we should ask when reading scripture: what does this text ask me to believe, to do, to repent of, and to give thanks for.[53] Scripture is inspired by God, we are told, so that it will be 'useful for teaching, for reproof, for correction, and for training in righteousness, so that everyone who belongs to God may be proficient, equipped for every good work' (Tim. 3: 16–17; NRSV).

Now we have two ways to understand why Gadamer says, when speaking of understanding as both reproductive and productive, 'Not just occasionally but always, the meaning of a text goes beyond its author... It is enough to say that we understand in a *different* way, *if we understand at all*.'[54] In the first place, understanding is not pure intuition from nowhere but construal from within one particular and contingent horizon among others. In the second place, the task of understanding is not completed, penultimately, to be sure, until the text as the voice of another has been applied to one's own situation and one has heard one's practices as well as one's beliefs addressed by that voice. Thus Jens Zimmermann writes in relation first to Calvin and then to pietism, 'The whole purpose of reading scripture is the restoration of our humanity to the fullness of the image of God in us as individuals and in society as a whole.... Reading is never an end in itself but always transforms the reader and results in action.'[55] This is a timely warning against the danger, to which analytic theology is not immune, of lapsing into scholasticism in the pejorative sense of the term, allowing metaphysics to become separated from spirituality (love of God) and ethics (love of neighbor).

Instead of thinking of the hermeneutical task as a means to the kerygmatic end, we might do better to think of interpreting both scripture and tradition as always already preaching, at least to oneself. When hermeneutics has holiness as its *telos*, philosophical hermeneutics can serve as an *ancilla theologiae*.

---

[52] *Truth and Method*, 307/306.
[53] I read this years ago in a pamphlet long since lost.
[54] *Truth and Method*, 296–7/296.
[55] In part 1 of *Recovering Theological Hermeneutics*, Jens Zimmermann argues that 'understanding *is* application' for Luther, Calvin, English Puritanism, and German Pietism. Quotations are from pp. 33 and 94.

14

Dark Contemplation and Epistemic Transformation

The Analytic Theologian Re-Meets Teresa of Ávila

Sarah Coakley

The philosophical theologian who has a respect for analytic philosophy may find herself in something of a methodological bind. On the one hand, the fierce clarity and apologetic incisiveness of the analytic tradition offers philosophical deliverances which the continental tradition, even at its best, is hard put to rival. On the other hand, the analytic approach can on occasion display a certain hermeneutical blindness which is nothing less than embarrassing to those trained in continental ways of reading.

This dilemma is particularly evident when complex texts from the 'mystical' traditions of Christianity are—for whatever philosophical purpose—under consideration. The 'apophatic rage'[1] which has overtaken post-Heideggerian continental philosophy of late, as a corrective to the perils of so-called 'onto-theology', has led to a renewed fascination with 'mystical theology'[2] in premodern

---

[1] The phrase was coined by Martin Laird, in his ' "Whereof we Speak": Gregory of Nyssa, Jean-Luc Marion and the Current Apophatic Rage', *Heythrop Journal*, 42 (2001), 1–12.

[2] In the sense of ps.-Dionysius (early 6th cent. CE), who first introduces the term, and to be distinguished from 'mysticism' in the modern, psychologized, transreligious, sense of William James. 'Mystical' as an adjective appears in early patristic writing to mean 'secret', 'mysterious'—as applied to readings of scripture or effects of the sacraments. 'Mystical theology' appears as a phrase for the first time in the title of a work by ps.-Dionysius, but he does not explicitly define it. From the work itself, we deduce that the term combines (1) the theological practice of negating positive ('kataphatic') claims about God (and, in Dionysius's case, even of negating the negations) and (2) the ascetic practice of 'contemplation', which may lead to passing states of 'ecstasy' (*ekstasis*) and 'union' (*henosis*) in which the mind goes beyond itself (*huper noun*) into darkness and unknowing. This darkness is however a 'brilliant' one in Dionysius, suffused with the 'overwhelming light' of the Trinity. For a brief and insightful contrast of the categories of 'mystical', 'mystical theology', and 'mysticism', see Andrew Louth, 'Mysticism', in Gordon S. Wakefield (ed.), *A Dictionary of Christian Spirituality* (London, SCM, 1983), 272–4. I do not

Christian traditions, and a somewhat questionable tendency to fuse this premodern inheritance with the Derridean project of 'deferral'. Nonetheless, the philosophical significance of 'apophaticism'[3] has been readily celebrated here, and for interesting cultural reasons.[4] In the same time-span, ironically, analytic

concur with Louth's charge in this article that Teresa of Ávila can be blamed for introducing the first lurch towards 'psychologized' modern interpretations of mystical states (even though a selective and misleading reading of her early work, the *Life*, led to this interpretation developing rather quickly after her death). William James's account of 'mysticism' in *The Varieties of Religious Experience* ([1]1902; London: Fontana, 1960) is very different from Dionysius's 'mystical theology', for it is a subset of James's more generic modern category 'religious experience': see n. 6, below.

[3] It is necessary also to give a working definition of 'apophaticism', given the confusion that has arisen during the current 'rage' to use the term carelessly, or to bleed its meanings into those of 'negative theology' (the term more commonly used in the West up to the postmodern period). The term *apophasis* literally means, in Greek, 'saying no', or 'saying negatively' (from the verb *apophemi*), making it ostensibly equivalent to the Latin *via negativa*; but the Greek word *apophasis* can also convey the meaning of 'revelation' (from the verb *apophaino*), thus giving it richer overtones than the Latin. We also need to distinguish between extra possible evocations of 'negative theology'/'negativity' in the Western tradition beyond that of merely *speaking* negatively. Here I propose extending a threefold typology of the meanings of 'negative theology' provided by Bernard McGinn in 'Three Forms of Negativity in Christian Mysticism', in John W. Bowker (ed.), *Sciences and Religions: Knowing the Unknowable about God and the Universe* (London: I. B. Tauris, forthcoming). (1) *The theological practice of 'unsaying' claims about God*, of negating the positive to express God's uniqueness and transcendence (NB this is the point of overlap between 'apophaticim'/negative theology and the *first* aspect of 'mystical theology' in the sense of ps-Dionysius (see n. 2, above)). The relation of the negating and the positive positing can vary. Some writers see them as dialectically related and mutually correcting; others insist that the negative pole is more fundamental and/or that even it has to be negated as well. (2) *The ascetic practice of detachment of the human will and/or desire* from false goals (Eckhart is a prime example). (3) *The paradoxical theology of divine absence-as-divine-affliction* (Luther's theology of the cross and John of the Cross's second night of spirit both fit into this mould). My addition is (4) *the distinctively modern expression of God's presence-as-absence* (Simone Weil, R. S. Thomas, come to mind: here the 'dazzling' nature of Dionysius's darkness seems suppressed, and modern atheism, as well as Kant's problematic *noumenal* darkness, hover in the background). Derrida's project of 'différance' and 'deferral' seems in continuity with (4), but also to involve a new, postmodern, reading of (1), perpetual 'unsaying', but without the ascetical practices of 'contemplation', or the assumption of revelatory 'kataphatic' ballast, which are found as the accompanying features in the premodern 'mystical theology' of ps.-Dionysius. On this problem see Mary-Jane Rubenstein, 'Dionysius, Derrida, and the Critique of Ontotheology', in Sarah Coakley and Charles Stang (eds.), *Re-Thinking Dionysius the Areopagite* (Oxford: Blackwell, forthcoming). I shall return to the contentious issue of whether the first of these categories of 'negative theology' (= *apophasis* in Greek) can imply an 'experience' of God, and if so, in what sense. It is this first type of 'negative theology' with which we are mainly concerned in this essay, although Teresa's narrative encodes elements of the second type as well.

[4] Oliver Davies and Denys Turner, in the introduction to their edited volume, *Silence and the Word: Negative Theology and Incarnation* (Cambridge, CUP, 2002), suggest that there are three main reasons for the renewed fascination with premodern forms of 'apophaticism' in the contemporary postmodern: (1) a prevalent cultural religious scepticism; (2) a philosophical engagement with radical 'difference'; and (3) the turn to 'experience': the 'privatisation and internalisation of religion' (ibid. 1–2).

philosophy of religion has developed an equal investment in Christian mystical traditions, but for a very different purpose. Its aim has been to provide some sort of positive 'justification'[5] for theistic claims by reference to the evidences of 'religious experience'.[6] Its sensitivity to the valences of apophatic speech in the same texts of mystical theology has been slight, however, in contrast to the insights of continental philosophy and theology on the same topic.

The purpose of this chapter is not so much to adjudicate between these two existing philosophical projects as to nudge creatively beyond them. In the spirit of the 'analytic theology' which this volume celebrates, the aim is to do richer justice hermeneutically to the texts of mystical theology than the analytic school of philosophy of religion has so far achieved, whilst retaining those traits of clarity and apologetic purpose which have been its positive hallmarks.

But to undertake this mediating task, I propose to introduce a third element into the discussion to help unsettle the unfortunate disjunction between analytic and continental traditions of philosophical theology. This manoeuvre may come as something of a surprise, but I trust it will prove efficacious. An initial *feminist* analysis of the recent discourses of analytic philosophy of religion on 'religious experience', I shall argue, provides a revealing means of exposing certain covert dilemmas which demand closer philosophical attention and analysis. Once we see that analytic philosophy of religion—whether consciously or not—has committed itself to the exploration of a (stereotypically) 'feminine' realm of subjectivity and affectivity in its project to give epistemic significance to mystical states, it becomes clear why its attempts to give veridical status to such experiences tend to be hampered whilst the deeper philosophical seriousness of 'female' mystical claims remains unanalysed. Only a closer attention to the subtleties of mystical discourse itself (including its apophatic manoeuvres), and to its *accompanying and repetitive bodily practices,* can help the analytic tradition beyond

---

[5] The philosophical notion of 'justification' is almost inexhaustibly complex, depending on whether one appeals to so-called 'internalist' or 'externalist' criteria (or a mixture). For these initial purposes I am using the term in a rather loose generic sense to mean 'an epistemically appropriate response', or 'a rationally defensible account of one's belief'; but the grounds or conditions for such can be almost endlessly debated. See Richard Swinburne, *Epistemic Justification* (Oxford: OUP, 2001), esp. 1–8, for a brief and clear introductory account of the basic definitions and distinctions in this area of philosophical debate.

[6] James's understanding of this category has in the main been taken for granted in analytic discussion: see again his *Varieties of Religious Experience,* esp. lecture 3. Although James gives two chapters of these Gifford Lectures to 'Mysticism' (lectures 16 and 17), and even discusses the Carmelites briefly, the primary evocation of 'religious experience' for him is an elevating and profound encounter of a sudden and short-term nature. The presumption that such short-term, high-point, 'experiences' are also what 'mystical theology' is about is precisely what is questioned in this chapter.

its usual confines of expectation at this point—or so I shall argue. And whereas Teresa of Ávila has long already been the favoured 'pin-up girl' of analytic philosophy of religion in its appeal to veridical religious experiences of a sporadic, Jamesian sort, I shall attempt to show that this reading of her has profoundly trivialized her work's deeper epistemic significance. She is no less of an 'apophatic' thinker, for a start, than her Carmelite confrère John of the Cross (a fact that is often overlooked); but she is also one who gives us (qua female contemplative, utilizing the autobiographical mode of discourse) particular insights into how epistemic function may be expanded and changed by bodily, contemplative practices *over the long haul*. To concentrate only on passing, albeit striking, moments of encounter with the divine in Teresa's early work[7] (as analytic philosophy of religion almost always does when appealing to her[8]) is thus profoundly misleading and distorting.

What follows in this chapter is part of a much larger epistemological project, and only a small slice of that undertaking can be discussed here. However, I shall proceed for these purposes in three stages. First, a playful feminist analysis of some of the most important turns to religious experience in analytic philosophy of religion in recent decades will supply a substantial opening section, which will then lead on, in the light of a feminist critique, to an analysis of how Teresa's project, sympathetically understood, might suggest how *contemplative practice* (as opposed to passing religious experiences) could help provide justification for certain sorts of theistic claim, and what role an apophatic sensibility would play in such a move. This final section will not only attempt to extend some of the main moves made by William Alston in his *Perceiving God*[9] in such a new way, but also respond to Alston's own recent attempt (in his unpublished Taylor Lectures[10]) to press his epistemological project in this apophatic direction. I shall conclude that Alston's new 'turn' has considerable potential, but one still in need of further development and critique.

---

[7] Most famously the vision of an angel with a dart, immortalized in Bernini's statue: *The Book of Her Life*, 29. 13, tr. Kieran Kavanaugh and Otilio Rodriguez, *The Collected Works of St. Teresa of Ávila*, i (Washington, DC: ICS Publications, 1987), 252, hereafter *Life*.

[8] See e.g. Michael Peterson, William Hasker, Bruce Reichenbach, and David Basinger (eds.), *Philosophy of Religion: Selected Readings* (Oxford: OUP, 2001), which opens with a section on 'Religious Experience', first featuring two visions from Teresa's *Life* (pp. 7–10), and then moving immediately to William James and William P. Alston (pp. 10–29).

[9] William P. Alston, *Perceiving God: The Epistemology of Religious Experience* (Ithaca, NY: Cornell UP, 1991), hereafter, *PG*.

[10] The Taylor Lectures, 2005, were delivered at Yale in October of that year by Nicholas Wolterstorff, on behalf of (the, alas, ailing) Bill Alston. They can be found on the web at http://www.goodnewsline.com/pastoral_resource/lecture.htm.

CONTEMPORARY RELIGIOUS EPISTEMOLOGY: THE TURN TO 'FEMININITY'?

I start by sketching what may seem an initially implausible thesis. As is well known, analytic philosophy of religion expended an enormous amount of creative energy in the last part of the twentieth century in the area of religious epistemology. It could well be said to have been the most important discussion point in the field in that period, and certainly the area in which the most important novelties of approach have been explored—whether in the discussion of what was there termed 'mysticism' and 'religious experience', or in the field of so-called 'Reformed epistemology'. *Why* has this explosion of interest occurred, and why now?

The most obvious answer to that question is to point to the upheavals of postmodern thought, and specifically to the collapse of so-called 'classical foundationalism', to which the 'Reformed epistemology' of writers such as Alvin Plantinga and Nicholas Wolterstorff was an explicit response. But I want to suggest in what follows that there was another, and more covert, subtext in these developments. For arguably it was an attempt to wrest into the sphere of public rationality and accountability, and to turn to *justificatory* effect, that nexus of associations more commonly, in the Enlightenment heritage, stereotypically associated with the woman: subjectivity, trust, the private realm, affectivity, and intimacy with the divine. Just as Freud, at the turn into the twentieth century, had explored a repressed realm—that of the 'unconscious'—by reference principally to *female* bodies, female case studies, so here (though arguably with even less consciousness of the gender implications) the repressed 'feminine' has been played out, appropriated, constrained into an already-assumed rationality for justificatory and explicative purposes.[11]

The trouble is (as I shall show in the next section) that when women's mystical texts, especially, are appealed to for evidences of such putatively truth-conducive experiences of God, there turns out to be a certain *excess* within them still

---

[11] Arguments about purported 'repression' tend to meet with the familiar tactic of denial. I can only point here to the evidences I shall go on to marshal, which involve noting when and how women, women 'mystics', and topics stereotypically associated with women, are treated in analytic philosophy of religion of a particular vintage, and how (at a time when the use of personal pronouns was only just beginning to become gender-fluid under certain political pressures) the feminine pronoun was sometimes utilized at interestingly revealing moments. The same time span also produced a new analytic interest in male religious thinkers (e.g. John Calvin, Jonathan Edwards) who exhibited concern for religious 'affections'; but I take this as an adjunct part of the phenomenon I am highlighting (the 'feminization' of religious rationality), not as a challenge to it.

unaccounted for, associated not least with their apophatic caveats and their bodily responses; there are, then, elements of their witness that will not quite *fit* the laudable epistemic purposes that these philosophers intend. The female mystical writers on whom they so much depend are saying something rather different from what these contemporary philosophers of religion hope to derive from them; and to take these women writers seriously would be to question, and even *transcend*, the forms of rationality that the philosophers vigorously defend in pursuit of the justificatory exposition of religious truth.

But let me first try to defend my suggestion that contemporary analytic philosophy of religion is engaged here in an unconscious interaction with the 'feminine' (in this stereotypical—not, note, *essentialist*—sense[12]). What seems to be at stake is an attempt to wrest the elusive private arena of religious affect into the realm of public accountability; and this can only be done by legitimating what we might playfully call certain epistemic 'soft centres': notably, the practices of 'credulity', 'testimony', and 'trust'. Let us consider three influential forms of such a religious epistemology of experience, before assessing the feminist implications that might flow from such a consideration. I shall briefly examine: the cumulative evidentialism of Richard Swinburne, as applied to 'religious experience'; the early 'Reformed epistemology' of Nicholas Wolterstorff and Alvin Plantinga; and the defence of God's perceivability on the analogy of sense experience in the work of William Alston. To be sure, the important (and at the time, novel) epistemic moves that were made in these three influential departures in analytic philosophy of religion have since had a long period of reception, critique, and refinement.[13] But if my argument is correct, there was something that—for all their different strategic ploys—hiddenly conjoined these approaches and still requires systematic attention and development.

Richard Swinburne on 'Religious Experience'

The place of 'religious experience'[14] in Swinburne's now classic repristination of arguments for the existence of God is, as it turns out, a crucial one. According

[12] I refer here to a set of stereotypical gender associations (the 'feminine') whose empirical verification is notoriously subject to methodological circularity; the stereotypes are thus at least arguably 'socially constructed'. 'Essentialism', in contrast, simply *assumes* that such gender associations are intrinsically attached to the female 'sex'. For a justly famous problematization of the 'sex'/gender division, see Judith Butler, *Gender Trouble* (New York: Routledge, 1990).

[13] See, for instance, Alvin Plantinga's three-volumed work on 'warrant', esp. the third volume —*Warranted Christian Belief* (New York: OUP, 2000); and Nicholas Wolterstorff's *Thomas Reid and the Story of Epistemology* (Cambridge: CUP, 2001).

[14] Richard Swinburne, *The Existence of God* (Oxford: OUP 1979; rev. edn., 1991, from which the pagination here is taken), 244–76, hereafter *EG*.

to Swinburne, the cumulative force of the other—more public—arguments (drawing on cosmology, the miraculous, etc.) is, on the Bayesian probability formula that he is employing, less than clinching. It is the appeal to the very different (because 'subjective' and 'private') experiences of God that feature in his chapter 13 (which cannot by definition be quantified mathematically in terms of the probability calculus) that ultimately sways the balance of probability over into the positive pole. So a lot hangs on 'subjectivity' here; and to make a lot hang on it, Swinburne has to do something with this subjective surd to make it epistemically respectable. 'Religious experiences', interestingly characterized mainly as discrete *appearances* (senses of something—a very big Something?—being *present*), have to be wrested into the public domain via 'principles' of 'credulity' and 'testimony', and thus made respectable by some fairly strict analogy to the way that the Enlightenment made the marginalized—though still public—category of *miracle* respectable: by torturing evidence, testing the quality and character of testimonials, and so on.[15] Swinburne admits here a necessary reliance on 'certain private and occasional manifestations by God to some men'.[16] The realm of privacy and the bedroom is suddenly exposed: 'some men' may even have to rely on the guiding judgement of their 'wife' (*sic*) to judge whether the apparition or personage seemingly appearing in the bedroom was really there or not ('my wife was awake, but did not see the man [in a toga disappearing up the chimney] and so probably he was not there', etc.).[17] We enter here the realm of the powerfully subjective; and for 1979 this was a daring departure for analytic philosophy of religion. How are we to *trust*, epistemically, the subjective, the private, the elusive? That was Swinburne's task to explore; and at some points in the text, at least, it was clear that this was implicitly a *gendered* matter.

But we need to probe a little more closely what Swinburne means by 'religious experience' in *The Existence of God*, before we can judge both the strengths and the frailties of his epistemic approach in this context. Immediately we confront a tangle that I am not sure if Swinburne himself fully sorts out. It appears at the outset of chapter 13 that the paradigm case for a 'religious experience' on Swinburne's view is something 'private and occasional',[18] a 'conscious mental going on' (Swinburne's general definition of an 'experience'), which is 'internal'[19] but nonetheless has the quality of inclining us to believe in the presence of an *external* object. Employing a famous distinction of Roderick Chisholm's between *epistemic* and

---

[15] Swinburne had already analysed such a process *vis-à-vis* external miracles in his early book, *The Concept of Miracle* (London: Macmillan, 1970). The concept of 'torturing evidence' comes from R. G. Collingwood.
[16] *EG* 244.   [17] *EG* 264.   [18] *EG* 244.   [19] *EG* 245.

comparative 'seeming'.[20] Swinburne opts for the former in his understanding of 'religious experience': it seems *epistemically* to the knowing subject that his religious experience is an experience of God—i.e. he is inclined to believe that God is *there*, not just to say that this looks *like* a picture of God.

The paradigm 'religious experience', then, is sensing the presence of 'a person, such as Mary or Poseidon', or '[of] Heaven', or a 'timeless reality beyond oneself'.[21] A religious experience seems therefore to be first and foremost a sporadic visitation—'private and occasional'—like an overt miracle but *inside*; and this is the model that dominates Swinburne's approach to the matter. However when he comes to complexify his understanding of religious experience by offering five types of such experience, he blurs this initial clarity. His first type, for instance (a 'seeing-as' God's handiwork of the night sky, which is not a sporadic visitation) does not easily fit his initial paradigm, whereas with his second and third types—that religious experience is the subjective reception of the perception of miracles (2), or more private 'visual sensations' such as dreams of angels (3)—we are in the heartland of Swinburne's normative view of such things. In his fourth and fifth categories, however, he is already slipping off the end of what he himself is going to be willing to deal with: these are 'certain sensations that are private' and not explicable in terms of normal public sensations (4), and apophatic states of experiencing through 'nothingness or darkness' (5). In order to yank this last category back into the realm of what Swinburne can even hope to deal with in his own terms, he comes up with a most strange parallel that such mystical darkness may be like feeling strongly 'that my hand behind my back is facing upwards rather than downwards, yet not because of having any sensations'.[22] This bizarre caricature of what might be going on in forms of 'mystical theology' gives the lie to Swinburne's ability to deal with darkness in mystical states according to the paradigm he has adopted at the outset.[23]

So Swinburne wants, first, for 'religious experiences' to be significantly *like* discrete conscious perceptual experiences of external objects, and all the better if they are 'forceful'.[24] Secondly, he then wields his crucial appeals to the

---

[20] See R. M. Chisholm, *Perceiving: A Philosophical Study* (Ithaca, NY: Cornell UP, 1957), ch. 4.

[21] *EG*, 247.

[22] *EG* 251.

[23] As a rather impatient essay by Richard Gale, criticizing Swinburne's project, underscores, Swinburne really needs an individual perceptual appearance in each case for his mode of argument here to work ('Swinburne and Religious Experience', in Alan G. Padgett (ed.), *Reason and the Christian Faith* (Oxford: OUP, 1994), 39–63; see 44). In my view, Gale is right to alert us to that problem, although wrong in his triumphant insistence that a firm disjunction can be drawn between *all* 'religious experiences' and sense experience, thus spoiling Swinburne's analogy altogether.

[24] *EG* 274.

'principle of credulity' and 'principle of testimony', without which, he memorably avers, we would all be stuck in the 'sceptical bog'[25] of assuming a kind of solipsistic disbelief of *everything* that we tell one another. The 'principle of credulity', then, according to Swinburne, is that '(in the absence of special considerations) things are probably as others are inclined to believe that they have perceived them'.[26] This must be conjoined with the 'principle of testimony', that '(in the absence of special considerations) the experiences of others are (probably) as they report them'.[27] Of course, these principles need checking: we don't believe *anything* anyone tells us or that they happen to believe themselves; and Swinburne presents us with four defeasibility criteria for testing when our scepticism should lock back into play:[28]

(1) if the subject is 'unreliable' or is operating under the influence of drugs or other mind-disturbing conditions;

(2) if the claim is being made in circumstances parallel to others that proved false;

(3) if 'background' evidence shows that the claim is unlikely; or

(4) if it appears likely that something else (other than God) caused my experience.

Now it will be immediately apparent that the sceptically inclined will triumphantly seize on the powerful potentials of these four defeasibility criteria to try and squash any individual claim to a veridical religious experience, especially where the religious experiences concerned—as in Swinburne's cases 4 or 5, discussed above—already appear to drop off the map of normal perceptual experience. And yet there remains the intriguing force of Swinburne's principles of credulity and testimony; and what exactly are we to make of them? They are not, note, a mere invitation to 'gullibilism'. As Caroline Franks Davis has rightly countered,[29] in a careful response to an attack by Michael Martin on Swinburne's position,[30] the principle of credulity, on Swinburne's understanding, does not claim to make the subject's purported religious experience *instantly* veridical. The first thing it claims to do—and this is vitally important—is to open the *possibility* of veridicality, or rather to stop any appeal to religious experience being sceptically dismissed from the outset as epistemically hopeless. The doors of my perception are made at least potentially open to the new, the unexpected. Of course, if I am *known* to be

---

[25] *EG* 254 n. 1. [26] *EG* 272.
[27] Ibid. [28] See *EG* 260–71.
[29] See her *The Evidential Force of Religious Experience* (Oxford: OUP, 1999), ch. 4.
[30] See Michael Martin, 'The Principle of Credulity and Religious Experience', *Religious Studies*, 22 (1986), 79–93.

a 'crackpot' or on LSD or—God forbid!—an 'unreliable' enthusiast, things may look different. But at least, first, the *possibility* of my being right about my experience as an experience of God is left open, and then—and this is the further and yet more significant move—the burden of proof is (vitally) thrown onto my sceptical attacker. Herein lies the subtle force of Swinburne's argument, to which in due course I shall continue to appeal.

We have seen enough already, however, to note that Swinburne's essentially evidentialist approach to religious experience is *strong* in providing an initial bulwark against what he calls the 'sceptical bog', by analysing the subtle, but important, epistemic force of credulity and testimony. Where it is *weak*, however, is in its failure (1) to construe the significance of apophatic claims or 'darkness' states; (2) to consider the possibility of important bodily reactions to religious experience (beyond anything other than a passing 'mental occurrence'); (3) to reflect upon repeated religious practices and their experiential effects (as opposed to sporadic and unpredictable moments of divine encounter); and (4) to register acknowledgement of the gendered associations of the argument. What, for instance, if the 'wife in the bedroom' were to undergo herself some actual *transformation* of consciousness or epistemic response not easily comprehensible to her Man of Reason husband? This would involve not simply a discussion about the presence (or absence) of Someone in the room, but a claim that her very capacity to see had undergone some change. These are complications that Swinburne's initial approach does not consider.

Nicholas Wolterstorff and Alvin Plantinga on 'Reformed Epistemology'

In some contrast to Swinburne's strategies for rendering religious experience epistemically respectable, we must consider the even more daring epistemological departures of Nicholas Wolterstorff and Alvin Plantinga in their ground-breaking book of 1983, *Faith and Rationality*.[31] Outlining there a notion of a 'Reformed Epistemology' that would take on the acknowledgment of the *collapse* of 'classical foundationalism', Plantinga suggested that such a classical foundationalism resided in the insistence that all our justified (and thus justifiable) beliefs must be founded in what is either (i) self-evident, (ii) incorrigible, or (iii) evident to the senses. But, following a lead in Calvin, Plantinga went on to suggest that there was nothing irrational in 'belief in *God*' being 'properly basic' to our epistemology, just as classical foundationalism

[31] Notre Dame, Ind.: Notre Dame UP, 1983.

assumed (wrongly) that *only* self-evidence, incorrigibility, or evidence to the senses could be so basic. An arena of religious conviction previously assumed by many to be dangerously 'subjective', even 'irrational', had suddenly been pronounced to be in no worse shape, epistemically considered, than many everyday—indeed utterly uncontentious—claims to justified belief. It would doubtless be fanciful to make anything much of Plantinga's sudden shift to the feminine pronoun at this crucial point in his argument;[32] and yet, nonetheless, there is something intriguingly gender-associated about this welcoming of the *unargued* religious/affective realm into the sphere of legitimated rationality:[33]

She can execute the maneuver known to dialectician and matador alike as 'escaping between the horns'. As a natural theologian she offers or endorses theistic arguments, but why suppose that her own belief in God must be based upon such argument;... Indeed she can follow Calvin in claiming that belief in God ought not to be based on arguments from the deliverances of reason or anywhere else. She can adopt a faith 'standpoint'.[34]

Plantinga then spends a good deal of time in this essay explaining why the apparent irrationality of this move is *not* irrational (in the fideistic sense) at all. It *is* reasonable even though it is not 'demonstrable' in an evidentialist sense.[35] As Nicholas Wolterstorff puts it elsewhere in the same book, one may be *justified* in one's belief without *justifying* one's belief.[36] And this, of course, is implicitly a major erosion of the stern facade of the Lockean, evidentialist Man of Reason whom we encountered in Swinburne's text; dangers of extremism might seem to lurk once more, irrationality or 'enthusiasm' to hover in the background, affectivity to lurch to the fore. 'Femininity'—at least as it was stereotypically construed in relation to certain key Enlightenment philosophers and theologians—is suddenly in new philosophical vogue.

---

[32] 1983 was after all a period when American philosophers were beginning to try out using feminine and masculine pronouns interchangeably, leaving one guessing about what might—consciously or unconsciously!—elicit a shift at a particular moment in any given argument. (I am not inclined to rest my case on this form of speculation, and have unsurprisingly received insistent denials about the significance of the issue from such as William Wainwright, Richard Swinburne, and Bill Alston, in correspondence responding to this line of argumentation.)

[33] I think here, following the 'liberal' Calvinist tradition at least, of Schleiermacher's famous dictum that he wished he had been born a woman, given (as he believed) her greater capacity than man for religious affection. In Plantinga's slightly later article on 'Reformed Epistemology' in P. L. Quinn and C. Taliaferro (eds.), *Companion to the Philosophy of Religion* (Oxford: Blackwell, 1997), 383–9, the Reformed epistemic knower is, somewhat intriguingly, feminine throughout. Whatever we make of that, the appeal here to the *affective* tradition of Jonathan Edwards, and to a 'rich *interior* spiritual life' as a proper basis for believing in God, is more clearly enunciated than in Plantinga's earlier essay.

[34] *Faith and Rationality*, 71; my emphasis.

[35] Ibid. 88.

[36] Ibid. 157.

It is here, however, that Wolterstorff's rather differently nuanced appeal to religious experience presents such an interesting contrast to Swinburne's. We have already underscored the different end to which Wolterstorff is moving: he does not seek to *extend* an evidentialist case for theism by a special appeal to religious experience, but rather to give an account of being rationally justified in one's belief *without* seeking to justify it *ab initio*.[37] In taking this tack, we note, Wolterstorff concedes that 'people come to the conviction that God exists in the most astonishing diversity of ways'.[38] The 'experiences' lying behind this conviction range from picking it up from their parents, through an acknowledgement of their sense of guilt, to 'falling into a mystic trance' and believing they have met God. Only this last option, note, is anything like Swinburne's essentially sporadic, individualistic, and *perceptual* model for 'experiencing' God. Wolterstorff acknowledges this bewildering diversity, and thus simultaneously admits the corporate or communal nature of much religious experience. But he also insists, as Swinburne does not, that our rationality is *always* situation-specific:

It has long been the habit of philosophers to ask in abstract, non-specific fashion whether it is rational to believe that God exists, whether it is rational to believe that there is an external world, whether it is rational to believe that there are other persons, and so on. Mountains of confusion have resulted. The proper question is always and only whether it is rational for this or that particular person in this or that situation, or for a person of this or that particular type in this or that type of situation, to believe so-and-so. Rationality is always *situated* rationality.[39]

Already, then, the ostensibly universal foundationalist grounds on which Swinburne still stands are here shifting and crumbling. Thus, when Wolterstorff introduces *his* own crucial appeal to the 'credulity principle', this time in the form of its explication in the philosophy of Thomas Reid, the game we are playing is a very different one. We recall that Swinburne took a generic/male adult as his given epistemic subject, wrenching him from any particular social context into the ether of dispassionate assessment; he then used the appeal to 'credulity' as a rather sweeping way of granting his 'private' perceptions some initial claim to veracity. In Wolterstorff's account of credulity, in contrast, we enter the realm of childhood, and explore the fundamental, not merely secondary, epistemic need to *trust*. For Wolterstorff endorses Reid's acute psychological analysis of how a child, rooted in family and community, learns from the start of life how to believe—and only then to doubt. As Reid puts it:

---

[37] See ibid.   [38] Ibid. 175.
[39] Ibid. 155. To be fair, there is a strand of Swinburne's thinking (written slightly after the 1st edn. of *The Existence of God*), that was subsequently to move in this direction also: see *Faith and Reason* (Oxford: OUP, 1991), ch. 2.

> The wise Author of nature hath planted in the human mind a propensity to rely upon human testimony before we can give a reason for doing so. This, indeed, puts our judgment almost entirely in the power of those who are about us in the first period of life; but this is necessary both to our preservation and to our improvement. If children were so framed as to pay no regard to testimony or authority, they must, in the literal sense, perish for lack of knowledge.[40]

So here the credulity and testimony principles are not something we wheel on when desperate to give veracity to internal, 'subjective', perceptions that otherwise would look epistemically fishy. No, they are principles of *all* rationality, reminding us of our epistemic rootedness in circles of trust and mutuality. Implicitly—though Wolterstorff does not major on this point—they remind us of the special power of the maternal, which (even if for some perhaps only in the first period of life) either inculcates an attitude of trust and security, or of fear and distrust. As Reid has it, the child initially is credulous of everything, and gradually becomes slightly more discerning and cynical as she finds herself on occasions betrayed or mistaken. If this is right, then epistemology has everything to do with families and upbringing, and not only that: by implicit extension—given the profound effect of such factors on families and their stability—it also has to do with social circumstances of peace or war, justice or oppression; with racial or gendered discrimination, or integration and equal 'rights'. These factors are scarcely disentangle-able from any analysis of primary human (and familial) 'trust'. Whereas Swinburne arguably opened the door just a chink for religious standpoint epistemology, then, Wolterstorff has here seemingly blown down the wall.[41] His Reidian move, as we shall shortly see, thus has important potential for a *feminist* perspective on epistemological issues, even though—at this early stage of the adventures of 'Reformed epistemology'—this was far from his mind. To this issue, however, I shall return in the final section of this chapter.

William P. Alston and 'Perceiving God'

The third, and final, moment in late twentieth-century analytic philosophy of religion that is important for our purposes is the magisterial effort, in William Alston's *Perceiving God* (1991), to give religious experience epistemic credibility as an authentic variant on the general category of 'perception'. This project, which fascinatingly straddles the evidentialist/non-evidentialist divide of my

---

[40] See *Faith and Rationality*, 151, citing Reid's *Essays on the Intellectual Powers of Man*, 6. 5.
[41] Yet this move does not result in relativism proper, as Wolterstorff's subsequent work on Reid makes clear.

first two examples in this section,[42] sets out to 'defend the view that putative direct awareness of God can provide justification for certain kinds of beliefs about God'.[43] Chapter 1, which sets out to give examples of such direct awareness from the Christian mystical tradition, is—unsurprisingly, perhaps—replete with women's mystical texts. Teresa of Ávila makes notable appearances, but only, we should note, as an exemplar of these particular sorts of 'direct' peak experiences in her early work, *The Life*, which ostensibly fit Alston's mould.[44] The use of women's religious experiences in this project, then, is done not to valorize 'feminine' affectivity in any obvious sense, let alone women's 'sensuality' (which is treated with great caution), but ultimately to put 'direct' encounters with God on a footing that is properly 'perceptual' and thus in no worse shape, epistemically, than that of ordinary sense experience. Rather than an intensification of stereotypical 'feminine' traits here, therefore, there is if anything the opposite: women's mystical narratives, however subtly expressed—however 'ineffable' in their own cognizance[45]—are pulled by various means into the direct perceptual arena of Alston's notable 'Theory of Appearing'.[46] But the overall impact of the argument, nonetheless, has this much in common with both Swinburne and the 'Reformed Epistemologists', however different their strategies: 'feminine', 'affective', or 'mystical' experiences, previously categories of dubious reputation or credibility to secular philosophy, are being made to do important new work, and thus to find a toe-hold of epistemic respectability.

---

[42] It is ostensibly not interested in evidential arguments for the existence of God at the outset (*PG* 4–5); but it finally comes round to this issue in the last chapter. This causes a certain ambiguity in the book's intentions. Also, the view of 'justification' in *PG* is seemingly a form of externalism, but elsewhere Alston has argued that an 'internalist constraint' has added value: see *PG* 75, and the reference there to Alston's *Epistemic Justification* (Ithaca, NY: Cornell UP, 1989). Alston might be said to be positioned therefore somewhere between Swinburnian evidentialism and the 'proper basicality' moves of Plantinga and Wolterstorff. His main claim to 'justification' of so-called 'Christian mystical perception' is that its reliability is *no less* defensible than is that of ordinary sense experience—and that, he claims, is a pretty tough test for 'justification', tougher than mere 'coherentism' or various forms of 'internalism': see *PG* 76.

[43] Ibid. 9.

[44] Ibid. 13, 15, 32. There is one citation from Teresa's later work *The Interior Castle* (ibid. 53), but this is to make a slightly different point about the so-called 'spiritual senses'. Alston has some trouble pulling 'sensory' material into his pre-established epistemic orbit, since (see ibid. 5) he wants the distinctive experience of God to be 'direct' and *'non-sensory'*; hence he has to reduce the important 'spiritual senses' tradition to a mere *linguistic* device to express the unique nature of the direct 'perceptual' encounter with God (ibid. 51–4).

[45] Alston does not wish to take claims to 'ineffability' very seriously, even Teresa's: ibid. 32: 'this is blown out of all proportion' (!). I shall return to this issue in sections II and III.

[46] According to this theory, there are at least some 'direct' and 'unanalyzable' perceptions which are not mediated through 'concepts': see my final section, below, for a critical assessment of this opening apologetic gambit in *PG*.

But, unsurprisingly, there is a certain price Alston pays in delimiting the aim of his undertaking in *Perceiving God* to this worthy apologetic goal. For he makes a revealing remark right at the start of his introduction about the limitations of his study. He acknowledges that, 'From a religious point of view... the chief value of the experience of God is that it enables us to enter into *personal relationships* with God; most importantly, it makes it possible for us to enjoy the relation of *loving communion* with God for which we were created. But my topic will be the function of the experience of God in providing *information* about God...'[47] We can well understand why Alston drives this initial wedge: he needs to delimit what he can, and cannot, deal with in this particular undertaking; and it is certainly not his intention—as subsequent work has shown—to decry the significance of deepening relationship with God in prayer.[48] But the initial rhetorical disjunction between relationships and information in *Perceiving God* is nonetheless a revealing one; for—as Alston's heroine Teresa would surely herself insist—what can we rightly say about God unless we first enter into and sustain this relationship with God, and unless we take into account the revolutionary epistemic implications of such progressive submission to the divine? As if realizing this,[49] but not willing to acknowledge the epistemic disassemblage and/or transformation of approach it might involve, Alston leans heavily at this point on his misleadingly excerpted snippets from female mystical texts, and jousts only briefly and defensively with the possibility that an 'affective' quality might be a key element in an epistemic response to perceiving God.[50] In interesting contrast to Wolterstorff on this point, Alston quickly reins back on this complicating supposition, declaring that 'mystical experience can [on the contrary] be construed as perception in the *same* generic sense of the term as sense perception'.[51] But surely the cat is out of the bag: what Alston surely knows, but cannot fully acknowledge here, is that his star-case Teresa of Ávila is telling him about a *transformed* epistemic capacity in which affectivity, bodiliness and the traditional mental faculties are in some unique sense (through the long practices of prayer) aligned and made responsive to God. As with our other two analytic examples, although in rather different

---

[47] *PG* 2; my emphases.
[48] He wrote to me, for instance, in private correspondence from the summer of 1998 ('Comments on Sarah Coakley's Ferguson Lectures', 2), that 'I agree with you that an ideal treatment of this epistemological problem would involve going much more fully into the distinctive features of full blown mystical practice, as we find it in Teresa, John, and other major mystics'. His recent Taylor Lectures are in a sense an attempt to do just this, as we shall see in the final section, below.
[49] See *PG* 12.
[50] *PG* 51.
[51] *PG* 66; my emphasis.

ways, it seems that the 'feminine' voice in Alston's text wishes to tell an importantly different story from that which the male philosopher educes from her. How, then, could that voice speak for herself? To that problem we now turn.

A FEMINIST ASSESSMENT: LETTING TERESA SPEAK FOR HERSELF

It is time to gather the strands from this initial analysis of creative recent moves in analytic epistemology of religion. Why, exactly, has it been so revealing to discuss what I have represented as the repressed 'femininity' in these texts? The answer, as I claimed at the outset of this chapter, is that once this turn to the 'feminine' has been detected as a uniting theme in the three rather different epistemological ploys I have surveyed, we are in a better position to assess both its achieved strengths and its undeveloped potential. The various analyses of 'trust', 'credulity', and 'testimony' which attend it have been shown to provide subtle, but indispensable, bulwarks against contemporary religious scepticism; and they represent—in a period of postmodernity and post-foundationalism—some of the most ingenious novelties that the analytic tradition has explored in its continuing apologetic quest. These are the new epistemic 'soft centres', as I put it, which may lay claim to enduring philosophical significance.

Yet we have also seen that this analytic turn to the 'feminine' has been marred by its stereotypical presumptions, its failure to do justice to the very 'excess' that the woman mystic herself alluringly represents. What is missing, in fact, in the analytic reading of 'feminized' religious experience, is an appreciation of precisely those traits and interests that the post-Kantian continental tradition, in contrast, has tended to foster of late: a hermeneutical subtlety and attention to the text; a sensitivity to 'apophatic' forms of speech; an interest in the integration of sustained bodily practice and epistemological investigation; a questioning of the hegemony of the intellect in a destabilized, postmodern self; and—last but not least—a fascination with gender itself. In principle, of course, all the sophistication and clarity of the analytic school could be used to further the investigation of these themes. It will be the task of the rest of my chapter, then, and in the spirit of a new 'analytic theology' that this volume celebrates, to begin to sketch such a way forward.

But to do this we must first let Teresa speak for herself. In lieu of the misleadingly excerpted snippets which are so regularly anthologized by the analytic school, and which focus only on high-point experiences (which

Teresa herself treats with great reserve[52]), let us consider what she has to say—first in the *Life*, and then in the more mature *Interior Castle*—about her long, hard progress towards mystical 'union'.

Life, 18

Before her discussion of the particular nature of the prayer of union in chapter 18 of her autobiography, Teresa has explained how her prayer has progressed from active, discursive meditation (stage one), through touches of special consolation in the 'prayer of quiet', as the faculties of memory, understanding, and will are gradually more unified (stage two), to a third stage, in which the faculties are 'almost in complete union', but not quite. She uses a gardening and watering metaphor to illustrate these stages—which, note, are ordered according to how *she* perceives their effects.[53] The first stage is hard work, hauling up buckets of water for the garden from a deep well; in the second the water has risen in the well and is more easily winched up; and in the third the water comes from a stream or spring. But in the fourth stage, in chapter 18, there is a downpour of rain from above in 'the fourth water'. At this point the self is completely unified in its epistemic response and taken up into God in a way that also temporarily suspends its bodily movements and its sensations. Yet in a way impossible to describe clearly (or at least not without metaphorical stretching and constant apophatic reminders) the sensual, the affective, and the intellectual are now all one, and Christ is all in all:

---

[52] See the whole section of the *Life*, chs. 22–9, which casts the incident of angel and spear (*vide* n. 7, above) in the context of careful consideration of the dangers of *misleading* bodily effects in prayer, and of the necessary spiritual discernment involved in distinguishing true from false apparitions of this sort. I discuss this issue in greater detail in my recent essay, 'Palliative or Intensification? Pain and Christian Contemplation in the Spirituality of the Sixteenth-Century Carmelites', in Sarah Coakley and Kay Kaufman Shelemay (eds.), *Pain and its Transformations: The Interface of Biology and Culture* (Cambridge, Mass.: Harvard UP, 2007), 77–100, esp. 86–9.

[53] There is thus an important difference, at least in Teresa's *Life*, from the approach of John of the Cross to the stages of spiritual ascent (his account in *The Ascent of Mt Carmel* and *The Dark Night* being couched in an 'objective' third-person narrative, and being ostensibly much less interested than Teresa in what one might call the epistemic significance of 'bodily effects'). But we must caution here against falling into stereotypical judgement about 'male' (supposedly superior) and 'female' (supposedly inferior) 'mysticism', as was characteristic of several generations of modern spiritual writing (of which Louth's article, *vide* n. 2, is a *Nachlass*). The particular insights about the bodily implications of the progression to union that Teresa brings—albeit later significantly modified in *The Interior Castle*—are arguably more deeply 'incarnational' in their significance for being interested in the body: on this point, see my longer discussion in Coakley and Shelemay (eds.), *Pain*, ch. 5.

In this fourth water the soul isn't in possession of its senses, but it rejoices without understanding what it is rejoicing in. It understands that it is enjoying a good in which are gathered together all goods, but this good is incomprehensible. All the senses are occupied in this joy in such a way that none is free to be taken up with any other exterior or interior thing.

In the previous degrees, the senses are given freedom to show some signs of the great joy they feel. Here in this fourth water the soul rejoices incomparably more; but it can show much less since no power remains in the body, nor does the soul have any power to communicate its joy. At such a time, everything would be a great obstacle and a torment and a hindrance to its repose. And I say that if this prayer is the union of all the faculties, the soul is unable to communicate its joy even though it may desire to do so—I mean while being in the prayer. And if it were able then this wouldn't be union.

How this prayer they call union comes about and what it is, I don't know how to explain. These matters are expounded in mystical theology; I wouldn't know the proper vocabulary. Neither do I know what the mind is; nor do I know how it differs from the soul or the spirit. It all seems to be the same thing to me, although the soul sometimes goes forth from itself. The way this happens is comparable to what happens when a fire is burning and flaming, and it sometimes becomes a forceful blaze. The flame then shoots very high above the fire, but the flame is not by that reason something different from the fire but the same flame that is in the fire. Your Reverence with your learning will understand this, for I don't know what else to say.

While the soul is seeking God in this way, it feels with the most marvelous and gentlest delight that everything is almost fading away through a kind of swoon in which breathing and all the bodily energies gradually fail. This experience comes about in such a way that one cannot even stir the hands without a lot of effort. The eyes close without one's wanting them to close; or if these persons keep them open, they see hardly anything...

Now let us come to what the soul experiences here interiorly. Let those who know how speak of it since it cannot be understood—much less put into words!

After having received Communion and been in this very prayer I'm writing about, I was thinking when I wanted to write something on it of what the soul did during that time. The Lord spoke these words to me: 'It detaches itself from everything, daughter, so as to abide more in me. It is no longer the soul that lives but I. Since it cannot comprehend what it understands, there is an understanding by not understanding'.[54]

The Interior Castle, 7. 2

This discussion in the *Life* was not, however, Teresa's last word on the matter of 'union': she was to change her mind, and in a very significant way, in the

---

[54] *Life*, 18. 1–2, 10, 14. 157–8, 161, 162–3. For the ironic use of rhetorical self-deprecation about intellectual matters in the *Life* ('Your Reverence with your learning will understand this...', etc.), see the important study of Alison Weber, *Teresa of Ávila and the Rhetoric of Femininity* (Princeton: Princeton UP, 1990). Such tropes largely fall away in Teresa's later work.

years that followed. The most significant feature of her spiritual maturation was her body's *habituation* to a (now non-sporadic) state of union. Whereas previously, as in the *Life*, passing experiences of union would leave her physically prostrate, now—in the close description of that state in *The Interior Castle*, 7—that union has become permanent, and her body is no longer afflicted by it. Rather, her embodied selfhood now exists in a curious tension between complete union and safety-in-God at one level ('the center of the soul'), and yet an equal sensibility of continuing trials, disturbances, and bodily fatigue at another:

The center of our soul, or this spirit, is something so difficult to explain, or even believe in, that I think, Sisters, I'll not give you the temptation to disbelieve what I say, for I do not know how to explain this center. That there are trials and sufferings and that at the same time the soul is in peace is a difficult thing to explain. I want to make one or more comparisons for you. Please God, I may be saying something through them...

The King is in His palace and there are many wars in his kingdom and many painful things going on, but not on that account does he fail to be at his post. So here, even though in those other dwelling places there is much tumult and there are many poisonous creatures and the noise is heard, no one enters that center dwelling place and makes the soul leave. Nor do the things the soul hears make it leave; even though they cause it some pain, the suffering is not such as to disturb it and take away its peace. The passions are now conquered and have a fear of entering the center because they would go away from there more subdued.[55]

In these two crucial passages in the *Life* and *The Interior Castle*, then, Teresa speaks for herself about the epistemic impact of mystical union (not merely of 'religious experiences'). We note especially the following distinguishing features of her narrative: the repeated 'apophatic' manœuvres in relation to both God and self;[56] the different bodily effects in the two texts—and their

---

[55] *The Interior Castle*, 7. 2. 10–11, in *Collected Works*, tr. Kavanaugh and Rodriguez, 437.

[56] Primarily in the sense of the *first* type of 'negative theology' ('apophaticism') enumerated above (n. 3), that of repeatedly unsaying what is said on account of the transcendent or mysterious subject matter involved: these topics are strictly indescribable in any other way. Note that Teresa is well aware that this linguistic strategy is part and parcel of what 'mystical theology' in the Dionysian tradition involves (see again n. 2, above); and she also takes for granted the other features of that Dionysian tradition: a commitment to practices of 'contemplation' leading one beyond the normal capacities of the mind, and a presumption of the authority of 'kataphatic' Christian claims in Bible and tradition. Despite being relatively unschooled scholastically as a woman, she has clearly absorbed from her confessors, and from some of her own reading, the assimilation of Dionysius in available Spanish authors such as Osuna and Laredo. On this reception, see Luis M. Girón Negrón, 'Dionysian Thought in 16th Century Spanish Mystical Writing', in Coakley and Stang (eds.), *Re-Thinking Dionysius the Areopagite*, forthcoming. A close attention to the full narrative of Teresa's life-history also reveals that the *second* type of 'negative theology' delineated in n. 3 (an ascetic detachment of the will and desire) features profoundly in her narrative as an intrinsic accompaniment to the first, linguistic, understanding of 'apophaticism' ('mystical theology', in her parlance).

implication, not just for Teresa herself, but for her community of sisters; the unification of the mental faculties; the subduing of the passions; and finally the infusion of the presence of Another (Christ).

Is it, then, we may ask by way of clarification, appropriate to call what Teresa describes about union in these two texts religious 'experiences' at all? The matter is made significant not simply because this is the modern categorization with which we started (along with virtually all analytic philosophers of religion), but on account of a recent reactive attempt by Denys Turner to deny that 'apophatic' or 'darkness' states in 'mystical theology' should be classified as 'experiences' at all.[57] An answer to this conundrum is not uncomplicated, not least because of Teresa's change of mind about the nature of 'union' between her earlier and later writings, as we have just seen. In the *Life*, her description of union is indeed of a passing state, and appears prima facie to fit William James's typological features of 'Mysticism' rather well ('ineffable', 'noetic', 'transient', 'passive').[58] However, on closer inspection, even this early description of union by Teresa does not really cohere with James's intents or understanding; for having thus promisingly set out his typology of 'mystical' characteristics, James goes into an excursus on matters largely irrelevant to disciplined religious life and its practices (the phenomenon of *déjà vu*, for instance, or the inhalation of chloroform!), which ploy distinctly muddies the picture; and when he does get back to the 'practices of orison', it is rather obvious from his footnotes that he has not read the Carmelites to the end of their narratives.[59] The later description by Teresa of sustained union in *The Interior Castle*, book 7, is thus not even discussed by James; and he appears to have little understanding of the epistemic implications of this enduring state of union, as opposed to a passing taste of it.

Still, it would be odd, I submit, to deny that either of these accounts of union by Teresa are 'experiences' (albeit ones of rather different sorts); indeed Teresa herself constantly appeals to 'experience' as one of her main claims to authority.[60] Turner's refusal of this category, then, has a strong element of polemical shadow-boxing, even though he is entirely right to insist that 'apophaticism' (or 'negative theology') comes in different brands, some of which do not obviously apply to 'experiences' as such, and especially not to

---

[57] See Denys Turner, *The Darkness of God: Negativity in Christian Mysticism* (Cambridge: CUP, 1995).

[58] James, *Varieties*, 367–8.

[59] Ibid. 369–85; the slightly later discussion of Teresa suggests, significantly, a reading only as far as bk 6 of *The Interior Castle* (ibid. 398).

[60] There is a useful discussion of this semantic issue in Edward Howells, *John of the Cross and Teresa of Ávila: Mystical Knowing and Selfhood* (New York: Crossroad, 2002), 94–5. Readers of Teresa in English should however beware of the way that the standard translations at points introduce the language of 'experience' when it is not in the original Spanish.

'Mysticism' as understood by James.[61] It is only by a careful reading of Teresa herself, then, that we can capture the particular epistemic significance of what she says, as opposed to what James, or Alston (or for that matter, Turner), would have her say.

Above all, when we let Teresa speak for herself we see that what contemporary analytic philosophy calls 'reason' and 'perception' have in union gone beyond their normal limits—have extended into that dark, ineffable realm that Swinburne found so strangely hard to explicate, and Alston averred was 'blown out of all proportion' to its actual significance.[62] However, whatever this state of union is, it is surely *this* that analytic philosophy of religion should be interested in when it attempts to explicate the significance of 'mystical theology' for epistemology. Here, we do not so much grasp or 'perceive' God, but more truly God grasps *us*—if at any rate we over time have fostered the special epistemic passivity that is the condition for the possibility of this graced contemplative occurrence. The French postmodern feminist, Luce Irigaray, in her celebrated essay 'La Mystérique', has at least some inkling of the epistemic profundity of such union when she challenges male philosophy of religion in her own inimitable way:

This is the place where consciousness is no longer master, where, to its extreme confusion, it sinks into a dark night that is also fire and flames. This is the place where 'she'—and in some cases he, if he follows 'her' lead—speaks about the dazzling glare which comes from the source of light that has been logically repressed, about 'subject' and 'Other' flowing out into an embrace of fire that mingles one term into another, about contempt for form as such, about mistrust for understanding as an obstacle along the path of jouissance and mistrust for the dry desolation of reason.[63]

Where then is the way *beyond* the analytic philosophers' attempts to wrest Teresa's rationality into their own assumed epistemic perspective—a way

---

[61] Thus it is correct to say that 'apophaticism 1' (see again n. 3) is about linguistic strategy and is not an experience as such; but in 'mystical theology', as we have seen, this practice is characteristically accompanied by that of contemplation and *ekstasis*, which at least once in the Dionysian corpus is explicitly called an 'experience': *Divine Names* 2. 9 (648B). Turner's main interest, however, is in the radical form of 'apophasis 2', which can indeed be said to cancel previous attachments to affirming 'experiences' of God; yet it seems artificial to deny that this practice has itself an 'experiential' dimension of sorts, as do apophaticisms 3 and 4. See Bernard McGinn's insightful review of Turner: *Journal of Religion*, 77 (1997), 309–11.

[62] See again, *PG* 32.

[63] 'La Mysterique', in *Speculum of the Other Woman* (Ithaca, NY: Cornell UP, 1985), 191. To cite Irigaray in this context is admittedly to open a psychoanalytic (Lacanian) can of worms entirely alien to the Carmelite context; but Irigaray's striking form of expression vividly brings home here the implicitly gendered dimension of the contemporary philosophical question about the nature of 'reason'. For an extended analysis and critique of Irigaray's significance for analytic philosophy of religion, see my 'Feminism and Analytic Philosophy of Religion', in William J. Wainwright (ed.), *The Oxford Handbook of Philosophy of Religion* (Oxford: OUP, 2005), ch. 20.

beyond the 'dry desolation of reason', as Irigaray has put it? How could Alston genuinely learn from the Teresa who so exercises him? Let us now consider this in the final section of this chapter. In so doing we shall also find ourselves returning to the intriguing features of 'trust', 'credulity', and 'testimony' that I noted earlier, and which I shall argue are capable of further, feminist gloss and extension.

CONTEMPLATION, APOPHATICISM, AND EPISTEMIC EXPANSION

In this section I am going to isolate three dimensions of Alston's important epistemological work which I believe are worthy of both critical evaluation and extension. They will thus forward my attempt to find a way to enunciate a *feminist* epistemology of 'contemplative practice',[64] but without abandoning the fundamental interest in the justification of truth claims over which Alston is primarily concerned. One of these aspects of Alston's work (which I shall call 'answering the epistemic circularity charge') involves an argument in *Perceiving God* that I believe to be both successful and important, although I shall suggest that it can be further bolstered by some relevant feminist philosophical reflections. Another aspect of Alston's approach (the account of 'doxastic practices', so-called) is in need of some significant modification, I suggest, if it is to be brought into alignment with Teresa's witness that what is happening in certain forms of 'mystical' texts is an *expansion* of epistemic capacity in which the 'woman' (in Irigaray's symbolic and subversive sense) shows the way. The last dimension of Alston's work (the turn to the 'apophatic') has been enunciated by him more recently than in *Perceiving God*, in his Yale Taylor Lectures of 2005; and here we see Alston struggling for the first time to bring his own recent experience of contemplative practice into relation to an argument about divine 'mystery'. This argument is admittedly not complete; but it shows Alston at least pressing towards an epistemic account of the significance of the 'apophatic' for the first time.

Clearly I can only claim to effect some creative new 'mystical marriage' of this sort between Alston and Teresa (!) if I can give a convincing account of the *positive* aspects of these three dimensions of Alston's thinking for a feminist religious epistemology. Let us now look briefly at each of them in turn, before providing our own systematic conclusions. In each case we shall find that a lesson also

---

[64] I prefer this title, for reasons I have argued above, to the categories of 'religious experience' or 'Christian mystical perception'.

comes back from our earlier discussion of 'trust', 'credulity', and 'testimony' in Swinburne and Wolterstorff, and is conjoined with a feminist extension.

Answering the Epistemic Circularity Charge

The first dimension thus outlined is an argument in which I find Alston to be largely successful, and in a way highly significant, potentially, for feminist epistemology—especially if it wishes, as I also so wish, to continue to operate within a realist metaphysic. This is the general epistemological argument that exercises Alston for three chapters of *Perceiving God* (chs. 2, 3, and 4), and we shall see how it relates to notions of credulity and trust that I discussed above. But it involves an exposition of the theory of credulity that potentially has much more 'teeth' than the earlier, rather vague, explorations of Wolterstorff to the effect that all our rationalities are socially located and rooted in communities.

The underlying epistemological theory adopted by Alston in chapter 4 of *Perceiving God* is a 'doxastic practice' approach, which is itself much indebted to Thomas Reid and to a lesser (but interesting) extent to the later Wittgenstein.[65] Alston argues that all 'socially established doxastic practices'—i.e. practices which are belief-forming—are 'innocent until proved guilty' (and here we note the Reidian move on credulity: trust *precedes* doubt). As Alston puts it, 'they all deserve to be regarded as *prima facie* rationally engaged in...pending a consideration of possible reasons for disqualification'.[66] Now here Alston shows—in a very clever move—that none of our 'basic doxastic practices' (those with provide basic access to the world) can be shown to be reliable without 'epistemic circularity', that is, without relying on the outputs of the practice itself. Thus we cannot, for instance, show the reliability of sense perception (SP) without *relying* on sense perceptions; and we cannot show the reliability of memory without *relying* on memory, and so on. So whatever epistemic claims we might want to make on the basis of what Alston (rather misleadingly) calls 'Christian Mystical Practice' (CMP)—by which he does not mean regular activities of meditation and contemplation, but rather sporadic perceptual occurrences—will be in no worse epistemological shape, in the absence of defeasibility rejoinders, than claiming, for instance, that I am now seeing this computer screen, or that I can remember that I had toast for breakfast.

[65] See *PG* 153: 'we will follow the lead of Thomas Reid in taking all our established doxastic practices to be acceptable as such, as innocent until proven guilty'; and the brief discussion of Wittgenstein that follows, in which Alston admits that he is 'far from a slavish follower' (ibid.).
[66] Ibid.

Now if this basic move is right, it might actually be very good news for feminists and feminist epistemology (although Alston does not remark on that[67]). This is because it can release feminist epistemology from the apparently forced retreat to the position of a *relativistic* 'standpoint' epistemology, marked by an epistemic circularity supposedly not suffered by other forms of knowledge.[68] Instead, we can join hands with the arguments of the feminist philosopher Sandra Harding in arguing that feminist standpoint epistemology is not intrinsically in contradiction with the goals of achieving 'objective knowledge', indeed that feminist epistemologies can on the contrary work to *expand* visions on the true away from the restrictions of a 'masculinist' approach.[69] An element of circularity in our epistemic reasoning is not a sign, necessarily, of solipsism or relativistic bias; on the contrary, it is a general feature of our most basic epistemological negotiations. And thus the expansion of vision to include the special epistemic perspectives of women, 'mystics', the poor, or the racially oppressed, can *contribute* to the 'objectivity' of our knowledge, rather than threatening it.[70]

Contemplative Activity as 'Doxastic Practice'

The second dimension of Alston's argument follows on from here, but provides him with an opportunity that he then, in my view, fails to exploit as richly as he could have done in *Perceiving God*. He has attempted a fair and sensitive treatment of at least aspects of 'CMP' in chapter 1 of his book, including starring roles in that exposition for Teresa herself. But when it comes to spelling out his theory of 'doxastic practices' in detail, he fails to see the application to which he could fit this theory in the light of the mystical texts he has earlier quoted. To understand what is going on here, we need to know precisely what Alston means by a 'doxastic practice'. His definition runs thus:

A doxastic practice can be thought of as a system or constellation of dispositions or habits, or to use a currently fashionable term, 'mechanisms', each of which yields a

---

[67] In private correspondence to the author he acknowledges reading some feminist epistemology, but does not evidence any strong appreciation of it.

[68] Recall that we saw above that Wolterstorff, in his early work in *Faith and Rationality* at least, does not completely see off the spectre of such relativism when he stresses the situation-specific nature of our epistemologies: see n. 41 above.

[69] See Sandra Harding, 'Rethinking Standpoint Epistemology: "What is Strong Objectivity?"', in Linda Alcoff and Elizabeth Potter (eds.), *Feminist Epistemologies* (New York: Routledge, 1993), 49–82: the argument is that we can have 'situated', 'realist' knowledge precisely *because* there is no such thing as a disembodied, unlocated knower. The more perspectives are taken account of, therefore, the stronger the 'objectivity' achieved.

[70] For a more developed critical discussion of 'standpoint' epistemology along these lines, see again my 'Feminism and Analytic Philosophy of Religion', esp. 506–9, 513–16.

belief as output that is related in a certain way to an 'input'. [Sense Perception], for example, is a constellation of habits of forming beliefs in certain ways on the basis of inputs that consist of sense experiences... [so] I suggest that our epistemic situation may be illuminated by thinking of our beliefs as formed by various practices...[71]

Or again, a little later:

I think of a doxastic practice as the exercise of a system or constellation of belief-forming habits or mechanisms, each realizing a function that yields beliefs with a certain kind of content from inputs of a certain type. Such functions differ in the width of the input and output types involved. The input type could be something as narrow as a certain determinant configuration of specific sensory qualia, and the output type something as narrow as a belief to the effect that the object in the center of the visual field is Susie Jones.[72]

But what, we might ask, if we do not restrict ourselves to such narrow conditions and examples? These have the ring of the factory workshop: in goes the raw material (the input) and out plops the belief, suitably mediated via the 'doxastic practice'. It is indeed a dryly *mechanistic* account. But is this really how 'belief-forming practices' of a more subtle and sustained form characteristically operate in the context of religious belief? Surely not. What if this analysis of 'doxastic practices' were extended to include meditative or contemplative practices such as Teresa enjoins us to? The gradual unification of the faculties, affections, and senses through these 'practices' here cause, if Teresa's witness is reliable, a breakthrough over time into *new* levels of perception and sensation, *new* ways of 'perceiving God' (including the paradoxical 'perception' of God as precisely *unknowable* noetically). And such phenomena would be unthinkable if one were restricted to what Alston takes to be the 'normal' perceptual and epistemic base; for in Teresa's case such developments specifically involve the body and the affections also as sites of knowing, and the strange and gradual unification of the mental faculties. And this is something quite different from the crude synchronic 'mechanism' of the slot-machine. No, rather we need to analyse how the 'doors of perception' swing open by degrees in response to a divine allure—how the *graced* invitation of contemplation slowly, and far from mechanically, discloses levels of epistemic response '*beyond*', as Irigaray puts it, 'the dry desolation of [masculinist] reason'.

It seems, then, that in addition to the basic first move of 'justifying' beliefs by means of the very 'doxastic practices' that produce them, we also need some stern supplementary means of pragmatic (or 'spiritual') testing where

---

[71] *PG* 153.   [72] *PG* 155.

ramified religious claims are concerned.[73] But this is not an arena in which we are left bereft philosophically, least of all by Teresa herself, or—for that matter—by recent developments in pragmatist or feminist epistemology. Teresa, throughout her works, but especially in her mature *Interior Castle*, is ever wont to stress the acid test of 'the fruits of the Spirit': it is a matter of such wise *discretio spirituum* by which one accords credibility to special mystical favours, on the one hand, or to new departures in monastic community life, on the other.[74] And it is striking that, in this regard, Teresa's voice finds an echo—however remotely—in the entirely secular discourses of contemporary feminist epistemology. Lynn Hankinson Nelson, for instance, has recently restressed the importance of the *community* nature of realistic epistemic testing. Reacting against the individualist tendencies of much analytic epistemology, she writes: 'Experience remains the heart of the matter, but it is inherently social rather than individualistic; for we experience the world through the lens of going projects, categories, theories, and standards, and all of these are generated by communities.'[75] In short, while more could be said about this suggested form of 'justification',[76] its social and communitarian nature acts as a vital bulwark against error, and Nelson's feminist assessment of this inter-subjective aspect importantly expands on, and refines, the basic Reidian openness to 'trust' and 'credulity'.

The Turn to the 'Apophatic'

We come, finally, to perhaps the trickiest aspect of 'Christian Mystical Perception', so-called, and one, as we saw, that was effectively shunned by

---

[73] Norman Kretzmann's critique of Alston is worth mentioning here ('Mystical Perception: St Teresa, William Alston, and the Broadminded Atheist', in Alan G. Padgett (ed.), *Reason and the Christian Religion: Essays in Honour of Richard Swinburne* (Oxford: Clarendon Press, 1994), 65–90). He is right that Alston does not supply a *strong* form of 'justification' of religious belief in *PG* (such as to make such religious claims 'deontologically' truth-conducive: ibid. 74); but he is misleading when he makes a 'broad-minded atheist' (has one ever met one?) the critical point of reference for the assessment of claims like Teresa's. (His view of Teresa is also seriously distorted by the same hermeneutical blindness that to some extent afflicts Alston in *PG*.) The fact is that Teresa herself supplies the necessary tools of discernment for bolstering her epistemic claims when she appeals to the 'fruits of the Spirit' *within faithful community*. The major difference from Alston's initial account of justification here is that it involves a 'diachronic' analysis which Kretzmann does not consider: on the advantages of such, see Swinburne, *Epistemic Justification*, ch. 7.

[74] This is a recurrent theme in the later work of Teresa, but it is summed up in her epithet in *The Interior Castle*, 7. 4, 6 (446): 'This is the reason for prayer, my daughters, the purpose of this spiritual marriage: the birth always of good works, good works'.

[75] Lynn Hankinson Nelson, 'Epistemological Communities', in Alcoff and Potter (eds.), *Feminist Epistemologies*, 142.

[76] Again, see the extended and illuminating discussion in Swinburne, *Epistemic Justification*, ch. 7, esp. 188–91. It could be held against Swinburne, however, that he does not adequately consider, in his account of 'diachronic justification', the role of a *community* in such diachronic investigation and testing.

Alston at the time of *Perceiving God*. What are we to make of Teresa's, and other mystics', tendency to 'unsay' whatever they *do* say of God in their accounts of contemplative practice and its goal in union? And how, if at all, can this 'apophatic' aspect relate to the quest to 'justify' their claims? When Teresa says, so emphatically, that in the state of union the soul 'understands by not understanding', is she, in effect, just politely clearing her throat? Is she, as the analytic school of philosophy often charges, sliding into conceptual muddle under the cover of a portentous appeal to 'mystery'? Or is there something about the nature of God, qua God, that makes such an intimate encounter with him in union entirely transcendent and *sui generis*, and thus inherently 'ineffable'?

The answer, I submit, is surely 'yes' to the last enquiry: God, being God, is unlike *any* Other, and thus by definition is not to be 'perceived' in a way straightforwardly akin to any other item in the universe (which is his own creation, after all).[77] Should we not then positively expect an 'experience' of God in contemplation to be epistemically unique, even bizarre? Yet this, of course, was precisely *not* what Alston was willing to admit at the time of writing *Perceiving God*; indeed, to have done so would in a way have undermined his own major opening gambit in the book—the enunciation of his so-called 'Theory of Appearing'. This theory, to my mind, sits in somewhat ambiguous relationship to the 'doxastic practice' arguments of the rest of the book, and certainly creates difficulties for the question of 'apophatic' claims. We cannot therefore evade a brief discussion of it before we look at Alston's more recent pronouncements on divine 'mystery'.

It is vital to the Alston of *Perceiving God*, as we have seen, that individualized and 'immediate' sense perceptions of ordinary objects be the normative analogue for 'Christian Mystical Practices'. Arguably this comes about because of the need to resist his main enemies whom he calls the 'conceptualists'— that is, *non-realist* post-Kantian epistemologists whom he feels he must see off early in his defence of a direct realism *vis-à-vis* perception. But this attempt to do a bold end-run around Kant involves, in my view, paying a high price in terms of hermeneutical credibility.[78] Everything at this stage of the book *seems* to depend on the 'Theory of Appearing', which is described thus: 'According to the Theory of Appearing the notion of X's appearing to S as so-and-so is

---

[77] Hence the persistent biblical reminders of the mortal danger, if not impossibility, of seeing God face to face.

[78] Several alternative responses could be made here, but space does not permit a lengthy analysis. (1) One could remain open to the possibility of 'pre-conceptual' experiences (e.g. by pre-linguistic children, whom Alston does not even consider), but still remain sceptical that their existence *guarantees* 'direct' perception of the sort that Alston thinks he needs. (2) One could return to Kant and argue that the 'recession from reality' view that Alston is countering is actually a misreading of him: his epistemology is set up precisely to guarantee a realist grasp of

fundamental and unanalyzable. And since this relationship, being unanalyzable, is not analyzable in terms of conceptualizations, beliefs, takings, or anything else of the sort, it really does have [a] non- or pre-conceptual character'.[79] According to this theory, then, Alston wants it to be possible (at least *occasionally*[80]) for something (including, in 'parallel' form, a big something called God?) to present itself unambiguously and unanalysably in such an immediate perception, and so altogether escape—at least in some circumstances—tainting 'conceptualization'. But this whole argument is, in my view, fragile, question-begging, and (not least) unnecessary, in the light of Alston's later important appeals to the socially constructed epistemic base of 'doxastic practices', which as we have seen can themselves yield true, justified beliefs.

Now it is possible that I—and many others—have misunderstood the precise intentions or scope of Alston's 'Theory of Appearing'.[81] Perhaps it is not as structurally significant for his religious epistemology as I have taken it to be. But probably the more important point for our current purposes is that taking the analogue of *perception* (of objects) as the presumed starting point for a discussion of direct and intimate 'experiences' of God may in any case have its own limitations and hermeneutical frailties. And again, we may here find a point of intriguing contact with feminist philosophy, albeit in a context not intended to be applied to the issue of God. Thus Lorraine Code, in her famous article 'Taking Subjectivity into Account',[82] asks why we should take what she calls 'perception

reality, not to undermine it (though God, of course, is off this map in Kant's view). (3) One could argue endlessly—and probably fruitlessly—about the number of nonconceptual 'perceptions' any adult could actually claim to have had, given the hermeneutical webs we are constantly engaged in: I am not sure this is empirically resolvable, nor whether Alston would regard this as a proper challenge to his position. (4) More to the point for our current purposes, one could be sceptical (as I am) that the Theory of Appearing helps us, in any case, to get at the specificity and uniqueness of *contemplative* encounter with the divine.

[79] *PG* 55.

[80] It seems to be a strangely *rare* eventuality to bear so much weight: see *PG* 27: 'however rarely...in adult experience'.

[81] In private correspondence Alston insists that the Theory is 'not an epistemological theory of any sort', and has nothing to do with 'truth' or 'metaphysics; it is *simply* a theory of 'perception' ('Comments on Sarah Coakley's Ferguson Lectures', undated, from the summer of 1998). I must admit that I find that claim puzzling, because surely the central argument of the *PG* is that perceiving God is in important respects *akin* to other forms of perception; whence it would follow that a claim to perceive God is as 'unanalyzable' and 'direct' (and also as potentially 'justified' in its non-viciously-circular practice), as perceiving everyday objects is. Hence this theory of perception would at least have inferred *implications* for theistic metaphysics, and surely this is intended in the unfolding of the book's logic. Indeed, when Alston boldly claims, as he first enunciates the Theory of Appearing, that 'x can't appear to me unless it exists' (*PG* 37), we must surely conclude that its status as a theory of perception bleeds inexorably into epistemic *and* metaphysical territory.

[82] Lorraine Code, 'Taking Subjectivity into Account', in Alcoff and Potter (eds.), *Feminist Epistemologies*, 15–48.

at a distance' as a *normative* epistemic model in basic questions of perception and recognition. What about knowing other *people*, she says: would this not yield a very different 'geography of the epistemic terrain'? Here Code strikes a distinctly Reidian note of her own: she points out that, 'Developmentally, learning what she or he can expect of other people is one of the first and most essential kinds of knowledge a child acquires'.[83] Indeed, it is arguably prior to, and logically requisite for, the learning of the basic skills of recognition and naming that attend the perception of objects. By analogical extension from Code's point, I would press the question: is not the knowing of *God* inculcated in persistent 'contemplative practice' much more akin to this knowing and loving of another, than it is akin to recognizing a mango in the marketplace?

In correspondence with Alston (much concerned with said mangoes![84]) I have put it to him that far more interesting for religious epistemology than the (contentious) 'preconceptual knowing' in the Theory of Appearing is a *different* sort of 'naked' knowing, the naked knowing of *contemplative* passivity. He replied, with typical generosity:

I find what you say very attractive and exciting. I am certainly convinced that contemplative prayer involves the kind of mental emptiness to make room for God, or rather to make room for our awareness of God, since God was there all along. This is very important, but at the moment *I don't know just how to make hay of it epistemologically.*[85]

But some years after writing this letter, Alston had dramatically changed his mind. He had himself risen to the challenge and had begun to 'make hay' precisely in the way suggested. His Taylor Lectures of 2005 are devoted to the topic of what he calls the Divine Mystery Thesis (DMT), that is, the claim that 'No concepts in the human repertoire can be truly applied to God as he is in

---

[83] Ibid. 15, 32. Code goes on: 'Other people are the point of origin of a child's entry into the material/physical environment both in providing or inhibiting access to that environment—in *making* it—and in fostering entry into the language with which children learn to name... Participators in childraising could not easily ignore the primacy of knowing and being known by other people in cognitive development, nor could they denigrate the role such knowledge plays throughout an epistemic history' (ibid. 32–3). In short, if Alston wanted to choose the *most* 'unanalyzable' features of perception, he might do better first to examine the newborn's 'direct' relation to the primary caregiver.

[84] Letter of 20 Dec. 1996: 'I am plumping for a mode (kind, species, form...) of cognition that does not, in itself, involve the application of concepts or any other form of conceptual thinking.... I don't go along with the current trend of doing obeisance to Kant on perception... I feel no need to square accounts with Kant.... I take "looking like a mango" to mean something like "looking the way mangoes typically look" (in that kind of light, from that perspective, etc., etc.).'

[85] Ibid., penultimate paragraph, my emphasis. Alston went on: 'Anyway, I plead guilty to not sufficiently "underscoring" in *PG* the difference between perceiving objects in the physical environment and perceiving God. Or rather, since I talked a lot about such differences, I plead guilty to not developing this in anything like the way you suggest...'.

himself'.⁸⁶ So here Alston is for the first time directly taking on the topic of 'apophaticism', or ostensibly so; and the contrast with his resistance to 'ineffability' in *Perceiving God* is striking. But more significantly, he devotes his second Taylor Lecture to an examination of 'whether a certain kind of experience might provide epistemic support for the DMT'; and now, for the first time, he chooses to investigate the *long-term discipline* of 'contemplative prayer', rather than passing 'religious experiences'. Taking the two contemporary Cistercians Thomas Merton and Thomas Keating as his key exponents for these purposes, he first clarifies the theses for which he is aiming to glean 'experiential' support:

(1) At its fullest development contemplation involves a union with God.
(2) This union involves God's sharing his life and, in particular, his knowledge of himself, with us.
(3) This enables us to have knowledge of God as he is in himself that is beyond concepts and other representations and as such far superior to any other knowledge we can have.
(4) The DMT.⁸⁷

So, finally, Alston is attending precisely to the questions that I had discussed with him some years earlier. After a succinct analysis of the relevant aspects of Merton's and Keating's texts, Alston produces a new version for himself of the 'credulity principle': 'What can be *indubitably* derived from the experience is how things seem to the subject...there is no alternative to taking the word of the reporters of the experiences as to what the experiences reveal to them'.⁸⁸ He then goes on to provide a set of '*reasons* for taking our guides at their word':

(A) They are in the best position to know what is happening, especially since such experiences are not shared with the population in general.

---

⁸⁶ Taylor Lecture 1, 1. The discerning reader may immediately see that this 'DMT' does not quite line up with any of the definitions of 'apophaticism' from the classical Christian heritage rehearsed above (n. 3). I shall come back to that point very shortly, below.

⁸⁷ Taylor Lecture 2, 17 (in continuing pagination from lecture 1: page numbers are not given in the web form of the lectures).

⁸⁸ Ibid. 18; my emphasis. In my view, this principle is formulated with insufficient caution: come back Swinburne, we might remark at this point, all is forgiven! I say this because Swinburne's defeasibility criteria surely ought to continue to have important balancing weight against *undiscriminating* 'credulity', even as we do indeed give the contemplative the initial benefit of the doubt. But we *do* have 'alternatives' to taking the contemplative exponents 'at their word' if they turn out to be alcoholic, psychotic, known liars, or 'unreliable' in other ways that their fellow contemplatives/friends/family members would certainly know of. More than Swinburne's own analysis underlines, then, the *community* context of assessment of 'fruits' proves especially significant in this realm of contemplative claims; for those claims need to be assessed in the light of long-term personal acquaintance and knowledge of the consistency, discipline, and charity of the person concerned.

(B) There are a significant number of witnesses that tell roughly the same story, thereby providing some interpersonal confirmation.
(C) What they report as the ultimate fulfillment of human potentialities is coherent with what is believed about God's intentions as creator in Christianity and in other theistic religions.
(D) The quality of the[ir] lives, the influence and the work of leading contemplatives gives us confidence that they know what they are talking about.[89]

But Alston's final conclusion is that, whereas (A)–(D) provide sufficient justifying support for theses (1)–(3), enunciated above, *they cannot help us with the DMT*, since '[our guides] do not attempt to lay out any inferential bridge from their experience, or from the first three conclusions to the DMT'.

Is this right, and if so, how much of a problem does it present? It seems to me that these questions can be answered quite simply, and in a twofold manner.

First, Alston seems to answer his own conundrum *in the only way that is needed for our current epistemological purposes* when he concludes that 'if, as I am assuming, we are accepting our guides' reports as to what is going on in their experience, it is a natural conclusion that no other, inferior knowledge could have a claim to be a knowledge of God as he is in himself'. In other words (to gloss Alston a bit further here): we already have sufficient justifying reasons, given the conditions outlined above, for believing the contemplative exponents' accounts of what it is to experience God in union, and for trusting them also in their particular kinds of claim to 'know' God in Godself. Moreover, and likewise, we also have sufficient reasons to take seriously their claim that 'apophatic' speech is the most accurate, appropriate (and in a somewhat paradoxical sense, *clear*[90]) way of speaking of both God and self in this relationship of union.

Secondly, I would claim that, underlyingly, Alston has set up his definition of the DMT in a misleading way, such that it ceases to be a theological *desideratum* to justify it experientially in any case. Indeed, as stated ('*No concepts* in the human repertoire can be truly applied to God as he is in himself'), it is a highly contentious claim, both theologically and philosophically; and granted that, it is pointless to agonize about whether contemplative 'experience' can give it veracity until one is certain that that outcome is desirable. Why do I say this? Because the DMT appears to hide within it a Kantian or neo-Kantian presumption (much beloved of the 'liberal' American theology that Alston so strongly contests) that 'God' is *inherently* off-limits epistemically—'dark' in the sense of Kant's noumenal no-man's-land—and

---

[89] Again, Taylor Lecture 2, 18; my emphasis.
[90] It is in this sense that the analytic desideratum of clarity can be attained in this area, i.e. clarity precisely about what can, and cannot, be said, and in what way.

thus rendering all human attempts to speak of him *equally* invalid. This view, note, contrasts most importantly with the 'apophaticism' of 'unsaying' in the Dionysian sense of 'mystical theology' (as discussed above in Teresa's case), and would be avidly contested by the Thomist tradition also, for which the doctrine of analogy and the possibility of the 'literal' application of the 'pure perfection terms' to God are basic postulates. But we need not stop to open this particular can of theological worms here, since our argument has already delivered what we wanted. In short, we are justified in believing the contemplatives' claims about God under the conditions described.

CONCLUSIONS

In this chapter I have attempted to contribute to the project of 'analytic theology' in the following ways. First, I have brought together the now-classic analytic interest in the epistemology of 'religious experience' with the current continental fascination with 'apophaticism', and goaded them both towards a closer attention to the texts of 'mystical theology' themselves. In that sense I have attempted a certain *rapprochement* of the sort that 'analytic theology' fundamentally proposes. Secondly, I have urged that a specifically feminist analysis and critique of the relevant analytic discourses is a fruitful one. It can chart a certain unconscious turn to the 'feminine' in the recent strategies of analytic religious epistemology (most productively in its exploration of the epistemic 'soft centres' of 'trust', 'credulity', and 'testimony'); but it can also expose a failure to attend to the actual voices of women mystics themselves, and to explore their distinctive epistemic significance. Teresa of Ávila has been falsely pedestalized as the favoured exemplar of merely passing 'religious experiences'; yet her own narratives of union (expressed characteristically in the paradoxical language of 'apophaticism') give us a much richer insight into the epistemic significance of sustained practices of contemplation, lived out, embodied, and spiritually tested in the context of religious community.

Thirdly, then, I have urged that the analytic school, for all its hermeneutical shortcomings, gives us enough tools in our epistemological tool-kit to make justified claims about God on the basis of such texts of mystical theology. No epistemic duties are flouted, and suitable grounds are explicated for presuming certain claims to 'mystical union' to be truth-conducive. A diachronic approach to justification is applied (to do justice to the narrative features of contemplative advance), as is a basic appeal to credulity and testimony, bolstered by pragmatic and spiritual appeals to 'fruits', and tempered, where necessary, by critical application of relevant 'defeasibility criteria'. Further, the use of 'apophatic' speech to describe such states of divine union, far from signalling the *end* of the applicability of the analytic approach, can be shown to be elegantly clear precisely about what can, and cannot, be said about God on the basis of contemplative union. Mystery and divine uniqueness can be evoked with a certain precision, and without falling into unnecessary and mindless obfuscation, as is the recurrent fear of the analytic school.

Finally, this argument has been feminist for one further reason also. It has explored a form of personal empowerment and epistemic expansion (in God) which has the capacity to transcend certain classic Western divisions of parts of the self—intellect and will, spirit and sensuality, soul and body—in which woman has always tended to be awarded the 'inferior' role in such dualisms. At a time when postmodern philosophy is declaring that there *is* no stable self, and feminism is wondering whether the self has been declared outmoded just as women were attaining to it, this represents an alluring third option. As we have seen, the trivializing of Teresa has been a long-established philosophical trope within the discourses of analytic philosophy of religion. 'Analytic theology' may, in contrast, represent a movement capable of retrieving her true epistemic and spiritual significance.

Index

Abelard, P., 68, 108–109, 113
actualism, *see* Barth: actualism
Adams, M., 185n55
Alexander of Hales, 109
Alston, W., 283, 292–95, 300, 301–11
Ammer, C. 84n67
analysis 36–42, 44, 46, 51, 63–64 *see also* analytic philosophy
    conceptual 3, 6, 22–25, 117–119, 123–128, 131n30, 157
    feminist 282–283, 311
    as theological method 42–50
analytic philosophy 2–7, 35–40, 54–55, 117–119, 162–168, 251–255, 271, 300
    and continental philosophy 37, 265, 280
    and narrative, 254–55
    as ahistorical, 21–22
    characterized, 3–7
    problems with 18, 29, 50, 51n29, 251–53
    as reductionistic 40
    of religion 58, 118–19, 136, 185, 215, 282–286, 292, 300, 312
analytic theology
    as ahistorical, 50, 87, 136; *see also* analytic philosophy: as ahistorical
    characterized, 7, 34–50, 54–55, 59–61, 117–119
    objections, 50–53
    vs. philosophy of religion, 118–119
analytic Thomism, 34n4
Anselm 39, 49, 62–63, 124, 168
anti-realism, 137, 138, 139, 140–42, 149–50
apophaticism, 19–21, 168, 280–81, 281n3, 298n56, 298–301, 305–11; *see also* mystical theology *and* negative theology
Aquinas, T., 100, 101, 108–12, 16, 184, 219–20, 233, 240
    on faith 101–102, 109–112
Aristotle 92–95, 98–100, 279 *see also* knowledge; Platonic/Aristotelian conception of
Arnauld, A., 240–41
Athanasius, 106–7
Augustine 39, 49, 56, 64, 168, 262–263
Austin, J. L., 178n31
authority, 207–209

Barr, J., 216n3
Barth, K. 28, 35n9, 46, 61, 117, 121n12, 216n4
    actualism, 172–74, 175
    on Scripture 172–186
Bavinck, H., 221n18
Baxter, R. 38n13
Belgic Confession, 190
Benedict XVI, 95–7
Berkhof, L. 7–8
bullshit 70–71
    analysis of 72–76
    intentional 72
    product 73–76

Calvin, J. 16, 45, 54, 187, 276, 279, 289–290
    see also Reformed epistemology *and* sensus divinitatis
Chisholm, R. 14, 286
Christology, 183–5
Chrysostom, J. 106, 110
classical doctrine of God 61–63
Clement of Alexandria 91, 111, 116, 168
    on faith 100–109, 112–114
    on gnosis 103–104
Code, L., 307–8
Cohen, G.A., 72–76
continental philosophy 17, 37, 155–156, 168, 271, 280, 282 *see also* analytic philosophy; and continental
cosmology, 246–7
Council of Trent, 241n1
Craig, W. L., 197
Crisp, O. 136, 150–51, 153, 218n12
Critchley, S., 17
Cross, R., 185n55
Cupitt, D. 2, 8

Davies, O. 281n4
Davis, C. F. 228n32, 288
Davis, S. T. 197
Derrida, 274–5, 281n3
Descartes, R. 14, 16, 24–25, 240–241, 269, 276
dialogic pluralism, 164–66
dogmatic theology, 139–42, 149–50, 215–220, 221

dogmatic theology (*cont.*)
  and religious experience, 226–32
  defined, 214
doxastic practice, 208n12, 301–5
Dummett, M. 11, 89–90

Edwards, J., 227n30
empiricism 13–14, 16, 21, 29, 269n21
epistemic justification, 118, 187–88, 282n5
epistemology of theology 54, 66–68
essentialism, 285

faith, characterized, 233
foundationalism 6–7
  classical 12, 16, 17, 159–163, 289–90
  doxastic 12, 14
  source 13–17, 26–28, 30
Franke, J., 12n17
Frankfurt, H. 55, 70, 72–75 *see also* bullshit
Freddoso, A., 176
Freud, S., 284

Gadamar, H. G., 274, 278–9
Gale, R., 287n23
Galileo, 234
glaube, *see* Kant: on belief
Geach, P. 89–90
God's Word, *see* Word of God
god of the philosophers 24–25, 61
Goldin-Meadow, S., 257
Gorrell, R., 84
Gould, S. J., 236–244
Grenz, S. 12n17, 34–35
Gunton, C. 43–46

Habermas, G., 197
Hankey, W., 99n22
Harding, S., 303
Harvey, V., 153
Hauerwas, 219n14
Haught, J., 241–44
Hegel, 277–8
Heidegger, M. 10, 18, 35, 37, 67, 70, 75–75, 167–168, 270–276, 278
hermeneutics, 272–9
Hobson, P., 256
Holy Spirit, internal instigation, 190, 202, 204–207, 210–212
Hume. D. 76, 89, 269
Hunsinger, G., 172–3
Husserl, E., 269, 271

Inge, W., 246, 247
Isocrates 92–95, 114
Iverson, J., 257

James, W., 281n2, 282n6, 299–300
justification, *see* epistemic justification

Kant, I. 27, 50n30, 51, 158, 163, 167–68, 267, 306n78
  and analytic theology, 120, 122, 123–130, 134, 135
  and synthetic theology, 130–34
  and the cosmological argument, 131–33
  influence on theology, 120–21
  on belief (*glaube*), 120, 122, 128–30, 133–34, 158–59
  on conceptual analysis, 123–8
  ontological argument, 123–4
kataphatic theology, 168; *see also* apophaticism
Kierkegaard, S., 269
knowledge
  and narrative, 258–260
  and second person experiences, 257–60
  and testimony 87–91
  of persons, 255–260
  Platonic/Aristotelian conceptions of 92–96
Kretzmann, N., 305n73

Lamont, J., 88n1
Langford, J., 234n4
Leekam, S., 256n15
Lemaître, G., 246
Lindbeck, G. 22, 47–50
Locke, 158, 163
logical positivism, 156–57

Marion, J. 24–25, 136n3, 267–68
McClaren, B., 80
McCormack, B., 173–4, 178, 179, 183
McFague, S., 71–2, 76–79, 84
McGrath, A. 34n7
McGrew, T., 197, 200–1
Melanchthon, P. 46, 217
Merleau-Ponty, M., 266, 267n9, 270
meta-epistemology, 159–60
metanarrative 13–14, 60
metaphor, 5n7, 19–20, *see also* models of theology: persuasive metaphor
models of theology
  persuasive metaphor 76–79
  perpetual conversation 79–83
Moltmann, J., 33n2, 56n3, 67, 71–72, 74n20, 79–84
Morris, T. V., 185
motives of credibility 87–89, 91 Muller, R., 219n13
Murphy, N., 265

Index

mystery in theology 9–10, 50, 52n31, *see also* apophaticism, mystical theology, *and* negative theology
mystical theology, 280–82, 297, 298n56, 299, 300, 311–12, *see also* apophaticism *and* negative theology

narrative 29, 59–60, 242–243
   and analytic philosophy 251–264
natural theology 28, 45–46, 126, 167, 189, 193–194, 198–204, 211, 215–232
   and religious experience, 223–26
   conceptions of, 217–219
negative theology 98–99, 281n3, 298n56, 299, *see also* apophaticism *and* mystical theology
Nelson, L. H., 305
non-overlapping magisterial, 236–7
Nussbaum, M., 255n10
Nyaya school of philosophy 92, 95 *see also* testimony

occasionalism, 176
onto-theology 9–10, 19, 167–168
Origen 56, 94, 105–106, 115
Owen, J. 27
   on faith 112–116

persons, knowledge of, *see* knowledge
phenomenology, 266–279
   hermeneutical, 273–79
Philo of Alexandria
   as precursor to scholasticism 100
Plantinga, A. 39n15, 49n28, 79, 184n55, 188, 190–195, 202–207, 253, 284–285, 289–293 *see also* Reformed epistemology
Plato 92–100, 276
postliberal theology 33, 35, 47–49 *see also* Lindbeck, G.
Preti, C., 73n16, 77–8
Price, H. H., 20–21
probability, dwindling, 190–201
properly basic belief, 188; *see also* foundationalism
pseudo-Dionysus, 280n2
Putnam, H., 71

Quine, W. V., 277–78

Rahner, K., 74, 75n27
Ramm, B., 175
rationalism 13, 16, 29
Rauser, R., 152

Rawls, J., 164
Rea, M., 138
realism, 138; *see also* anti-realism
reason
   procedural, instrumental and substantive use of 41–44, 218, 219–220
Reformed epistemology 16n23, 45, 284–285, 289, 290n33, 292
religion
   as being overly accommodating toward science, 239–44
   as constructively engaging science, 244–47
   as selectively ignoring science, 238–39
   as wholly independent of science, 236–38
   characterized, 235
religious experience, 286–96, 298–301
   and dogmatic theology, 226–32
   and natural theology, 223–26
   nature of, 220–23
Reno, R. R., 1n1
revealed theology, 119
Richardson, A., 71n2
Ricouer, 273
Rorty, 265, 274n33

Sarfati, J., 239n8
Schleiermacher, F. 27, 67n27, 277–278, 290n33
   and dogmatic theology, 139–42
   on religion, 145–49
   on religion and philosophy, 148–49
   on theology, 137, 139–45, 149–50
science, characterized 235
Scopes Trial, 234
scripture
   divine character of, 171–2
   inspiration, 171, 187, 188–89
   see also Word of God
second person experience, 257–60
Sellars, W., 160
sensus divinitatis see Reformed epistemology *and* Plantinga, A. *and* Calvin, J.
Sheehan, T., 11
speech-acts, 177–79
Spiegler, G., 142n3
Swinburne, R. 36, 51, 88, 136, 189–90, 194n8, 199–200, 222n21, 285–291, 293, 300, 305n76, 309n88
synthetic theology, 124, 130–34
systematic theology
   as analytic theology 54–69
   as perpetual bull session 84
   defined, 214

systematic theology (*cont.*)
  nature of 55–56
  skepticism about 80–83
  value of analytic approaches to 37–38

Taylor, R. C., 100
Teresa of Ávila 30, 280–283, 293–306, 311–312
testimony, 201–204
  authoritative, 207–12
  nonreductive accounts of vs. reductive accounts of 89–91
theology
  and metaphysics, 150–54
  and phenomenology, 266–72
  see also analytic theology,
    models of theology, mystical theology, negative theology, synthetic theology, *and* systematic theology
tradition, 276–7
transubstantiation, 240–41

truth
  correspondence theory of 49–50
  deflationary theory of 47
  epistemic theory of 47–48 *see also* postliberal theology *and* Lindbeck, G.
  in theology 46–50
Turner, D., 281n4, 299–300

union, mystical, 296–300

van Fraassen, B 4, 23–24, 252–253, 261
Vanhoozer, K., 178–79, 180
van Inwagen, 207

Westphal, M. 8–12, 28–30, 137n5
White, A. D., 234
Williams, B., 253
Winston, D., 100
Wolterstorff, N. 51n30, 121n11, 289–92, 294, 303n68
Word of God, 171–72, 173–175, 179–80
Wright, N. T., 197

Printed in Great Britain
by Amazon